MAINTAINING AND REPAIRING PCS
LAB GUIDE

Vice President and Publisher: Natalie E. Anderson
Associate VP/ Executive Acquisitions Editor, Print: Stephanie Wall
Executive Editor, Media: Richard Keaveny
Executive Editor: Chris Katsaropoulos
Editorial Assistant: Lora Cimiluca
Product Development Manager: Eileen Bien Calabro
Senior Media Project Manager: Steve Gagliostro
Media Project Manager: Alana Meyers
Director of Marketing: Margaret Waples
Senior Marketing Manager: Jason Sakos
Career Channel Marketing Manager: John Wannemacher
Marketing Assistant: Ann Baranov
Customer Service Representative: Rebecca Scott
Managing Editor: Lynda Castillo
Production Project Manager: Lynne Breitfeller
Manufacturing Buyer: Natacha Moore
Cover art: Michael R. Hall

This book was set in Futura MD BT, Times New Roman, and Arial by Cathy J. Boulay, Educational Technologies Group. It was printed and bound by Bind-Rite Graphics. The cover was printed by Phoenix Color Corp.

Written and edited by Marcraft Production Staff: Charles Brooks, Caleb Sarka, Paul Havens, Wanda Dawson, Evan Samaritano, Cathy Boulay, and Anthony Tonda

Technical review: Caleb Sarka, Wanda Dawson, and Stuart Palmer

Pearson Education Ltd.
Pearson Education Singapore Pte. Ltd.
Pearson Education Canada, Ltd.
Pearson Education—Japan

Pearson Education Australia Pty. Limited
Pearson Education North Asia Ltd.
Pearson Educación de Mexico, S.A. de C.V.
Pearson Education Malaysia Pte. Ltd.

10 9 8 7 6 5 4 3 2 1
ISBN 0-13-613682-6

Trademark Acknowledgments

PREFACE

The authors, and Marcraft International, have been producing computer services training materials since 1988. In particular, Marcraft publishes comprehensive theory and hands-on lab texts that assist students in studying for and passing the Computing Technology Industry Association (CompTIA) certification exams.

CompTIA is an organization that has established introductory certification criteria for service professionals in the computer industry. Most notably, CompTIA has created and sponsors the A+, Network+, i-Net+, Server+, and Security+ Certification Examinations. The A+ exam is designed to certify entry-level technicians for the installation, maintenance, and repair of desktop computer hardware and software. The Network+ exam is designed to serve as an introductory certification for network administration, focusing on Client/Server operating systems used with Local Area Networks (LANs). The i-Net+ Certification is designed specifically for any individual interested in pursuing Internet-related careers. The Server+ exam is designed for individuals who will be supporting and repairing servers. The Security+ exam is for individuals who will be supporting networks and websites that have direct Internet access and need to be protected from intruders.

For more information on CompTIA and these exams, visit *http://www.comptia.org*.

Organization

The A+ Certification Lab Guide provides an excellent hands-on component to emphasize the theoretical materials provided in the A+ Certification Training Guide. Applying chapter concepts developed in the textbook to these lab exercises is crucial in preparing for a successful career as a computer technician. The Lab Guide contains fifty-four lab procedures, which are divided into the following lab groups:

Lab Group 1 – *Hardware Setup* – Consists of labs covering the setup of the computer hardware, which includes the configuration of the bootup sequence, CMOS passwords and resources, and setting up the computer storage parameters. Also included in this lab group are the common troubleshooting procedures that take advantage of both hardware and software techniques.

Lab Group 2 – *Operating Systems* – Provides extensive instruction on the operation of the Windows 2000 Professional, and Windows XP Professional operating systems. Operational features include navigation, Plug-and-Play, tools and resources, computer management, and installing peripheral equipment for operation under the operating systems.

Lab Group 3 – *System Administration Tools* – Covers the administration of the computer operating systems and covers all operational aspects of the computer and its operating system. Utilization of the included operating system tools is also covered in depth. This includes system information, disk management, accessories, domain names, the Registry, safe operating system mode, log files, and virus protection.

Lab Group 4 – *Network Management* – Provides instruction on setting up and maintaining a computer network, which includes connecting to the Internet. The student will acquire the knowledge and skill sets that will enable them to troubleshoot a computer network with an understanding of the different features of the Internet.

Lab Group 5 – *System Maintenance* – Consists of maintaining a computer system, which includes keeping the system current with the latest updates and upgrades. This group concludes with operating system faults, which will provide an understanding of problems that can occur with many operating systems.

These labs are written to be performed on single operating system computers. However, they have been tested on multi-boot machines. There will be variances in lab procedures when running them on the multiple operating system computers. The OS fault labs will cause major problems in the system and SHOULD NOT be performed on multi-boot machines. Contact Marcraft International if you have any questions concerning how these labs are to be performed.

Pedagogy

Each lab begins with a set of objectives to be achieved through the procedure and a list of items required to carry out the procedure. Icons are employed throughout each procedure to describe its nature.

Each procedure ends with a set of lab-specific questions designed to permit students to assess their understanding of the lab.

Upon completion, the student should have learned the required knowledge and skill sets as defined by the CompTIA A+ Certification objectives.

Table of Contents

LAB GROUP 2 – OPERATING SYSTEMS

LAB GROUP 3 – SYSTEM ADMINISTRATION TOOLS

LAB GROUP 4 – NETWORK MANAGEMENT

LAB GROUP 5 – SYSTEM MAINTENANCE

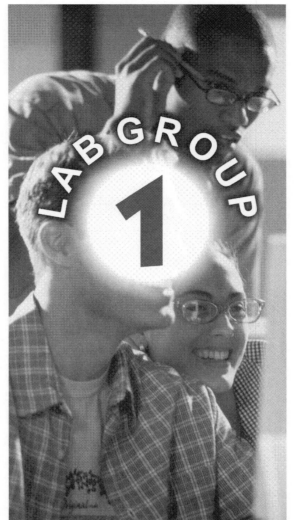

LAB GROUP 1

HARDWARE SETUP

Removing and Installing Hardware Components

OBJECTIVES

1. Disassemble the PC-compatible desktop/tower computer system.
2. Verify the correct orientation of interface cables.
3. Assemble the PC-compatible desktop/tower computer system
4. Boot up the system.

Hardware

RESOURCES

1. Phillips screwdriver
2. PC-compatible desktop/tower computer system — Customer-supplied desktop/tower hardware system **OR** Marcraft Computer Repair Trainer **OR** suitable PC hardware trainer
3. Windows 2000 installed
4. Windows Millennium Edition installed

DISCUSSION

In this procedure you will start a computer to verify that it is operating properly. Then you will disassemble the computer and reassemble it. You will go through all the steps of disassembly except actually taking the drives and motherboard out of the system. This is not necessary because it is just a matter of common sense and using a screwdriver. Then you will reassemble the computer, applying the correct orientation of power and interface cables, along with the computer's front panel connections.

Most PCs are capable of working with several different types of disk storage devices. The drives that are normally included as standard equipment with a PC are a $3\frac{1}{2}$ inch floppy-disk drive (FDD), a multi-gigabyte hard-disk drive (HDD), and a CD-ROM drive. These units can typically be found in the front section of the system unit as illustrated in Figure 2-1.

Figure 2-1: Typical Drive Units

Computer case manufacturers use a variety of construction methods in the case manufacturing process. Some case styles allow for the removal of the face plate simply by pulling. Most others require that the side panels be removed first. Look at the housing carefully before attempting to open it. A screwless case will usually allow the front plate to be removed simply. If you see screws securing the side panels to the back of the computer housing, chances are the face plate cannot be removed first.

Hardware

PROCEDURE

1. **Boot up the computer**
    ____a. Push the power button to turn the computer on. The computer should do a quick memory test (some numbers will count on the screen).
    ____b. The computer will boot up to a Software menu.
    ____c. Choose *Microsoft Windows Millennium Edition* by pressing the **DOWN ARROW** key once.
    ____d. Press **ENTER**, and the computer will boot into Microsoft Millennium Edition.
    ____e. Use the path *Start /Shut Down*, and then select **Shut down** from the drop-down menu in the *Shut Down Windows* dialog box.
    ____f. Click on the **OK** button. The computer will close Millennium Edition and shut down.

NOTE: The computer will shut down Millennium Edition and the power will turn off automatically.

2. **Identify adapter cards**
    ____a. Unplug the power cord from the back of the computer.
    ____b. Remove the screws on the back panel of the computer cover.
    ____c. Take the cover and side panels off. Refer to Figure 2-2 for appropriate housing styles.
    ____d. Identify the video card. It is the one that the monitor is plugged into.

Figure 2-2: Removing the Computer Cover

___e. Record the slot that it is plugged into in Table 2-1. Slots are numbered from right to left starting at slot 1. See Figure 2-3.

___f. Identify the modem card. It is the card with the two telephone ports in the back of it.

___g. Record which slot it is installed into in Table 2-1.

___h. Identify the network card. It is the one with the oversized phone port. (An RJ-45 jack that serves as the physical network port.)

___i. Record the slot in Table 2-1.

Figure 2-3: Numbered Slots

3. **Disconnect external cables (see Figure 2-4)**

Figure 2-4: Disconnect External Cables

___a. Disconnect the keyboard from the back of the computer.

___b. Disconnect the PS/2 mouse.

___c. Disconnect the phone cable.

___d. Disconnect the RJ-45 network cable.

___e. Disconnect the printer cable if you have one.

4. **Disconnect all internal cables**

___a. Disconnect the IDE ribbon cable from the hard drive.

___b. Disconnect the IDE ribbon cable from the CD-ROM.

___c. Disconnect the IDE ribbon cable(s) from the system board.

___d. Disconnect the FDD ribbon cable from the floppy-disk drive.

___e. Disconnect the FDD ribbon cable from the system board.

___f. Remove all the cables from the computer.

5.   Disconnect power supply connections
_____a.   Disconnect the power connector from the hard drive.
_____b.   Disconnect the power connector from the CD-ROM.
_____c.   Disconnect the power connector from the floppy drive.
_____d.   Disconnect the power connector from the system board.

6.   Remove the adapter cards
_____a.   Unscrew the video card from the back panel, and then remove it and place it into an antistatic bag.
_____b.   Repeat Step a to the modem card.
_____c.   Repeat Step a to the network card.

7.   Disconnect all front panel connections (see Figure 2-5)

Figure 2-5: Front Panel Connections

_____a.   Remove the power switch connector.
_____b.   List the color of the wires in Table 2-2.
_____c.   Remove the speaker connector.
_____d.   List the color of the wires in Table 2-2.
_____e.   Remove the power LED connector.
_____f.   List the color of the wires in Table 2-2.
_____g.   Remove the hard drive channel 1 LED connector.
_____h.   List the color of the wires in Table 2-2.
_____i.   Remove the hard drive channel 2 LED connector.
_____j.   List the color of the wires in Table 2-2.
_____k.   Remove the reset switch connector.
_____l.   List the color of the wires in Table 2-2.

For all practical purposes, the disassembly of the computer is now complete. From this point you could also remove the drives and motherboard from the case, but this is a simple mechanical procedure that takes little time. We are now going to reassemble the computer.

8.   Connect the front panel connections (see Figure 2-5)
_____a.   Find the power LED connector and connect it to the motherboard where it is labeled Power LED. See Table 2-2 if needed.
_____b.   Find the reset switch connector and connect it to the motherboard where it is labeled Reset.
_____c.   Find the power switch connector and connect it to the motherboard where it is labeled Power Switch.

____d. Find the hard-disk drive LED Channel 1 connector and connect it to the motherboard where it is labeled HDD1 LED.

____e. Find the hard-disk drive LED Channel 2 connector and connect it to the motherboard where it is labeled HDD2 LED.

____f. Find the speaker connection and connect it to the motherboard where it is labeled Speaker.

9. Install the adapter cards

Make sure the cards are lined up properly with the slots. It will require a firm push to get the cards reseated in the motherboard expansion slot.

____a. Install the video card into the slot recorded in Table 2-1 and screw it into the back panel.

____b. Install the modem card into the slot recorded in Table 2-1 and screw it into the back panel.

____c. Install the network card into the slot recorded in Table 2-1 and screw it into the back panel.

10. Connect the power supply (see Figure 2-6)

Figure 2-6:
Connecting the
Power Supply

NOTE: All the connectors are keyed to plug only in one way.

____a. Plug the ATX power connector into the system board.

____b. Plug the power connector into the floppy-disk drive.

____c. Plug the power connector into the hard-disk drive.

____d. Plug the power connector into the CD-ROM drive.

The disk drives are connected to the system through flat ribbon cables. The cables are different sizes so there should be no problem with mixing them up. However, it is possible to connect some disk drive signal cables in reverse. Pay attention to the small color stripe, usually red, that runs along one edge of the cable. This is the Pin-1 indicator stripe and points to the #1 pin of the interface on both ends, as illustrated in Figure 2-7. There are some floppy and hard drive cables that enable you to connect a second disk drive on the same cable. Though it has become very common to see this done with hard drives, it's no longer a common occurrence with floppy drives. On floppy drive cables one end has a twist in the middle of the ribbon cable to tell the computer which drive is A: and which one is B:. The connector at the end of the cable is designated as the drive A: connector.

The floppy-disk drive allows the system to load programs and data from a removable diskette. The hard-disk drive is a sealed unit and has no removable parts. It runs as long as power is applied to the system. The CD-ROM, like the floppy drive, allows the system to load programs from a removable CD. CDs hold large quantities of data that can be read by the system, are removable, and can be exchanged for one holding different data as desired.

11. Connect the ribbon cables

____a.   Connect the floppy-disk drive to the ribbon cable as in Figure 2-7.

____b.   Connect the system board to the ribbon cable, striped side to pin 1.

____c.   Connect the power cord to the computer.

____d.   Turn the computer on.

____e.   Does the LED on the floppy-disk drive turn on immediately?

____f.   Turn the power off.

____g.   Unplug the power supply.

____h.   If you answered *No* to Step e above, skip to Step j.

____i.   The cable is on backwards if you answered *Yes* to Step e. Reconnect it correctly.

____j.   Connect the hard-disk drive cable to the motherboard in the Primary IDE controller, striped side to pin 1.

____k.   Plug the middle of the connector into the hard drive, striped side to pin 1, and plug the end into the CD-ROM drive, striped side to pin 1.

12. Connect the external cables

____a.   Plug the keyboard into the lower connection. Make sure the orientation is correct, otherwise you could bend pins and ruin the keyboard.

____b.   Plug the mouse into the port just above the keyboard, again checking orientation.

____c.   Plug the monitor back into the video card. The connector is keyed and can only be plugged in one way. Be careful not to bend pins, as this will ruin the monitor.

____d.   Plug in the power cord.

____e.   Replace the cover of the computer.

____f.   Screw in the cover screws.

Figure 2-7: Connecting the Ribbon Cable

NOTE: Reassembly is complete. You need to reboot the computer to see if it is still working properly.

13. Boot up the computer

____a.   Push the power button to turn the computer on. The computer should do a quick memory test (some numbers will count on the screen).

____b.   The computer will boot up to a Software menu.

____c.   Choose *Microsoft Windows Millennium Edition* by pressing the **DOWN ARROW** key once.

____d.   Press **ENTER**.

____e.   The computer will boot into Microsoft Millennium.

____f.   Click on the **Start** button on the lower left.

____g.   Click on **Shut Down**.

____h.   The *Shut Down Windows* dialog box appears.

____i.   Click on the scroll arrow in the middle of the box.

____j.   Select **Shut down**.

____k.   Click on the **OK** button.

____l.   Replace the cover of the computer.

____m.   Screw in the cover screws

TABLES

Table 2-1

Adapter Card	Slot
Video Card:	
Modem Card:	
Network Card:	

Table 2-2

Cable	Color
Power Switch:	
Speaker:	
Power LED:	
IDE 1st channel:	
IDE 2nd channel:	
Reset:	

Feedback

LAB QUESTIONS

1. What does the colored stripe on a disk drive's signal cable indicate?

2. When connecting the floppy-disk drive signal cable to the floppy-disk drive, what precaution should be taken?

3. How do you shut down Windows Millennium Edition?

4. How do you identify a Network Interface Card (NIC)?

5. What will happen if you plug a floppy drive cable in backwards?

6. How many wires are on the power connectors for a hard drive?

7. Counting away from the keyboard connector, in which direction are the slots in a motherboard labeled?

Working with CMOS

Hardware

OBJECTIVES

1. Show the boot sequence of the PC-compatible desktop/tower computer system.
2. See the extended memory count.
3. Change settings in CMOS.
4. See the LED sequence.
5. Detect hard-disk drives.
6. Boot to operating system.

RESOURCES

1. PC-compatible desktop/tower computer system — Customer-supplied desktop/tower hardware system **OR** Marcraft Computer Repair Trainer **OR** suitable PC hardware trainer
2. Windows Millennium Edition installed

DISCUSSION

In this lab you will learn about the booting sequence of a computer, observing what the computer checks before going on to the next sequence of events. The sequence will be manipulated so that it will either skip checking something or stop booting up because of a diagnostic check. You will learn how to set up hard drives easily in CMOS.

```
Copyright 1993-1997  IGS
    VGA / VESA BIOS Ver 2.0413
    Video Memory Size: 8MB
```

PROCEDURE

1. **Pause the bootup process**
   ____a.   Turn the computer on.

Depending on the video card in the system, you may see a Video ROM message flash on the screen. Some video cards display this message whereas others do not. If so, this will tell you the video card type and amount of memory on the card, if recognized, as shown in Figure 3-1.

Figure 3-1: Bootup Process Video ROM Message Screen

_____b.   When the computer is counting memory press the **PAUSE** key.

The *PAUSE* key allows you to pause the bootup process so that you can see some key processes happening. Notice that the bottom of the screen says you can press the *DEL* key to enter setup or press the *ESC* key to bypass the memory test as shown in Figure 3-2. We will be entering CMOS later. Notice that at the bottom there are a CMOS BIOS date and a serial number; these would be useful in an upgrade.

```
  Award Modular Bios v4.5IPG, An Energy Star Ally
  Copyright (C) 1984-1997, Award software, Inc.

   (2a5kfr3c) 11/A

   AND-K6 (tm)/333 PCU Found
   Memory Test:  9572K OK




   Press DEL to enter SETUP
   11/19/97-Ali-15214-23-2A5KFR3CC-00
```

Figure 3-2: Bootup Memory Test Complete

_____c.   Press the **SPACE** key to continue the memory test.

_____d.   After the memory count is done a Plug and Play BIOS extension should pop up. Press **PAUSE** and record the copyright date info in Table 3-1.

_____e.   Press the **SPACE** key to continue.

_____f.   The Plug and Play BIOS should find a CD-ROM drive.

_____g.   Press the **PAUSE** key.

_____h.   Record the CD-ROM type and number in Table 3-2.

_____i.   Press the **SPACE** key.

_____j.   A *System Configuration* box should come up, as shown in Figure 3-3.

Figure 3-3: System Configuration

```
                        Award Software, Inc.
                        System Configuration

  CPU              : AMD-K6(tm)-2        Base Memory       :       640 K
  Co-Processor     : Installed           Extended Memory   :    130048 K
  CPU Clock        : 400Mz               Cache Memory      :       512 K

  Diskette Drive  A : 1.44M, 3.5 in.      Display Type      :     EGA/VGA
  Diskette Drive  B : None                Serial Ports(s)   :     3F8 2F8
  Hard Disk Drive C : LBA, Mode 4, 4299MB Parallel Ports(s) :         378
  Hard Disk Drive D : None                Bank0 DRAM Type   :    EDO DRAM
  Hard Disk Drive E : CDROM, Mode 4       Bank1 DRAM Type   :        None
  Hard Disk Drive F : None                Cache L2 Type     :   Pipe-Burst

  PCI device listing...
  Bus No.  Device No.  Func. No.  Vendor/Device  Class   Device Class        IRQ
     0         2          1       10B9   5219     0101    IDE Controller       14
     0         3          0       1013   00B8     0300    Display Controller   NA
     0         4          0       10EC   8139     0200    Network Controller   11

  Verifying DMA Pool Data ............
```

_____k.   Press the **PAUSE** key.

_____l.   This is the system information. Fill out Table 3-3 as completely as you can.

_____m.   Below the *System Configuration* box is a PCI device listing. In Table 3-4 record the Device No., Device Class, and IRQ numbers used for each device.

_____n.   Press the **SPACE** key to continue.

_____o. The computer will boot to the software menu. Choose either **Microsoft Windows 2000 Professional** or **Microsoft Windows Millennium Edition**.

_____p. Turn the power off on the computer by flipping the power switch on the back of the power supply.

2. Standard CMOS Setup Utility

_____a. Turn the power on.

_____b. Press the **DEL** key when the computer is counting memory. The *CMOS Setup Utility* screen appears as shown in Figure 3-4.

```
                    CMOS Setup Utility
           - Copyright © 1984-2000 Award Software

    ┌──────────────────────────┬──────────────────────────┐
    │ Standard CMOS Features   │ Frequency/Voltage Control │
    │                          │                           │
    │ Advanced Bios Features   │ Load Setup Defaults       │
    │                          │                           │
    │ Advanced Chipset Features│ Set Supervisor Password   │
    │                          │                           │
    │ Integrated Peripherals   │ Set User Password         │
    │                          │                           │
    │ Power Management  Setup  │ Save & Exit Setup         │
    │                          │                           │
    │ PnP / PCI Configuration  │ Exit Without Saving       │
    │                          │                           │
    │ PC Health Status         │                           │
    └──────────────────────────┴──────────────────────────┘
    Esc : Quit                  ▲▼ ►◄  : Select Item
    F10 : Save & Exit Setup     (Shift)F2  : Change Color

              Time, Date, Hard Disk Type...
```

**Figure 3-4:
CMOS Setup Utility
Screen**

_____c. Press **ENTER** on *Standard CMOS Features*.

_____d. Here you can change the date, time, floppy-disk drive type, hard-disk drive settings, video display type, and what errors to halt the boot process on.

_____e. Use the **DOWN ARROW** key to highlight the *Halt On* area as shown in Figure 3-5.

_____f. Press the **PAGE DOWN** key to change the settings.

_____g. Enter all possible options in Table 3-5.

_____h. Set it to halt on all errors.

_____i. Press the **ESC** key to exit the *Standard CMOS Features Setup* screen and return to the **Main menu**.

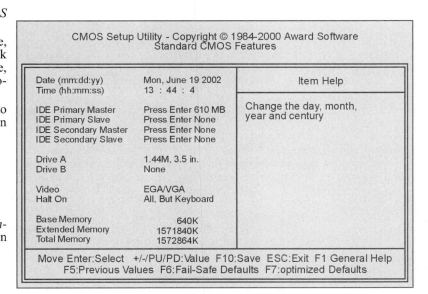

Figure 3-5: Standard CMOS Features Screen

___j.   Press **F10** to save changes and exit CMOS.

___k.   Press **Y**.

___l.   Press **ENTER** to confirm.

___m.   Turn the power off.

___n.   Unplug the keyboard.

___o.   Turn the computer on.

___p.   Record the message from the screen into Table 3-6.

___q.   Turn the computer off.

___r.   Plug the keyboard in; make sure it is oriented the correct way.

3.   **CMOS BIOS Features Setup**

___a.   Turn the computer on.

___b.   Press the **DEL** key to enter CMOS setup.

___c.   Press the **DOWN ARROW** key once to highlight *Advanced BIOS Features*.

___d.   Press **ENTER**. The BIOS features screen will appear as shown in Figure 3-6.

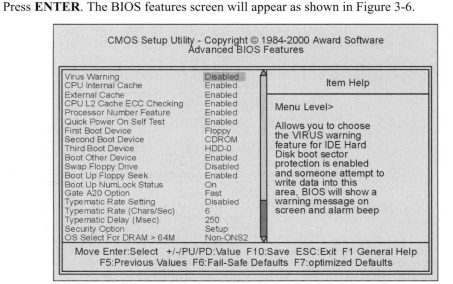

Figure 3-6: The Advanced BIOS Features Screen

___e.   Check the bootup floppy seek; make sure that it is enabled. Press **PAGE DOWN** to change.

___f.   Arrow to **Quick Power On Self Test**.

___g.   Press **PAGE DOWN** to disable it.

___h.   Press the **ESC** key.

___i.   Press **F10** to save and exit CMOS.

___j.   Press **Y**.

___k.   Press **ENTER** to confirm.

___l.   Watch the memory test. Record what has changed in Table 3-7 .

___m.   Press the **DEL** key after memory stops counting to enter CMOS setup.

___n.   Arrow down to **Advanced BIOS Features**.

___o.   Press **ENTER**.

___p.   Arrow down and change the *Quick Power On Self Test* to enabled.

___q.   Press **ESC**.

___r.   Press **F10** to save and exit.

___s.   Press **Y**.

___t.   Press **ENTER** to confirm.

___u.   Turn the power off.

4. The drive LED sequence

____a.   Turn the power on.

____b.   Watch the LED on the front of the case. Record the order in which the floppy-disk drive LED and the hard-disk drive LED come on in Table 3-8.

____c.   Let the computer boot to the software menu.

____d.   Arrow down once to select **Microsoft Windows Millennium Edition**.

____e.   Press **ENTER**.

____f.   Windows Millennium Edition will boot up.

____g.   Click on **Start**.

____h.   Click on **Shut Down**.

____i.   Then in the *Shut Down Windows* dialog box select **Shut down**.

____j.   Click on the **OK** button.

____k.   The computer will shut down and turn off.

TABLES

Table 3-1

Table 3-2

Table 3-3

System Information			
CPU Type:		**Base Memory:**	
Coprocessor:		**Extended Memory:**	
CPU Clock:		**Cache Memory:**	
Drive A:		**Display Type:**	
Drive B:		**Serial Ports:**	
Primary Master:		**Parallel Ports:**	
Primary Slave:		**Cache L2 Type:**	
Secondary Master:		**SDRAM at Rows:**	
Secondary Slave:		**EDO RAM at Rows:**	
Power Management:		**Fast-Page RAM at Rows:**	

Table 3-4

	System Configuration	
Device No.	Device Class	IRQ Number

Table 3-5 Standard CMOS Setup

	Halt On	

Table 3-6 Keyboard Removed

Table 3-7 Quick Power On Self Test Disabled

Table 3-8 Drive LED Sequence

LAB QUESTIONS

Feedback

1. How do you enter a CMOS setup screen on most BIOS?

2. How do you pause the bootup process?

3. What is the box that appears on bootup and has a lot of information about the computer called?

4. How do you save changes and exit CMOS setup?

5. What does the Quick Power On Self Test do?

CMOS Passwords and Resources

OBJECTIVES

1. Use Advanced BIOS Features setup
2. Use CMOS passwords.
3. Learn about power management settings.
4. Learn about integrated peripherals.

Hardware

RESOURCES

1. PC-compatible desktop/tower computer system—Customer-supplied desktop/tower hardware system **OR** Marcraft Computer Repair Trainer **OR** suitable PC hardware trainer
2. Windows Millennium Edition installed
3. Phillips screwdriver

DISCUSSION

CMOS settings may differ from manufacturer to manufacturer. Passwords for computers can give you the necessary security for your computer. One of the biggest problems faced when repairing computers is CMOS user passwords. You need to know what to do if the computer you are trying to repair has a password and you don't know what it is. The way to get around this is to clear the CMOS settings. This will clear out the password, but it will also clear out any custom settings that may have been set up.

PROCEDURE

1. **Prepare the system for adding a bootup password**
   ____a.   Start the computer.
   ____b.   Press **DELETE** to enter CMOS when prompted on the bottom of the screen.
   ____c.   Arrow down to **Advanced BIOS Features** and press **ENTER**.
   ____d.   Arrow down to highlight **Security Option**.

_____e.   Press **PAGE DOWN** to change it from Setup to System as shown in Figure 4-1.

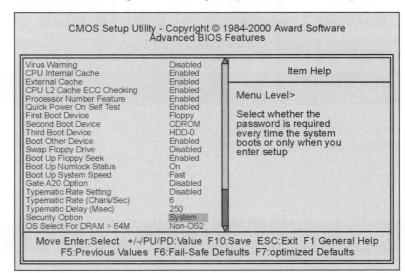

Figure 4-1:
Advanced BIOS
Features Screen

_____f.   Press **ESC**.
_____g.   Press **F10**.
_____h.   Press **Y**.
_____i.   Press **ENTER** to save and exit CMOS. The computer will reboot.

2. Set up User Password for CMOS entry
_____a.   Press **CTRL+ALT+DELETE** to reboot the computer.
_____b.   Press the **DELETE** key when the computer is counting memory.
_____c.   Arrow over and highlight **Set User Password**.
_____d.   Press **ENTER**.
_____e.   The *Enter Password* box will appear as in Figure 4-2.

CMOS Setup Utility - Copyright © 1984-2000 Award Software

Standard CMOS Features	Load Bios Defaults
Advanced BIOS Features	Load Setup Defaults
Advanced Chipset Features	Set Supervisor Password
Integrated Peripherals	Set User Password
Power Management Setup	Save & Exit Setup
Pnp / Pci Configuratio	Enter Password:	out Saving
PC Health Status	

Esc : Quit   ↑↓ ←→ : Select Item
F10 : Save & Exit Setup

Change/Set/Disable Password

Figure 4-2:
The Enter Password
Box

_____f.   Type **marcraft** for the user password.
_____g.   Press **ENTER**.

____h.   Type **marcraft** again to confirm it.
____i.   Press **ENTER**.
____j.   Press **F10**.
____k.   Press **Y** to save and exit CMOS.
____l.   Press **ENTER**.
____m.   The computer will reboot.

NOTE: Your bootup process now requires a password for the operating system to begin loading.

____n.   When prompted to enter password, type **marcraft**.
____o.   The computer will boot to the software menu as in Figure 4-3.

Please select the operating system to start

Microsoft Windows 2000 Professional
Microsoft Windows Millennium Edition

Use ↑ and ↓ to move the highlight to your choice
Press Enter to choose.

For troubleshooting and advanced startup options for Windows 2000, Press F8.

**Figure 4-3:
The Software Menu**

3.   **Disable the User Password**
____a.   Press **CTRL+ALT+DELETE** to reboot the computer.
____b.   Press **DELETE** to enter CMOS when prompted.
____c.   Enter **marcraft** when prompted.
____d.   Arrow over and highlight **Set User Password**.
____e.   Press **ENTER**.
____f.   Leave it blank and press **ENTER**. This should disable the password.
____g.   Press a key to continue.
____h.   Press **F10**.
____i.   Press **Y**.
____j.   Press **ENTER** to save and exit CMOS.
____k.   Press **DELETE** to enter CMOS. You should not be prompted for a password.

NOTE: There may come a time when you do not know the password and will need to get into CMOS setup. We will enable the password again and show you how to clear it and proceed to enter CMOS.

____l.   Arrow over to **User Password**.
____m.   Press **ENTER**.
____n.   Type **marcraft**.
____o.   Press **ENTER**.
____p.   Type **marcraft** again.
____q.   Press **ENTER** and confirm it.

_____r.   Press **F10**.

_____s.   Press **Y**.

_____t.   Press **ENTER** to save and exit CMOS.

_____u.   Let the computer boot to the Password Prompt.

_____v.   Turn the computer off.

4.   Clear the CMOS Settings

_____a.   Unplug the computer.

_____b.   Remove the screws from the computer cover.

_____c.   Remove the computer case cover.

_____d.   Remove the CMOS battery.

_____e.   Use the system board documentation to locate the jumper for clearing the CMOS settings.

NOTE: The J32 jumper, shown in Figure 4-4, is for clearing the CMOS on the Marcraft MC-8000 Trainer. See the system board book on other computers.

Figure 4-4:
Jumper JP32

_____f.   In this example, move the jumper from pins 2 and 3 to pins 3 and 4, turn the computer on, and count to 20. (Use the procedure from your system board documentation for any other computer.)

_____g.   Turn the computer off and then return the jumper back to pins 2 and 3 on JP32.

_____h.   Turn the computer on and press the **DELETE** key during the memory count. The password should be gone.

_____i.   Press the **ESC** key and then press the **ENTER** key to reboot.

_____j.   Record the error message that appears when rebooting in Table 4-1.

_____k.   Press **F1** to continue booting.

_____l.   Replace the case cover.

_____m.   Screw on the cover.

_____n.   Press **CTRL+ALT+DELETE** to reboot

_____o.   Press the **DELETE** key to enter the CMOS setup.

NOTE: The default CMOS settings will be fine except that the time may have been reset to the BIOS date. If the time is reset, we can change it in CMOS by following Step 5 below.

5.   Change the Date and Time in CMOS

_____a.   Press **ENTER** on the *Standard CMOS Setup*.

_____b.   Highlight the month.

____c.   Press **PAGE DOWN** on the month to change it to the desired month as shown in Figure 4-5.

____d.   Highlight the day.

____e.   Press **PAGE DOWN** or **UP** to change it to the correct day.

____f.   Highlight the year.

____g.   Press **PAGE DOWN** or **UP** to change it to the correct year.

____h.   Highlight the hour.

____i.   Press **PAGE DOWN** or **UP** to change it to the correct hour.

____j.   Highlight the minute.

____k.   Press **PAGE DOWN** or **UP** to change it to the correct minute.

____l.   Press **ESC** to Exit.

```
 CMOS Setup Utility - Copyright © 1984-2000 Award Software
                  Standard CMOS Features

 Date (mm:dd:yy)        Mon, June 19 2002        Item Help
 Time (hh:mm:ss)        13 : 44 : 4
                                             Change the day, month,
 IDE Primary Master     Press Enter 610 MB    year and century
 IDE Primary Slave      Press Enter None
 IDE Secondary Master   Press Enter None
 IDE Secondary Slave    Press Enter None

 Drive A                1.44M, 3.5 in.
 Drive B                None

 Video                  EGA/VGA
 Halt On                All, But Keyboard

 Base Memory                     640K
 Extended Memory             1571840K
 Total Memory                1572864K

 Move Enter:Select  +/-/PU/PD:Value  F10:Save  ESC:Exit  F1 General Help
      F5:Previous Values  F6:Fail-Safe Defaults  F7:optimized Defaults
```

Figure 4-5: Standard CMOS Features Screen

Power management in CMOS helps preserve power usage on a computer. Integrated peripherals are the input/output devices that are included on the motherboard. These are USB (universal serial bus), serial ports or COM ports, parallel ports (for printers and scanners), IDE hard drive controllers, and floppy-disk drive controllers.

We will now deal with Power Management Setup in the CMOS. Power Management is sometimes used for computers that are always on, but mostly it is used for battery-powered computers like laptops. By changing these settings you will be able to save power. You will also be able to let the computer know on which type of activity it should "wake up."

6.   Power Management Setup

____a.   Arrow down to highlight **Power Management Setup**.

____b.   Press **ENTER**.

____c.   Arrow down to highlight **Power Management**, and press **ENTER**.

____d.   Press **PAGE DOWN** to change it to **Min Saving** as shown in Figure 4-6.

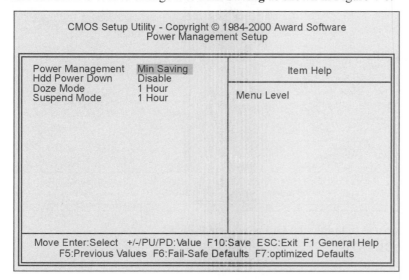

**Figure 4-6:
Power Management
Screen**

_____e.   Record the values in Table 4-2.
_____f.   Press **PAGE DOWN** again so it displays **Max Saving**.
_____g.   Record these values in Table 4-2.
_____h.   Press **PAGE DOWN** until it displays **User Defined settings**.
_____i.   Press the **ESC** key twice to return to the *Main* menu.

The Integrated Peripherals Setup can set the On-Chip Primary IDE to be enabled or disabled. We will get into this in more detail in the next lab along with the FDC Controller.

The On-Chip USB Controller can be either enabled or disabled. USB is a relatively new serial bus type, allowing up to 127 devices to be connected simultaneously through one USB port. It also allows for "hot-swapping" devices easily, which means changing the devices while the computer is still powered on. See the *A+ Certification Concepts & Practice* book for more on USB devices.

The Init Display First has a selection PCI slot (default) or AGP slot. This simply tells the computer what slot to "snoop" first for the video card. If the correct slot is listed here it will make booting up slightly faster.

The Onboard Serial Port setting is one of the most used settings in this CMOS section. It allows you to select what COM port you want each serial port to be. The main reason this is important is that old modems work best if they are on one of the standard COM ports: 1, 2, 3, or 4. In order for the IRQ of the modem not to conflict with the IRQ of the COM port you must either change the modem or change the setting in CMOS. Usually you would just disable COM 2 and set the modem to use the COM 2 settings.

The Onboard Parallel port allows you to change the mode in which the parallel port operates. This is important because some devices, such as scanners, require the parallel port to operate in ECP mode in order to communicate correctly. This is where you would change those settings.

7.   Integrated Peripherals setup
_____a.   Arrow up to highlight **Integrated Peripherals**.
_____b.   Press **ENTER**. The Integrated Peripherals screen will appear as in Figure 4-7.

**Figure 4-7:
Integrated
Peripherals Screen**

_____c.   Arrow down to highlight the **Onboard Serial Port 1**.
_____d.   Press **PAGE DOWN**.
_____e.   Record all options available for Serial Port 1 in Table 4-3.
_____f.   Change the setting back to **Auto**.

____g.   Press **ESC**.
____h.   Press **F10**.
____i.   Press **Y**.
____j.   Press **ENTER** to confirm and exit CMOS setup.

8.   **Verify that the computer is still booting properly**
____a.   The computer will boot up to the software menu.
____b.   Arrow down to select **Microsoft Windows Millennium Edition**.
____c.   Press **ENTER**.
____d.   Windows Millennium Edition will boot up.
____e.   Click on **Start**.
____f.   Click on **Shut Down**.
____g.   In the *Shut Down Windows* dialog box select **Shut down**.
____h.   Click on the **OK** button.

TABLES

Table 4-1

Error Message	

Table 4-2

Power Management	Min Saving	Max Saving
HDD PowerDown		
Doze Mode		
Suspend Mode		

Table 4-3

Options Available for Serial Port 1		

Feedback

LAB QUESTIONS

1. When will a user be prompted for a password if the Security Option is "Setup"?

2. When will a user be prompted for a password if the Security Option is "System"?

3. How do you reboot the computer without pushing the reset switch or the power switch?

4. How do you get into the CMOS of a computer if you don't know the system password that it is asking for?

5. When clearing the CMOS settings with the jumper, what time will the computer be set to?

6. What computer system is Power Management most useful to and why?

7. How many Serial Port settings can be set up in CMOS?

Configuring and Troubleshooting HDD Settings

Hardware

OBJECTIVES

1. Auto-detect IDE drives in CMOS.
2. Use CMOS IDE modes.
3. Learn about CD-ROM setup considerations.
4. Explore IDE cable configurations.
5. Explore IDE device Master/Slave jumper settings.

RESOURCES

1. PC-compatible desktop/tower computer system — Customer-supplied desktop/tower hardware system **OR** Marcraft Computer Repair Trainer **OR** suitable PC hardware trainer with Windows 2000 and Millennium Edition installed
2. Faulted hardware components — User-supplied faulted IDE cable **OR** Marcraft Basic Hardware/Software Fault Set (faulted IDE cable)

DISCUSSION

You need to enter the BIOS's CMOS Configuration Setup program during bootup and set several parameters to match the type of HDD being installed. Before exchanging or reformatting a hard-disk drive, it is always advisable to make backups of the drive's contents and record its configuration parameters.

There are certain pieces of information that should be known, and configurations that should be verified, before inserting the drive into the disk drive bay. In particular, the drive's type parameters should be verified, and its physical Drive Select or Master/Slave setting should be made.

For some drives, this information is contained in an information booklet that comes with the drive. Other drives include this information on a sticker that is mounted on the drive itself. In these cases, it is somewhat difficult to access the information after the drive has been installed in the system unit.

Figure 5-1 depicts the relationship of the hard-disk drive to the rest of the system. In addition, it shows the hard-disk drive's information and control signal paths between the drives and the system board (through the signal cables).

Figure 5-1:
HDD-Related
Components

Hardware

PROCEDURE

1. Auto-Detection

_____ a.   Turn the computer on.

_____ b.   Press **Reset** to reboot the computer; and then press **DELETE** to enter CMOS setup.

_____ c.   Press **ENTER** to go into **Standard CMOS Features**.

_____ d.   Arrow down to highlight **IDE Auto-Detection**, and press **ENTER**. The IDE Primary Master setup is opened as shown in Figure 5-2.

```
CMOS Setup Utility - Copyright © 1984-2000 Award Software
                     IDE Primary Master

  IDE HDD Auto-Detection    Press Enter          Item Help

  IDE Primary Master        Auto           Menu Level>
  Access Mode               Auto
                                           To auto-detect the
  Capacity                  41176 MB       HDD's size, head... on
                                           this channel
  Cylinder                  19710
  Head                      16
  Precomp                   0
  Landing Zone              19709
  Sector                    255




  Move Enter:Select   +/-/PU/PD:Value  F10:Save  ESC:Exit  F1 General Help
        F5:Previous Values  F6:Fail-Safe Defaults  F7:optimized Defaults
```

Figure 5-2:
IDE Primary
Master Screen

___e. Press the **ENTER** key to begin the auto-detection process.

___f. Press the **ESC** key twice to access the main menu and then use the **ARROW** keys to highlight **Integrated Peripherals**.

___g. Press the **ENTER** key.

___h. Make sure that the On-Chip IDE Channel 0 and Channel 2 are both enabled, and press the **ESC** key.

___i. Press **F10**, **Y**, and **ENTER** to save and exit CMOS. The computer will reboot.

2. Check configuration

___a. Press the **PAUSE** key on the keyboard at the *System Configuration* screen. See Figure 5-3.

___b. At the bottom of the screen under *Device Class* find *IDE Controller*.

___c. Record the IRQ(s) that it is using in Table 5-1; press **SPACE**.

___d. Press **CTRL+ALT+DELETE** to reboot the computer.

3. Disable 2nd channel IDE (1)

___a. Press **DELETE** to enter CMOS when prompted.

___b. Arrow over to **Integrated Peripherals** and press **ENTER**.

___c. Arrow down to **OnChip IDE Channel 1**. See Figure 5-4.

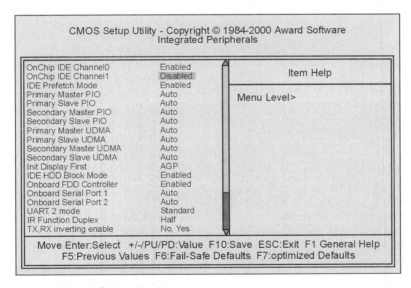

Copyright © 1984-2000 Award Software, Inc.
System Configuration

CPU	: AMD-K6(tm)-2	Base Memory	:	640 K
CPU ID /ucode ID	: Installed	Extended Memory	:	130048 K
CPU Clock	: 400Mz	Cache Memory	:	512 K

Diskette Drive A	: 1.44M, 3.5 in.	Display Type	:	EGA/VGA
Diskette Drive B	: None	Serial Ports(s)	:	3F8 2F8
Pri Master Disk	: LBA, Mode 4, 4299MB	Parallel Ports(s)	:	378
Pri Slave Disk	: None	Bank0 DRAM Type	:	EDO DRAM
Sec.y Master Disk	: CDROM, Mode 4	Bank1 DRAM Type	:	None
Sec. Slave Disk	: None	Cache L2 Type	:	Pipe-Burst

PCI device listing...

Bus No.	Device No.	Func. No.	Vendor/Device		Class	Device Class	IRQ
0	2	1	10B9	5219	0101	IDE Controller	14
0	3	0	1013	00B8	0300	Display Controller	NA
0	4	0	10EC	8139	0200	Network Controller	11

Verifying DMA Pool Data ....

Figure 5-3: System Configuration Screen

CMOS Setup Utility - Copyright © 1984-2000 Award Software
Integrated Peripherals

OnChip IDE Channel0	Enabled	Item Help
OnChip IDE Channel1	Disabled	
IDE Prefetch Mode	Enabled	
Primary Master PIO	Auto	Menu Level>
Primary Slave PIO	Auto	
Secondary Master PIO	Auto	
Secondary Slave PIO	Auto	
Primary Master UDMA	Auto	
Primary Slave UDMA	Auto	
Secondary Master UDMA	Auto	
Secondary Slave UDMA	Auto	
Init Display First	AGP	
IDE HDD Block Mode	Enabled	
Onboard FDD Controller	Enabled	
Onboard Serial Port 1	Auto	
Onboard Serial Port 2	Auto	
UART 2 mode	Standard	
IR Function Duplex	Half	
TX,RX inverting enable	No, Yes	

Move Enter:Select +/-/PU/PD:Value F10:Save ESC:Exit F1 General Help
F5:Previous Values F6:Fail-Safe Defaults F7:optimized Defaults

Figure 5-4: Integrated Peripherals Screen

___d. Press **PAGE DOWN** to disable it.

___e. Press **ESC** to return to the *Main* menu.

___f. Press **F10**, **Y**, and **ENTER** to save and exit CMOS.

4. Enable 2nd channel IDE

____a. Press **Pause** on the *System Configuration* screen.
____b. Record what IRQ(s) the IDE Controller is using now in Table 5-2.
____c. Press **SPACE**.
____d. Press **CTRL+ALT+DELETE** immediately.
____e. Press **DELETE** to enter CMOS when prompted.
____f. Go into the *Integrated Peripherals* screen again and enable the 2nd channel IDE.
____g. Arrow down to the **IDE Primary Master PIO** and press **PAGE DOWN**.
____h. Record all selections in Table 5-3.
____i. Set it back to **Auto**.

These selections are for different supported modes that hard drives offer. The standard mode is 4. Since most CMOS settings auto-detect, there is no need to do anything with these settings. The only reason to modify them would be if a hard drive from an older system were installed into a newer system. The older system would have partitioned and formatted the drive in mode 1, for instance. In order for the new computer to recognize the drive, it would have to force mode 1 or repartition and format the drive. All the information on the hard drive would be lost.

5. Other HDD options

____a. Arrow down to **IDE HDD Block Mode**; press **PAGE DOWN** to see the different selections. See Figure 5-5.

```
          ROM PCI/ISA BIOS (2A5KFDAA)
          INTEGRATED PERIPHERALS SETUP
               AWARD SOFTWARE, INC.
┌────────────────────────────┬────────────────────────────┐
│ On-Chip IDE Controller  : Enabled  │ Parallel Port Mode    : ECP+EPP │
│ The 2nd channel IDE     : Disabled │ ECP Mode Use DMA      : 1       │
│ IDE Primary Master PIO  : Auto     │ Parallel Port EPP Type: EPP1.9  │
│ IDE Primary Slave PIO   : Auto     │                                 │
│ IDE Secondary Master PIO: Auto     │                                 │
│ IDE Secondary Slave PIO : Auto     │                                 │
│ IDE Primary Master FIFO : Enabled  │                                 │
│ IDE Primary Slave FIFO  : Disabled │                                 │
│ IDE Secondary Master FIFO: Disabled│                                 │
│ IDE Secondary Slave FIFO: Disabled │                                 │
│ IDE HDD Block Mode      : Enabled  │                                 │
│                                    │                                 │
│ Onboard FDC Controller  : Enabled  │                                 │
│ Onboard UART 1          : Auto     │                                 │
│ UART 1 Operation mode   : Standard │ ESC : Quit       ↑↓→← :Select Item│
│                                    │ F1  : Help    PU/PD/+/- : Modify │
│ Onboard UART 2          : Auto     │ F5  : Old Values  (Shift)F2 : Color│
│ UART 2 Operation mode   : Standard │ F6  : Load BIOS Defaults         │
│                                    │ F7  : Load Setup Defaults        │
│ Onboard Parallel Port   : 278/IRQ5 │                                 │
└────────────────────────────┴────────────────────────────┘
```

**Figure 5-5: Integrated Peripherals Screen
(Different Selections)**

Some BIOS offer an option called "block mode." Block mode is a performance enhancement that allows the grouping of multiple read or write commands over the IDE/ATA interface so that they can be handled on a single interrupt.

Interrupts are used to signal when data is ready to be transferred from the hard disk; each one interrupts other work being done by the processor. Newer drives, when used with supporting BIOS, allow you to transfer as many as 16 or 32 sectors with a single interrupt. Since the processor is being interrupted much less frequently, performance is much improved, and more data is moving around with less command overhead, which is much more efficient than transferring data one sector at a time.

NOTE: Some systems can have trouble running disks in block mode, even if they are supposed to allow it. You may have better luck with the drive or system if it is disabled.

____b. Select **Enabled**.
____c. Press **ESC** to exit the *Main* menu.
____d. Arrow over to the **Advanced BIOS Features Setup** and press **ENTER**.

____ e.   Arrow down to **First Boot Device**. See Figure 5-6.

____ f.   Press **PAGE DOWN** and record all the selections into Table 5-4.

____ g.   Select **Floppy** for the *First Boot Device*.

____ h.   Select **HDD-0** for the *Second Boot Device*.

____ i.   Select **HDD-1** for the *Third Boot Device*.

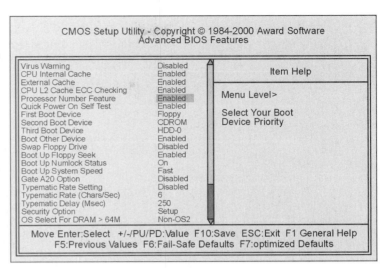

The EIDE interface has been redefined from IDE to allow faster transfer rates as well as to handle more storage capacity and to control non−hard drive units, such as tape drives or CD-ROM drives. The EIDE interface is often described as ATAPI (AT Attachment Peripheral Interconnect) or Fast ATA (Fast AT Attachment). ATA-2 is the latest version.

Figure 5-6: Advanced BIOS Features Screen

Most new operating systems now come with a bootable CD-ROM. Table 5-4 shows how it would be very easy to make the CD-ROM the first boot device so that you can install the operating system without a bootable floppy disk. The ATAPI interface became the industry-wide standard of the EIDE controller, allowing CD-ROM drive manufacturers to build in ATAPI-compliant drives so that software drivers are not necessary. Without this interface bootable CD's would not have been possible.

____ j.   Press **ESC** to return to the *Main* menu.

____ k.   Press **F10**, **Y**, and **ENTER** to save and exit CMOS.

IDE Troubleshooting

The first section is dedicated to installing the hardware of a typical hard-disk drive unit. The final section of the procedure concentrates on the diagnostic and troubleshooting aspects associated with typical HDD units.

You previously entered the BIOS's CMOS Configuration Setup program, and detected parameters to match the type of HDD being installed. Drive Type information for SCSI drives normally requires that the CMOS configuration be set to "none installed" to operate correctly.

Before exchanging or reformatting a hard disk drive, it is always advisable to make backups of the drive's contents and record its configuration parameters.

The drive's type parameters should be verified, and its physical Drive Select or Master/Slave setting should be made. These parameters may be in an information booklet that comes with the drive or on a sticker that is mounted on the drive itself. In some cases, it is somewhat difficult to access the information after the drive has been installed in the system unit, so the instructor should record this information in a more easily read location.

The Master/Slave setting will normally be Master if the unit is the primary or the only HDD in the system. This is the default setting from the factory. The CD-ROM is the Slave unit by default.

Hard drives are very sensitive to physical damage. If you drop a hard drive even from 4 inches above the table, there is no guarantee that it will still work. The heads on the hard drive will crash on the disk and create bad or unreadable sectors, especially if sector 0 is involved. Then the drive table and information will be lost and the drive will be unusable.

1.   Standard configuration

____a.   Refer to the HDD documentation to determine the Drive Select or Master/Slave jumper settings.

____b.   Obtain the drive's parameter information from the driver or information booklet and record it in Table 5-5.

____c.   Check to make sure that all the screws are secure in the drive and that it is not loose. See Figure 5-7.

SMALL
SCREWS

Figure 5-7:
Hard Drive Mounting
Screws Are Secure

NOTE: IDE drives use a single wide signal cable. As you know from Lab 2, the signal cable must be aligned correctly at both the drive and controller ends. The stripe must be aligned with the #1 pin at both ends. All new cables are keyed to prevent backwards installation.

____d.   Verify the connection of the signal cables to the HDD, the CD-ROM, and the HDD controller on the system board.

____e.   Turn the computer on.

____f.   Press **DELETE** to enter CMOS when prompted.

____g.   Go into Standard CMOS setup.

____h.   The Primary Master should be the HDD. Press **ENTER** to verify it is set to "*Auto*".

____i.   Make sure all other hard drives are set up for **Auto** detection, and be sure the "*Access Mode*" is also set to *Auto*. Change the settings if they are not set to *Auto*.

____j.   Press **ESC** to view the *Main* menu.

____k.   Press **F10**, **Y**, and **ENTER** to save and exit CMOS.

____l.   Verify that the computer boots up to the software menu where you have the choices of **Microsoft Windows 2000 Professional** or **Microsoft Windows Millennium Edition**.

____m.   Turn the computer off.

2.   Master IDE devices

____a.   Connect the CD-ROM and hard-disk drive to the same ribbon cable (the original HDD cable). Verify that the hard-disk drive is set to "Master" on the Drive Select jumper. Verify that the CD-ROM's Master/Slave configuration jumper is set to "Master".

____b.   Turn the computer on.

____c.   Record the results in Table 5-6.

____d.   Turn the computer off.

3. **Master CD-ROM, Slave HDD**
   ____a. Change the jumper on the hard-disk drive to the Slave setting.
   ____b. Turn the computer on.
   ____c. Press **DELETE** to enter CMOS.
   ____d. Enter *Standard CMOS setup*.
   ____e. Note the differences in Table 5-7.
   ____f. Press **F10**, **Y**, and **ENTER** to save and exit CMOS.
   ____g. Record the results in Table 5-8.
   ____h. Turn the computer off.

4. **Master HDD, Slave CD-ROM**
   ____a. Change the CD-ROM Drive Select jumper back to the Slave position.
   ____b. Change the hard drive jumper back to the Master position.
   ____c. Turn the computer on.
   ____d. Record the results in Table 5-9.
   ____e. Turn the computer off.

As you can see, it doesn't matter which drive is set to Master as long as there is only one drive set to Master. However, if the slave device had been a hard drive instead of a CD-ROM the computer would have tried to boot from the IDE-0 every time. If it wasn't bootable you would have received an error message.

5. **Incorrect IDE cable orientation**
   ____a. Unplug the 80-pin cable from the CD-ROM and HDD.
   ____b. Plug the 40-wire CD-ROM cable into the HDD.
   ____c. Turn the computer on.
   ____d. Record the results in Table 5-10.
   ____e. Turn the computer off.

6. **Marcraft Fault Set**
   ____a. Open the Marcraft Fault Set and get the faulted IDE cable.
   ____b. Install the cable to the system board, HDD, and CD-ROM, making sure it is oriented the correct way.
   ____c. Turn the computer on and record the results in Table 5-11.
   ____d. Turn the computer off.

7. **Return all cables and jumpers to their original configuration.**

TABLES

Table 5-1

Table 5-2

Table 5-3

Available Selections for the IDE Primary Master PIO		

Table 5-4

Available Selections for the Boot Sequence	

Table 5-5

HDD Parameters from Information Book or Sticker		
Cylinders	Heads	Sectors

Table 5-6

Table 5-7

Table 5-8

Table 5-9

Table 5-10

Table 5-11

PROCEDURE - 5

Feedback

LAB QUESTIONS

1. Where should you look to find hard drive parameters?

2. Does your BIOS offer block mode?

3. What has made bootable CD's possible?

4. Is it possible to boot from a Zip disk?

5. How would you change your boot sequence to boot from the floppy drive?

6. Before exchanging a hard-disk drive what should be done first?

7. Name two configurations for HDD jumper settings used in this lab.

8. What is the default setting for a CD-ROM from the factory?

9. If you have two drives, one master and one slave, does it matter which device is plugged into the center or end of an IDE cable?

10. If two hard drives are both set to slave on one cable, what will happen?

Using Multimeters (Optional)

Hardware

OBJECTIVES

1. Measure resistance on a speaker.
2. Measure voltage from a power supply.

RESOURCES

1. PC-compatible desktop/tower computer system — Customer-supplied desktop/tower hardware system **OR** Marcraft Computer Repair Trainer **OR** suitable PC hardware trainer
2. Digital multimeter with leads
3. A good fuse
4. A bad fuse

DISCUSSION

This lab will help you to measure various electrical quantities on a computer. The multimeter can be used to measure resistance, current, and potential across a circuit.

PROCEDURE

1. **Resistance on speaker**
   ____a. Remove the side panel from the computer.
   ____b. Rotate the multimeter dial to 200 ohms.
   ____c. Hold the red lead on the exposed end of the red wire that connects the system speaker.
   ____d. Hold the black lead on the exposed end of the black wire that connects the system speaker.
   ____e. Record the reading of the meter in Table 6-1.

2. **Voltages**
   ____a. Turn on the power to the computer.
   ____b. Look for the 20-pin ATX power connector that is plugged into the board. It should look similar to location 1 in Figure 6-1.

Figure 6-1: Power Supply Connector

_____c. Rotate the multimeter dial to 20 Vdc.
_____d. Firmly secure the black connector of the multimeter into a black connector of one of the 4-pin internal drive power connectors (location 2).
_____e. Insert the red multimeter connector into each pin on the ATX connector and record their respective voltages in Table 6-2.

NOTE: *The pin number is small and may be labeled on the back wire side of the connector. The yellow wire should be pin one.*

_____f. Check the voltage at each pin of the 4-pin internal drive power connector and record the values in Table 6-3.
_____g. Turn the computer off.
_____h. Replace the side panel.

3. Fuses
_____a. Obtain the two fuses, one good and one bad, from your instructor.
_____b. Rotate the multimeter dial to 200 ohms.
_____c. Touch the two leads together and record the multimeter reading in Table 6-4. You are now establishing a datum or zero point of no resistance.
_____d. Without touching the leads together, record the multimeter reading in Table 6-5.
_____e. Place one lead on one end of the good fuse.
_____f. Place the other lead on the other end of the good fuse. Be sure that your fingers or the leads are not touching each other.

NOTE: *The only path for electricity to flow is through the fuse.*

_____g. Record the multimeter reading in Table 6-6.
_____h. Place one lead on one end of the bad fuse.
_____i. Place the other lead on the other end of the bad fuse. Be sure that your fingers or the leads are not touching each other.

NOTE: *The only path for electricity to flow is through the fuse.*

_____j. Record the multimeter reading in Table 6-7.
_____k. Return all your equipment to your instructor.

TABLES

Table 6-1

Speaker Resistance:	

Table 6-2

ATX Voltages			
Pin No.	Voltage	Pin No.	Voltage
1		11	
2		12	
3		13	
4		14	
5		15	
6		16	
7		17	
8		18	
9		19	
10		20	

Table 6-3

4-Pin Internal Drive Power Connector Voltages			
Pin No.	Voltage	Pin No.	Voltage
1		3	
2		4	

Table 6-4

Zero Resistance:	

Table 6-5

Maximum Resistance:	

Table 6-6

Good Fuse Resistance:	

Table 6-7

Bad Fuse Resistance:	

Feedback

LAB QUESTIONS

1. How many pins does an ATX power connector have?

2. The multimeter can be used to measure what?

3. What is the total range of voltages across the power supply?

4. What options does your multimeter support for dc voltage?

5. What should be the resistance of a good fuse?

Hardware Troubleshooting

OBJECTIVES

1. Unplug the keyboard.
2. Unplug the mouse.
3. Disable the L2 cache.
4. Unplug the video card.
5. Unplug the RAM.
6. Unplug the FDD interface cable.
7. Unplug the power to the FDD, CD-ROM, HDD, and motherboard.

Hardware

RESOURCES

1. PC-compatible desktop/tower computer system — Customer-supplied desktop/tower hardware system **OR** Marcraft Computer Repair Trainer **OR** suitable PC hardware trainer

2. Faulted hardware components — user-supplied faulted hardware components (defective mouse, defective DIMM module, defective FDD cable, defective options power connector) **OR** Marcraft Basic Hardware/Software Fault Set

DISCUSSION

This lab will familiarize you with some of the errors associated with bad devices. You will receive different messages from the computer depending on which device has a problem. You will explore a fault with IDE connectivity and various no-signal problems.

PROCEDURE

1. **Establish the "Halt On" setting in the CMOS Setup utility**
   ____a. Turn the computer on.
   ____b. Press the **DELETE** key to enter the *CMOS Setup utility*.
   ____c. Press **ENTER** to enter the *Standard CMOS Setup*.
   ____d. Change the *Halt On* setting to **All errors**, and press the **ESC** key.
   ____e. Press the **F10** key and **ENTER** to save the change and exit the CMOS Setup utility.

Figure 7-1: Unplug the Keyboard

BACK OF
SYSTEM
UNIT

KEYBOARD

SYSTEM
BOARD

2. Keyboard

_____a. Verify that the computer is off; if it is not, shut it down.

_____b. Unplug the keyboard connector from the back of the computer, as shown in Figure 7-1.

_____c. Turn the computer on.

_____d. Record your observations about any errors given in Table 7-1.

_____e. Turn the computer off.

_____f. Plug in the keyboard.

BACK OF
SYSTEM
UNIT

PS/2 MOUSE

Figure 7-2: Unplug the Mouse

3. Mouse

_____a. Unplug the mouse (it may be serial or PS/2), as shown in Figure 7-2.

_____b. Plug in the Marcraft faulted mouse.

_____c. Turn the computer on.

_____d. When the Operating System selection screen comes up, select **Windows 2000 Professional** and press **ENTER**.

_____e. Once the operating system has started, try moving the mouse. Record your observations in Table 7-2.

_____f. Press **ALT+F4** with the keyboard.

_____g. Verify that _Shut Down_ is selected; you may need to use the **UP/DOWN ARROW** keys.

_____h. Press **ENTER** to shut down the computer.

_____i. Replace the original mouse.

4. L2 Cache

_____a. Turn the computer on and press **DELETE** to enter CMOS setup.

_____b. Use the arrow keys to browse for **L2 Cache**, usually in _Advanced Settings_.

NOTE: The L2 Cache is sometimes called the External Cache.

_____c. Disable L2 Cache by pressing the +/- keys or by pressing **ENTER** and using the arrow keys.

_____d. Save settings and exit CMOS Setup.

_____e. Boot the computer to Windows 2000 Professional.

_____f. Record your observations in Table 7-3.

_____g. Restart the computer and enter CMOS Setup as before.

_____h. Repeat Steps b-d, only this time enable L2 Cache.

_____i. Turn the computer off.

5. Video card

____a. Remove the side panel of the computer.
____b. Unplug any external connections to the video card, such as the monitor, for example.
____c. Unscrew the mounting screw of the video card.
____d. Pull the card out of its slot, either a PCI or AGP slot, as shown in Figure 7-3.

Figure 7-3: Unplug the Video Card

____e. Turn the computer on and record your observations in Table 7-4.
____f. Turn the computer off.
____g. Replace the video card in its slot.
____h. Replace the mounting screw.
____i. Replace any external connections.

6. RAM

____a. Unplug all extended memory from the motherboard. Be careful with the clamps on the ends of the memory slots, as shown in Figure 7-4.

____b. Insert the Marcraft faulted memory from the fault set.

____c. Turn the computer on and record your observations in Table 7-5.

____d. Turn the computer off.

____e. Replace the memory in their original slots.

Figure 7-4: Unplug Memory

Figure 7-5: Unplug
Floppy Interface

7. FDD interface

____a. Unplug the floppy-disk drive interface at the end connected to the floppy drive, as shown in Figure 7-5.

____b. Plug in the Marcraft faulted floppy interface.

____c. Turn the computer on.

____d. Record your observations in Table 7-6.

____e. Turn the computer off.

____f. Replace the floppy drive interface to its original location.

8. FDD power

____a. Unplug the floppy-disk drive power connector.

____b. Turn the computer on.

____c. Record your observations in Table 7-7.

____d. Turn the computer off.

____e. Replace the floppy drive power connector to its original location.

9. CD-ROM power

____a. Unplug the power connector to the CD-ROM, as shown in Figure 7-6. Do not unplug the interface cable.

____b. Turn the computer on.

____c. If the hard drive and CD-ROM are on the same cable, record the error of the non-booting system in Table 7-8. Skip to Step i.

____d. When the *Operating System selection* screen comes up, select **Windows 2000 Professional** and press **ENTER**.

____e. Once Windows has booted move the mouse and double-click on **My Computer**.

____f. Record the icons listed on the right in Table 7-9.

____g. Close *My Computer* by clicking on the X in the top right part of the window.

____h. Shut down Windows by clicking on **Start/Shut Down** and clicking on **OK**.

____i. Turn the computer off and replace the CD-ROM power connector into its original location.

Figure 7-6: CD-ROM Connections

10. HDD power

___a. Unplug the power connector to the hard drive, as shown in Figure 7-7.

___b. Turn the computer on and record your observations in Table 7-10.

___c. Turn the computer off and replace the hard drive power connector.

11. Motherboard

___a. Unplug the motherboard power connector, as shown in Figure 7-8.

___b. Turn the computer on and record your observations in Table 7-11.

___c. Turn the computer off.

___d. Replace the motherboard power connector.

Figure 7-7: Hard Drive Connections

Figure 7-8: Power Connectors

TABLES

Table 7-1

No Keyboard Connected:	

Table 7-2

No Mouse Connected:	

Table 7-3

L2 Cache Disabled:	

Table 7-4

No Video Adapter:	

Table 7-5

No Memory:	

Table 7-6

No Floppy Drive Interface:	

Table 7-7

No Floppy Drive Power:	

Table 7-8

No CD-ROM Drive Power:	

Table 7-9

My Computer Contents:	

Table 7-10

No Hard Drive Power:	

Table 7-11

No Power to Motherboard:	

LAB QUESTIONS

1. What type of mouse did you use?

2. How many memory modules did you remove?

3. What slot does your video card use?

4. What item do you think was missing from My Computer during the CD-ROM steps?

5. Why do you think there are different results between (1) a non-powered CD-ROM set to Slave with a hard drive as the master on one cable and (2) a non-powered CD-ROM set to Master on its own cable?

Feedback

Research and Design a Media Center Computer

OBJECTIVES

1. Examine a media center computer system specification.
2. Explain the reasons for the selection of each system component.
3. Determine how individual system components will be connected.
4. Based on the given specification, design a media center computer system and identify the required components (use fill-in-the-blank graphic).

Hardware

RESOURCES

1. Books
2. Newspapers
3. Magazines
4. Computer with Internet access

DISCUSSION

Once experience has been gained using a basic computer system, it becomes increasingly evident that the computer can be used to do much more than what is possible using the basic computer configuration. Due to the lack of Internet connectivity, even the research conducted in the previous procedure required the use of a computer having more capabilities than those provided by the basic system.

In this lab procedure, the student will use his or her research skills to locate suitable components providing the capabilities required for a media center computer meeting the specified system specification. Armed with the system specification, the previous research experience should be used to determine which components would be required in order to assemble such a system. Once again, the book, newspaper, magazine, computer, and Internet resources of the local library will prove to be very helpful.

Media center computers and their specific operating systems are designed to manage the digital affairs of modern mediates, such as those who not only wish to watch movies, but edit them as well. Media savvy creators enjoy making family slide shows, or recording every episode of a favorite TV show. Accordingly, media center systems vary depending on the digital lifestyles of their owners.

For example, digital photographic and video editors can perform production work using the high-end tower desktop PC system shown in Figure 8-1. As a large tower desktop, it can be connected directly to a home office monitor, rather than to a living room entertainment center. Its full surround sound speaker system provides accurate audio playback for high-end video productions.

**Figure 8-1: A System for
Performing Photographic
and Video Editing**

Alternately, the media center PC shown in Figure 8-2 has the appearance of a stereo component, and is better suited for the living room as part of whole house entertainment center. Its location is not conducive for use with editing chores, Internet browsing, or e-mail compositions, although it would be capable of such activity.

**Figure 8-2: A System for
Recording and Managing
Television Broadcasts**

More appropriate for such tasks, and others as well, is the full-featured laptop media center (MCE) PC shown in Figure 8-3. The portability of such a machine makes it suitable for use as a primary home office machine, easily handling e-mail, spreadsheet work, and web browsing. In addition, it can move easily into the living room to record television programming, play music, or display photo slide shows on a big screen.

Figure 8-3: A Laptop Media Center PC

Due to the unique designs, styles, and purposes being assigned for contemporary media center computer systems, care must be taken in the selection of which components to use. While determining how to put the specified media center computer system together, remember that the customer will need to understand why the specified key components were selected, and how they are connected into the system.

PROCEDURE

1. Examine the media center computer system specification provided below. Consider the components necessary for the construction of a media center computer system to meet this spec.

    - Processor: Intel 2.8GHz Pentium D

    - Chipset: Intel® 945P express chipset

    - Chassis: Anodized aluminum heatsink case with passive cooling technology

    - Operating System: Microsoft Windows XP Media Center Edition 2005

    - TV Tuners:

        - NTSC: Dual ISF-certified cable/satellite tuners with full hardware MPEG-2 compression, a 3D comb filter, noise reduction for advanced personal video recorder (PVR) activities, with independent S-video, RF, and RCA audio input jacks

        - ATSC: Single HDTV tuner to receive free, over-the-air high definition TV broadcasts in North America; additional rear jack for a second HDTV tuner

    - FM Tuner: Stereo FM terrestrial radio tuner

- Audio:
  - Intel high definition audio 8-channel CODEC
  - 5.1/6.1/7.1 digital surround sound
  - 192-kHz/24-bit audio output and SPDIF out interface (Optical Toslink)
  - Dolby Digital, DTS Analog Decoding, and SPDIF Pass-through
  - Two channel audio inputs
- Graphics:
  - PCI Express x16
  - Nvidia GeForce 6600GT 128-bit, 16.0GB/sec memory bandwidth; 4.0 billion fill rate, 375 million vertices per second; 1000-MHz memory data rate; 8 pixels per clock (peak); 400-MHz RAMDACs
  - Proprietary passive cooling system, with no fans
  - High-speed GDDR3 memory
  - DVD/HDTV MPEG-2 decoding, up to 1920x1080i resolutions
  - Integrated HDTV encoder
  - Advanced adaptive de-interlacing
  - WMV9 decode acceleration
  - OpenGL 2.0 optimizations and support
  - Microsoft DirectX 9.0 Shader Model 3.0 support
  - DVI, VGA, and Component (YPbPr) outputs
- Storage:
  - Internal: Two 3.5-inch SATA2 consumer-grade hard drives; support for 320 GB to 800 GB total internal storage
  - Mounting: Anti-vibration and anti-sound screwless design, with proprietary passive cooling system
  - External: Supports USB 2.0 and IEEE1394 (Firewire) storage
  - Network: Support for a terabyte A/V storage server; support for additional multiple terabytes of network storage; integrated support for Microsoft Media Center 2005
  - Disc Changer: Support for the Ice Vault 200-disc changer; support for multiple Ice Vaults for more than 1000 DVDs
- Optical Disk Drive:
  - Multi-format, progressive scan dual-layer DVD/CD recorder
  - Slot-loading sleek design for reduced noise
  - Records up to 8.5 GBs per dual-layer DVD
  - 2.4x DVD +R DL; 5x DVD-RAM writing; 8x DVD-R writing; 4x DVD-RW writing; 8x DVD+R writing; 4x DVD+RW Writing; 24x CD-R writing; 16x CD-RW writing; 24x CD-ROM reading; 8x DVD-ROM reading; buffer under-run protection; DVD super MULTI read/write support
- Memory:
  - 1 GB DDR2 533 MHz PC4200
  - Dual-channel memory architecture
  - 4 x 184-pin DIMM sockets

- Networking: 10/100/1000 Base-T Gigabit Ethernet LAN
- Expansion Ports:
  - USB 2.0: 2x Front Panel, 4x Rear Panel
  - IEEE1394 (Firewire): 1x Front Panel, 1x Rear Panel
- Power:
  - 550-watt, internal, fanless power supply with overpower protection
  - Rounded heatsink design
  - 115/230V switching

2. The media center computer system specification presented in the previous step is designed to provide the most advanced home entertainment features available today. It regards performance, rather than cost, as the most important selection criteria. Research these individual components to determine their desired features, and why they have been included in the specification. Then, fill in the appropriate tables with your findings. Indicate whether each component feature is internal or external to the media center computer, and describe its performance. If necessary, increase the number of rows provided in the tables, and be ready to explain each component feature to the customer.

Table 8-1: Intel 2.8 GHz Pentium D Processor

Int/Ext	Description	Performance

Table 8-2: Intel 945P Express Chipset

Int/Ext	Description	Performance

Table 8-3: Aluminum Heatsink Chassis with Passive Cooling System

Int/Ext	Description	Performance

Table 8-4: Windows XP Media Center Edition 2005 Operating System

Int/Ext	Description	Performance

Table 8-5: Dual NTSC Tuner with Hardware Encoding

Int/Ext	Description	Performance

Table 8-6: ATSC HDTV Tuner

Int/Ext	Description	Performance

Table 8-7: Stereo FM Terrestrial Radio Tuner

Int/Ext	Description	Performance

Table 8-8: Audio

Int/Ext	Description	Performance

Table 8-9: Graphics

Int/Ext	Description	Performance
	Nvidia GeForce 6600GT video card	

Table 8-10: Storage

Int/Ext	Description	Performance

Table 8-11: Optical Disk Drive

Int/Ext	Description	Performance

Table 8-12: Memory

Int/Ext	Description	Performance

Table 8-13: Networking

Int/Ext	Description	Performance

Table 8-14: Expansion Ports

Int/Ext	Description	Performance

Table 8-15: Power

Int/Ext	Description	Performance

3. Using Figure 8-4 as an example, determine where the individual external components will connect to the media center computer system. Figure 8-5 depicts the logical speaker locations for a 7.1 surround sound speaker system.

Figure 8-4: Media Center Computer System External Connections

Figure 8-5: Logical 7.1 Surround Sound Speaker Locations

4. Design a media center computer system, based on the given specification. Fill in the blanks using the graphic shown in Figure 8-6 to identify the various internal and external system components.

- System unit
- 9-in-1 memory card reader
- Monitor
- FM antenna
- Wireless mouse
- Wireless keyboard
- Surround sound
- Wireless keyboard/mouse receiver
- Remote control
- Front access ports
- DVD W/R drive with Lightscribe

Figure 8-6: A Media Center Computer System

Feedback

LAB QUESTIONS

1. What's the difference between a 6.1 and 7.1 surround sound system?

2. What is the main advantage of using a fanless power supply with a media center computer system?

3. Where should the center channel speaker be physically located?

4. How fast can high-speed GDDR3 memory operate?

5. What makes the selection of a full-featured laptop media center (MCE) PC so attractive?

6. Why would high-end video production not be performed on a living room entertainment center?

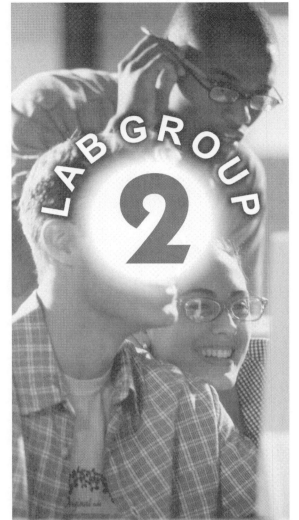

LAB GROUP 2

OPERATING SYSTEMS

Performing an Attended Installation of Windows XP Professional

OBJECTIVES

1. This lab will teach you how to perform an unattended installation of Windows XP Professional.

Operating System Technology

RESOURCES

1. PC-compatible desktop/tower computer system—Customer-supplied desktop/tower hardware system **OR** Marcraft Computer Repair Trainer **OR** suitable PC hardware trainer running Windows XP Professional
2. The Windows XP Professional CD

DISCUSSION

The installation of Windows XP Professional is mostly automatic process. Once the setup process begins, very little user interaction is required until the very last phases. The XP Professional CD is bootable and upon the system being rebooted, will begin the installation process automatically. The average installation time is approx 60 minutes.

PROCEDURE

1. **Install Windows XP Professional**
   ___a.   Make sure your machine is set to boot from the CD-ROM drive. If you are not sure how to do this, consult your system documentation for information about accessing the BIOS settings.

Figure 9-1: Text Mode Setup Portion of the Installation

    b.   Insert the Windows XP Professional CD into your CD-ROM drive and reboot the machine. When the computer reboots, the *Text Mode* setup portion of the installation begins as shown in Figure 9-1. During this time you will asked if you need in install any third-party SCSI or Raid drivers. You only have a few seconds to press the **F6** key and install the drivers before setup continues.

    c.   After a short time the *Welcome to Setup* screen is displayed as shown in Figure 9-2.

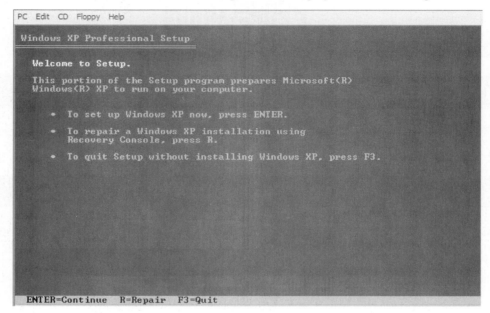

Figure 9-2: Welcome to Setup Screen

    d.   Press **ENTER** to continue with Setup.

    e.   The Windows XP Licensing Agreement appears as illustrated in Figure 9-3. After reading the terms of the license, press **F8** to accept the terms and continue the installation. If you do not accept the agreement, Setup will not continue.

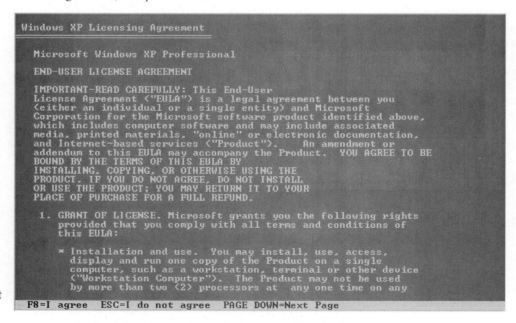

Figure 9-3: Windows XP Licensing Agreement

___f.　After you accept the Licensing Agreement, Setup proceeds to the *Disk Partitioning* portion as shown in Figure 9-4. If you have multiple partitions, Setup will list them and let you choose which one to install XP Professional to.

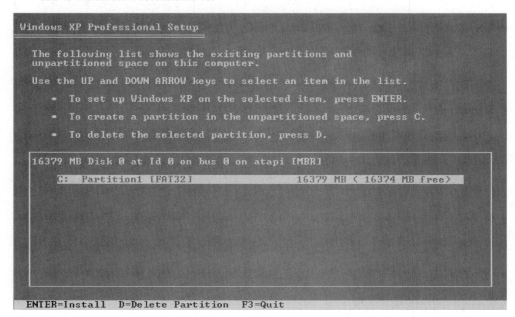

Figure 9-4: Disk Partitioning Portion

___g.　Once you have determined which partition to install to, press **ENTER** to continue.

___h.　Figure 9-5 shows the *Format* screen where you can decide how the drive should be formatted (FAT or NTFS). NTFS offers many advantages over FAT in terms of file security. Highlight "Format the partition using the NTFS file system and press **ENTER**.

```
Windows XP Professional Setup

  Setup will install Windows XP on partition

  C:  Partition1 [FAT32]                  16379 MB < 16374 MB free>

  on 16379 MB Disk 0 at Id 0 on bus 0 on atapi [MBR].

  Use the UP and DOWN ARROW keys to select the file system
  you want, and then press ENTER. If you want to select a
  different partition for Windows XP, press ESC.

     Format the partition using the NTFS file system <Quick>
     Format the partition using the FAT file system <Quick>
     Format the partition using the NTFS file system
     Format the partition using the FAT file system
     Convert the partition to NTFS
     Leave the current file system intact <no changes>




  ENTER=Continue   ESC=Cancel
```

Figure 9-5: Format Screen

_____i.   Setup will display a window, shown in Figure 9-6, warning that formatting the disk will delete all files from it. Press **F** to format the drive and continue.

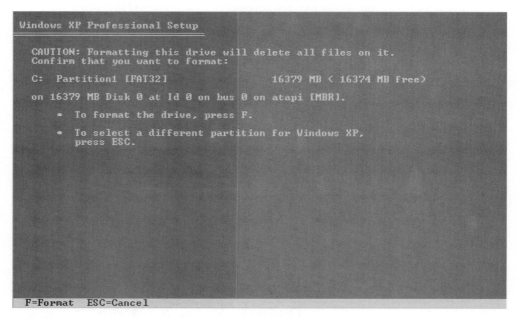

Figure 9-6:
Warning Screen

_____j.   Figure 9-7 shows the Format in progress.

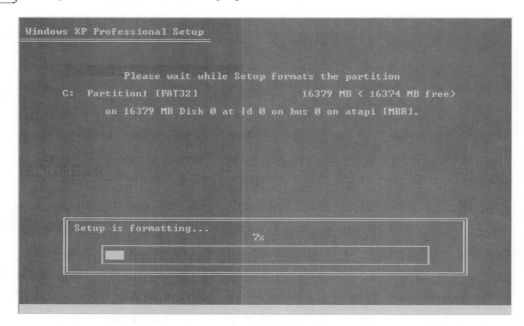

Figure 9-7:
Formatting Screen

_____k.   After the format process is complete, Setup will install the files needed to complete the next phase of the install process, then restart the computer as shown in Figure 9-8 and Figure 9-9.

**Figure 9-8:
Install Process**

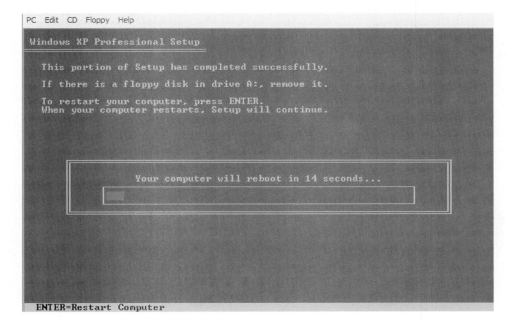

**Figure 9-9: Restarting
the Computer**

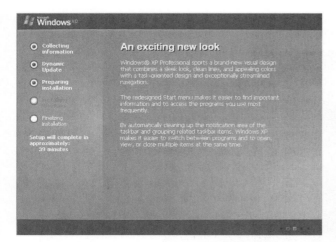

Figure 9-10: GUI Mode

____l.   After the *Text-Mode* portion of setup completes and the system restarts, Setup enters the *GUI mode* portion of the installation as shown in Figure 9-10.

____m.   After a period of time, the *Regional and Language Options* page is displayed as shown in Figure 9-11. Make sure the settings are correct for your area and click **Next**.

Figure 9-11:
Regional and Language
Options Page

____n.   The *Personalize Your Software* screen is next as shown in Figure 9-12. Fill in the appropriate information and click **Next** To continue.

Figure 9-12:
Personalize Your
Software Screen

____o.   Figure 9-13 shows the *Product Key* entry screen. Enter the 16 digit product ID and click **Next**.

Figure 9-13: Product Key Entry Screen

____p.   Figure 9-14 is the *Computer Name and Administrator Password* entry screen. Enter a name for your computer and choose a password for the Administrator account.

Figure 9-14: Computer Name and Administrator Password Entry Screen

_____q.   Figure 9-15 is the *Date and Time Settings* entry screen. Make sure the information is correct for your area and click **Next.**

Figure 9-15:
Date and Time
Settings Entry
Screen

_____r.   If Setup detects an installed Network Adapter, Setup will install network components after the *Date and Time Settings* screen as shown in Figure 9-16.

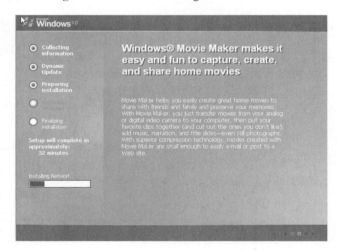

Figure 9-16:
Installing Network
Components

___s.   Figure 9-17 shows the *Network Settings* entry screen. You should normally choose the **Typical settings** option if you want Setup to automatically configure networking components. Typical components include Client for Microsoft Networks, File and Print Sharing for Microsoft Networks, and TCP/IP.

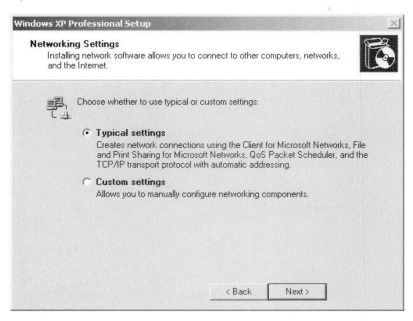

Figure 9-17: Network Settings Entry Screen Components

___t.   After selecting the Network Settings, Setup displays the *Workgroup or Computer Domain* name entry screen as seen in Figure 9-18. Enter the appropriate information and click **Next**.

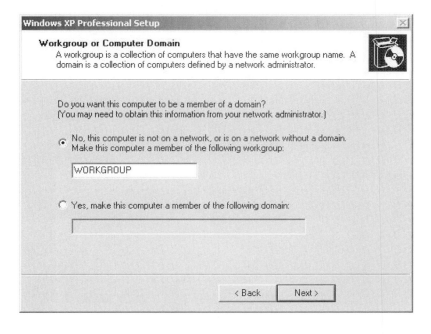

Figure 9-18: Workgroup or Computer Domain Name Entry Screen

_____u.   After clicking **Next** at the *Workgroup or Computer Domain* entry screen.

Setup continues with the final portion of the installation.

It may take from 15 to 60 minutes for the process to finish. Once finished the system will restart and you will be prompted to Logon for the first time.

Feedback

LAB QUESTIONS

1.   What are the two main stages of the XP Professional installation process?

2.   What are the choices available when the system asks you about formatting the partition you wish to install XP Professional to?

3.   What do the "Typical" network settings include?

Navigating Windows XP

Operating System Technology

OBJECTIVES

1. Explore the Start menu.
2. Use My Computer.
3. Add a program to the Quick Launch toolbar.
4. Remove a program from the Start menu.
5. Add a program to the Start menu.
6. Customize the Start menu.
7. Change the Taskbar view to Classic view.

RESOURCES

1. PC-compatible desktop/tower computer system — Customer-supplied desktop/tower hardware system **OR** Marcraft Computer Repair Trainer **OR** suitable PC hardware trainer running Windows XP Professional

DISCUSSION

Windows XP looks significantly different than either Windows Me or Windows 2000. In Figure 10-1 you can see that the desktop now is missing the icons for *My Computer*, *Network Neighborhood*, and *My Documents*. The only icon that is still there is the *Recycle Bin*, which has moved to the bottom right by default. In the lab we will show you where to locate these icons. We will also show you how to add the programs that you use frequently to the Quick Launch toolbar and *Start* menu for quick access without cluttering up your desktop. The last thing to show you is how to change the operation of the *Start* menu back to the way it operates in Windows 2000.

Figure 10-1: The Windows XP Desktop

**Operating
System
Technology**

PROCEDURE

1. **Navigate to My Computer from the Windows XP Start menu**

   ___a.   Boot the computer into Windows XP.

   ___b.   Click on the **Start** button with your mouse. Figure 10-2 shows
   the *XP Start* menu.

   ___c.   Click on the **My Computer** icon.

   ___d.   My Computer in XP is arranged according to device type as
   shown in Figure 10-3.

**Figure 10-2: The
Windows XP Start Menu**

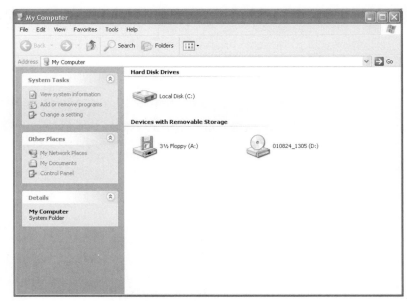

**Figure 10-3: My
Computer in
Windows XP**

   ___e.   Notice the links on the left side of *My Computer.*
   You can quickly open useful programs or folders by
   single-clicking on any of these links, just as if you
   were in Internet Explorer.

   ___f.   Click on **System Tasks** and the links located below
   that heading, then hide them.

   ___g.   Click on **System Tasks** again to bring the links
   back.

   ___h.   Click on **View system information**. This brings up
   the *System Properties* box, as in Figure 10-4, which
   is identical to the *System Information* icon located
   in the Control Panel.

   ___i.   Close the *Systems Properties* box by clicking on the
   X on the upper-right corner.

**Figure 10-4: The Systems
Properties Dialog Box**

___j.   Click on **Change a setting** to change the view to Control Panel, as in Figure 10-5.

___k.   Click on **Back** in the upper-left corner to return to *My Computer*.

___l.   Click on **Start**, and then hover the mouse over the *All Programs* arrow, as in Figure 10-6. This will open up the *Programs Menu* that is similar to the *Programs* menu in Window Me and Windows 2000. This is used the same way, so we won't go into the functionality of this *Programs Menu*.

Figure 10-5: The Control Panel

Figure 10-6: The Windows XP All Programs Menu

___m.   Click on the desktop to exit from the *Start* menu.

2.   Add programs to the Quick Launch toolbar

___a.   Let's make sure that the computer is using the Quick Launch toolbar. Right-click on the Taskbar on the bottom of the screen. Make sure not to click on an area where a program is running. You should get the menu shown in Figure 10-7.

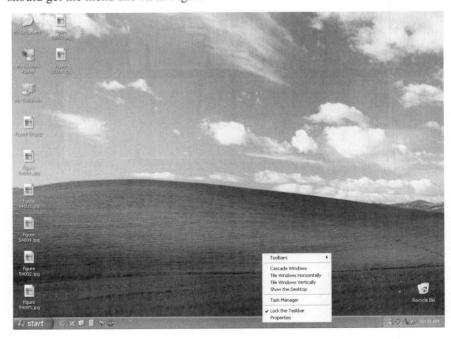

Figure 10-7: The Taskbar Menu

_____b.   Hover the mouse over the word **Toolbars**, then make sure that the Quick Launch toolbar is checked as in Figure 10-8. If it is not checked, click on it.

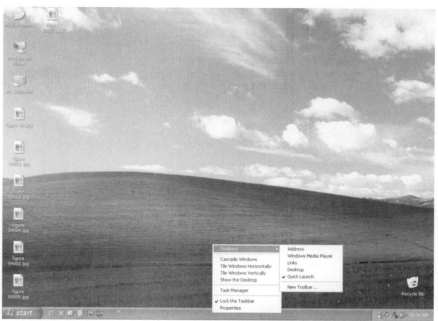

**Figure 10-8:
Enabling the Quick
Launch Toolbar**

_____c.   Right-click on the Taskbar on the bottom and click on **Lock the Taskbar** to unlock it. This will give you the ability to move items in the Taskbar.

_____d.   Click on the second set of dots to widen the Quick Launch toolbar, as in Figure 10-9.

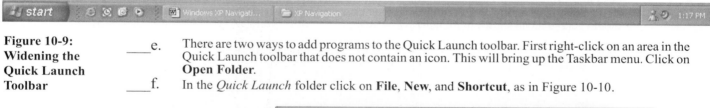

**Figure 10-9:
Widening the
Quick Launch
Toolbar**

_____e.   There are two ways to add programs to the Quick Launch toolbar. First right-click on an area in the Quick Launch toolbar that does not contain an icon. This will bring up the Taskbar menu. Click on **Open Folder**.

_____f.   In the *Quick Launch* folder click on **File**, **New**, and **Shortcut**, as in Figure 10-10.

**Figure 10-10:
Adding Shortcuts to
Quick Launch
Folder**

____g. This will bring up the Create Shortcut wizard seen in Figure 10-11. If you know the complete path to the program you could type it in the box. We will use the other method. Click on **Browse** to bring up the *Browse for Folder* dialog box.

____h. Click on the + next to My Computer, C Drive, Program Files, and Messenger to get to the *msmsgs* icon shown in Figure 10-12.

Figure 10-11: The Create Shortcut Dialog Box

Figure 10-12: Locate Program for Quick Launch Toolbar

____i. Click on **OK**.

____j. You will now see the path and program typed into the *Create Shortcut* dialog box. Click on **Next**.

____k. You need to type in a name for the program; by default the file name is in the box. Just type **Microsoft Messenger** to replace the file name in the box.

____l. Click on **Finish**.

____m. Your *Quick Launch* folder should now have a Microsoft Messenger Shortcut Icon in it as shown in Figure 10-13.

____n. Close the *Quick Launch* folder by clicking on the **X** in the upper-right corner.

____o. Notice the *Messenger* icon in the Quick Launch toolbar. Hover the mouse over the icon. You should see the Microsoft Messenger name appear above the icon.

____p. Now right-click on the Taskbar and click on **Lock the Taskbar** to lock it.

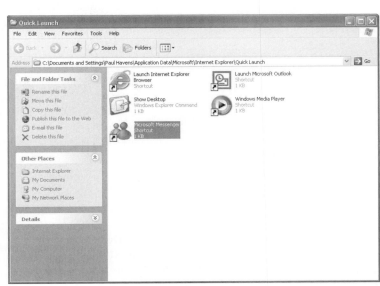

Figure 10-13: Microsoft Messenger Icon Added to Folder

____q.   Notice that the Taskbar is locked wherever you had the dots positioned. Take the time to unlock the Taskbar and position the dots in an area where all the icons can be visible, but there isn't a lot of extra space, and then lock the Taskbar.

____r.   Another way to add icons to the Quick Launch toolbar is to drag the programs into the toolbar. Click on **Start**.

____s.   Click on **All Programs**, then **Accessories** as in Figure 10-14.

**Figure 10-14:
The Accessories
Menu**

____t.   When clicking on the **Calculator** icon you need to right-click and hold-and-drag the icon down to the Quick Launch toolbar, then release the right mouse button.

____u.   A menu will display similar to Figure 10-15; select **Copy Here**. This will keep the shortcut in the *Programs* menu and create an additional one on the Quick Launch toolbar.

____v.   Let's test the shortcut by clicking on the **Calculator** icon. The calculator should display.

____w.   Click on the **X** to close Calculator.

____x.   We will now delete the icons in the Quick Launch toolbar. Right-click on the **Calculator** icon and select **Delete** from the menu as shown in Figure 10-16.

**Figure 10-15:
Right-Drag Options**

Copy Here
Move Here
Cancel

**Figure 10-16: Deleting a
Shortcut from the Quick
Launch Toolbar**

Open
Run as...
Pin to Start menu

Send To   ▶

Cut
Copy

Create Shortcut
Delete
Rename

Properties

_____y. You will get the *Confirm File Delete* dialog box. Click on **Yes** to send the Calculator shortcut to the Recycle Bin.

_____z. Repeat Steps x and y for the *MSN messenger* icon. Notice that the dialog box changed for MSN messenger; this is because we are deleting a shortcut instead of an actual file.

3. Customize the Start menu

_____a. Click on **Start**.

_____b. Right-click on **Tour Windows XP** and select **Remove from This List** as in Figure 10-17.

_____c. Notice that the icon is now gone. We will now replace the icon.

_____d. This menu displays the programs most used to replace the icon we need to run the Windows XP Tour. Click on **All Programs**, **Accessories**, and **Tour Windows XP**.

_____e. When the *Tour Windows XP* dialog box comes up, click on **Cancel**.

_____f. Click on **Start**. You will now see the *Tour Windows XP* icon back on the left-hand side as in Figure 10-18.

Figure 10-17: Removing Icon from Start Menu

Figure 10-18: The Start Menu

_____g. For further customization right-click on the **Start** menu and select **Properties**.

_____h. The *Taskbar and Start Menu Properties* dialog box comes up as in Figure 10-19.

_____i. Click on **Customize** to the right of *Start* menu.

_____j. Click on **Small Icons** to select it.

_____k. Now click on the **Advanced** tab at the top.

_____l. On this tab, you can select which folder and options you want to have on the *Start* menu and how to display them. Record all 15 main options in Table 10-1 (do not include the *how to display* options).

_____m. Click on **OK**.

Figure 10-19: Start Menu Properties

____n.   Click on **Start**. The menu should now have small icons as in Figure 10-20. Notice the small icons for the programs underneath the logon name.

____o.   Right-click on the **Start** button and click on **Properties**.

____p.   Click on **Customize**.

____q.   Change the icons back to the large size and click on **OK**.

4.   **Customize the Taskbar**

____a.   Click on the **Taskbar** tab at the top of the *Taskbar and Start Menu Properties* box as shown in Figure 10-21.

**Figure 10-20: Start
Menu with Small Icons**

**Figure 10-21:
Taskbar Properties**

____b.   Notice the options at the top. We have done *Lock the taskbar* and *Show Quick Launch* by using the right-click menu on the Taskbar.

____c.   Click on **Group similar taskbar buttons** to uncheck it. Notice the Internet Explorer Taskbar item and how it changes.

____d.   Click on **OK**.

____e.   Now click on the **Internet Explorer** icon on the Quick Launch toolbar four times and launch four different Internet Explorer windows.

____f.   Notice how each has its own *Taskbar* button.

____g.   Now right-click on the **Start** menu and select **Properties**.

____h.   Click on the **Taskbar** tab at the top.

**Figure 10-22:
Customize
Notifications
Window**

____i.   Now click on **Group similar taskbar buttons** and click on **Apply**. Explain what happens to the Internet Explorer buttons in Table 10-2.

____j.   The customizable part on the bottom lets you add or remove the clock from the bottom right corner. It also lets you choose which icons you want to display or hide.

____k.   Click on **Customize**.

____l.   Figure 10-22 shows an example of the customizable options. Click on the **volume** icon and change it to *Hide when inactive*. Click on **OK**.

____m.   The bottom right corner should now have an arrow as in Figure 10-23. Click on the arrow to see the *Volume* icon.

____n.   Click on **Customize** and change the *Volume* icon to *Always show* and click on **OK**. The *Volume* icon should reappear in the corner.

Figure 10-23: Hidden Icons Symbol

5. **Change the Start menu to the classic Windows 2000 display**
   ____a. Click on the **Start Menu** tab inside the *Taskbar and Start Menu Properties* box.
   ____b. Select **Classic Start** menu.
   ____c. Click on **OK**.
   ____d. Click on the **Start** button.
   ____e. Describe how the *Start* menu changes in Table 10-3.
   ____f. Right-click on the **Start** button and select **Properties**.
   ____g. Select **Start Menu** and click on **OK**.

TABLES

Table 10-1

Table 10-2

Table 10-3

Feedback

LAB QUESTIONS

1. How do you get to My Computer in Windows XP?

2. How do you scroll to installed programs in Windows XP?

3. Name two ways to add programs to the Quick Launch toolbar.

4. How is System Properties opened in Windows XP?

5. How do you change the Start menu back to the classic Start menu?

Windows 2000 Plug-and-Play

OBJECTIVES

1. Remove network adapter.
2. Install network adapter with Plug-and-Play.
3. Remove modem.
4. Install modem with Plug-and-Play.

Operating System Technology

RESOURCES

1. PC-compatible desktop/tower computer system—Customer-supplied desktop/tower hardware system **OR** Marcraft Computer Repair Trainer **OR** suitable PC hardware trainer with Windows 2000 installed
2. A Windows 2000 Plug-and-Play network adapter installed
3. A Windows 2000 Plug-and-Play modem installed
4. Network connection (optional)

DISCUSSION

The performance of Plug-and-Play (PnP) has improved with easy installation of PnP hardware in new systems. Windows 2000 doesn't require that you restart the computer as much as with previous operating systems. If a device is not PnP-compatible you may be able to install it manually through *Add/Remove Hardware* in the Control Panel. You may need the drivers provided by the manufacturer unless Windows has them already. In this lab you will install a PnP modem and network adapter with Windows 2000.

PROCEDURE

1. **View network adapter in Device Manager**
   ___a. Boot to the Windows 2000 desktop.
   ___b. Right-click on **My Computer** and select **Properties**.
   ___c. Click on the **Hardware** tab and click on **Device Manager**.
   ___d. You will see a list of device types attached to the computer.
   ___e. Look for the section called *Network adapters* and expand it by clicking on the plus (+) sign next to the icon.

_____f.   The window should look similar to Figure 11-1. Record the name of the network adapter in Table 11-1.

Figure 11-1:
Network Card in Device
Manager

_____g.   Right-click on the network adapter and click on **Uninstall**.
_____h.   You will be prompted to *Confirm Device Removal*. Click on **OK**.

2.   Remove network adapter
_____a.   Close all windows and shut down the computer.
_____b.   Open the computer case.
_____c.   Remove any external cables from the network card.
_____d.   Remove the mounting screw of the network adapter.
_____e.   Gently pull the adapter out of its expansion slot and set the adapter and screw aside.

3.   View hardware changes
_____a.   Turn on the computer and boot to the Windows 2000 desktop.
_____b.   Right-click on **My Computer** and select **Properties**.
_____c.   Click on the **Hardware** tab and click on **Device Manager**.
_____d.   Record your observations in Table 11-2.
_____e.   Close all windows and shut down the computer.

4.   Add network adapter
_____a.   Gently insert the network card back into the available expansion slot.
_____b.   Add the mounting screw of the network adapter.
_____c.   Plug in any external cables that you removed previously.
_____d.   Turn the computer on and boot to the Windows 2000 desktop.
_____e.   The network adapter will install automatically. You may not see any dialog windows. Navigate to **Device Manager** as in previous steps.
_____f.   Record your observations in Table 11-3.
_____g.   If you are connected to a LAN double-click on **My Network Places** from the desktop.
_____h.   Double-click **Computers Near Me**. If you are connected you should see other computers in the window.

5. **An alternative approach**
   ____a. From Device Manager right-click on the network adapter and choose **Uninstall**.
   ____b. Confirm the *Device Removal* by clicking on **OK**.
   ____c. Right-click the top icon (the computer name STATION01, for example) and choose **Scan for hardware changes** as in Figure 11-2.

Figure 11-2: Scan for Hardware Changes

____d. The computer should detect an Ethernet adapter. You will see a window similar to Figure 11-3. The words "Ethernet controller" will change to the specific name of the network adapter.

____e. Notice that the adapter is now installed in Device Manager. Close all windows.

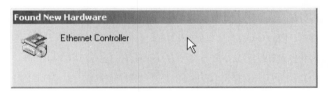

Figure 11-3: Found New Hardware

6. **Repeat Steps 1 through 4 with the Plug-and-Play modem**

7. **Test the modem**
   ____a. Navigate to **Device Manager**.
   ____b. Look for the modem and right-click on its icon. Click on **Properties**.
   ____c. Click on the **Diagnostics** tab.
   ____d. Click on the **Query Modem** button. If the modem is installed the computer will communicate with the modem. Responses to commands will appear in the window, similar to Figure 11-4.
   ____e. Close all open windows.
   ____f. Shut down the computer.

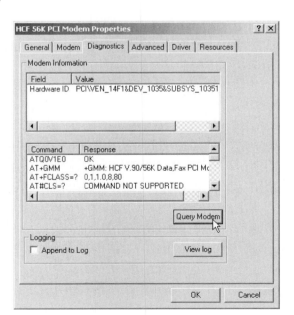

Figure 11-4: Sample Modem Query

TABLES

Table 11-1

Network Adapter:	

Table 11-2

Observations After Removal:	

Table 11-3

Observations After Adding:	

Feedback

LAB QUESTIONS

1. What does PnP stand for?

2. Why can PnP be useful?

3. What is an alternative way of installing a non-PnP device?

4. Will you see any dialog windows when installing a PnP device?

5. How can you scan for hardware changes while the computer is running?

Navigating Windows 2000

Operating System Technology

OBJECTIVES

1. Understand directory structure.
2. Create a Notepad document.
3. Cut, copy, paste, and rename files.
4. Search for files.
5. Change Windows Explorer views.
6. Modify folder options.
7. Use Control Panel.
8. Configure appearance.

RESOURCES

1. PC-compatible desktop/tower computer system—Customer-supplied desktop/tower hardware system **OR** Marcraft Computer Repair Trainer **OR** suitable PC hardware trainer with Windows 2000 Professional installed

DISCUSSION

It is important to know how to use the interface of Windows 2000. At first glance it may look similar to the Windows 9x environment, but the operation of Windows 2000 is somewhat different. This lab will familiarize you with some of the basic commands associated with navigating Windows 2000. You will learn how to change the appearance of windows, a few basic Control Panel settings, and folder options.

PROCEDURE

1. **Navigation and directory structure**
   ___ a. Boot the computer to Windows 2000.
   ___ b. Move your mouse to the bottom left of the screen and click on **Start**.
   ___ c. Follow the path *Start/Programs/Accessories/Windows Explorer*, similar to Figure 12-1. Click on the down arrows if necessary.

Figure 12-1: The Desktop and Start Menu

    d.   The file system on the computer is organized into a group of folders. Double-click through the path *My Computer/C:/WINNT*. On the right-hand window pane you can see the content of that folder.

NOTE: If the configuration is such that you do not see the folder's content, it will be necessary to click on the "Show Files" link to view the folder's content.

    e.   Click on the (**C:**) drive and then click on **File/New/Folder**, as shown in Figure 12-2.

Figure 12-2:
Windows Explorer

    f.   Type **YourInitials** for the name of the folder and press **ENTER**.
    g.   Move the folder into the *WINNT* folder by clicking and holding the mouse, dragging the folder on top of the folder, and releasing the mouse.
    h.   Close Windows Explorer by clicking on the "**X**" in the top right of the window.
    i.   On the desktop, double-click on **My Computer**.
    j.   Right-click the (**C:**) drive, and click on **Properties**. Record the free space in Table 12-1.
    k.   Click on **OK** for *Local Disk (C:) Properties*.
    l.   Open the (**C:**) drive by double-clicking on the icon. Open the *WINNT* Folder.
    m.   Look for the *YOURINITIALS* folder you just created. Right-click on it and select **Delete**.
    n.   When you are asked to confirm, click on **Yes**.
    o.   Close all open windows.

2.   Create a Notepad document
    a.   Open *Notepad* by navigating the path *Start/Programs/Accessories/Notepad*. This simple text-edit program will now start.
    b.   Maximize the program by clicking on the center button in the top right of the title bar.
    c.   Type **This is a test** in the document. Click on **File/Save**.
    d.   Type **YourName.txt** for the filename.
    e.   Select the menu to the right of *Save in:*

____f. Select Local Disk (**C:**). The window should look similar to Figure 12-3.

Figure 12-3: Save Dialog

____g. Click on **Save**.
____h. Close *Notepad*.

3. Create a shortcut

*NOTE: In the following procedures, if the My Computer window opens in a full-sized window or maxi-
mized, you will not be able to see your desktop. If so, click on the "square" button at the right corner of the title bar to restore it to its previous size. You can then resize the window, if necessary, to
see the desktop.*

____a. Open *My Computer*. Double-click on **C:**
____b. Look for the file *YourName.txt*. Right-drag it to the desktop and choose
        Create Shortcuts Here, as shown in Figure 12-4.
____c. You have just created a shortcut to the text file.

*NOTE: This is a convenient way of accessing programs and files. Double-clicking a
shortcut will open the file or program that is referenced.*

____d. Close any open windows.

**Figure 12-4: Right-Drag
Options**

4. Cut, copy, paste, and rename files
____a. Right-click the **Shortcut to YourName.txt** and click on **Copy**.
____b. Go through the path *My Computer/(C:)*. Right-click in any blank space, and click on **Paste**.

*NOTE: This Copy/Paste method can be used for duplicating any file, program or shortcut to any folder or
location within the Windows realm.*

____c. Right-click the shortcut you just made and click on **Rename**.
____d. Type **YourName2 Shortcut** and press the **ENTER** key on the keyboard.
____e. Right-click the shortcut you just renamed and choose **Cut**.
____f. Right-click the desktop and choose **Paste**.
____g. Delete the two shortcuts (*Shortcut to YourName.txt* and *Shortcut to YourName2*) from the desktop
        by clicking on the first, holding the **CTRL** key on the keyboard, and clicking on the second.
____h. Release the **CTRL** key, and right-click on one and choose **Delete**.
____i. Choose **Yes** to confirm the deletion of the two files.

NOTE: Notice that you are only deleting shortcuts to the file, not the actual "YourName.txt" file.

_____ j. Right-click the **Recycle Bin** on the desktop, choose **Empty Recycle Bin**, and confirm by clicking on **Yes** when prompted.

_____ k. Close all open windows.

5. Search for files

_____ a. Navigate the path *Start/Search/For Files or Folders*.

_____ b. Type **YourName.txt** into the *Search for files or folders named:* field.

_____ c. Choose **Look In Local Disk (C:)** as in Figure 12-5.

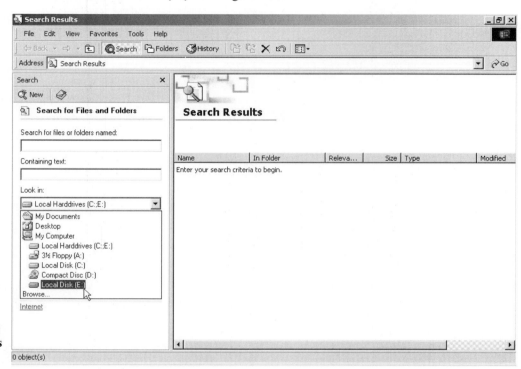

Figure 12-5: Search for Files and Folders

_____ d. Click on **Search Now**.

_____ e. You should see the file "YourName.txt" appear in the right-hand window pane. Notice the information you can see about the file.

_____ f. You may need to use the scroll bar in the bottom of the window to see additional information about the file. Record the desired information in Table 12-2.

NOTE: You can now manipulate the file found in the same manner as using Windows Explorer.

_____ g. Delete *test.txt* by right-clicking on the file's icon and choosing **Delete**. Choose **Yes** when prompted.

NOTE: Delete the actual file, not the shortcut, in the RECENT folder.

_____ h. Close all open windows.

6. Windows Explorer views

_____ a. Open *My Computer*.

_____ b. Navigate the path *C:\WINNT*. If necessary click on **Show files** on the left-hand column.

_____ c. Click on the **View** menu. Record the item with a "dot" in Table 12-3.

____d.   Change your view to **Details**. Observe the window. It should look similar to Figure 12-6.

**Figure 12-6:
Details View**

____e.   Look for the *Windows Explorer* application. Record its size in Table 12-4.

____f.   Change your view to **Thumbnails**.

____g.   Right-click on a blank space in the folder and choose **Arrange Icons/By Type**.

____h.   Scroll down to find a bitmap image and double-click on your selection. Record the filename in Table 12-5.

____i.   An image-editing program such as *Paint* should open. Observe it and close the program.

____j.   Now change your view of the *WINNT* folder to **Large Icons**, **Small Icons**, and **List** in turn. Observe the differences in each.

____k.   Close all windows.

7.   Folder Options

____a.   Open *My Computer.*

____b.   Click on **Tools/Folder Options**. In this window you can change settings on browsing local items, file types, and offline file configurations.

____c.   Click on the **View** tab. The window should look similar to Figure 12-7.

____d.   Scroll down and verify that *Show My Documents on the Desktop* is checked. Click on **Apply**.

____e.   Click on **OK**.

____f.   Now uncheck the same item in the *Folder Options* window. Record your observations in Table 12-6.

____g.   Recheck the item.

____h.   Click on **OK** and close all windows.

8.   Basic Control Panel

____a.   Open the Control Panel using the path *Start/Settings/Control Panel*.

____b.   Record how many objects exist in Table 12-7.

____c.   Double-click the **Mouse** icon.

____d.   Click on the **Motion** tab.

____e.   Increase the speed to **Fast**, and move the mouse.

____f.   Decrease the speed to **Minimum**, and move the mouse.

Figure 12-7: Folder Options View

___g.   Change the speed back to **Normal** and click on **OK**.

___h.   In Control Panel double-click the **Keyboard** icon.

___i.   Change the Cursor blink rate to its *fastest* setting. Observe the cursor on the left.

___j.   Change the Cursor blink rate to its *slowest* setting. Observe the cursor on the left.

___k.   Click on **Cancel** and close all open windows.

9.   Windows appearance

___a.   Right-click on the desktop and click on **Properties**. In this window you can change settings for your background, screen saver, windows colors, screen effects, and display adapter settings.

___b.   Click on the **Appearance** tab.

___c.   Choose the **Brick** scheme and click on **Apply**.

___d.   Choose **3D Objects** under the item drop-down menu.

___e.   Follow the path *Color/Other*.

___f.   Click on a color of your choice as in Figure 12-8, and then click on **OK**.

Figure 12-8: Color Palette

___g.   Click on **Apply**. Record the color you chose in Table 12-8.

___h.   Change the *Scheme* back to **Windows Standard** and click on **OK**.

TABLES

Table 12-1

Hard Drive Free Space:	

Table 12-2

In Folder:	
Size:	
Type:	
Modified:	

Table 12-3

View Item with a "Dot":	

Table 12-4

Size of Explorer Application:	

Table 12-5

Bitmap Image Filename:	

Table 12-6

Table 12-7

Table 12-8

Feedback

LAB QUESTIONS

1. How are the Start menu and file system organized?

2. What is the mouse operation used for moving a folder?

3. What is the method used in this lab for creating a shortcut?

4. What are four common operations for file manipulation?

5. How is the file search window similar to Windows Explorer?

6. What is the Folder Options window used for?

7. What is the Display Properties window used for?

8. What is the "Thumbnails" view?

9. What are the two areas of the Control Panel used in this lab?

10. What are the 3D objects?

Working with Printers in Windows 2000

**Operating
System
Technology**

OBJECTIVES

1. Install a printer.
2. Explore printer properties.
3. Print a test page on the printer.

RESOURCES

1. PC-compatible desktop/tower computer system — Customer-supplied desktop/tower hardware system **OR** Marcraft Computer Repair Trainer **OR** suitable PC hardware trainer with Windows 2000 installed
2. A printer connected to the computer with power turned on
3. Manufacturer's printer drivers (optional)

DISCUSSION

This lab will help you install a printer with Windows 2000. The procedure for installing the drivers may vary depending on the model of your printer. You will then explore the properties of the printer and print a test page.

PROCEDURE

1. **Install printer**
   ___ a.   Boot to the Windows 2000 desktop.
   ___ b.   Navigate the *Start/Settings/Printers* path.
   ___ c.   In the window that opens double-click on **Add Printer**.
   ___ d.   The *Add Printer Wizard* will appear. Click on **Next**.
   ___ e.   The *Local printer* and *Network printer* options will appear as in Figure 13-1. Verify that *Local printer* and *Automatically detect and install my Plug and Play printer* are selected. Click on **Next**.
   ___ f.   If Windows is unable to detect a Plug-and-Play printer, click on **Next** to install the printer manually.

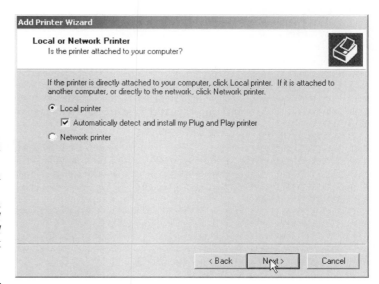

Figure 13-1: Add Printer Wizard

____g. Click on **LPT1** (unless otherwise directed by your instructor) from the list that appears. This is the port that is typically used on a computer for printing. Click on **Next**.

____h. Referring to Figure 13-2, scroll down the "*Manufacturers:*" list to click on the appropriate manufacturer for your printer. Scroll down the "*Printers:*" list and select the appropriate model of your printer. If your printer is not listed, insert the CD provided by the manufacturer, click on **Have Disk**, specify the location, click on **OK**, and follow the prompts to install the printer.

Figure 13-2:
Printer Selection

Figure 13-3: Completing the Add Printer Wizard

____i. Record the manufacturer and model of the printer in Table 13-1. Click on **Next**.

____j. You will be prompted to specify a name for the printer. Use the default and click on **Next**.

____k. Choose **Do not share this printer**. This will be used in a later procedure. Click on **Next.**

____l. You will be prompted to print a test page; select **No**. Click on **Next**.

____m. You will see a window similar to Figure 13-3. Verify the information and click on **Finish**.

____n. After files are copied verify that the printer now appears in the *PRINTERS* folder.

2. View Printer Properties and test page

____a. Double-click the printer you have just installed.

____b. A window similar to Figure 13-4 will appear. Click on **Printer/Properties**.

Figure 13-4:
The Printer Window

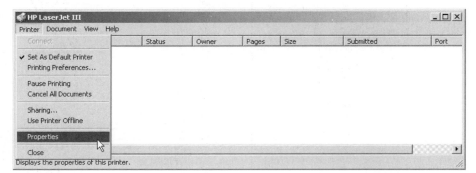

____c.   The properties of the printer will now open to the *General* tab. From this tab you can change the name, location, comments, and printing preferences of the printer. Click on the **Print Test Page** button.

____d.   A window similar to Figure 13-5 will appear. Verify that the test page has printed correctly and click on **OK**.

Figure 13-5: Test Page Dialog

____e.   On the test page that has printed look for the "*Driver name:*" information. Record the name of the driver in Table 13-2.

____f.   Click on the **Ports** tab. This shows information about the communication ports available on your computer. From this window you can Add, Delete, and Configure ports.

____g.   Click on the **Advanced** tab. From this tab you can change the printer's availability schedule, spool settings, defaults, print processing format, and separator page settings.

____h.   Click on the **Security** tab. From this window you change access privileges from users on your computer.

____i.   Click on the **Device Settings** tab. It may look similar to Figure 13-6. The settings in this window are specific to your printer. You can change various paper and cartridge settings from this window.

____j.   Click on **OK** and close all open windows.

____k.   Shut down the computer.

Figure 13-6: Device Settings

TABLES

Table 13-1

Printer	
Manufacturer:	
Model:	

Table 13-2

Printer Driver Name:	

Feedback

LAB QUESTIONS

1. Did you install a local printer or a network printer?

2. On what port is the printer installed?

3. Did you share the printer?

4. What can you do from the Advanced tab?

5. What are some possible settings from the Device Settings tab?

Windows 2000 Accessories

OBJECTIVES

1. Learn about Power Options.
2. Learn about Accessibility Options.
3. Learn about Regional Options.
4. Learn about Sounds and Multimedia.

Operating
System
Technology

RESOURCES

1. PC-compatible desktop/tower computer system — Customer-supplied desktop/tower hardware system **OR** Marcraft Computer Repair Trainer **OR** suitable PC hardware trainer with Windows 2000 installed
2. Sound card and speakers

DISCUSSION

This lab will explore some of the various system customizing options in Windows 2000. The Power Options are useful if the system is on a laptop. These features can be used to turn off the monitor and hard disks to conserve energy and battery life. Accessibility Options can be used to help people with audio and visual impairments by making sounds at various keyboard events and showing visual alerts. Regional Options can change language and various country specific settings on the computer. You can change the default sounds for different events.

PROCEDURE

1. **Power Options**
   ___a. Boot to the Windows 2000 desktop.
   ___b. Navigate the path *Start/Settings/Control Panel*.
   ___c. Double-click on **Power Options**. You will see a window similar to Figure 14-1.

Figure 14-1: Power Options

____d.   Record your *Turn off monitor* and *Turn off hard disks* settings in Table 14-1.

____e.   Change the *Turn off monitor* setting to **After 1 min** and click on **Apply**.

____f.   Do not move the mouse or press any keys for one minute and record your observations in Table 14-2.

____g.   Move the mouse and change the *Turn off monitor* setting back to its original state.

____h.   Click on **OK** for the *Power Options* properties.

Figure 14-2: Accessibility Contrast Options

2.   **Accessibility Options**

____a.   From the Windows 2000 Control Panel double-click on **Accessibility Options**.

____b.   Click on the **Display** tab. You will see a window similar to Figure 14-2.

____c.   Select **Use High Contrast**. Click on **Apply**.

____d.   Record your observations in Table 14-3.

____e.   Uncheck *High Contrast* and click on **Apply** to restore the display to its original state. You may need to resize the Taskbar by dragging the edge down to its original position.

____f.   In *Accessibility Options* click on the **Mouse** tab.

____g.   Select **Use MouseKeys**. Click on **Apply**.

____h.   Look at the keyboard and verify that the num lock light is on. If it is not, press the **NUM LOCK** key.

____i.   There are arrow keys on the numeric keypad on the right-hand side of the keyboard. Up is 8, down is 2, left is 4, and right is 6. Press up and record your observations in Table 14-4.

____j.   Uncheck *Use MouseKeys* and click on **Apply** to restore the option back to its original state.

____k.   Click on **OK** to close the *Accessibility Options* window.

3.   **Regional Options**

____a.   From the Windows 2000 Control Panel double-click on **Regional Options**. You will see a window similar to Figure 14-3.

**Figure 14-3:
Regional Options**

    b.   Under the *General* tab record your locale in Table 14-5.

    c.   Under the *Numbers* tab record the digit grouping in Table 14-5.

    d.   Under the *Currency* tab record the currency symbol in Table 14-5.

    e.   Under the *Time* tab record the time format in Table 14-5.

    f.   Under the *Date* tab record the date separator in Table 14-5.

    g.   Under the *Input Locales* record the uppermost input language in Table 14-5.

    h.   Click on **OK** to close the *Regional Options* window.

4.   Sounds and Multimedia

    a.   From the Windows 2000 Control Panel, double-click on **Sounds and Multimedia**. You will see a window similar to Figure 14-4.

Figure 14-4: Sound and Multimedia Properties

    b.   Click on the **Asterisk** event.

    c.   Record the "Name:" in Table 14-6. This is the name of the sound file that Windows plays when the corresponding event has occurred.

    d.   If you have a sound card and speakers, press the play button and you will hear the sound.

    e.   Click on the **Audio** tab. Record the preferred device for sound playback in Table 14-7.

    f.   Click on the **Advanced** tab under sound playback.

    g.   Record the speaker setup in Table 14-8.

    h.   Click on **OK** to close the *Advanced* window.

    i.   Click on the **Hardware** tab.

    j.   Record the number of devices listed in Table 14-9.

    k.   Browse for the CD-ROM in the device listing and double-click on it.

    l.   Record the name of the window that appears in Table 14-10.

    m.   Click on **OK** to close the window that you just opened.

    n.   Click on **OK** to close the *Sound and Multimedia Properties*.

    o.   Close the Control Panel.

    p.   Shut down the computer.

TABLES

Table 14-1

Power Options Properties	
Turn off monitor:	
Turn off hard disks:	

Table 14-2

Observations After One Minute:	

Table 14-3

Display Observations:	

Table 14-4

Observations of Use MouseKeys:	

Table 14-5

Regional Options	
Your Locale:	
Digit Grouping:	
Currency Symbol:	
Time Format:	
Date Separator:	
Input Language:	

Table 14-6

"Asterisk Event" Sound File Name:	

Table 14-7

Preferred Device for Sound Playback:	

Table 14-8

Speaker Setup:	

Table 14-9

Number of Hardware Devices:	

Table 14-10

Name of Window:	

LAB QUESTIONS

1. What two settings are available for a power scheme?

2. What features of accessibility were demonstrated in this lab?

3. Where would you go to change the language of the system?

4. The Regional Options/Date feature does what?

5. What is one way to change the hardware settings of an audio card in Windows 2000?

Feedback

Windows 2000/XP Startup Modes

OBJECTIVES

1. Restart and try various startup options.

Troubleshooting

RESOURCES

1. PC-compatible desktop/tower computer system — Customer-supplied desktop/tower hardware system **OR** Marcraft Computer Repair Trainer **OR** suitable PC hardware trainer with Windows 2000 or Windows XP installed
2. A PS2 mouse
3. A LAN connection

DISCUSSION

In this lab we will explore different startup options that appear when pressing the *F8* key at startup. These options can be useful for troubleshooting system problems. The Windows Advanced Options Menu includes the following default options:

- Safe Mode
- Safe Mode with Networking
- Safe Mode with Command Prompt
- Enable Boot Logging
- Enable VGA Mode
- Last Known Good Configuration (your most recent setting that worked)
- Directory Services Restore Mode (Windows domain controllers only)
- Debugging Mode
- Boot Normally (Windows 2000 only)
- Start Windows Normally (Windows XP only)
- Reboot (Windows XP only)
- Return to OS Choices Menu (Windows XP only)

Safe Mode will start Windows with a minimal set of drivers used to run Windows, including mouse, monitor, keyboard, hard drive, base video, and default system services. You can enter Safe Mode with Networking or Safe Mode with Command Prompt by selecting the appropriate mode. VGA mode is useful when you have installed a video driver and have configured it incorrectly. If the computer starts with a blank screen or you see random lines all over the screen, you may choose VGA mode to start Windows.

This mode will start the computer with the base video settings (640 X 480, 256 Colors). Boot Logging starts Windows and logs services that load or do not load to C:\winnt\ntbtlog.txt. Last Known Good Configuration starts Windows using the Registry information saved at the last proper shutdown. Directory Services Restore is used for Windows domain server systems. Debugging Mode starts Windows and sends debug information through the serial port to another computer. In Hardware Profiles you can change Windows startup to select a designated profile. Hardware Profiles can be useful for saving hardware-specific information when transporting a hard drive between two computers. One can do this without the need to reinstall all the devices on each system at every startup.

This procedure is compatible with both Windows 2000 and Windows XP. There are subtle differences, however, and you might want to do this procedure in both Windows 2000 and Windows XP.

PROCEDURE

Troubleshooting

1. **Safe Mode**
   ___a. Turn on the computer (restart if it is already on) and boot to Windows 2000 or Windows XP.
   ___b. When the screen displays the text *"Starting Windows, For Troubleshooting and Advanced Startup Options for Windows 2000, press F8 "*, press the **F8** key on the keyboard. (This is not displayed in Windows XP; you just keep pressing the **F8** key over and over again until you get the Advanced Options Menu.)
   ___c. You will see the Advanced Options Menu. Safe Mode is selected by default. Press **ENTER**.
   ___d. Once Windows starts you will see an information window about Safe Mode. Click on **OK**.
   ___e. Right-click the desktop and select **Properties** from the drop-down menu to open the *Display Properties* window, and click on the **Settings** tab.
   ___f. While in Safe Mode, Windows gives limited options on many things. Click on the **Colors** drop-down menu. Record your observations in Table 15-1.
   ___g. Click on the **Cancel** button.
   ___h. From the desktop, double-click the **My Network Places** icon.
   ___i. Double-click on **Entire Network**.
   ___j. Double-click on **Microsoft Windows Network**.
   ___k. You will see a dialog window similar to Figure 15-1. During Safe Mode, you cannot view the network. Click on the **OK** button.
   ___l. Close all windows and restart.

Figure 15-1: Unable to Browse Network Dialog

2. **Safe Mode with Networking**
   ___a. When the computer has restarted, boot the computer to Windows 2000 and press the **F8** key as before.
   ___b. From the *Windows 2000 Advanced Options Menu* scroll down by pressing the **DOWN ARROW** on the keyboard. Select Safe Mode with Networking and press **ENTER**.
   ___c. Once Windows starts you will see an information window about Safe Mode. Click on **OK**.
   ___d. From the desktop, double-click the **My Network Places** icon.
   ___e. Double-click on **Entire Network**.
   ___f. Double-click on **Microsoft Windows Network**.
   ___g. You should see your workgroup in the window. Double-click on it and record your observations in Table 15-2.
   ___h. Close all windows and restart.

3. Safe Mode with Command Prompt

____a. When the computer has restarted, boot the computer to Windows 2000 and press the **F8** key as before.

____b. From the *Windows 2000 Advanced Options Menu* scroll down and select **Safe Mode with Command Prompt**. Press **ENTER**.

____c. The operating system will boot to a command prompt. (C:\>). Type **dir** and press **ENTER** to view the contents of the drive.

____d. Record the amount of bytes free in Table 15-3.

____e. Type **explorer** and press **ENTER**. This will start the Windows Explorer.

____f. You will receive the Safe Mode message. Click on **OK**.

____g. Drag the title bar of cmd.exe (the command prompt) to the right.

____h. Record the changes to the operating environment as a result of typing **explorer** in Table 15-4.

____i. In the command line type **exit** and press **ENTER**.

____j. Click on the **Start** menu and select **Shut Down**.

____k. Select **Restart** from the drop-down menu and click on **OK**.

4. Boot Normally

____a. When the computer has restarted, boot the computer to Windows 2000 and press **F8** as before.

____b. From the *Windows Advanced Options Menu* scroll down and select **Boot Normally in Windows 2000** or **Start Windows Normally** in Windows XP. Press the **ENTER** key.

____c. Use Windows Explorer to delete the file *c:\WINNT\ntbtlog.txt* in Windows 2000 and *c:\Windows\ntbtlog.txt* in Windows XP. You may need to click on **Show files** if you cannot view the contents of the *System* folder.

____d. You have just deleted the boot log text file that Windows uses to log activity when *Enable Boot Logging startup* is selected. Close all windows and restart the computer.

5. Boot Logging

____a. When the computer has restarted, boot the computer to Windows 2000 and press **F8** as before.

____b. From the *Windows 2000 Advanced Options Menu* scroll down and select **Enable Boot Logging**. Press **ENTER**. Windows will now create a boot log file (*C:\WINNT\ntbtlog.txt*) to record its activity at startup.

____c. Once Windows has started you can view the contents of the logged file. From the desktop double-click on **My Computer**.

____d. Double-click on **(C:)**.

____e. Double-click on **WINNT** (Win2K) or **Windows** (WinXP).

____f. Click on **Show files** if necessary. Its hyperlink is located on the left-hand portion of the window.

____g. Scroll down and double-click on **ntbtlog**.

____h. *Notepad* will open the file. The window will appear similar to Figure 15-2. You can now view the boot log that contains all loaded and not-loaded drivers. Record the date that appears on the first line of the file in Table 15-5.

____i. Scroll down and view the contents of the file.

____j. Close all windows and restart the computer.

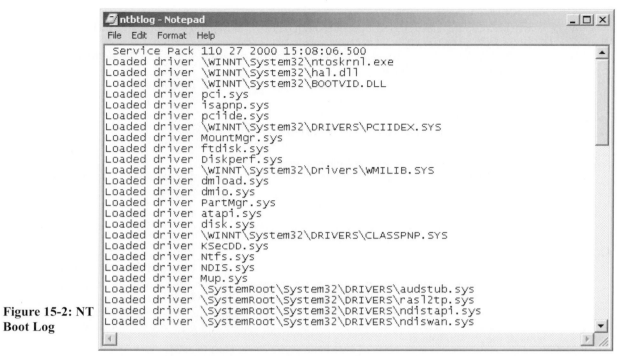

Figure 15-2: NT Boot Log

6. **VGA Mode**
    ____a.   When the computer has restarted, boot the computer to Windows 2000 and press **F8** as before.
    ____b.   From the *Windows 2000 Advanced Options Menu* scroll down and select **Enable VGA Mode**. Press **ENTER**.
    ____c.   When Windows has started, right-click the desktop and click on **Properties**.
    ____d.   Click on the **Settings** tab.
    ____e.   Record the settings for Colors and Screen area in Table 15-6.
    ____f.   Close all windows and restart the computer.

7. **Last Known Good Configuration**
    ____a.   When the computer has restarted, boot the computer to Windows 2000 and press **F8** as before.
    ____b.   From the Windows 2000 Advanced Options Menu scroll down and select **Last Known Good Configuration**. Press **ENTER**.
    ____c.   If you have made hardware profiles previously in Windows you can select them and boot to them. Press **L** to switch to the Last Known Good configuration.
    ____d.   Profile 1 should be selected. Press **ENTER**. If you pressed *D* your options would change to the default configuration.

8. **Hardware Profiles**
    ____a.   When Windows has started, right-click on **My Computer** and select **Properties**.
    ____b.   Click on the **Hardware** tab.
    ____c.   Click on the **Hardware Profiles** button.
    ____d.   A window similar to Figure 15-3 will appear. From this window you can add and delete hardware profiles. Click on **Cancel**.
    ____e.   Close all windows and shut down the computer.

**Figure 15-3:
Hardware
Profiles**

TABLES

Table 15-1

Colors Drop-Down Menu Observations

Table 15-2

Network Observations:	

Table 15-3

Bytes Free on C:\ at Command Prompt

Table 15-4

Operating Environment Changes Observations

Table 15-5

Boot Log Date:	

Table 15-6

Display Colors:	
Display Screen Area:	

Feedback

LAB QUESTIONS

1. How many startup options are included with Windows 2000 by default?

2. What does Safe Mode do?

3. When can VGA mode be useful?

4. How would you access the Start menu when in Safe Mode with Command Prompt?

5. Under what circumstances could Hardware Profiles be useful?

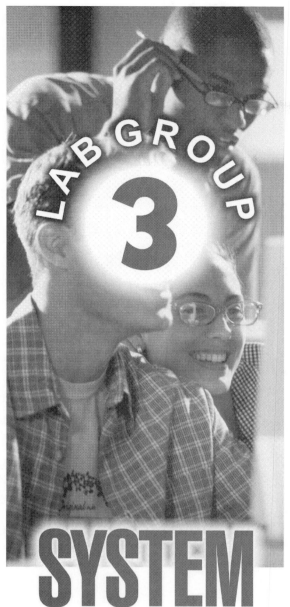

LAB GROUP

3

SYSTEM ADMINISTRATION TOOLS

Using Windows 2000 Administrative Tools

**Operating
System
Technology**

OBJECTIVES

1. View Component Services (COM+).
2. View Data Sources (ODBC).
3. View Event Viewer.
4. View Local Security Policy.
5. Use a Performance Counter.
6. View Services.
7. View Telnet Server Administration.

RESOURCES

1. PC-compatible desktop/tower computer system — Customer-supplied desktop/tower hardware system **OR** Marcraft Computer Repair Trainer **OR** suitable PC hardware trainer with Windows 2000 installed

DISCUSSION

COM+ is a set of services based on extensions of Microsoft Transaction Server (MTS) and the Component Object Model (COM). The idea of COM applications is not at all new. It's simply the term used to refer to groups of COM components developed to work together. A COM application example is Microsoft Excel, which consists of a primary executable and accompanying application extension DLLs for spell checking, Visual Basic functionality, and so on. Some of what differentiates a COM+ application is written into the component code, and some is defined through the Component Services administrative tool.

COM+ is a part of the Microsoft Management Console (MMC). MMC does not perform administrative functions, but works with tools that do. MMC can be used to create, save, and open administrative tools (called MMC consoles) that manage the hardware, software, and network components of your Windows system. MMC is a feature of Windows 2000, Windows NT, Windows 95, and Windows 98. The Component Services Console Tree can use the console tree of the Component Services administrative tool to view the applications, components, and security roles.

**Operating
System
Technology**

PROCEDURE

1. **Component Services**
   ____a.   Boot the computer to Windows 2000.
   ____b.   Navigate the path *Start/Settings/Control Panel*.
   ____c.   Double-click **Administrative Tools**. The window should look similar to Figure 16-1.

**Figure 16-1:
Administrative Tools**

   ____d.   You should now see the shortcuts to the eight administrative tools provided in Windows 2000.
   Double-click **Component Services**.

NOTE: You may need to maximize the window and resize the window pane.

   ____e.   Expand the *Component Services* icon that appears by clicking on the plus (+) sign next to the *Component Services* icon.
   ____f.   Click on the plus (+) sign next to the *Computers* icon.
   ____g.   Then click on the plus (+) sign next to the *My Computer* icon.
   ____h.   Expand the *COM+ APPLICATIONS* Folder. This corresponds to the applications installed on this computer. You can change the properties of an application by right-clicking the application and then clicking on **Properties**.
   ____i.   Record the three items that appear in Table 16-1.
   ____j.   Expand the *Distributed Transaction Coordinator*. This contains the Transaction List, which displays current transactions in which the computer is participating. It also contains Transaction Statistics.
   ____k.   Click on the **Transaction Statistics**. In the right-hand window pane, information such as performance, types, speed, and maximum and minimum response time for the transactions in which a computer participates is displayed. The window should look similar to Figure 16-2 on the next page.

**Figure 16-2:
Component Services**

_____1.   Close the *Component Services* window.

2.   Data sources

Open Database Connectivity (ODBC) can be used to access data from a variety of database management systems. An ODBC driver allows ODBC-enabled programs to get information from ODBC data sources. DSN stands for Data Source Name.

_____a.   From the *ADMINISTRATIVE TOOLS* folder double-click **Data Sources (ODBC)**.
_____b.   The window that opens will look similar to Figure 16-3.

Figure 16-3: ODBC

___c.   Read the explanation at the bottom of the window. Click on the **System DSN** tab.

___d.   Record the explanation about a System DSN from the bottom of the window in Table 16-2.

___e.   Click on the **File DSN** tab. This area of ODBC allows a connection to a specific database file.

___f.   Click on the **Drivers** tab. Count how many drivers are installed; you may need to scroll down.

___g.   Record the number of drivers in Table 16-3.

___h.   Click on the **Tracing** tab. Read its description in the bottom of the window.

___i.   Click on the **Connection Pooling** tab. Read its description in the bottom of the window.

___j.   Click on the **About** tab. Record its description in Table 16-4.

___k.   Close the ODBC Data Source Administrator.

3.   Event Viewer

Event viewer is a useful tool for diagnosing hardware, software, and system problems with Windows. When an error occurs it will usually be logged for later viewing in Event Viewer. If log warnings show that a disk driver can only read or write to a sector after several retries, the sector is likely to go bad eventually. Logs can also confirm problems with software. If a program crashes, a program event log can provide a record of activity leading up to the event.

___a.   From the *ADMINISTRATIVE TOOLS* folder double-click on **Event Viewer.**

___b.   The window should look similar to Figure 16-4. There are three areas of Event Viewer: Application Log, Security Log, and System Log.

**Figure 16-4:
Event Viewer**

___c.   The System Log is highlighted by default. Items are sorted by latest date first in the right-hand window pane. There are three types of events: Warnings, Errors, and Information. Look at the first item in the list. Record the required information in Table 16-5.

_____d. Click on the **Application Log** and view any information that it contains. This area records any errors or information that applications encounter with Windows.

_____e. Click on the **Security Log**.

_____f. Record how many events appear in Table 16-6. Here Windows will monitor and record actions that are viewed as security violations.

_____g. Close *Event Viewer*.

4. Local Security Settings

Local Security Settings is used to configure security policies for the local computer. These settings include the Password policy, Account Lockout policy, Audit policy, IP Security policy, user rights assignments, recovery agents for encrypted data, and other security options. Local Security Policy is only available on Windows 2000 computers that are not domain controllers. If the computer is a member of a domain, these settings may be overridden by policies received from the domain.

_____a. From the *ADMINISTRATIVE TOOLS* folder double-click **Local Security Policy**.

_____b. The window should look similar to Figure 16-5.

**Figure 16-5:
Local Security
Settings**

_____c. Expand **Account Policies**.

_____d. Click on **Password Policy**.

_____e. Record the Maximum password age in Table 16-7. The Maximum password age is the time a password will remain the same until the user is prompted to change it.

_____f. Expand **Local Policies**.

_____g. Click on **User Rights Assignment**.

_____h. View the right-hand window pane and scroll down to "*Shut down the system*".

_____i. Double-click on **Shut down the System**, and a window similar to Figure 16-6 appears.

_____j. The users that have rights to this operation will be listed. From this window you can add and delete users assigned to shut down the system. Record the users assigned to this task in Table 16-8.

_____k. Click on **OK**.

_____l. Click on **Security Options** under *Local Policies*.

**Figure 16-6:
Local Security
Policy Setting**

___m.   Record the first policy that is listed in Table 16-9.
___n.   Click on **IP Security Policies** on Local Machine.
___o.   Record the three policies in Table 16-10.
___p.   Close *Local Security Settings*.

5.   Performance

The performance console collects and displays real-time data about memory, disk, processor, network, and other activity in a graph, histogram, or report form.

___a.   From the *ADMINISTRATIVE TOOLS* folder double-click **Performance**.

NOTE: Notice that the System Monitor is selected on the left-hand window pane by default. There are no graphs selected by default.

___b.   Click on the large plus (+) button above the graph in the right-hand window pane to add a computer.
___c.   By default the performance object is set to *Processor* and the counter selected is *% Processor Time*.
___d.   Click on **Add**.
___e.   Click on **Close**.
___f.   You are now monitoring how much the processor is used in terms of time. Start a few programs like *Internet Explorer* and *Notepad* and then close them.
___g.   Observe the changes in the chart. The window will look similar to Figure 16-7.

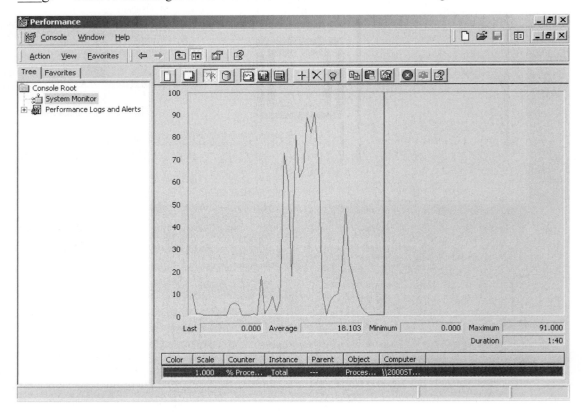

**Figure 16-7:
Performance
Charting**

___h.   Notice the key at the bottom of the window. It shows the color of the line, scale, and other information about the chart.

_____i.   As before, click on the (+) button.

NOTE: You can add more than one graph on the same chart. When you add another line to the chart, the Performance console will automatically choose an available color for the graph.

_____j.   This time select **Memory for the Performance object**. You may need to scroll the drop-down menu.
_____k.   Select **% Committed Bytes In Use** as the counter. You may need to scroll up in the list.
_____l.   The window should look similar to Figure 16-8.

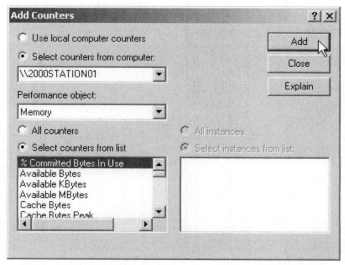

**Figure 16-8:
Add a Counter**

_____m.   Click on **Add**.
_____n.   Click on **Close**.
_____o.   Record the Color of the % Processor Time and % Committed Bytes In Use lines in Table 16-11.
_____p.   As before, start a program, but this time do not close it, just minimize it.
_____q.   Record your observations of the % Committed Bytes In Use line in Table 16-12.
_____r.   Close *Performance* and any other programs you have started in this step, but do not close the *Administrative Tools* window.

6.   Services

The Services console is used to manage the services on your computer, set recovery actions to take place if a service fails, and create custom names and descriptions for services so that you can easily identify them.

_____a.   From the *ADMINISTRATIVE TOOLS* folder double-click **Services**.
             These are services listed on the right-hand window pane.

NOTE: From this window you can see all the services that are running, either by default from Windows 2000 or from installed programs that add a service.

_____b.   Double-click the **Alerter Service**. From this window you change the properties for starting the service, add an action when the service fails, or change its Log On properties.
_____c.   Read its Description and click on **Cancel**. You can see the status of the service; it will be either Started or blank (implying stopped).
_____d.   Count how many services have been started and record this in Table 16-13.
_____e.   Close *Services*.

7. **Telnet Server Administration**

Telnet is a service that allows you to "telephone-net" into another computer. Originally it was designed to view information on a remote computer (hundreds of miles away) as if you were sitting at that computer. Today we just use the Internet for this type of long distance communication, but telnet can still be a useful tool. The Telnet Server is built into Windows 2000 to allow remote computers access through a telnet client. The client can be invoked by typing "telnet" from the command line.

____a. From the *ADMINISTRATIVE TOOLS* folder double-click on **Telnet Server Administration**. You will see a window similar to Figure 16-9.

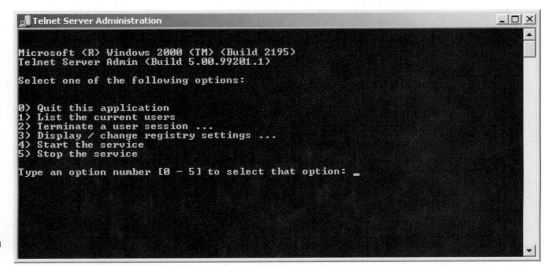

Figure 16-9: **Telnet Server Administration Window**

____b. Type **4** and press **ENTER** to start the service.

NOTE: After the service has started, other computers connected on the LAN can connect to the computer via the command prompt. A remote computer can connect by typing "telnet" and the IP address of a computer with the Telnet Server running.

____c. Stop the telnet service by typing **5** and pressing **ENTER**.
____d. Enter **0** to quit the *Telnet Server Administration*.
____e. Close all open windows, and shut down the computer.

TABLES

Table 16-1

Com+ Applications Folder:	

Table 16-2

System DSN Explanation:	

Table 16-3

Number of ODBC Drivers:	

Table 16-4

ODBC About Description:	

Table 16-5

Event Viewer System Log - First Event	
Type:	
Date:	
Source:	

Table 16-6

Security Log Events:	

Table 16-7

Maximum Password Age:	

Table 16-8

Users Assigned to Shut Down the System:	

Table 16-9

First Listed Policy:	

Table 16-10

IP Security Policies:	

Table 16-11

	Colors
% Processor Time:	
% Committed Bytes in Use:	

Table 16-12

Table 16-13

Number of Services Started:	

Feedback

LAB QUESTIONS

1. How many items did you have in the Application Log of Event Viewer?

2. How can Event Viewer be useful?

3. What is an automatic feature of the Performance console?

4. Which option in Telnet Server Administration starts the service?

5. How would you navigate to view all the services that are running?

Using Windows 2000 Computer Management

Operating
System
Technology

OBJECTIVES

1. View various areas of Computer Management.
2. Use Task Manager.

RESOURCES

1. PC-compatible desktop/tower computer system — Customer-supplied desktop/tower hardware system **OR** Marcraft Computer Repair Trainer **OR** suitable PC hardware trainer running Windows 2000

DISCUSSION

Windows Computer Management provides access to administration tools for managing disks as well as local and remote computers. Some of the tools included are Event Viewer, System Information, Performance Logs and Alerts, Shared Folders, Device Manager, Local Users and Groups, and Disk Defragmenter. These can be useful tools for viewing the hardware and software components of your computer.

PROCEDURE

1. **Start Computer Management**
   ___a. Boot the computer to Windows 2000.
   ___b. Open Computer Management through the path *Start/Settings/Control Panel*. Double-click on **Administrative Tools** and double-click on **Computer Management**. The window will look similar to Figure 17-1.
   ___c. Click on **Event Viewer**. Notice the contents in the right-hand window pane. This is the same Event Viewer that you have used in previous labs.

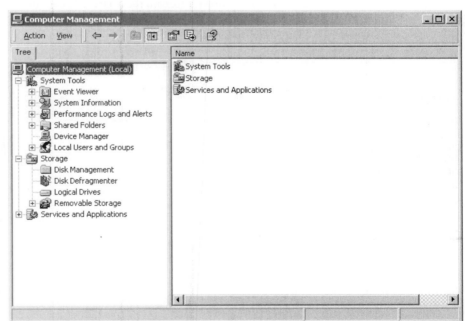

Figure 17-1: Computer Management

2. System Information

____a.   Click on **System Information**. If you have used "msinfo32" in Windows 98 or Me this will look familiar. From this menu you can view properties of your hardware resources and components, software environment, and Internet Explorer settings.

____b.   Expand *System Information* and click on **System Summary**.

____c.   Record the required fields in Table 17-1.

____d.   Click on **Hardware Resources** and expand the folder.

____e.   From this window you can view properties such as I/O Address Ranges, Memory Ranges, and device IRQ settings. Click on **I/O**. Record one of the Address Ranges of the PCI bus in Table 17-2.

____f.   Click on **IRQs** and record the IRQ of the keyboard in Table 17-3.

____g.   Expand **Components** under **System Information**.

____h.   Click on **Display**. Record the required fields in Table 17-4.

____i.   Expand the *PORTS* folder and select **Serial**.

____j.   View the information displayed. Record the COM1 Baud Rate in Table 17-5.

____k.   Select **Parallel** and view the information displayed.

____l.   Expand **Software Environment** under *System Information*.

____m.   Select the **DRIVERS** folder and view the information displayed.

____n.   Select **Startup Programs**. This area can be useful for optimizing system performance. If your system is running slower than normal you may have unnecessary programs running.

____o.   Collapse System Information by clicking on the minus (-) sign next to its icon.

3. Performance Logs and Alerts

____a.   From *Computer Management* expand **Performance Logs and Alerts**.

____b.   You will see three areas: Counter Logs, Trace Logs, and Alerts. These logs can be initialized from the Performance area of Administrative tools. Collapse Performance Logs and Alerts.

4. Shared Folders

____a.   From *Computer Management* expand **Shared Folders**.

____b.   Click on the **Shares Icon**. From this window you can see all the folders that are shared from your computer.

____c.   Click on **Shares**. Record the Shared Folders in Table 17-6.

____d.   Click on **Sessions**. From this area you can view any remote users attached to your computer.

____e.   Click on **Open Files**. From this area you can view which files are being accessed over the network. Record any open files in Table 17-7.

____f.   Collapse *Shared Folders*.

Figure 17-2: Device Manager

5. Device Manager

____a.   From Computer Management click on **Device Manager**. The window should look similar to Figure 17-2.

____b.   This area can perform the same functions as Device Manager in Windows 98 or 95. This is a useful tool for viewing any conflicts or hardware setup problems with various components on the computer. Expand **Mice and other pointing devices**.

___c.   Record any items listed in Table 17-8.

___d.   Click on the **View** menu and select **Devices by connection**. From this view you can see a hierarchical structure of connections to the computer.

___e.   Click on the **View** menu and select **Resources by type**.

___f.   Expand the **Interrupt request (IRQ)** list.

___g.   Look for the keyboard and double-click on its icon.

___h.   You will see a properties window appear, it will look similar to Figure 17-3. Click on the **Resources** tab.

___i.   From this window you can view the I/O range and IRQ of the device. Record the Input/Output Range(s) of the keyboard in Table 17-9.

___j.   Click on **Cancel**.

6.   Local Users and Groups

___a.   From *Computer Management* double-click the **Local Users and Groups** icon to expand it.

___b.   Click on **Users**.

___c.   By default two users are set up by Windows: Administrator and Guest. Guest is disabled by default. Double-click on **Guest**.

___d.   You will see a window similar to Figure 17-4. The account is disabled by default. *Uncheck Account* is disabled.

Figure 17-3: Keyboard Properties

Figure 17-4: Guest User Properties

___e.   Click on **OK**.

___f.   Click in a blank space in the window.

___g.   Click on the **Action** menu and **Select New** user.

___h.   From this window you can create a new user to log on the computer. They can log on locally or over the network. Click on **Close**.

___i.   Click on **Groups** and record the description of Administrators in Table 17-10.

NOTE: You may need to double-click the icon next to the name to view the user's properties.

___j.   Collapse *Local Users and Groups*.

7.   Storage

___a.   From *Computer Management* expand **Storage**.

___b.   Click on **Disk Management**.

___c.   From this window you can view partitioning information, similar to the fdisk command in DOS.

___d.   Record the file system of (C:) in Table 17-11.

___e.   Click on **Disk Defragmenter**. Disk Defragmenter moves the pieces of each file or folder to one lo-cation on the volume, so that each occupies a single, contiguous space on the disk drive. Regular defragmentation will improve system performance.

___f.   Click on **Volume (C:)**.

___g.   Click on the **Analyze** button.

___h.   In a moment the *Analysis Complete* dialog will appear. Click on **View Report**.

___i.   Read the *Most fragmented files* section and click on **Close**.

___j.   The window should look similar to Figure 17-5. Depending on system speed and percent frag-mented the defrag may take from 5-60 minutes. If time permits, click on **Defragment**.

Figure 17-5:
Disk Defragmenter

___k.   Click on **Logical Drives**.

___l.   You will see A:, C:, D:, and any other physical drives installed on your computer. You can dou-ble-click on each one and view its properties.

___m.   Expand **Removable Storage**. From this area you can manage backup devices on the computer.

8.   Services and Applications

___a.   From *Computer Management* expand Services and Applications.

___b.   Click on **Services**. As you have seen before, these are the services running on the computer.

___c.   Expand **Indexing Service**. This Service indexes all the files and folders on the computer for easy searching. Record any catalog items in Table 17-12.

___d.   Close *Computer Management* and all windows.

9. **Task Manager**

___ a. From the Windows 2000 desktop press **CTRL+ALT+DELETE** on the keyboard.

___ b. Click on the **Task Manager** button.

___ c. Click on the **Applications** tab. If you have any applications running, such as Microsoft *Word* or *Internet Explorer*, you can view their status and end them if necessary.

___ d. Click on the **Processes** tab. This displays all services, applications, and other processes running on the system. Record how many processes are running in Table 17-13.

___ e. Click on **View/Select Columns**. The window will look similar to Figure 17-6.

___ f. From this window you can add columns that display advanced information about a process. Select all the columns by clicking in the box to the left of each name and placing a check mark.

___ g. Click on **OK**. You can now view more information about a specific process. You may need to use the horizontal scroll bar.

___ h. Look at the *System Idle Process* and record its Memory Usage in Table 17-14.

___ i. Click on the **Performance** tab.

___ j. From this tab you can view a graphical representation of CPU Usage and Memory Usage. Record the value for Total Physical Memory (K) in Table 17-15.

___ k. Close *Task Manager*.

___ l. Close all open windows, and shut down the computer.

Figure 17-6: Select Columns

TABLES

Table 17-1

System Information - System Summary	
OS Name:	
Version:	
Total Physical Memory:	
Available Physical Memory:	

Table 17-2

Sample PCI Bus Address Range:	

Table 17-3

Keyboard IRQ:	

Table 17-4

Display Information	
Adapter Name:	
Adapter Type:	
Resolution:	
Bits / Pixels:	

Table 17-5

COM1 Baud Rate:	

Table 17-6

Shared Folders	

Table 17-7

Open Files:	

Table 17-8

Items Listed in Mice and Other Pointing Devices:	

Table 17-9

Keyboard Input / Output Ranges:	

Table 17-10

Administrators Description:	

Table 17-11

File System of (C:):	

Table 17-12

Indexing Service Catalogs:	

Table 17-13

Processes Running on System:	

Table 17-14

System Idle Process Memory Usage:	

Table 17-15

Total Physical Memory:	

LAB QUESTIONS

1. What can System Information be used for?

2. How can you view all the shared folders of the system?

3. What can Device Manager be used for?

4. What default users are set up by Windows?

5. What does Disk Defragmenter do?

Feedback

Windows XP Plug-and-Play

Operating System Technology

OBJECTIVES

1. Remove Network Interface Card (NIC).
2. Install NIC with Plug-and-Play capabilities.
3. Remove modem.
4. Install modem with Plug-and-Play capabilities.

RESOURCES

1. PC-compatible desktop/tower computer system — Customer-supplied desktop/tower hardware system **OR** Marcraft Computer Repair Trainer **OR** suitable PC hardware trainer with a Plug-and-Play modem and NIC installed under Windows XP

DISCUSSION

This procedure is very similar to procedure 11. We wanted to show you how the Plug-and-Play installations have improved with each Windows operating system. In this procedure we will again have you remove the network adapter and modem and reinstall them. This lab should go very fast since you have already performed these tasks once.

PROCEDURE

1. **Remove the Network Interface Card (NIC)**
   ___ a. Boot to the Windows XP desktop.
   ___ b. Press and hold the **Windows** key (located next to the left ALT key) then press the **Pause** key (upper-right keyboard next to the 10 key). This should bring up the *System Properties* box.
   ___ c. Click on the **Hardware** tab.
   ___ d. Click on **Device Manager**.
   ___ e. Click on the + next to *Modems* and *Network Adapters* as in Figure 18-1.
   ___ f. Record the devices in Tables 18-1 and 18-2.
   ___ g. Right-click on the network card and select **Uninstall**.
   ___ h. In the *Confirm Device Removal* dialog box click on **OK**.
   ___ i. Now click on **Start** and **Shut Down**.

Figure 18-1: XP Device Manager

      j.   Select **Shut Down** and click on **OK** to turn off the computer.

      k.   After unplugging the computer, remove the network interface card from the computer.

      l.   Boot up the computer into Windows XP.

      m.   Press the **Windows** key + **Pause** key to bring up System Properties.

      n.   Click on **Hardware** then **Device Manager**.

      o.   Notice that the network adapter is not installed.

      p.   Now click on **Start/Shutdown** and select **Shut Down**.

> **WARNING**
>
> On ATX machines you must make sure to unplug the computer to prevent damage to the computer. ATX machines have a 5-volt supply to the motherboard even when off.

2. **Install NIC with Plug-and-Play capabilities**

      a.   Install the network card into the trainer.

      b.   Make sure to connect the network cable and fasten the screw.

      c.   Boot the computer to Windows XP desktop.

NOTE: There should not have been any Found New Hardware dialog boxes. Since the hardware was already installed it still exists in Windows XP and will install the software automatically.

      d.   Press the **Windows Key + Pause** to bring up System Properties.

      e.   Click on the **Hardware** tab, then **Device Manager**.

      f.   The network card should now be in Device Manager again.

      g.   Make sure it matches what you recorded in Table 18-1.

3. **Repeat Steps 1 and 2 for the modem**

TABLES

Table 18-1

Network Adapter:	

Table 18-2

Modem:	

Feedback

LAB QUESTIONS

1. How do you remove drivers in Windows XP?

2. Why must you unplug ATX computers before removing or installing adapter cards?

3. What is the key combination used to bring up System Properties?

4. Do any dialog boxes appear when installing previously installed hardware in Windows XP?

5. Is there usually any interaction between the user and the operating system when installing Plug-and-Play devices?

Using Windows XP Control Panel

Operating System Technology

OBJECTIVES

1. Explore Control Panel using Category View.
2. Switch to Classic View.

RESOURCES

1. PC-compatible desktop/tower computer system — Customer-supplied desktop/tower hardware system **OR** Marcraft Computer Repair Trainer **OR** suitable PC hardware trainer running Windows XP Professional

DISCUSSION

In Windows XP the Control Panel has changed to Category View. In this lab procedure we will show you how to use the categories to get tasks accomplished. We will also show you how to switch the view back to the Classic View. Most technicians use this view because they know what they are looking for, whereas the Category View is useful for non-technical users. The final thing we will show you is how to use the system restore function to keep your computer backed up.

PROCEDURE

1. **Use the Category View in Control Panel**

    ___a.   Click on **Start/Control Panel**.
    ___b.   Control Panel should display as in Figure 19-1. (If Control Panel displays in the Classic View you may have to click on Category View in the upper-left corner.)

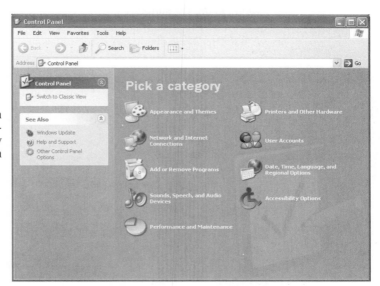

Figure 19-1: Control Panel: Category View

____c.   Click on **Appearance and Themes**.

Here is where you would change the theme, background, screen saver, and screen resolution by clicking on the different tasks. You can also click on the normal Control Panel icons at the bottom of the window as shown in Figure 19-2. We will not explain all the tasks from here on out, but will go through each category.

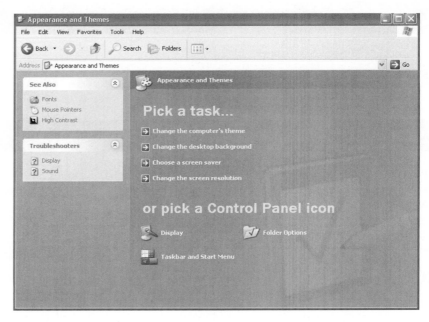

Figure 19-2:
Appearance and
Themes Category

____d.   Click on the **Up** button.
____e.   Click on **Printers and other hardware**.
____f.   Record all the tasks that can be accomplished here in Table 19-1.
____g.   Click on the **Up** button.
____h.   Click on **Network and Internet Connections**.
____i.   Record the tasks that can be accomplished here in Table 19-2.
____j.   Click on the **Up** button.
____k.   Click on **User Accounts**.
____l.   A *User Accounts* dialog box comes up as in Figure 19-3. Click on the **X** to close the box.

Figure 19-3: User
Accounts

____m.   In Tables 19-3 through 19-7, record the tasks that can be accomplished in each remaining category.

NOTE: Some icons do not bring up another category screen. They run programs such as User Accounts. Simply explain which program these icons run.

2.   Switch the view to Classic Control Panel view
____a.   Click on **Switch to Classic View** on the upper-left side of the *Control Panel* window.
____b.   This will switch it to the Classic View as in Figure 19-4. Click on **Switch to Category View** to change it back.

Figure 19-4: Classic Control Panel

____c.   Click on the **X** in Control Panel to close it.

TABLES

Table 19-1

Table 19-2

Table 19-3

Table 19-4

Table 19-5

Table 19-6

Table 19-7

Feedback

LAB QUESTIONS

1. How do you access the Control Panel in Windows XP?

2. How do you change views from Classic View to Category View?

3. Which category is where users can change the theme, background, screen saver, and screen resolution?

4. How do you change views from Category View to Classic View?

5. How many Control Panel category icons are located in the Control Panel window in Category View?

Working with Device Manager

OBJECTIVES

1. Understand how to use Device Manager to view and manage hardware attached to your system.

RESOURCES

1. PC-compatible desktop/tower computer system — Customer-supplied desktop/tower hardware system **OR** Marcraft Computer Repair Trainer **OR** suitable PC hardware trainer running Windows XP Professional

**Operating
System
Technology**

DISCUSSION

Device Manger allows you to view all of the devices currently attached to your machine and the status of that device. From Device Manager you can view the current settings, view the name and version number of a device driver file, reconfigure the resources for a device, update the drivers, remove, enable and disable devices as well as troubleshoot devices.

PROCEDURE

1. **Access Device Manager**

   ____a. Device Manager may be accessed either of two ways. The first way is by double-clicking on the **System** icon in the Control Panel and choosing the **Hardware** tab then clicking on the **Device Manager** button as shown in Figure 20-1, or by right-clicking on **My Computer** and choosing **Properties** as shown in Figure 20-2, then the **Hardware** tab, then clicking the **Device Manager** button. Either way you will arrive at the same place.

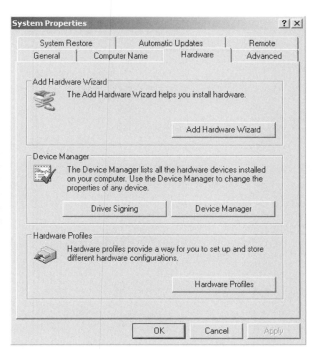

Figure 20-1: The Device Manager Button

**Figure 20-2:
Selecting
Properties**

Figure 20-3: Device Manager Window

____b.   Clicking the **Device Manager** button opens the *Device Manager* window, as shown in Figure 20-3. It displays a list of the devices attached to your machine.

____c.   Clicking the **Plus** sign next to the *Device* category expands the category and displays the contents, as shown in Figure 20-4.

Figure 20-4: The Category Expands

_____d. To view the settings for a particular device double click on it or right click on it and select **Properties**. For this lab choose the **IDE ATA/ATAPI controllers. Click the plus** sign next to the category then double click on the **Primary IDE Channel** to display it's properties, as shown in Figure 20-5.

_____e. The *General* tab displays the current status of the device as well as listing the type of device, the manufacturer of the device and it's location on the system bus. You may also trouble shoot the device from here if it is not functioning correctly.

_____f. Click on the **Advanced Settings** tab, as shown in Figure 20-6. In the case of the IDE controller you are shown information about the type of the device, the transfer mode, and what mode the drive is currently running in.

Figure 20-5:
Primary IDE
Channel
Properties

Figure 20-6: Advanced Settings Tab

_____g. Click on the **Driver** tab, as shown in Figure 20-7. The *Driver* tab provides information about who wrote the drive, when it was written, the driver version, and if it is digitally signed by the writer.

Figure 20-7: Driver Tab

___h.   Click on the **Driver Details** button. A detail window opens as shown in Figure 20-8 and Windows dis-plays which files are in use for the device.

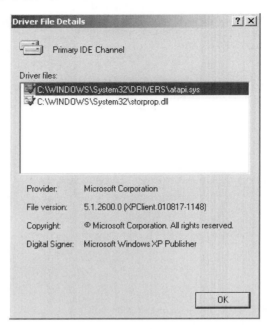

Figure 20-8: A Detail Window

___i.   Click **OK** to close the details window and click on the **Resources** tab. The *Resources* tab displays the physical address of the hardware on the system bus as shown in Figure 20-9. If there were to be a re-source conflict with another device, the conflict would be noted in the grey box at the bottom.

Figure 20-9: The Resources Tab

___j.   If you were to encounter a resource conflict, Windows may let you try an alternate resource con-figuration to solve the conflict. You may also disable or uninstall a device from Device Manager.

2. Disable or uninstall a device

____a. In Device Manager, right-click on the device as shown in Figure 20-10. Choose either **disable** or **uninstall** from the pop-up menu.

**Figure 20-10:
Right-clicking on
the Device**

____b. If you choose **disable** Windows displays a warning message, as shown in Figure 20-11.

**Figure 20-11:
Disable Warning
Message**

____c. If you choose **uninstall**, Windows displays the warning message shown in Figure 20-12.

If you disable a device it will no longer function and will have a red "X" next to its name in Device Manager. To enable the device again, right-click on it and choose **enable**. Windows will then re-enable the device. A re-boot may be needed to restore functionality.

As shown in Figure 20-5 above, Windows also provides a *Troubleshooting* button on the *General* tab of the device's properties. If you are having a problem with the device, click the **Troubleshoot** button and Windows will launch the appropriate wizard to try and help you resolve the problem.

Figure 20-12: Uninstall Warning Message

Feedback

LAB QUESTIONS

1. Describe the function of Device Manager. How does it help you maintain your system?

2. How do you find details on a device's drivers in Device Manager?

3. How do you disable a device in Device Manager? Do you get a warning?

Installing Printers in Windows XP

**Operating
System
Technology**

OBJECTIVES

1. Install a printer.
2. Share a printer.
3. Install a network printer.
4. Uninstall a network printer.

RESOURCES

1. PC-compatible desktop/tower computer system — Customer-supplied desktop/tower hardware system **OR** Marcraft Computer Repair Trainer **OR** suitable PC hardware trainer running Windows XP Professional
2. A printer connected to the printer locally
3. A shared network printer
4. Print drivers if necessary

DISCUSSION

In this lab we will install a printer locally on the machine. We will also install a network printer and print a test page. In Windows XP, connecting to a network printer becomes almost automatic. We use a Hewlett-Packard LaserJet 1100 printer. The results may vary with different printers.

PROCEDURE

1. **Install a printer on the parallel port**
   ____a.   Boot the computer into Windows XP.
   ____b.   Plug the printer into the trainer's parallel port, LPT1.
   ____c.   Now plug in the printer and turn it on.
   ____d.   In the Taskbar a message will appear that new hardware is found, and that Windows is installing the drivers; then it will finally say the hardware is installed and ready for use. No user interaction is necessary if the driver is available either locally or at the Windows Update site; the computer just fetches the driver automatically.
   ____e.   Click on **Start**.

___f. Click on **Printers and Faxes**. The *Printers and Faxes* window will appear as in Figure 21-1.

Figure 21-1: XP Printers and Faxes

___g. Right-click on the newly installed printer and select **Properties**.

___h. The printer's *Properties* box will come up as in Figure 21-2.

Figure 21-2: XP Printer Properties Box

2. Share a printer in Windows XP

___a. Click on the **Sharing** tab.

___b. Select **Share this printer**.

___c. Share the printer with the name of Marcraft.

___d. Click on **OK**.

___e. Close the printer's *Properties* box by clicking on the **X**.

3. Connect to a network printer in Windows XP

___a. Now click on **Start** and then click on **Printers and Faxes**.

___b. On the left side click on the words **Add a printer**.

Figure 21-3: Add Printer Wizard

____c. The Add Printer Wizard comes up as in Figure 21-3. It states that if you have a Plug-and-Play printer you do not need to use this wizard. Since we are installing a network printer click on **Next**.

____d. The *Local or Network Printer* dialog box comes up as in Figure 21-4, select **A network printer** if it is not already selected and click on **Next**.

Figure 21-4: Local or Network Printer Dialog Box

____e. The *Specify a Printer* dialog box comes up. Make sure to click on **Connect to this printer** and click on **Next** to browse for the printer.

____f. The *Browse for Printer* box comes up as in Figure 21-5. Double-click the computer of the workstation next to you or a specific computer as specified by your Instructor. This will expand it to the printer name shared on it.

Figure 21-5: Browse for Printer Dialog Box

____g. Double-click on the **Printer share name**. In this lab procedure it should be *Marcraft*.

____h. The *Default Printer* dialog box opens up as in Figure 21-6. Select no to not have this printer be the default printer. Click on **Next**.

____i. A *Completing the Add Printer Wizard* dialog box comes up. Click on **Finish**.

____j. Your *Printers and Faxes* window should still be open. Verify that the printer is installed. Record the name of the network printer in Table 21-1.

Figure 21-6: Default Printer Dialog Box

4. **Uninstall a printer in Windows XP**
   ____a.   Right-click on the network printer and select **Delete**.
   ____b.   A *Printers* dialog box comes up asking you if you are sure you want to remove your connection to the printer on the server. Click on **Yes**.

TABLES

Table 21-1

Name of Printer:	

Feedback

LAB QUESTIONS

1. How do you install a local Plug-and-Play printer in Windows XP?

2. How do you share a printer on a network in Windows XP?

3. How do you get to the Add Printer Wizard in Windows XP?

4. When adding a network printer how do you browse the network for available printers?

5. How does a network printer display in the Printers and Faxes window?

Disk Management in Windows 2000

OBJECTIVES

1. Use Disk Cleanup.
2. Back up a file.
3. Restore a backup.
4. Compress a file.
5. Encrypt a file.

Troubleshooting

RESOURCES

1. PC-compatible desktop/tower computer system — Customer-supplied desktop/tower hardware system **OR** Marcraft Computer Repair Trainer **OR** suitable PC hardware trainer with Windows 2000 installed
2. A blank 1.44 MB floppy disk

DISCUSSION

This lab will discuss some common disk management procedures. You can use storage media such as a CD-R, high-capacity floppy, tape drive, DVD-R, or secondary hard drive. Windows has a backup utility that can be used to schedule backups of your files. It is a good practice to clean unnecessary files off your hard drive. Windows has a utility called Disk Cleanup that can delete some of these files for you. Windows has a built-in file compression utility, but there are many third-party utilities available as well. For security reasons you may need to encrypt your files. The Encrypting File System (EFS) included with Microsoft Windows 2000 is based on public-key encryption. Each file is encrypted using a randomly generated file encryption key. Each file has a unique file encryption key, making it safe to rename. If you move a file from an encrypted folder to an unencrypted folder on the same drive, the file remains encrypted. If you copy an unencrypted file into an encrypted folder, the file remains unencrypted. You don't have to decrypt a file to open it and use it. EFS automatically detects an encrypted file and locates a user's file encryption key from the system's key store to open the file. In this lab you will create, back up, restore, compress, and encrypt a WordPad Document.

PROCEDURE

1. **Disk Cleanup**
   ____a.   Boot the computer into Windows 2000.
   ____b.   Navigate the path *Start/Programs/Accessories/System Tools* and select **Disk Cleanup**.

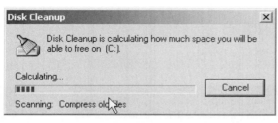

Figure 22-1: Calculating Cleanup Space

____c. When prompted to select the drive to clean up, select the **C: Drive** and click on **OK**. You will see a window similar to Figure 22-1 calculating the space to clean up.

____d. After the calculation has completed, record the entries in "Files to delete:" that have a check mark in Table 22-1.

____e. Select **Recycle Bin** and **Temporary files** by clicking in the box to the left of their respective icons. A check mark will appear.

____f. Click on the **More Options** tab. You will see two areas: Windows components and Installed programs.

____g. Click on the **Clean up** button under *Windows Components*. You will see a window similar to Figure 22-2.

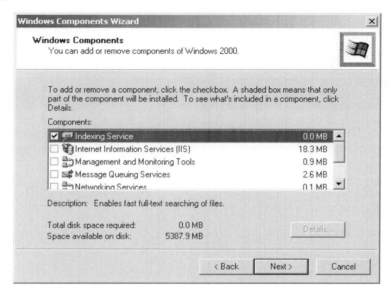

Figure 22-2: Add/Remove Windows Components

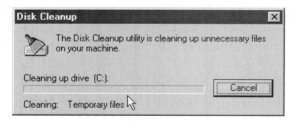

Figure 22-3: Cleaning Up Files

NOTE: You can check or uncheck items from this window to add or remove Windows components. This window can also be accessed through Control Panel/Add/Remove Programs.

____h. Click on **Cancel**.

____i. Click on **OK** to close the *Disk Cleanup* window for C:.

____j. Confirm the "Are you sure" question by clicking on **Yes**. You will see a window similar to Figure 22-3.

____k. When the cleanup has completed close all windows.

2. Create a file

____a. From the Windows 2000 desktop double-click on **My Documents**.

____b. Create a *WordPad* Document by clicking on **File/New/WordPad Document**.

____c. Type **YourName** as the name of the document.

____d. Close all windows.

3.   Backup

____a.   Navigate the path *Start/Accessories/System Tools/* and then select **Backup** from the *System Tools* menu. You will see the *Welcome* screen.

____b.   Click on the **Backup** tab. You will see a window similar to Figure 22-4. From this area you can select drives or folders to back up on one of the media types.

Figure 22-4: Select Items to Back Up

____c.   In the left pane, click on **System State** to highlight it, but do not place a checkmark in the box next to it.

____d.   Record the items that appear in the right-hand window pane in Table 22-2.

____e.   Click on the **MY DOCUMENTS** folder and put a checkmark in the box next to the icon.

NOTE: You will be able to do this backup on a floppy as long as the MY DOCUMENTS folder is small enough.

____f.   Record the drive and filename of the backup (in the bottom left of the window) in Table 22-3.

____g.   Insert a blank floppy into the floppy drive.

____h.   Click on the **Start Backup** button. You will see a window similar to Figure 22-5.

____i.   Enter "**your name**" for the Backup description.

____j.   Enter "**your name**" for the label to identify the media if it is overwritten.

____k.   Click on the **Start Backup** button. You will see a *Backup Progress* window.

____l.   When the backup has completed, click on **Close**.

____m.   Close the *Backup* window.

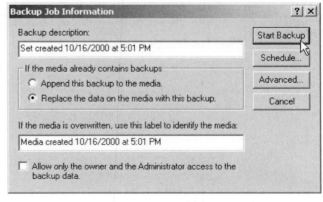

Figure 22-5: Backup Job Information

4. Delete a file

____a.   From the Windows 2000 desktop double-click the **My Documents** icon.

____b.   Right-click on the document that you created earlier and select **Delete**.

____c.   Confirm by clicking on **Yes**.

____d.   Close all windows.

5. Restore the backup

____a.   Open the *Windows Backup* utility by navigating the path *Start/Programs/Accessories/System Tools/* and then selecting **Backup**. You will see the **Welcome** screen.

____b.   Click on the **Restore** tab.

Figure 22-6: Confirm Restoration Dialog

____c.   In the right window pane, double-click **File** to expand it.

____d.   Expand the backup with Your Name on it by double-clicking it.

____e.   Place a check mark next to the C: drive to restore the files that were backed up.

____f.   Click on the **Start Restore** button.

____g.   Confirm restoration by clicking on **OK**. You will see a window similar to Figure 22-6.

____h.   Make sure the source file to back up has the correct filename and path, and click on **OK**.

____i.   After the restore has completed, click on **Close**.

____j.   Close all windows.

6. Test the restoration

____a.   From the Windows 2000 desktop double-click on **My Documents**.

____b.   Record your observations about the files in this folder in Table 22-4.

NOTE: The remainder of this lab can be performed only if you have an NTFS partition on your hard disk. Consult your instructor before performing Steps 7 and 8 below.

7. Compress a file

____a.   From the Windows 2000 desktop double-click on **My Documents**.

____b.   Double-click on your *WordPad* document that was just restored.

____c.   To add some size to the file, enter 10 lines of the character **X** with the keyboard. (You can hold down the key for one line, and copy and paste the rest.)

____d.   Close the document. When prompted, click on **Yes** to save the changes.

**Figure 22-7:
Advanced
Attributes**

____e.   Right-click on the document and choose **Properties**.

____f.   Record its "Size on disk" in Table 22-5.

____g.   Click on the **Advanced** button. You will see a window similar to Figure 22-7.

____h.   Select **Compress contents to save disk space**. Click on **OK**.

____i.   Click on the **Apply** button.

____j.   Record the new "Size on disk" in Table 22-6.

8.   Encrypt a file

____a.   From the properties of the document click on the **Advanced** button again.

____b.   Select **Encrypt contents to secure data**, which will turn the compression option off.

____c.   Click on **OK** to close the *Advanced Attributes* window.

____d.   Click on **OK** to close the *File Properties* window. You will see a window similar to Figure 22-8.

```
┌─────────────────────────────────────────────────────────┐
│ Encryption Warning                                    [X] │
├─────────────────────────────────────────────────────────┤
│  ⚠   You have chosen to encrypt a file that is not in an │
│      encrypted folder. The file can become decrypted when │
│      it is modified.                                      │
│                                                           │
│      Because files saved in encrypted folders are         │
│      encrypted by default, it is recommended that you     │
│      encrypt the file and the parent folder.              │
│                                                           │
│      What do you want to do?                              │
│                                                           │
│      ○  Encrypt the file and the parent folder            │
│      ◉  Encrypt the file only                             │
│                                                           │
│  ─────────────────────────────────────────────────────  │
│  ☐ Always encrypt only the file    [  OK  ]  [ Cancel ]   │
└─────────────────────────────────────────────────────────┘
```

Figure 22-8: Encryption Warning

____e.   Click on the radio button next to *Encrypt the file and the parent folder* to select it and click on **OK**.

____f.   While the file is selected you will see "Attributes: Encrypted" in the right-hand portion of the *My Documents* window.

____g.   Close all open windows, and shut down the computer.

TABLES

Table 22-1

Files to Delete:	

Table 22-2

System State (right-hand pane):	

Table 22-3

Backup Drive and Filename:	

Table 22-4

Observation About Files:	

Table 22-5

File Size on Disk:	

Table 22-6

New File Size on Disk:	

Feedback

LAB QUESTIONS

1. What are some storage medias?

2. What does EFS stand for?

3. What are two ways to access Add/Remove Windows components?

4. By what ratio was a file compressed in this procedure?

5. Using the methods in this lab, can you encrypt and compress a file at the same time?

Working with the Windows 2000 Registry

OBJECTIVES

1. Use RegEdit to change a string.
2. Export the Registry and view its size.

Troubleshooting

RESOURCES

1. PC-compatible desktop/tower computer system — Customer-supplied desktop/tower hardware system **OR** Marcraft Computer Repair Trainer **OR** suitable PC hardware trainer with Windows 2000 installed

DISCUSSION

Windows 2000 stores its configuration information in a database called the Registry. The Registry contains information for users, system hardware, software, and other settings. For example, to run a program at startup you could add the string "programname.exe" to the key "*HKEY_LOCAL_MACHINE\Software\Microsoft\Windows\CurrentVersion\Run*." Windows constantly references the Registry during its operation. Incorrectly editing the Registry may severely damage your system. If you do damage your system, you may be able to repair the Registry or restore it to the same version you were using when you last successfully started your computer. You may resort to reinstalling Windows if the system is damaged beyond repair, but you may lose any changes that have been made in the Registry. The Registry is organized hierarchically as a tree made up of keys, subkeys, hives, and value entries. There are three types of values: String, Binary, and DWORD. Two Registry editors are included with Windows 2000: REGEDT32 and REGEDIT. In RegEdit the keys have icons similar to the folder icons in windows. With Regedt32 you can set the security for Registry keys. Also, in Regedt32 you can view or edit the value data types REG_EXPAND_SZ and REG_MULTI_SZ. With both RegEdit and RegEdt32 you can edit the Registry of another computer on the network if you have administrative rights and the Remote Registry Service is running on the other computer. In this lab we will use RegEdit to change some basic colors on the computer. We will be editing the string "*My Computer\HKEY_USERS\45 CHARACTER\Control Panel\Colors\Menu*", where 45 CHARACTER is a unique identification number assigned to the user. There should be only one registered user on the computer, the Administrator. The Menu string is 212 208 200 (Gray) by default. In this Registry string there are three numbers that each range from 0 to 255. They represent a value in their respective colors: red, green, and blue. Four basic colors are listed in Figure 23-1 as an example.

Figure 23-1: Basic Colors

RED	GREEN	BLUE	RESULTS
0	0	255	All blue in color
0	255	0	All green in color
255	0	0	All red in color
212	208	200	The default Windows gray

Troubleshooting

PROCEDURE

1. **Edit a string**
   ____a.   Boot to the Windows 2000 desktop.
   ____b.   Start Microsoft Registry Editor by clicking on **Start/Run**. Type **regedit** and click on **OK**.
   ____c.   You will see a window similar to Figure 23-2. Expand HKEY_USERS by clicking on the plus (+) sign next to its icon.

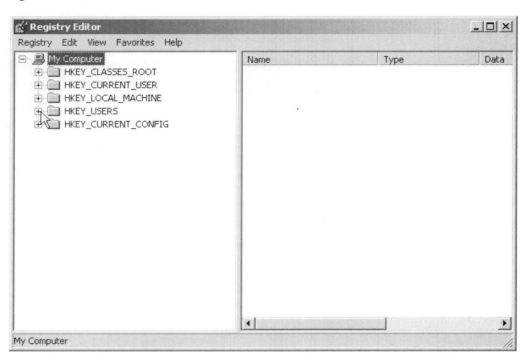

**Figure 23-2:
RegEdit.exe**

   ____d.   Expand the 45 CHARACTER key. It could be s-1-5-127520070-1808537768-1060284298-500, for example.
   ____e.   Expand the CONTROL PANEL key.
   ____f.   Click on the **COLORS** key.
   ____g.   In the right-hand window pane look for the string value *Menu* and record its "type" in Table 23-1.
   ____h.   Double-click the *Menu* string. Your screen should look similar to Figure 23-3.
   ____i.   Record the "Value data" in Table 23-2.
   ____j.   Enter **0 255 0** for the Value data, and click on **OK**.
   ____k.   Close the Registry Editor and restart the computer.

Figure 23-3: Editing a String

2. View the results

____a. Once the computer has restarted to Windows, click on the **Start** menu.

____b. Record your observations in Table 23-3.

____c. Right-click the desktop and select **Properties**.

____d. Click on the **Appearance** tab.

____e. Under the *Item:* drop-down menu select **Menu**.

____f. To the right of the drop-down menu is a field called **Color**. Click on it and then click on **Other**.

____g. You will see a window similar to Figure 23-4. Record the Red, Green, and Blue values in Table 23-4.

____h. Enter **212** for the Red value.

____i. Enter **208** for the Green value.

____j. Enter **200** for the Blue value.

____k. Click on **OK** to close the *Color* box.

____l. Click on **OK** to close the *Display Properties* window.

____m. Restart the computer.

Figure 23-4: Menu Color Properties

3. View Registry string value

____a. Once the computer has restarted, start the Registry Editor and browse to the *Menu* string as in Steps 1a-f.

____b. Double-click the *Menu* string as before.

____c. Record your observations about the value of the string in Table 23-5.

____d. Close the *Edit String* window.

4. **Export Registry**

___a. In the menu bar, click on the **Registry** menu and then select **Export Registry**. You will see a window similar to Figure 23-5.

Figure 23-5:
Export Registry File

___b. Under *Export* range click on the **All** radio button.

___c. In the *Save in* box confirm that the default location is *MY DOCUMENTS*. If it is not, change the default location to **MY DOCUMENTS**.

___d. In the *File name* box enter **sample registry export** for the filename and click on **Save**.

___e. After a few moments the Registry files will be exported to MY DOCUMENTS. Close the Registry Editor.

___f. From the Windows desktop, double-click the **My Documents** icon.

___g. Right-click the "sample registry export" and click on **Properties**.

___h. Enter its size in Table 23-6.

___i. Close all windows.

TABLES

Table 23-1

"Menu" Key Type String:	

Table 23-2

Menu "Value Data":	

Table 23-3

Reboot Observation with New Value Data:	

Table 23-4

Color Palette Values		
Red	Green	Blue

Table 23-5

Reboot Observation with Restored Value Data:	

Table 23-6

File Size of Sample Registry Export:	

LAB QUESTIONS

1. What are three things that the Registry keeps track of?

2. If you damage the Registry beyond repair, what may you have to do?

3. What advantages does RegEdt32 offer?

4. What is the correlation between the Red, Green, and Blue values of the Menu color and the Registry string that you changed?

5. What conclusions can you make about the correlation between Windows' operation and its Registry?

Feedback

Windows 2000 Virus Protection

Troubleshooting

OBJECTIVES

1. Manually scan the C: drive for viruses.

RESOURCES

1. PC-compatible desktop/tower computer system — Customer-supplied desktop/tower hardware system **OR** Marcraft Computer Repair Trainer **OR** suitable PC hardware trainer with Windows 2000 installed

2. Anti-virus package - McAfee VirusScan utility **OR** other user supplied anti-virus utility

DISCUSSION

Viruses can harm the operation of your system. When visiting questionable Web sites, or opening infected e-mail, you may get a virus that causes your system to operate strangely. Viruses can delete documents, system files, or other files on your computer. They can be spread to other users through e-mail, the Internet, or any other electronic means of communication. It is important to rid the computer of any viruses and perform preventive maintenance on your system. It is also important to have the latest .DAT files, which define the known viruses, because new viruses appear every day. McAfee can also update its files on your computer directly from their Web site. This lab will help you to use McAfee VirusScan to scan the hard drive on your computer.

PROCEDURE

1. **Manual scan for viruses**

____a. Boot to the Windows 2000 desktop.

____b. Double-click the **McAfee VirusScan Central Shortcut** on the desktop.

____c. If you are prompted to perform a scan because one has not been preformed before, click on **No**.

____d. You will now see a window similar to Figure 24-1. Click on the **Scan** button.

____e. Highlight **Local Disk (C:)**.

____f. Click on the **Settings** button.

Figure 24-1: McAfee VirusScan

Figure 24-2:
Scan Settings

g. Record the items selected under "What to scan" in Table 24-1.

h. Click on the **All files** radio button.

i. Click on the **Action** tab. You will see a window similar to Figure 24-2.

j. Click on the down arrow to open the "*When a virus is found*" menu so that it expands and record the options in Table 24-2.

k. Click on the **Exclusion** tab.

l. From this window you can add or remove folders to be excluded during a scan. Record the item that is excluded in Table 24-3.

m. Click on **OK** to close the *Scan Settings* window.

n. Click on the **Activity Log** button. You will see a window similar to Figure 24-3.

o. Click on the **Log Settings** button.

p. Record the Items under "Enable logging for" in Table 24-4.

q. Click on **OK** to close the *Log Settings* window.

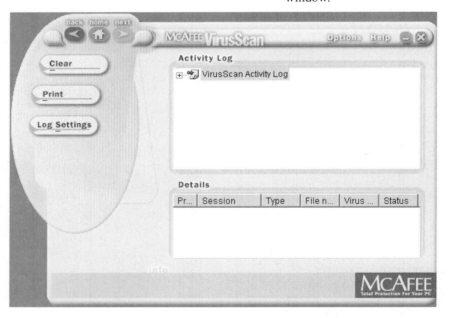

Figure 24-3:
Activity Log

r. Click on the **VirusScan Activity Log** and then expand it by clicking on the + sign next to the icon.

s. Click on the **VirusScan Log**, if it exists, to highlight it.

t. Click on the **Clear** button.

u. Click on the **Back** button in the upper-left portion of the window to return to the previous scan window.

v. Click on the **Scan Now** button and the virus scan will begin. It may take several minutes.

w. Record your observations of the bottom of the window in Table 24-5. What do you think it is showing?

2. View results

____a.   If any viruses are detected you should choose to delete the file affected.

____b.   Immediately after the scan is finished a window similar to Figure 24-4 will open. Click on **OK** to the result window.

____c.   Click on the **Activity Log** button.

____d.   Expand the **VirusScan Activity Log**.

____e.   Expand the **VirusScan Log**.

____f.   You will see an item with the current date and time of the scan you just performed. Expand the item.

____g.   Click on **Scan Settings**.

____h.   Under the *Details* window you can see various information about the scan. Record the required values in Table 24-6.

____i.   Click on **Scan Summar**y and record the required details in Table 24-7.

____j.   Close the *McAfee VirusScan* window.

Figure 24-4: Scan Results

3. VirusScan Console

____a.   In the System Tray there is an icon that looks like a magnifying glass. This is the **VirusScan Console**. Double-click on it. You will see a window similar to Figure 24-5.

Figure 24-5: VirusScan Console

____b.   Double-click on **Scan Drive 'C'**.

____c.   Click on the **Schedule** tab. You can specify when an automatic scan should take place from this window.

____d.   Click on **Enable** and record the options to run in Table 24-8.

____e.   Click on **Cancel** and Close the *VirusScan Console* window.

4. Virus Shield

____a.   In the system tray there is an icon that looks like a V inside a shield. It may have a red circle with a slash in front of it. This is the **Virus Shield**. It can be made to monitor actions during normal operation. Double-click on it.

____b.   If the System Scan is disabled; enable it.

____c.   Press **CTRL+ALT+DELETE** and click on **Task Manager**.

____d.   Click on the **Performance** tab.

___e. Arrange your screen so that you can see the Memory Usage of Task Manager and System Scan Status at the same time. The screen should look similar to Figure 24-6.

**Figure 24-6:
View Both Windows at
Once**

___f. Click on the **Disable** button and then the Enable button in System Scan and record the differences of memory usage in Table 24-9.

NOTE: We already know that programs take up system resources when they're running. This program also scans every file that is accessed.

___g. Test this by opening a program like *Internet Explorer* and looking at the Last file scanned and the Scanned statistics for the number of files scanned.
___h. Record the names of the other three tabs of the *System Scan Status* window in Table 24-10.
___i. Disable **System Scan**, close all open windows, and shut down the computer.

TABLES

Table 24-1

What to Scan:	

Table 24-2

"When a Virus is found" Options:	

Table 24-3

Excluded Item:	

Table 24-4

"Enable logging for":	

Table 24-5

Scan Observations

Table 24-6

Details Window - Required Values	
Scan Engine Version:	
Scan Item 1:	
Scan All Files	

Table 24-7

Scan Summary Details	
Virus in Memory:	
Files Infected:	

Table 24-8

Schedule Options:		

Table 24-9

Differences	
Memory Used During Disable:	
Memory Used During Enable:	

Table 24-10

System Scan Tabs:	

Feedback

LAB QUESTIONS

1. Approximately how many files did you scan for viruses?

2. What other drives were available in "Where & What" when doing a scan of drive C:?

3. Where would you view the date and time of your last scan?

4. Where would you go to have the C: drive scanned once a day?

5. Why is it important to have the latest virus .DAT files?

Windows XP System Restore

Troubleshooting

DISCUSSION

System Restore automatically tracks changes to your computer at specific intervals to create restore points. Restore points can be scheduled or manually created. They also are automatically created before any changes are made to the system configuration. These restore points only back up system and program files.

System Restore, by default, is set up to monitor and restore all partitions on all drives in your system. It also monitors all installations of all applications or drivers that users install through normal delivery mechanisms like CD-ROMs, floppy drives, and so on. If you accidentally delete a monitored program file (such as .exe or .dll files) or they have become corrupted, you can restore your computer to a state that existed before those changes occurred.

System Restore does not lose your personal files or passwords. It does not restore any files located in the *My Documents* folder. It does not restore any files with common data file name extensions, such as .doc or .xls. To keep your personal data files completely safe from System Restore writing over them, save them in the *My Documents* folder.

If a program was installed after the restore point that you are restoring, the program will most likely be uninstalled. Data files that were created with that program will not be lost; however, you will have to reinstall the program to use the data files.

PROCEDURE

1. **Set up the amount of drive space to be used by System Restore**
   ____a. Open **System Restore** by navigating the *Start\All Programs\Accessories\System Tools\System Restore* path, as shown in Figure 25-1.

Figure 25-1: Opening System Restore

_____ b.   The *Welcome to System Restore* screen will appear, as shown in Figure 25-2.

Figure 25-2: System Restore Welcome Screen

Figure 25-3: System Properties/System Restore Tab

_____ c.   The *Welcome* screen contains a brief explanation of the System Restore utility, an area to select whether you wish to *Restore my computer to an earlier time*, or *Create a restore point*. On the left-hand side is a link to the *Advanced* settings for System Restore. Click on **System Restore Settings**. In a single hard drive system, you will receive a Properties page like the one in Figure 25-3. (In multiple-drive systems, the page will offer options for obtaining the status of the different drives.)

___d. Notice the check box at the top of the screen. Turning off System Restore disables the function on all drives. Leave the box cleared. For computers with a single drive skip to Step e. Highlight drive C from the list and click on the **Settings** button. The *System Restore* settings for the selected drive are displayed.

___e. You may move the slider to increase or decrease the amount of disk space allocated for the Restore Points. Click on **OK** to close the *Drive Settings* dialog box (multiple drives only), then click on **OK** to close the *System Properties* screen.

2. Restore your system from an existing Restore Point

___a. Make sure *Restore my system to an earlier time* is selected and click on **Next** to continue. The *Select a Restore Point* wizard opens, as shown in Figure 25-4. Notice that there is a calendar on the left side of the wizard. The dates displayed in bold contain restore points that you may use to restore your system to that date.

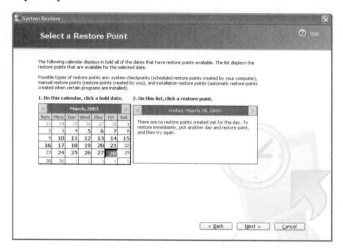

Figure 25-4: Select a Restore Point Wizard

___b. Choose the closest date to the current day with a valid restore point and click on it once.

___c. Notice that the right side changes to what was done for the computer to create the restore point. In Figure 25-5 the restore point created on March 26, 2003 had multiple restore points created and each one has a time associated with it. For yours it should have one checkpoint and display a system checkpoint with the time. If there are multiple restore points on that day, select the one latest in the day and click on **Next**.

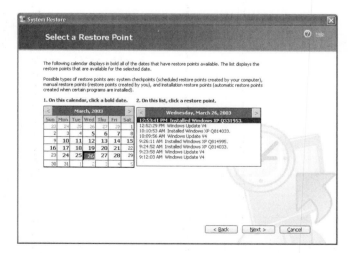

Figure 25-5: Restore Point Date with Multiple Restore Points

_____d.   Clicking on **Next** will cause the *Confirm Restore Point Selection* screen to appear, as shown in Figure 25-6. This screen provides the date and time of the restore point being used.

**Figure 25-6:
Restore Point
Confirmation
Screen**

Figure 25-7: System Restore Process

_____e.   Click on **Next** to begin the restore process.

_____f.   The wizard collects some information about the system and then logs off. It then starts the restore process as shown in Figure 25-7.

_____g.   After the restore process is finished, the system will be restarted, and then the desktop appears and the System Restore wizard displays the results as shown in Figure 25-8. If the restore process failed, you would be advised to choose another Restore Point, and try again.

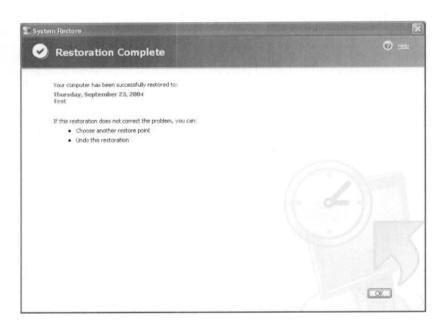

**Figure 25-8:
System Restore
Results Screen**

3. **Create a system restore point**

____a.   We will now manually create a system restore point. Open the System Restore wizard from the *Start* menu as before. This time select **Create a Restore Point** and click on **Next** to continue.

____b.   You will be asked to provide a name for the restore point. The name you choose should be representative of the purpose of the point, such as "New Driver" or the current date. For this lab we will enter the date. Enter the current date in the *Restore point description* text box, as shown in Figure 25-9, and click on **Create** to continue.

Figure 25-9: Restore Point Description

____c.   The system will create the restore point, and when done will display confirmation that the point has been created, as shown in Figure 25-10. Click on **Home** when finished to return to the *Welcome to System Restore* screen.

Figure 25-10: Restore Point has been Created

Feedback

LAB QUESTIONS

1. What does System Restore monitor by default in a system restore point?

2. How do you adjust the amount of disk space allocated to System Restore?

3. Is it possible to turn off System Restore?

4. What do you use to restore the system to an earlier restore point?

5. What do you use to create a system restore point?

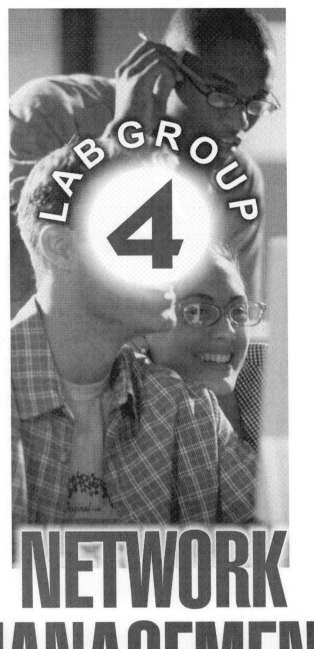

LAB GROUP

4

NETWORK MANAGEMENT

Using TCP/IP in Windows 2000

Networking

OBJECTIVES

1. Configure the Command Prompt window to improve visibility.
2. Use the IPCONFIG utility to examine your current TCP/IP configuration.
3. Use the ARP utility to map IP addresses to physical MAC addresses.
4. Use the NETSTAT utility to examine all current network connections.
5. Use the NBTSTAT utility to resolve Windows computer names on the network.
6. Use the NET VIEW utility to list all shared devices on a network node.
7. Use the TRACERT utility to test data packet routing and timing.
8. Use the PING utility to test other network nodes.

RESOURCES

1. PC-compatible desktop/tower computer system — Customer-supplied desktop/tower hardware system **OR** Marcraft Computer Repair Trainer **OR** suitable PC hardware trainer with 128 MB RAM
2. Windows 2000 operating system (installed)
3. Network Interface Card (installed)
4. Internet access through a network connection or modem

DISCUSSION

Windows provides several networking tools, called TCP/IP utilities, which can assist you in troubleshooting networking problems and determining how your network is performing. These tools are also present in Windows 2000. The functionality of the utilities will change depending on whether you are using a network server, a direct network connection via a modem, or a network workstation. Because of this variability, if a step does not function as described below, move on to the next step.

Networking

PROCEDURES

As before, you will access these tools through the *Command Prompt* window. In this lab procedure you will modify the *MS-DOS Command Prompt* window to increase the visibility of the displayed information. When completed, you will use the IPCONFIG /all command to list all current network parameters. The ARP command will map your network host's IP address to a NIC's MAC address. You will use the NETSTAT command to identify your current network connections, and the NBTSTAT command to resolve the Windows computer names of the other nodes you are connected to on the network. The NET VIEW command will list the nodes on your LAN and the shared devices on one of these nodes. You will use the TRACERT command to test data packet routing to a remote host, and to examine the time required for it to travel between points. Finally, you will use the PING command to test for responsiveness from a network node.

NOTE: The information actually displayed when running these utilities will vary greatly depending on your particular network configuration. The examples provided below will not match your results.

1. **Modify the Command Prompt window to increase visibility**
   ____a.   Boot the computer into Windows 2000.
   ____b.   Navigate the path *Start/Programs/Accessories/Command Prompt* to open the *MS-DOS Command Prompt* window.
   ____c.   Right-click the Command Prompt title bar and select **Properties** from the pop-up contextual menu.
   ____d.   Click on the **Colors** tab.
   ____e.   Click on the white color selector box, as seen in Figure 26-1, to change the background to white.
   ____f.   Click on the **Screen Text** radio button to select it.
   ____g.   Click on the black color selector box to change the text color to black.
   ____h.   Click on the **OK** button to close the *Properties* window.
   ____i.   Click on the **OK** button to change the window properties for the current window only.

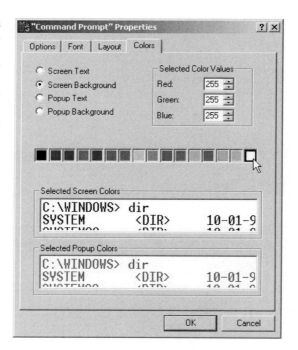

Figure 26-1: Command Prompt Properties Window

IPCONFIG

The IPCONFIG utility allows you to see your current IP address and other useful network configuration information. The command "IPCONFIG /all" will display the complete network information for the host computer you are using. As shown in Figure 26-2, this utility will identify the current network configuration, including the IP address and physical MAC address. If you are using DHCP to provide your IP address, you can use the "/release" and "/renew" switches to force the DHCP server to withdraw the current IP address lease, or drop the current lease and grab a new one.

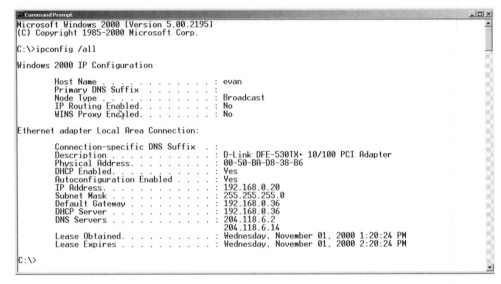

Figure 26-2: IPCONFIG /all

NOTE: IPCONFIG /all is used to display the current network configuration.

1.   Run IPCONFIG to display your network configuration

_____a.   At the MS-DOS command prompt, type **ipconfig ?** and press the **ENTER** key. Review the usage notes for IPCONFIG.

_____b.   At the command prompt, type **ipconfig /all** and press the **ENTER** key.

_____c.   Record the listed information for your client workstation in Table 26-1.

ARP

The Address Resolution Protocol (ARP) utility can be used to identify addressing information by examining the contents of the ARP caches on either the client or the server. It is primarily used to map IP addresses to physical MAC addresses.

1.   Run ARP to resolve your client and current network connections

_____a.   At the command prompt, type **arp** and press the **ENTER** key. Review the usage notes for ARP.

___b. At the command prompt, type **arp -a** and press the **ENTER** key. This will show information similar to Figure 26-3.

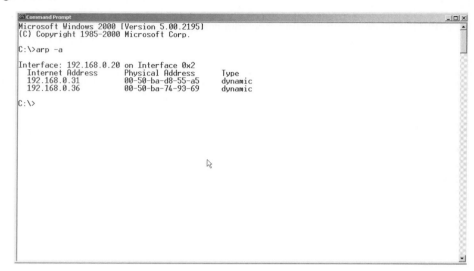

**Figure 26-3: arp - a
Command Prompt
Window**

NOTE: ARP is used to map IP addresses and physical MAC addresses.

___c. Record the IP address of your host computer, as shown in the Interface line, in Table 26-2.
___d. Record the IP and MAC addresses in Table 26-3.

NETSTAT

The command "netstat -e" displays the number of data packets transmitted and received, and the number of errors generated, as shown in Figure 26-4. The command "netstat -r" displays a list of all of the current connections and shows which are active.

NOTE: NETSTAT is used to display statistics about the current session.

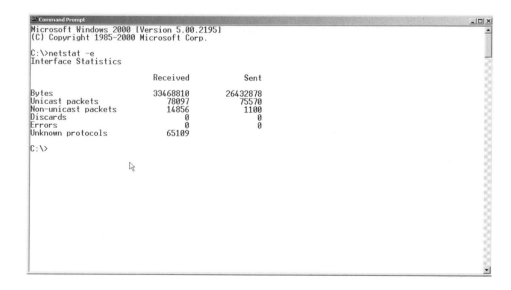

**Figure 26-4: netstat - e
Command Prompt
Window**

1.   Run NETSTAT to examine the current network connection

____a.   At the command prompt, type **netstat ?** and press the **ENTER** key. Review the usage notes for NETSTAT.

____b.   At the command prompt, type **netstat -e** and press the **ENTER** key to display packet statistics.

____c.   At the command prompt, type **netstat -r** and press the **ENTER** key. This will show your network connection information similar to Figure 26-5.

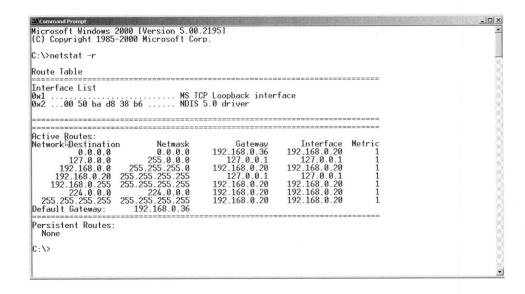

```
Command Prompt                                                              _|□|x|
Microsoft Windows 2000 [Version 5.00.2195]
(C) Copyright 1985-2000 Microsoft Corp.

C:\>netstat -r

Route Table
===========================================================================
Interface List
0x1 ........................... MS TCP Loopback interface
0x2 ...00 50 ba d8 38 b6 ...... NDIS 5.0 driver

===========================================================================

Active Routes:
Network Destination        Netmask          Gateway       Interface  Metric
          0.0.0.0          0.0.0.0     192.168.0.36    192.168.0.20      1
        127.0.0.0        255.0.0.0       127.0.0.1       127.0.0.1      1
      192.168.0.0    255.255.255.0    192.168.0.20    192.168.0.20      1
     192.168.0.20  255.255.255.255       127.0.0.1       127.0.0.1      1
    192.168.0.255  255.255.255.255    192.168.0.20    192.168.0.20      1
        224.0.0.0        224.0.0.0    192.168.0.20    192.168.0.20      1
  255.255.255.255  255.255.255.255    192.168.0.20    192.168.0.20      1
Default Gateway:      192.168.0.36
===========================================================================
Persistent Routes:
  None

C:\>
```

Figure 26-5: netstat -r Command Prompt Window

NBTSTAT

The NBTSTAT (NetBIOS over TCP STATistics) utility shows the Windows NetBIOS names for the connected computers, and lists their IP addresses and the status of the connection. This allows you to check connections made with the Windows Network Neighborhood tool. The "nbtstat -c" command displays the NetBIOS names of the hosts you are connected to, and the IP addresses they map to.

1.   Run NBTSTAT to resolve your client's current network connections

____a   At the command prompt, type **nbtstat** and press the **ENTER** key. Review the usage notes for NBTSTAT.

____b.   At the command prompt, type **nbtstat -c** and press the **ENTER** key. This will show you remote host identification information similar to Figure 26-6.

```
Command Prompt                                                                    _|□|×|

C:\>nbtstat -c

Local Area Connection:
Node IpAddress: [192.168.0.20] Scope Id: []

              NetBIOS Remote Cache Name Table

       Name            Type      Host Address     Life [sec]
    -----------------------------------------------------------
       MARCRAFT2   <20>  UNIQUE      192.168.0.74        567
       EDITOR      <20>  UNIQUE      192.168.0.27        585
       YU-WEN      <20>  UNIQUE      192.168.0.15        560

C:\>
```

Figure 26-6: nbtstat -c Command Prompt Window

NET VIEW

The NET VIEW command lists all of the computers currently connected to your Local Area Network (LAN). It can also display all of the shared devices associated with a particular network host. The format for displaying shared devices is "net view *your server name*", where the server name is the actual NetBIOS name of the workstation or server you are connected to. For example, "net view \\accounting" will resolve a list of all of the shared devices supported by the server named "accounting".

1. **Run NET VIEW to list the nodes on the LAN and display the shared devices on a node**
   ____a.   At the command prompt, type **net view ?** and press the **ENTER** key. Review the usage notes for NET VIEW.
   ____b.   At the command prompt, type **net view** and press the **ENTER** key to list all of the nodes connected to your LAN. Your results should be similar to Figure 26-7.

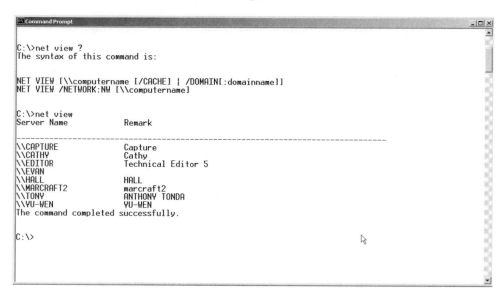

```
Command Prompt                                                                    _|□|×|

C:\>net view ?
The syntax of this command is:


NET VIEW [\\computername [/CACHE] | /DOMAIN[:domainname]]
NET VIEW /NETWORK:NW [\\computername]


C:\>net view
Server Name            Remark

-------------------------------------------------------------
\\CAPTURE             Capture
\\CATHY               Cathy
\\EDITOR              Technical Editor 5
\\EVAN
\\HALL                HALL
\\MARCRAFT2           marcraft2
\\TONY                ANTHONY TONDA
\\YU-WEN              YU-WEN
The command completed successfully.


C:\>
```

Figure 26-7: net view ? Command Prompt Window

____c.   Record the host names listed by NET VIEW in Table 26-4.

____d.   At the command prompt, type **net view *host name*** and press the **ENTER** key. In this command, you should replace *host name* with the NetBIOS name of one of the hosts listed in Table 26-4. This will show the shared devices on a particular host computer, as seen in the example shown in Figure 26-8.

```
Command Prompt                                                    _ □ ×

C:\>net view \\cathy
Shared resources at \\cathy

Cathy

Share name    Type        Used as   Comment

------------------------------------------------------------------
C             Disk
CALEB         Disk        (UNC)
CD            Disk
DC-700        Disk
DC200         Disk
DC700-LG      Disk
DOWNLOADS     Disk
HP            Print
IC100D        Disk
IC100DLAB     Disk
IC100DSUP     Disk
PI-100        Disk
PRINTER DOCS  Disk
TEMP          Disk
TONY          Disk
WAECLASS      Disk
The command completed successfully.

C:\>_
```

Figure 26-8: NET VIEW Command Prompt Window

TRACERT

The command "tracert *hostname*", where *hostname* is the IP address or DNS name of a host, will trace the path of a network connection to that remote host. This command will display the number of hops and the IP addresses of the routers that a data packet has traveled through in order to reach the remote host. It will also measure the time (in milliseconds) it takes for the data packet to travel from point to point on this route.

If you are having trouble connecting to a specific destination, the question then becomes: Is the problem at the destination, or at one of the routers along the way? TRACERT will detect whether a particular router along the current path is not functioning. If a router does not respond, the response time values are marked with an asterisk [*], indicating that the data packet timed out. TRACERT will also indicate if a router is slow. You can determine this by looking at the time it takes for a packet to get through a particular router. As you can see in Figure 26-9, the time delay is calculated three times for each router in the chain. The median of the three values should be used to evaluate the time it took to get the data packet through the router.

Figure 26-9: TRACERT Command Prompt Window

1. **Run TRACERT to check a remote network connection**

   ____a.   At the command prompt, type **tracert** and press the **ENTER** key. Review the usage notes for TRACERT.

   ____b.   At the command prompt, type **tracert www.mic-inc.com** and press the **ENTER** key to trace the route to the Marcraft server.

   ____c.   Record the IP address associated with www.mic-inc.com in Table 26-5.

PING

The PING command is one of the key tools for troubleshooting TCP/IP. PING sends a data packet to a specified IP address and returns it to your machine. If the IP address is not currently active, you will receive a message stating that the transaction has timed out. If you are having trouble connecting to a network, PING can be used to test the functionality of TCP/IP on your own machine. If you are able to PING the loopback address (127.0.0.1) and your own network IP address, you can be fairly sure that TCP/IP on your host computer is working properly. The next step is to test the IP address for your network server and/or your default gateway. As a final test you can PING the IP address of a remote host server.

NOTE: Can't remember your IP address, or the IP address of the local server? Run IPCONFIG to get your IP address and the address of the host DNS server and gateway, or you can look up the data in Table 26-1.

1. **Run PING to check the status of a TCP/IP connection**

   ____a.   At the command prompt, type **ping** and press the **ENTER** key. Review the usage notes for PING.

   ____b.   At the command prompt, type **ping 127.0.0.1** and press the **ENTER** key to test TCP/IP on your local host computer.

_____ c.   At the command prompt, type **ping xxx.xxx.xxx.xxx**, where *xxx.xxx.xxx.xxx* is the host IP address listed in Table 26-1. Now press the **ENTER** key to test your local TCP/IP connection. Your screen should appear similar to Figure 26-10.

```
Command Prompt                                                          _ □ ×

C:\>ping 127.0.0.1

Pinging 127.0.0.1 with 32 bytes of data:

Reply from 127.0.0.1: bytes=32 time<10ms TTL=128
Reply from 127.0.0.1: bytes=32 time<10ms TTL=128
Reply from 127.0.0.1: bytes=32 time<10ms TTL=128
Reply from 127.0.0.1: bytes=32 time<10ms TTL=128

Ping statistics for 127.0.0.1:
    Packets: Sent = 4, Received = 4, Lost = 0 (0% loss),
Approximate round trip times in milli-seconds:
    Minimum = 0ms, Maximum = 0ms, Average = 0ms

C:\>ping 192.168.0.20

Pinging 192.168.0.20 with 32 bytes of data:

Reply from 192.168.0.20: bytes=32 time<10ms TTL=128
Reply from 192.168.0.20: bytes=32 time<10ms TTL=128
Reply from 192.168.0.20: bytes=32 time<10ms TTL=128
Reply from 192.168.0.20: bytes=32 time<10ms TTL=128

Ping statistics for 192.168.0.20:
    Packets: Sent = 4, Received = 4, Lost = 0 (0% loss),
Approximate round trip times in milli-seconds:
    Minimum = 0ms, Maximum = 0ms, Average = 0ms

C:\>_
```

Figure 26-10: PING Command Prompt Window

_____ d.   At the command prompt, type **ping xxx.xxx.xxx.xxx**, where *xxx.xxx.xxx.xxx* is the IP address listed in Table 26-5. Press the **ENTER** key to test your connection to the remote server at Marcraft. You should see a screen similar to Figure 26-11.

```
Command Prompt                                                          _ □ ×

C:\>ping 206.61.210.100

Pinging 206.61.210.100 with 32 bytes of data:

Reply from 206.61.210.100: bytes=32 time=60ms TTL=252
Reply from 206.61.210.100: bytes=32 time=70ms TTL=252
Reply from 206.61.210.100: bytes=32 time=20ms TTL=252
Reply from 206.61.210.100: bytes=32 time=20ms TTL=252

Ping statistics for 206.61.210.100:
    Packets: Sent = 4, Received = 4, Lost = 0 (0% loss),
Approximate round trip times in milli-seconds:
    Minimum = 20ms, Maximum = 70ms, Average = 42ms

C:\>_
```

Figure 26-11: PINGing Command Prompt Window

_____ e.   Close all open windows, and shut down the computer.

TABLES

Table 26-1

Host Name:	
Primary DNS Suffix:	
Node Type:	
IP Routing Enabled:	
WINS Proxy Enabled:	
Description:	
Physical Address:	
DHCP Enabled:	
Autoconfiguration Enabled:	
IP Address:	
Subnet Mask:	
Default Gateway:	
DHCP Server:	
DNS Servers:	
Lease Obtained:	
Lease Expires:	

Table 26-2

Host Computer Interface IP Address:	

Table 26-3

IP and MAC Addresses		
IP Address	**Physical MAC Address**	**Type**

Table 26-4

Net View Host Names:	

Table 26-5

IP Address for www.mic-inc.com:	

PROCEDURE - 26

Feedback

LAB QUESTIONS

1. What command will display the connection path from your terminal to a remote Internet address?

2. Where do you enter the command to run a TCP/IP utility program?

3. What TCP/IP utility can be used to locate a slow router on a Wide Area Network such as the Internet?

4. Which command will resolve the IP and physical MAC addresses of the nodes connected to your network?

5. What TCP/IP utility can be used to identify the IP address of a site when given a DNS name?

Networking with Windows 2000

OBJECTIVES

1. Share a folder and test access.
2. Share a printer and test printing.
3. Map a drive to a shared resource.
4. Add a Network Place.

Networking

RESOURCES

1. Two PC-compatible desktop/tower computer systems — Customer-supplied desktop/tower hardware systems **OR** Marcraft Computer Repair Trainers **OR** suitable PC hardware trainers (with Windows 2000 installed) connected through a TCP/IP LAN
2. Internet Access for the "Add Network Place" section

DISCUSSION

This lab will perform some basic operations with peer-to-peer networks in Windows 2000. You will learn how to share folders, and check the ability of another user to connect and view the contents of that folder. Through "My Network Places" you can view contents of the LAN and create shortcuts to FTP sites. You will learn how to add a Network Place such as a File Transfer Protocol site, and how to map a drive to a folder that is shared on another computer in the Local Area Network (LAN).

PROCEDURE

1. **Share a folder**

    ___a. On your local machine (Machine 1) boot to the Windows 2000 desktop.

    ___b. Double-click on **My Computer**.

    ___c. Double-click on **Local Disk (C:)**.

    ___d. Create a new folder in the C: drive and name it **YOURNAME SHARED**.

    ___e. Double-click the **YOURNAME SHARED** folder.

    ___f. Create a text document by clicking on **File/New/Text Document** as in Figure 27-1.

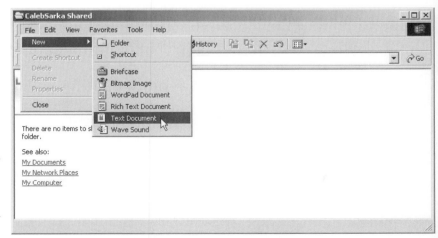

Figure 27-1: Create a Text Document

___g. Use the default *New Text Document* by pressing the **ENTER** key.

___h. Click on the **Back** button in the top left-hand corner of the window.

___i. Right-click the **YOURNAME SHARED** folder and choose **Sharing**.

___j. Select the **Share this folder** radio button.

___k. Click on the **Permissions** button.

___l. A window similar to Figure 27-2 will open. The default "Everyone" group will be listed in the top pane of the window. From this pane you can add users and change their individual permissions in the bottom pane.

___m. Click on **OK** twice. The folder is now shared.

2. Test access

___a. On your partner's machine (Machine 2) boot to the Windows 2000 desktop.

___b. Double-click the **My Network Places** icon.

___c. Double-click on **Computers Near Me**. This displays the computers in your local workgroup.

___d. Look for the icon of (Machine 1) and double-click on it.

___e. You should see the folder that was just created and shared. Double-click on it and record its content in Table 27-1.

___f. You have just accessed a shared recourse over the LAN. Close all windows.

3. Share a printer

___a. From your local computer (Machine 1) navigate the path *Start/Settings/Printers*.

___b. Right-click the printer that you installed earlier and choose **Sharing**.

___c. Click on the **Shared as** radio button as in Figure 27-3.

Figure 27-2: Sharing Permissions

Figure 27-3: Sharing a Printer

___d. Use the default name for the share, and then click on the **Additional Drivers** button.

___e. From this window you can select drivers for machines that may not have Windows 2000, and need to access the printer over a LAN. Click on **Cancel**.

___f. Click on **OK** to close the printer's *Properties* window.

4. Test printer access

___a. From your partner's desktop (Machine 2) click on the **My Network Places** icon.

___b. Double-click on **Computers Near Me**.

___c. Look for the icon of (Machine 1) and double-click on it.

___d. Right-click the printer that you have just shared and select **Connect**.

_____e.   After a connection window similar to Figure 27-4 has appeared and closed, close all windows.

Figure 27-4: Connecting to a Printer

_____f.   Double-click the **My Computer** icon.
_____g.   Double-click the **Control Panel** icon.
_____h.   Double-click on **Printers**.
_____i.   Double-click the printer that you had connected to previously.
_____j.   From the Printer select **Properties**.
_____k.   Click on the **Print Test Page** button. The test page should now print from the printer attached to (Machine 1).
_____l.   Click on **OK** to close the dialog window that opens, and then click on **OK** to close the printer's _Properties_ window.
_____m.   Close all windows.

5.   Map a drive to a shared resource
_____a.   From your partner's desktop (Machine 2) click on the **My Network Places** icon.
_____b.   Double-click on **Computers Near Me**.
_____c.   Look for the icon of (Machine 1) and double-click on it.
_____d.   Look for the folder that was created and shared earlier (YOURNAME SHARED), and right-click on it, then select **Map Network Drive**. The window should look similar to Figure 27-5.

Figure 27-5: Map Network Drive

_____e.   For the _Drive:_ field select the first available letter, E: for example. Record the drive letter selected in Table 27-2.
_____f.   Verify that the _Reconnect at logon_ field is selected. This will map the drive to the shared resource every time that you log on to the LAN. Click on **Finish**.
_____g.   Close all windows. You have now mapped a drive to a shared resource.
_____h.   Verify the drive connection by double-clicking on **My Computer**. You will see the name of the folder you have just connected to, followed by the drive letter selected.
_____i.   Close all windows.

6. **Add Network Place**

____a.   From the desktop of your computer double-click the **My Network Places** icon.

____b.   Double-click on **Add Network Place**.

____c.   The Add Network Place Wizard, similar to Figure 27-6, will appear. Click on the *some examples* hyperlink.

Figure 27-6: The Add Network Place Wizard

____d.   Read the three things that appear in the Examples list and record them in Table 27-3.

____e.   Type **ftp://ftp.microsoft.com** in the text box, and then click on **Next**.

____f.   Verify that the *Log on anonymously* field is checked. Most FTP sites allow an anonymous logon to view public files. Click on **Next**.

____g.   Enter "*Your Name's* connection to Microsoft's FTP server" in the text box and click on **Finish**.

____h.   The window should automatically open, similar to Figure 27-7. Record the number of items in Table 27-4.

Figure 27-7: Connecting to the Microsoft FTP Server

____i.   Close the window and you should see My Network Places still open. Record any new items in Table 27-5.

____j.   Close all open windows and shut down the computer.

TABLES

Table 27-1

Content of Shared Folder:	

Table 27-2

Drive Letter Selected:	

Table 27-3

Network Place Examples:	

Table 27-4

Number of Items:	

Table 27-5

My Network Places - New Items:	

Feedback

LAB QUESTIONS

1. What is the default group added to a newly shared folder?

2. What can My Network Places be used for?

3. What does Computers Near Me display?

4. What are additional printer drivers used for?

5. Why is anonymous logon used?

Windows XP TCP/IP Setup

OBJECTIVES

1. Install the TCP/IP protocol.
2. Administer clients, protocols, and services.
3. Set print and file sharing.
4. Administer bindings for the client.

Networking

RESOURCES

1. PC-compatible desktop/tower computer system — Customer-supplied desktop/tower hardware system **OR** Marcraft Computer Repair Trainer **OR** suitable PC hardware trainer with 128 MB RAM, Windows XP operating system, and NIC installed
2. Internet access through a network connection or modem.
3. Internet Explorer 6.0
4. Windows XP CD-ROM

DISCUSSION

TCP/IP (Transmission Control Protocol/Internet Protocol) is used in many types of local area networks (LANs), but it is also used as the standard communications protocol for the Internet. TCP/IP is the most popular network protocol in use, primarily due to the fact that, unlike other network protocols (IPX/SPX, AppleTalk, etc.) no single vendor owns the rights to it. TCP/IP was originally created by the U.S. Department of Defense Advance Research Projects Agency (DARPA) to provide resilient service on networks that include a wide variety of computer types. Due to its beginnings as a protocol for military computer networks, TCP/IP is very resistant to hacking. Therefore, it is considered to be the most secure of all the network protocols. TCP/IP uses a system that assigns a unique number to every node on the network. This number is known as the IP address. All devices on a TCP/IP network need a unique IP address in order to function. An IP address is a set of four numbers that range in value between 0 and 255, and each number is separated by a period. It can be very time-consuming to manually assign IP addresses and subnet masks to every computer and device on the network. For this reason, many network administrators assign these IP addresses by automatic Dynamic Host Configuration Protocol (DHCP) addressing. DHCP enables the host server to automatically assign IP addresses and subnet masks every time a client computer begins a network session.

Networking

PROCEDURE

1. **Open the TCP/IP Properties window**

    ___a.   Turn on the computer.

    ___b.   Right-click on the **My Network Places** icon on the desktop, then select **Properties** from the pop-up menu to open the *Network Connections* window.

    ___c.   Right-click on the **Local Area Connection** icon and select **Properties** from the drop-down menu to open the *Local Area Connection Properties* window. It should appear similar to Figure 28-1.

    ___d.   Click on the **Install** button to open the **Select Network Component Type** window.

    ___e.   Click on **Protocol** to select it and then click on the **Add** button.

    ___f.   Record the Network Protocols available in Table 28-1.

    ___g.   Click on the **Cancel** button twice to return to the *Local Area Connection Properties* window.

    ___h.   The *General* tab shows the current protocols, services, and clients installed on your computer. Record each of these items in Table 28-2.

    ___i.   Get the appropriate TCP/IP network configuration information from your ISP, Network Administrator, or instructor and record this information in the appropriate locations in Table 28-3.

Figure 28-1: Local Area Connection Properties Window

2. **Record the current TCP/IP settings**

    ___a.   Uncheck the box next to **Internet Protocol (TCP/IP)**.

    ___b.   Click on the **OK** button.

    ___c.   Click on the **Yes** button when prompted for the removal of the other protocols.

    ___d.   If you entered *Yes* for DHCP, click on the **Cancel** button and skip to Step 3.

    ___e.   At the *General* tab, record the specified IP address and subnet mask in Table 28-4. Your screen should appear similar to Figure 28-2.

Figure 28-2: IP and Subnet Configuration Information

___f.   Click on the **Advanced** button to open the *Advanced TCP/IP Properties* window. It should appear similar to Figure 28-3.

Figure 28-3: Advanced TCP/IP Properties Window

___g.   Click on the **DNS** tab and record the DNS server information, if any, in Table 28-4.
___h.   Click on the **Cancel** button to close the *Advanced TCP/IP Properties* window.
___i.   Click on the **Cancel** button to close the *Internet Protocol TCP/IP Properties* window.

3.   Delete the TCP/IP Protocol
___a.   Uncheck the box next to **Internet Protocol (TCP/IP)**.
___b.   Click on the **OK** button.
___c.   Click on the **Yes** button when prompted for the removal of the other protocols.

4.   Attempt to Access the Internet
___a.   Click on the **Internet Explorer** icon in the Quick Launch toolbar, to open Internet Explorer.
___b.   Close the message box that appears, and then close Internet Explorer.
___c.   Open Internet Explorer again.
___d.   Click on the **Refresh** button.
___e.   In Table 28-5, describe the message you receive.
___f.   Click on the **Connect** button. You should receive a message similar to the one in Figure 28-4.
___g.   Close all windows that are open.

Figure 28-4: Unable to Connect to Internet Message

5.   Install the TCP/IP Protocol
___a.   Use the path *Start/Settings/Control Panel* to open the *Control Panel* window.
___b.   If the *Limited* view is presented, click on the *View all Control Panel options* hyperlink to see all of the *Control Panel* icons.
___c.   Double-click the **Network Connections** icon.
___d.   Double-click the **Local Area Connections** icon in the *Network Connections* window.

    e.   Click on the **Support** tab, as shown in Figure 28-5.

    f.   In Table 28-6, record the information as it appears.

    g.   Click on the **General** tab again.

    h.   Click on the **Properties** button to open the *Local Area Connection Properties* window.

    i.   Place a checkmark next to **Internet Protocol (TCP/IP)** and the other options will automatically be selected as well.

    j.   Click on the **OK** button to install the TCP/IP protocol.

6.   **Confirm the installation of the protocols**

    a.   In the *Local Area Status* window, click on the **Support** tab.

    b.   In Table 28-7, record the settings.

    c.   Click on the **Close** button.

Figure 28-5: Support Tab

7.   **Configure all TCP/IP settings**

    a.   If you are using DHCP, skip to Step i.

    b.   Right-click the **Local Area Connection** icon and select **Properties** from the drop-down menu.

    c.   Click on **Internet Protocol (TCP/IP)** to highlight it.

    d.   Click on the **Properties** button to open the *Internet Protocol (TCP/IP) Properties* window, as shown in Figure 28-6.

Figure 28-6: TCP/IP Properties Window

    e.   Enter the information that you collected from your instructor in the appropriate spaces.

    f.   Click on the **OK** button twice to confirm the configuration settings.

    g.   Turn off the computer.

TABLES

Table 28-1: Network Protocols

Table 28-2: Current Protocols, Services, and Clients Installed

Table 28-3: Assigned TCP/IP Configuration Settings

IP Address:	
Subnet Mask:	
Primary DNS Server:	
Secondary:	

Table 28-4: Current TCP/IP Configuration Settings

IP Address:	
Subnet Mask:	
Primary DNS Server:	
Secondary:	

Table 28-5

Table 28-6

Address Type:	
IP Address:	
Subnet Mask:	
Default Gateway:	

Table 28-7

Address Type:	
IP Address:	
Subnet Mask:	
Default Gateway:	

Feedback

LAB QUESTIONS

1. Which protocol is used to set the IP address?

2. For whom was TCP/IP created?

3. What system is used to automatically assign IP addresses and subnet masks to every computer and device on the network?

4. Which control panel is used to administer your network connection?

5. Name two advantages to using the TCP/IP protocol.

Testing TCP/IP Connections

Networking

OBJECTIVES

1. Test TCP/IP connection.
2. Configuring Advanced Settings.

RESOURCES

1. PC-compatible desktop/tower computer system — Customer-supplied desktop/tower hardware system **OR** Marcraft Computer Repair Trainer **OR** suitable PC hardware trainer running Windows XP Professional

DISCUSSION

This lab procedure will test your settings using the *ping* command and will verify your settings by using the *ipconfig* command.

Figure 29-1 depicts the *Internet Protocol (TCP/IP) Properties* page. Your settings may be different from what is shown in the figure, this is expected. If your settings include having *Obtain an IP ad-dress automatically then your settings will be blank, again this is expected. If not selected then select* **Use the following IP address:** and enter an address that is within the useable range for your network, in this example we are using IP Address:192.168.1.111, Subnet mask: 255.255.255.0, Default gateway: 192.168.1.1.
Select **Use the following DNS server addresses:** and enter the value of your DNS Server, we are using 192.168.1.2 in our example. Click **OK** three times to save and close all *Network Connection windows*.

Figure 29-1: Internet Protocol (TCP/IP) Properties

PROCEDURE

1. **Test TCP/IP connections**

____a. Open a *command prompt*, as shown in Figure 29-2, by typing **cmd** at the *Task Bar Start/Run* prompt and then pressing the **ENTER** key.

Figure 29-2:
Opening a
Command
Prompt

____b. From the command prompt type **ipconfig /all** then press **ENTER**. Figure 29-3 depicts the IP configuration information for *Bookp*c. In Table 29-1, record the following information display on your screen:

- Host Name
- Primary DNS Suffix
- Physical Address
- DHCP Enabled
- IP Address
- Subnet Mask
- DNS Servers

```
C:\>ipconfig /all

Windows IP Configuration

        Host Name . . . . . . . . . . . . : bookpc
        Primary Dns Suffix  . . . . . . . : eittraining.com
        Node Type . . . . . . . . . . . . : Unknown
        IP Routing Enabled. . . . . . . . : No
        WINS Proxy Enabled. . . . . . . . : No
        DNS Suffix Search List. . . . . . : eittraining.com

Ethernet adapter Local Area Connection:

        Connection-specific DNS Suffix  . :
        Description . . . . . . . . . . . : SiS 900 PCI Fast Ethernet Adapter
        Physical Address. . . . . . . . . : 00-07-95-E4-5B-9A
        Dhcp Enabled. . . . . . . . . . . : No
        IP Address. . . . . . . . . . . . : 192.168.1.111
        Subnet Mask . . . . . . . . . . . : 255.255.255.0
        Default Gateway . . . . . . . . . : 192.168.1.1
        DNS Servers . . . . . . . . . . . : 192.168.1.2

C:\>_
```

Figure 29-3:
Displaying the
TCP/IP Configuration

_____c.   Obtain the IP address of another computer in your network and record it in Table 29-2, then at the command prompt type **ping** *(other IP Address)* and press **ENTER**. In Figure 29-4 we have used the IP address of **192.168.1.2** and pressed **ENTER** to obtain the results seen in Figure 29-4.

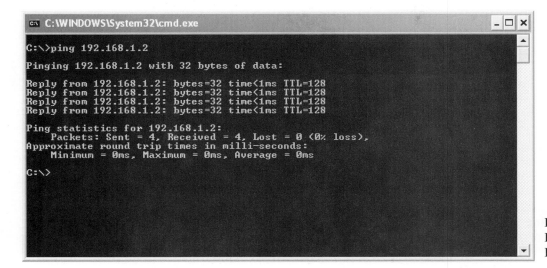

**Figure 29-4:
Pinging Another
IP Address**

_____d.   To obtain the *physical address (MAC address)* of the computer you just pinged type at the command prompt **arp –a** and press **ENTER**. Your results will be similar to those displayed in Figure 29-5, however the IP address and MAC address will be different since each MAC address and IP address must be unique.

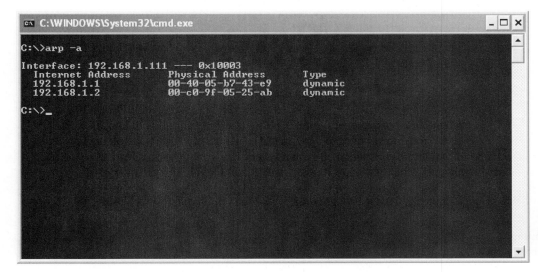

**Figure 29-5:
Using ARP to
Determine a
MAC Address**

2. **Ping a non-existent and bogus IP address**

____a. From the command prompt type in **ping** (an IP address that does not exist on your network) and press **ENTER**. Figure 29-6 shows pinging 192.168.1.55, an address that doe not exist on this network.

Figure 29-6: Using ARP to Pinging a Non-existent IP Address

____b. From the command prompt type **ping 192.168.1.256** and press **ENTER**. Figure 29-7 shows the type of error that is displayed when you attempt to ping a bogus address.

Figure 29-7: Pinging a Bogus IP Address

3. **Configure the default gateway**

____a. Open *Network Connections,* then open *Local Area Connections*, then open *Local Area Connection*, in the *Local Area Connection Status* dialog box select **Properties** and highlight **Internet Protocol TCP/IP and click on Properties** to open the *TCP/IP Properties* dialog box. Tab down to the *Default Gateway* and type in the gateway address for your network. Figure 6.3.12 illustrates the default gateway as 192.168.1. Press **OK** to save your changes.

Figure 29-8: Configuring the Default Gateway

____b. If you have a functioning gateway/router then you can ping a remote IP address to test your gateway. For an example of a valid Gateway address see Figure 29-9.

Figure 29-9: Pinging a Valid IP Address via a Gateway

4. **Assign multiple IP addresses**

___a.   Open your Internet Protocol (TCP/IP) Properties, as performed in step 3a. Click the **Advanced** button to bring up the *Advanced TCP/IP Properties* dialog box, click **Add** and enter **192.168.1.75** for the IP address and tab to the Subnet Mask the default value will be 255.255.255.0 then click **Add** to save the new address. Figure 29-10 illustrates *TCP/IP Address* dialog box with the additional IP address entered. Click **OK** twice and then **Close** to save the changes.

Figure 29-10: Configuring Multiple IP Addresses

___b.   From the command prompt type **ping 192.168.1.75** and press **ENTER**. You should see a reply from the .175 address. If you do not recheck the information you typed in step 4a, make sure that no other computer has been assigned this IP address. If one has, change your address to one that is not conflicting.

___c.   At the command prompt type **ipconfig /all** and press **ENTER**. Figure 29-11 shows that the one network card now has two IP addresses assigned to it.

```
C:\WINDOWS\System32\cmd.exe                                    _ □ ×
C:\>ipconfig /all

Windows IP Configuration

        Host Name . . . . . . . . . . . . : bookpc
        Primary Dns Suffix  . . . . . . . : eittraining.com
        Node Type . . . . . . . . . . . . : Unknown
        IP Routing Enabled. . . . . . . . : No
        WINS Proxy Enabled. . . . . . . . : No
        DNS Suffix Search List. . . . . . : eittraining.com

Ethernet adapter Local Area Connection:

        Connection-specific DNS Suffix  . :
        Description . . . . . . . . . . . : SiS 900 PCI Fast Ethernet Adapter
        Physical Address. . . . . . . . . : 00-07-95-E4-5B-9A
        Dhcp Enabled. . . . . . . . . . . : No
        IP Address. . . . . . . . . . . . : 192.168.1.75
        Subnet Mask . . . . . . . . . . . : 255.255.255.0
        IP Address. . . . . . . . . . . . : 192.168.1.111
        Subnet Mask . . . . . . . . . . . : 255.255.255.0
        Default Gateway . . . . . . . . . : 192.168.1.1
        DNS Servers . . . . . . . . . . . : 192.168.1.2

C:\>
```

Figure 29-11: Checking the Computers IP Addresses

___d.   Remove the second IP address by returning to the *Advanced TCP/IP Properties* dialog box, select **192.168.1.75** then click on the **Remove** button to remove the address. Click **OK** three times to confirm and save your changes. Double check your work by running **ipconfig /all** again, you should see only one IP address assigned to the card.

TABLES

Table 29-1

Host Name:	
Primary DNS Suffix:	
Physical Address:	
DHCP Enabled:	
IP Address:	
Subnet Mask:	
DNS Servers:	

Table 29-2

LAB QUESTIONS

1. Referencing the IP and subnet mask used in this lab, define both the host and network portions of the IP address.

2. What is the MAC address of your network card?

3. What steps would be needed to change your TCP/IP settings to automatically receive an IP address from a DHCP server?

4. What are the valid starting addresses for a Class 'C' address?

Feedback

CHALLENGE

Change your IP address to 168.1.1.1 with a subnet mask of 255.255.0.0 and attempt to ping another client in the 192 network. If you are successful explain why, if you were not successful explain what would need to be done to get replies from the other client.

Networking with Windows XP

Networking

OBJECTIVES

1. Share drives, folders and files.
2. Set up drive mapping to a folder on another computer.
3. Connect to a shared network resource.
4. Add a Network Place.

RESOURCES

1. Two PC-compatible desktop/tower computer systems — Customer-supplied desktop/tower hardware systems **OR** Marcraft Computer Repair Trainers **OR** suitable PC hardware trainers with 128 MB RAM, Windows XP operating system, and NIC installed
2. Working network connection

DISCUSSION

This lab will perform some basic operations with peer-to-peer networks in Windows 2000. You will learn how to share folders, and check the ability of another to connect and view the contents of that folder. Through "My Network Places" you can view contents of the LAN and create shortcuts to FTP sites. You will learn how to add a Network Place such as a File Transfer Protocol site, and how to map a drive to a folder that is shared on another computer in the Local Area Network (LAN).

PROCEDURE

1. **Share folders with other users of the network**
   ____a. Open Windows Explorer.
   ____b. Click on the plus sign (+) next to **My Computer** to expand the directory.
   ____c. Double-click on the Local Disk (**C:**) drive to expand the directory tree.
   ____d. With the C: drive highlighted, click on the **File** menu and select **New** and then **Folder**.
   ____e. Type your first initial and last 4 characters of your last name, the word shared, and press the **ENTER** key.
   ____f. Right-click your new folder and select **Sharing and security** from the pop-up menu.

_____g. Place a checkmark in the box next to **Share this folder on the network**, and uncheck the box next to **Allow network users to change my files**, shown in Figure 30-1.

Figure 30-1: Sharing a folder on the Network

_____h. Click on the **OK** button to save the shared settings.
_____i. Click on the **Start** button and select **Run** from the menu.
_____j. Type **Notepad** and click on the **OK** button to open the *Notepad* window.
_____k. Type your name and your computer name in the *Notepad* window.
_____l. Click on the *File* menu and select **Save As**.
_____m. Click on the **My Computer** button on the left side of the *Save As* window.
_____n. Double-click on the **C:** drive.

Figure 30-2: Creating and Saving a Text File to be Shared

_____o. Double-click on the folder you just created.
_____p. In the *File name:* text box, type **Shared.txt** and click on the **Save** button, as shown in Figure 30-2.
_____q. Close all windows.

2. Test access to the shared folder
_____a. Once your partner has finished the above steps, double-click on **My Network Places.**
_____b. Double-click on **Entire Network**.

____c.   Double-click on **Microsoft Windows Network**.

____d.   Double-click on your workgroup or domain name.

____e.   Look for the icon of your partner's computer and double-click it.

____f.   You should see the folder that your partner created. Double-click on it and record the content of the folder in Table 30-1.

____g.   You have just accessed a shared resource over the LAN. Close all windows.

3.   Set Full Access permissions for a shared folder

____a.   Double-click on **My Computer**.

____b.   Double-click on the **C:** drive.

____c.   Right-click your new folder and select **Sharing and security**.

____d.   Place a checkmark next to **Allow network users to change my files**, as shown in Figure 30-3.

____e.   Click on the **OK** button to save your settings and close the window.

NOTE: Now anyone can change the files that are in this folder.

Figure 30-3: Allowing Users to Change Files

4.   Share a printer

____a.   Go to the computer that is going to host the shared printer and navigate the *Start/Settings/Printers* path.

____b.   Right-click on the computer that you installed the printer on previously and choose **Sharing**.

Figure 30-4: Sharing a Printer

____c.   Click on the radio button next to **Share this printer**, as shown in Figure 30-4.

____d.   Use the default name for the share.

____e.   Click on the **Additional Drivers** button.

____f.   From this window you can select drivers for machines that may not have Windows XP, and need to access the printer over a LAN. Click on the **Cancel** button.

____g.   Click on the **OK** button to close the *Printer Properties* window.

____h.   Close all other windows.

PROCEDURE - 30

5. Test printer access

____a.   Go to your desktop and double-click on the **My Network Places** icon.

____b.   Double-click on **Entire Network**.

____c.   Double-click on **Microsoft Windows Network**.

____d.   Double-click on your workgroup or domain name.

____e.   Double-click on the name of the computer that hosts the printer that you just shared.

____f.   Right-click the printer and select **Connect**.

____g.   After a connection window similar to Figure 30-5 has appeared and closes, close all windows.

____h.   Double-click the **My Computer** icon.

____i.   Double-click the **Control Panel** icon.

____j.   Double-click on **Printers and Faxes**.

____k.   Double-click the printer that you had connected to previously.

____l.   From the *Printer* select **Properties**.

____m.   Click on the **Print Test Page** button. The test page should now print from the shared printer.

____n.   Click on the **OK** button to close the dialog window that opens.

____o.   Click on the **OK** button to close the *Printer Properties* window.

____p.   Close all windows.

Figure 30-5: Connecting to a Shared Printer

6. Map a network drive in Windows Explorer

____a.   Double-click on the **My Computer** icon on the desktop.

Figure 30-6: Browsing to a Folder to Map to

____b.   Click on the **Tools** menu and select **Map Network Drive**.

____c.   Click on the drop-down menu next to **Drive:** and make sure the next consecutive drive letter is chosen.

____d.   Click on the **Browse** button as shown in Figure 30-6.

____e.   Double-click on **Microsoft Windows Network** and then your workgroup or domain name.

____f.   Double-click on the **C:** drive.

____g.   Click on the folder that your partner created and shared, and then click on the **OK** button.

____h.   Click on the check box next to **Reconnect at logon** in order to re-create the mapped drive, as shown in Figure 30-7.

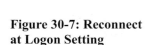

Figure 30-7: Reconnect at Logon Setting

____i.   Click on the **Finish** button.

____j.   Close all windows.

NOTE: You have now mapped a drive to a shared resource.

____k. Verify the drive connection by double-clicking on **My Computer**. You will see the name of the folder you have just connected to, followed by the drive letter that it was given during the mapping under the *Network Drives* section.

____l. Close all windows.

7. Add Network Place

____a. From the desktop of your computer double-click the **My Network Places** icon.

____b. Double-click on **Add Network Place**.

____c. The *Add Network Place Wizard*, similar to Figure 30-8, will appear.

____d. Click on the **Next** button.

____e. Click on **Choose another network location** and click on the **Next** button.

____f. Read the Service Providers that appear in the next window and record them in Table 30-2.

____g. Click on the **View some examples** link below the text entry box.

____h. Take note of the types of places that can be added with this wizard.

____i. Type **ftp://ftp.microsoft.com** in the text box, and then click on the *Examples* link below the text entry box.

____j. Click on the **Next** button.

____k. Verify that the **Log on anonymously** field is checked. Most FTP sites allow an anonymous logon to view public files.

____l. Click on the **Next** button.

____m. Enter *Your Name's* **connection to Microsoft's FTP server** in the text box, substituting your name for the words *Your Name's*.

____n. Click on the **Finish** button.

____o. The Internet Explorer window should automatically open, similar to Figure 30-9. Record the number of items in Table 30-3.

Figure 30-8: Add a Network Place Wizard

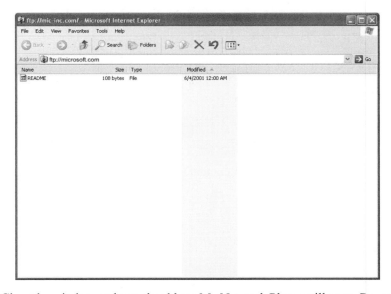

Figure 30-9: Internet Explorer Window

____p. Close the window and you should see My Network Places still open. Record any new items in Table 30-4.

____q. Close all open windows and shut down the computer.

TABLES

Table 30-1

Content of Shared Folder:	

Table 30-2

Service Providers:	

Table 30-3

Number of Items:	

Table 30-4

Feedback

LAB QUESTIONS

1. What can My Network Places be used for?

2. What are additional printer drivers used for?

3. When mapping a shared resource from another computer, what does it look and act like?

4. Why is anonymous logon used?

IE 6.0 Internet Client Setup

Networking

OBJECTIVES

1. Run the Internet Explorer browser client.
2. Browse the Internet.
3. Configure the Outlook Express e-mail client.
4. Check your e-mail.
5. Configure Internet Explorer.

RESOURCES

1. Two PC-compatible desktop/tower computer systems — Customer-supplied desktop/tower hardware systems **OR** Marcraft Computer Repair Trainers **OR** suitable PC hardware trainers with Windows XP Operating System Installation CD and NIC installed
2. Internet access through a network connection
3. A valid e-mail account
4. Internet account configuration information from your instructor, network administrator, or ISP

DISCUSSION

One of the fastest growing areas of microcomputer use is in the field of wide area networking. The advent of the World Wide Web, and the use of associated client applications called *web browsers*, has enabled millions of non-technical users to access the Internet. This, in turn, has led to a greater need for web-related technical assistance.

A successful computer technician must have the ability to identify concepts and capabilities relating to the Internet and basic procedures for setting up a system for Internet access. That is the purpose of this lab. The subsequent labs will cover Internet-related topics such as Telnet, FTP, and the Internet domain name system.

The most widely used web browser applications are Microsoft's Internet Explorer (IE) and Netscape's Navigator. Both of these applications are provided free for educational or personal noncommercial use, and can be downloaded from the company's Web site. Of course, you will need to have a web browser already installed and configured in order to download these browsers.

Fortunately, Windows XP comes with IE already installed as part of the operating system. Using an Internet browser to locate and download applications, demos, drivers, and patches is one of the primary skills needed by every computer technician.

Networking

PROCEDURE

In this lab procedure you will configure your network Internet browser and e-mail clients. In order to fill in some of these parameters, you will need to acquire information from your ISP, instructor, or network administrator. Then you will browse the Internet using the Internet Explorer 6.0 (IE6) web browser, as shown in Figure 31-1. You will then configure your e-mail client (Outlook Express) and check your e-mail.

**Figure 31-1:
Internet Explorer
Web Browser**

If you are working in a classroom environment, it may be necessary to uninstall these features from the system for the next class. In this case, consult with your instructor before uninstalling anything from the system.

1. **Record the configuration information for your Internet network connection**
   ___a.   Boot up the computer.
   ___b.   Record the Internet configuration information you received from your instructor, network administrator, or ISP in Table 31-3.

2. **Run Internet Explorer**
   ___a.   Double-click the **Internet Explorer** icon on your desktop.
   ___b.   In the *Windows XP - Microsoft Internet Explorer* window, click on the **Maximize** button in the upper-right corner.
   ___c.   Click on the **Help** menu and select **About Internet Explorer**.
   ___d.   Record the current version number in Table 31-1.
   ___e.   Click on the **OK** button to close the *About Internet Explorer* window.
   ___f.   Close Internet Explorer.

3. **Explore the Internet with the Internet Explorer browser**
   ___a.   Click on the **Start** button and select **Run** from the *Start* menu.
   ___b.   In the *Open* box, type **www.arstechnica.com** and then click on the **OK** button.
   ___c.   Press the **CTRL+D** keys simultaneously to add the current page to your *Favorites* list.

4. **Search the Internet to find a driver for an HP DeskJet 6127 printer**
   ___a.   Click on the **Address** box and type **www.hp.com** to access the Hewlett-Packard Website.
   ___b.   Press the **ENTER** key.
   ___c.   Click on the link labeled **support & drivers** as shown in Figure 31-2.

Figure 31-2: Selecting the Drivers Link from the HP Website

   ___d.   Click on the link labeled **HP driver downloads, software updates and patches**.
   ___e.   Scroll down the list of company names and click on the hyperlink labeled **Hewlett Packard**.
   ___f.   In the box labeled *Enter model product number:* type **DeskJet 6127** and click on the double arrows to the right.
   ___g.   Select your operating system by clicking on the **Microsoft Windows XP** link.
   ___h.   Click on the **hp deskjet 6127 printer software/driver: Corporate users - Network and USB** link.
   ___i.   Scroll down and click on the **download now** button.
   ___j.   Click on the **Save** button when the *File Download* box appears.
   ___k.   Save the file to your *Download* directory.

5. **Find a map showing the location of Marcraft International, Inc.**
   ___a.   Click on the **Address** box, type **www.yahoo.com**, and press the **ENTER** key.
   ___b.   In the list of site features, click on **Maps** as shown in Figure 31-3.

Figure 31-3: Selecting the Maps Link at Yahoo.com

_____c. In the *Address* box type **100 N. Morain St**.

_____d. In the *City/State/Zip* box type **Kennewick, WA 99336**.

_____e. Click on the **Get Map** button.

_____f. When the page finishes downloading, press the F11 key on your keyboard to view the full screen image.

NOTE: There are various features to enlarge or reduce the map size and detail. The area viewed can also be shifted in any direction by clicking on the arrow next to the compass direction.

_____g. Click on the link labeled **Driving Directions: To this location** as shown in Figure 31-4.

Figure 31-4: Selecting Driving Directions

_____h. Enter the address of your current location in the **Enter a Starting Address** section.

_____i. Click on the **Get Directions** button.

_____j. Record the distance to Marcraft in Table 31-2.

6. Configure the Outlook Express e-mail client

_____a. Click on the **Outlook Express** icon in the *Quick Launch* toolbar at the bottom of the screen.

_____b. Click on the **Tools** menu and select **Accounts**.

_____c. On the **Mail** tab, click on the **Add** button and select **Mail.**

_____d. Enter your name as listed in Table 31-3a into the *Display name* box, then click on the **Next** button.

_____e. Enter your e-mail address as listed in Table 31-3b into the *E-mail address* box, then click on the **Next** button.

_____f. Enter your POP3 server name or address as listed in Table 31-3c into the *Incoming mail* box.

_____g. Enter your SMTP server address as listed in Table 31-3d into the *Outgoing mail* box. Click on the **Next** button to continue.

    h.   Enter your POP3 Login Name as listed in Table 31-3e into the *Account name* box.

    i.   Enter your POP3 password as listed in Table 31-3f into the *Password* box, then click on the **Next** button.

    j.   Click on the **Finish** button to continue.

    k.   Click on the **Close** button.

7.   **Use and configure the Outlook Express mail client**

    a.   Click on the **Maximize** button in the upper-right corner.

    b.   Click on the **Send/Receive** button in the toolbar.

    c.   Click on the **Tools** menu and select **Options.**

    d.   Click on the **Maintenance** tab in the *Options* window.

    e.   Click on the check box to select **Empty messages from the 'Deleted Items' folder on exit** as shown in Figure 31-5.

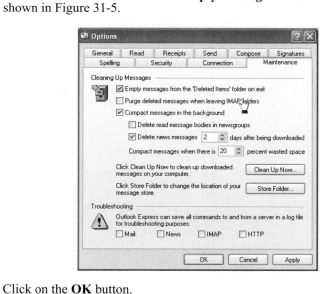

Figure 31-5: The Empty messages form Deleted Items Setting

    f.   Click on the **OK** button.

    g.   Close Outlook Express.

8.   **Configure the Internet Explorer browser**

    a.   Click on the **Internet Explorer** icon in the Taskbar to open IE.

    b.   Press the **F11** key to return to standard view.

    c.   Click on the **Address** box, type **www.zdnet.com/zdnn/**, and press the **ENTER** key.

    d.   Click on the **Tools** menu and select **Internet Options**.

    e.   Click on the **General** tab, and under *Home page* click on the **Use Current** button.

    f.   Click on the **Apply** button to make ZDNet News your home page.

    g.   Click on the **Advanced** tab.

    h.   Scroll down to locate the *Use inline AutoComplete* function, and then click on the check box to select it, as shown in Figure 31-6.

Figure 31-6: Select AutoComplete

____i.   Click on the **OK** button to turn on AutoComplete and exit the *Internet Options* window.
____j.   Close all open windows and shut down the computer.

TABLES

Table 31-1

Version Number:	

Table 31-2

Distance to Marcraft:	

Table 31-3

a.) Name:	
b.) E-mail Address:	
c.) POP3 Server Address:	
d.) SMTP Server Address:	
e.) POP3 Login Name:	
f.) POP3 Password:	

Feedback

LAB QUESTIONS

1. List five of the required configuration items that must be obtained from your ISP or network administrator when you are setting up Internet client applications.

2. State at least one Internet-related skill that is used by computer technicians.

3. What kind of Internet site is Yahoo.com?

   Hint: Click on Company Info at the bottom of www.yahoo.com.

4. How do you open the window that controls the advanced settings for Internet Explorer?

5. How do you set the current Web page as your home page?

Internet Explorer Security Settings

OBJECTIVES

1. Learn how to use Internet Explorer's built in security settings to protect the system and the user and the system from some of the hazards associated with browsing the Internet.

RESOURCES

1. PC-compatible desktop/tower computer system — Customer-supplied desktop/tower hardware system **OR** Marcraft Computer Repair Trainer **OR** suitable PC hardware trainer running Windows XP Professional

DISCUSSION

Internet Explorer settings are managed via the Internet Options entry located in the Tools listing in the Internet Explorer toolbar or through the Internet Options icon located in Control Panel.

PROCEDURE

1. **Use Internet Explorer's built in security settings**

   ____ a. Open Internet Explorer and click on **Tools** located in the tool bar, as shown in Figure 32-1.

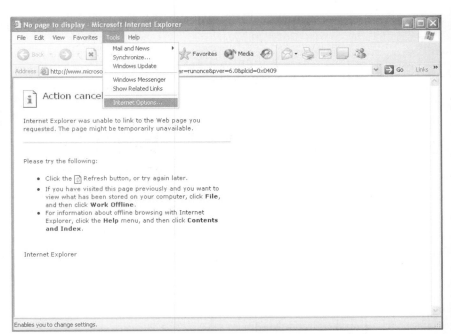

Figure 32-1: Selecting Tools Located in the Tool Bar

Figure 32-2:
The Internet
Options
Window

_____ b. The *Internet Options* window opens, as shown in Figure 32-2. The tabs dealing with Internet security options are labeled *General*, *Security*, and *Privacy*.

_____ c. The *General* tab allows you change settings affecting items like the default home page, temporary Internet files (cookies, cached Web pages, and the history of Websites you have visited). Click on the **Settings** button located in Temporary Internet Files section.

_____ d. Figure 32-3 shows the *Settings* window for the temporary Internet settings. This box contains settings that control how often the system should check for newer versions of the Web pages you have visited, the location of the folder that holds the files accumulated while using the Internet. These items are saved to help a Web page load faster the next time you visit. You will also note a setting that controls how much disk space is allocated to saving those Internet files. On a system with limited disk space, you may want to decrease the amount of space allocated.

Figure 32-3:
The Settings
Window

_____ e. In addition, you may also change the location of the folder used to store the files, as well as view the files currently contained in the folder and also view any Web page controls that were downloaded.

_____ f. Close the *Settings* window by clicking **OK.** Click on the **Security** tab to display the window, as shown in Figure 32-4.

Figure 32-4: The
Internet Options
Window, Security
Tab

___g.   The *Security* tab contains settings that allow you to assign certain Websites to various security zones. The Internet zone contains all Websites that have not been assigned to another zone. The Local Intranet zone would contain all the Websites contained on a local network (such as internal Web pages), the trusted zone would contain all the Web sites you have deemed safe and unlikely to damage the system, and conversely the Restricted sites would contain Web sites that are know to contain potentially dangerous content.

**Figure 32-5:
The Trusted
Sites Window**

___h.   To add a site to a zone, click on the name of the zone once to highlight and click the **Sites** button, as shown in Figure 32-5 and enter the name of the site. The same procedure is used to add sites to the Restricted zone and to the Intranet zone.

___i.   To change the security settings associated with a particular click the button labeled **Custom Leve**l. The *Security Settings* window opens, as shown in Figure 32-6.

___j.   These settings control how Internet Explorer handles various objects associated with Web pages such as ActiveX controls or Java Scripting. Sometimes Web pages can contain malicious objects designed to damage your system. Restricting how these objects interact with your system can help prevent viruses or Trojans being downloaded to your system without your knowledge.

___k.   The last tab that deals with Internet security is the *Privacy* tab, as shown in Figure 32-7. The *Privacy* tab controls how Internet Explorer handles cookies. Cookies are small text files placed on the system by some Websites to track usage.

**Figure 32-6:
The Security
Settings Window**

**Figure 32-7:
The Privacy Tab**

Figure 32-8:
The Advanced
Privacy Settings
Window

____l. By default the settings are set at a medium level. Moving the slider up and down changes the level of basic privacy used and displays a definition of that setting. It is also possible to import privacy settings from another location if you have a custom set you wish to use by clicking on the **Import** button and selecting the location of the stored settings.

____m. Click the **Advanced** button to open the *Advanced Privacy settings* window, as shown in Figure 32-8.

____n. By default, Internet Explorer is set to accept all cookies. This is to allow frequently visited Web pages to remember you from your last visit. Place a checkmark in the box labeled *Override automatic cookie handling*. This will activate the other settings options available, as shown in Figure 32-9.

Figure 32-9:
Override Automatic
Cookie Handling

Figure 32-10: Set to Prompt for Every Cookie

____o. You may change the settings by clicking the radio button next to the appropriate choice. Blocking all cookies will prevent all Websites from putting cookies on the machine. This will cause problems with Web sites that require cookies to be enabled in order to function correctly. Clicking the radio button next to *Prompt will cause Internet Explorer to ask permission before allowing a cookie to be placed on the system.* It will do this for every cookie.

____p. When Internet Explorer is set to prompt for every cookie, it will display a message informing you that a Website wishes to place a cookie on the system, as shown in Figure 32-10 and asking you how to proceed. You have 2 choices; you can either allow the cookie or block it. Note the checkbox labeled *Apply my decision to all cookies from this Website.* Placing a checkmark in the box before choosing *Allow* or *Block* will make that choice the default for all cookies associated with that site.

Feedback

LAB QUESTIONS

1. What functions do the Security settings in Internet Explorer control?

2. What are the Security Zones used for? Why would you want to use them?

3. What function does a cookie serve? Why would you want to use them?

Installing Wireless LANs

OBJECTIVES

1. Know how to use a wireless access point.
2. Know how to install a wireless PCI/PCMCIA (or PC card).

Computer Networking

RESOURCES

1. Two PC-compatible desktop/tower computer systems with Windows XP Professional installed
2. Single commercial router (Suggested: wireless 4-port 802.11a, 802.11b, or 802.11g router)
3. Wireless card

DISCUSSION

Establishing a wireless connection for a home can be very useful in certain situations. Homes where wiring Ethernet cabling is too expensive, and where distances between computers are too long, are good candidates for wireless connections. Also, networks with a large number of laptops may require a wireless network to fully take advantage of the portability that laptops provide.

Access Points vs. Routers

For a wireless Internet connection, various types of cards can be used to facilitate network connectivity. For a standard desktop/tower PC, the most common card type is a PCI wireless network card, which uses the PCI slot in a computer. For a laptop, it's common to use a PCMCIA wireless network card, which uses the PCMCIA slot in a laptop. Built-in wireless connections are also now enabled in certain categories of laptops, and even in some desktop motherboards. Generally speaking, however, you will need to be able to install and configure a wireless network card.

Finally, wireless cards can use many different protocols, depending on what specifications you require. These specifications include speed, bandwidth, and encryption.

802.11a

The 802.11a wireless LAN standard calls for operation in the 5 GHz radio band using Orthogonal Frequency Division Multiplexing (OFDM). 802.11a supports data rates ranging from 6 to 54 Mbps. 802.11a products became available in late 2001. Several problems with radio propagation in the 5 GHz band have prohibited the wide acceptance of 802.11a products:

- There is a path loss of 6.9 dB going from 2.4 GHz to 5.3 GHz. This means that almost five times as much RF power is required to cover the same distance.

- RF propagation through barriers such as walls is somewhat poorer at 5 GHz, so link budgets may suffer additional losses.

- It is very difficult to manufacture a 5 GHz system on conventional printed circuit board material.

- 802.11a products are not compatible with later 802.11b/g products.

802.11b

The 802.11 standards committee finalized the wireless LAN standard (IEEE Std. 802.11b-1999) in late 1999. To provide the higher data rates, 802.11b uses Complementary Code Keying (CCK), a modulation technique that makes efficient use of the radio spectrum.

The 802.11b standard provides for operation using radio frequencies in the 2.4 GHz band. Most wireless LAN installations today comply with 802.11b, which is also the basis for Wi-Fi certification from the Wireless Ethernet Compatibility Alliance (WECA). These products have been available since the year 2000.

Many home technology contractors for wireless LANs are selecting products based on the 802.11b standard, which has proven to be very popular; however, the 802.11g standard is gaining in popularity due to its higher transmission speed of 54 Mbps and interoperability with 802.11b networks. IEEE 802.11b defines two pieces of equipment. One is a desktop computer or, more often, a portable laptop with a wireless Network Interface Card (NIC), and the other is an Access Point (AP) that acts as a bridge between the wireless networked computers and a Distribution System (DS). DS is the term used in the standard for a wired LAN.

The infrastructure mode of operation consists of at least one AP connected to the DS and can be configured with one of the two following options:

- **Basic Service Set (BSS)** − An AP provides a local bridge function for the BSS. All wireless stations communicate with the AP and no longer communicate directly. All frames are relayed between wireless stations by the AP.

- **Extended Service Set (ESS)** − An ESS is a set of infrastructure BSSs in which the APs communicate among themselves to forward traffic from one BSS to another. This facilitates movement of wireless stations between BSSs.

The ad hoc mode operates as an Independent Basic Services Set (IBSS) or peer to peer. The wireless stations communicate directly with each other; however, not every station might be capable of communicating with every other station due to the range limitations. No access points exist in an IBSS; therefore, all stations need to be within range of each other for reliable communications.

Home RF

HomeRF is a wireless Local Area Network (LAN) standard supported by the HomeRF Working Group. HomeRF is not compatible or interoperable with the 802.11 family of wireless LANs. The HomeRF working group formed in 1998 to develop a standard for economical wireless home communications but has since disbanded. HomeRF 1.0 supported a transmission rate of 1.0 Mbps. HomeRF 2.0 increased the speed to 10 Mbps. But the 802.11b and 802.11g wireless network standards, due to their growing popularity and wide industry support, have replaced HomeRF as the dominant standard for home wireless networks.

Bluetooth

Bluetooth wireless technology connects one device to another using a short-range radio link. This standard evolved from early work and engineering studies performed by Ericsson Mobile Communications in 1994. The Bluetooth project focused on the feasibility of designing a low-power/low-cost radio interface between mobile phones and their accessories.

A Bluetooth radio consists of an RF transceiver, a baseband link control with associated link management software, and an antenna subsystem. The radio uses frequency-hopping, spread-spectrum technology to support both point-to-point and point-to-multipoint connections.

Under the current specification, up to eight Bluetooth-enabled devices can automatically configure themselves into a "piconet," with one master and seven slaves. Although a piconet can comprise no more than eight devices, its coverage can be extended by attaching one of the slaves to other piconets. Most Bluetooth implementations support a range of up to 10 meters and speeds up to 700 kbps for data or isochronous voice transmission.

The signal hops among 79 frequencies, at 1-MHz intervals, to give a high degree of interference immunity. RF output is specified as 0 dBm (1 mW) in the 10-meter mid-range version and -30 to $+20$ dBm (100 mW) in the longer range version.

Bluetooth wireless technology eliminates the need for numerous, often proprietary, cable attachments for connection of practically any kind of communication device. Connections are instant and are maintained even when devices are not within line of sight.

Radio frequency operation is in the unlicensed Industrial, Scientific, and Medical (ISM) band at 2.4 to 2.48 GHz, using a spread-spectrum, frequency-hopping, full-duplex signal at up to 1600 hops/s.

PROCEDURE

Computer Networking

NOTE: For this lab, we use the router as the access point. While we will make no modifications to the router, we will require some configurations for this lab.

1. **Configure the wireless router**
   ___a.   Take the documentation from the router. Locate what IP address the router initially uses.
   ___b.   Click on the **Start** button, scroll to, and click on **Internet**.

____c.   Connect to the **IP address** specified in the router's documentation, as shown in Figure 33-1.

Figure 33-1:
Accessing the Router
via a Browser

____d.   From any of the workstations connected to the router, connect to the router using the specified IP address mentioned in your router's documentation.

____e.   Log in using the **user name** and **password** provided by the documentation, unless otherwise specified.

____f.   Click on the **Wireless** menu button, and enable the **wireless connection**, as shown in Figure 33-3.

NOTE: For purposes of this lab, the wireless connection will have no security. This is not necessarily a good practice for the home.

Figure 33-3:
Enabling the Wireless
Connection

____g.   Apply all settings as required, and then exit the browser program.

2.   Install the card

NOTE: Always follow the directions that the documentation for your card provides. In this example, we use the D-Link DWL-520.

____a.   To avoid confusion, disconnect the network wire running between HTI-1 and the router.

____b.   Insert the **D-Link** CD-ROM into HTI-1. An *autorun* screen will appear.

____c.   Click on the **Install Driver/PC Utility** for the appropriate network card.

____d.   Click on **Next**.

____e.   Verify that the installation folder is appropriate, and click on **Next**.

____f.   Click on **Finish**.

____g.   Click on **No, I will restart my computer later**, and then click on **Finish**.

____h.   Turn **off** HTI-1.

____i.   Open your case, and **install** the PCI card.

____j.   Attach the **antenna** to the computer, as shown in Figure 33-4.

____k.   Turn **on** HTI-1.

____l.   When you restart your computer, a new window named *Found new Hardware* will appear. Select the **Install the software automatically** option, and click on **Next**.

____m.   Click on **Finish** to finalize the installation.

____n.   Double-click the **Network** icon in the system tray named *Wireless connection*, as shown in Figure 33-5.

Figure 33-4: Screwing an Antenna to a Network Card

Figure 33-5: Locating the Icon in the System Tray

____o.   Find your wireless network and connect to it. You will need to check the box **Allow me to connect to the selected wireless network, even though it is not secure**, as shown in Figure 33-6.

Figure 33-6: Connecting to a Wireless Network

2. **Test your connection**

NOTE: Because not all networks have Internet access, we will test the connection using a utility called ping.

    ____a.   Go to computer HTI-1. Click on the **Start** button and scroll to **All Programs**, **Accessories**, and click on **Command Prompt**.

    ____b.   Type in **Ping HTI-2** and press the **ENTER** key.

    ____c.   Verify and show the instructor that you are able to properly ping HTI-2.

    ____d.   Go to computer HTI-2. Click on the **Start** button and scroll to **All Programs**, **Accessories**, and click on **Command Prompt**.

    ____e.   Type in **Ping HTI-1** and press the **ENTER** key.

    ____f.   Verify and show the instructor that you are able to properly ping HTI-1.

Feedback

LAB QUESTIONS

1. What are the usual effective range and speeds for data transfer using the Bluetooth protocol?

2. What is the difference between ESS and DSS?

3. What is the maximum data transmission speed for HomeRF 2.0?

4. What radio frequency does 802.11a use?

Using Network OS Services

OBJECTIVES

1. Configure DHCP.
2. Configure NAT.

**Computer
Networking**

RESOURCES

1. Two PC-compatible desktop/tower computer systems with Windows XP Professional installed
2. Router (Suggested: Wireless 4 port 802.11a, 802.11b, or 802.11g Router)

DISCUSSION

One problem that can arise in a home network is the need to assign all of the computers in your home an individual IP address. In a TCP/IP network, every computer that is part of the network requires an IP address to be able to send data, like files and images, to each other. However, keeping track of what computer has what IP address assigned can be difficult. Fortunately, there is an automated method of IP address assignments.

This is accomplished via DHCP, or Dynamic Host Configuration Protocol. When a computer that is running a DHCP client is booted, it requests an IP from the DHCP server. The server has been assigned a block of IPs, and enters this range of addresses when the DHCP parameters are first set up. The DHCP server will assign the IP for a "lease period" that's pre-determined. This could be a matter of hours to unlimited.

In fact, ISPs can use DHCP to assign an IP address whenever a computer initiates an Internet connection. In the case of an ISP, the lease time can be for the duration of an Internet session, or it may be for a specific time.

There are two ways to allocate IP addresses, statically and dynamically. The dynamic allocation is the most common method. The router will assign the first available IP address from its pool to the next computer that requires an IP address. The static IP address allocation method is more involved. Entered into a table is a network card's MAC Address. A MAC address is a string of letters and numbers that are used to uniquely identify a piece of networking equipment. Using this MAC address, you can assign which network cards, and by extension, computers, can be assigned which specific IP addresses. This can be very useful if a certain computer needs to be given a specific IP address to function as a server for a certain application.

PROCEDURE - 34

While DHCP will help supply your network with enough IP addresses to use, a problem develops if you only have one IP address supplied by your ISP, but you would like all the computers in your network to be able to access the Internet. While one solution is to purchase more IP addresses from your ISP, this idea can be rather expensive. Another solution is to use Network Address translation (NAT).

NAT is used in local area networks to have the LAN use one set of IP addresses, and in turn, data is routed to a central point to interact with the Internet. The central point usually is either a router, or a computer with two network cards that serves as a router. In addition, because the NAT handles routing, there is some ability to choose what to route and what not to route to the internal computers, acting in some ways like a firewall. However, because of this routing, certain applications may be unable to run initially, because the ports haven't been properly defined.

A computer's connections are split up into numerous ports. There are up to 65535 ports total. A port can be considered as a way of identifying specific communication between computers. Certain applications use specific ports. For instance, the port used to send and receive data via the HTTP protocol is port 80. A list of some of the better known applications and their ports are shown in a Figure 34-1.

Figure 34-1:
Well-Known Ports

SERVICE	WELL-KNOWN PORT NUMBER
FTP	21, 20
Telnet	23
SMTP Mail	25
HTTP (WWW)	80
POP3 (Mail)	110
News	144
HTTP	443
PPTP	1723
IRC	6667

It is possible to route an application to use a different port than the well-known port. NAT assumes that ports should be closed by default, so unless ports are defined, the application cannot access the Internet. Usually, certain ports on residential routers are activated by default, including HTTP, and the ports required to send and receive e-mail.

Furthermore, depending on the application, ports may use the UDP protocol, the TCP protocol, or both for communication of data. UDP stands for User Datagram Protocol, which is a connectionless protocol. As a result, the need for error correction is very low. Instead, a broadcasting approach is utilized.

The TCP protocol stands for Transmission Control Protocol. You might recognize TCP as the first part of the phrase TCP/IP. Unlike UDP, TCP is a connection-oriented protocol. This means that a connection has to be verified and monitored between the sender and the receiver of data at all times. While this means reliable data transfers, this also can mean increased workload on both computers for data verification.

And finally, an application also can utilize a trigger port. A trigger port is a port that is first used to notify that a certain connection is to be activated. At that point, another port, or set of ports, are activated to be used.

PROCEDURE

Computer Networking

1. **Configure the router**
   ___a. Using HTI-2, open up a browser window.
   ___b. In the address bar, type in the IP address of the router, and click **ENTER**.
   ___c. As shown in Figure 34-2, type in the user name and click on OK. Then, use the appropriate context menus to locate the DHCP options.

NOTE: The IP address of the router may be different than the one shown. Consult your manual, or your instructor to determine which IP is the IP address of the router.

   ___d. If the DHCP server is not activated, activate it now, and apply. If you are instructed to reboot the router, allow the router to reboot, re-login, and then go back to the DHCP options.
   ___e. Change the range of the IP addresses. Change the range of the last set of numbers in an IP address to **0-100**, as shown in Figure 34-3. Note that this means that in your network, you can now support up to 100 IP addresses being assigned by the server. Click **Apply**. If the server must reboot, reboot the server, then re-login.

**Figure 34-2:
Accessing the Router
Using a Browser**

**Figure 34-3:
Assigning IP
Addresses**

___f.   Change the lease time to a different time interval.

___g.   Locate the Static DHCP menu. If required, enable the **Static DHCP** option, and reboot and re-login as needed.

___i.   Using computer HTI-1, click the **Start** button, scroll to **All Programs**, scroll to **Accessories**, and click **Command Prompt**.

___j.   Type in **IPCONFIG /all,** and press **ENTER**.

___k.   Locate the Physical Address for the Local Area Connection. This is the MAC address. Write this down in Table 34-1.

___l.   Ignoring the dashes, insert in the MAC address of HTI-1 into *Static IP address*.

___m.   Assign an IP address so that the last number is 2. Your static IP configuration should now resemble Figure 34-4.

**Figure 34-4:
Static IP
Addressing**

___n.   Click **Apply**, and reboot and re-login as necessary.

2. Network Address Translation

___a.   While logged into the router, locate the section that deals with opening and closing TCP and UDP ports. Consult the manual of your router for additional help. For instance, the DLink and SMC routers name these sections Virtual Server and Special Applications.

___b.   Certain brands of routers already have certain ports opened ahead of time because they are very common. If your router already has some ports opened, list up to 3 of them in Table 34-2.

_____c.   Create a new port rule, by entering in a port number. In this case, we will use port *5900*. Enter in the value **5900** under public port number, indicate that this is a **UDP** connection, and assign this to the IP address of **HTI-2**. Enter the value 5900 under the private port number as well. The result should resemble Figure 34-5, depending on the make and the model of the router you are using.

What this has created is a rule, that when a connection from the Internet is made to the router, on port 5900 using a UDP connection, to route the connection to computer HTI-2's port 5900.

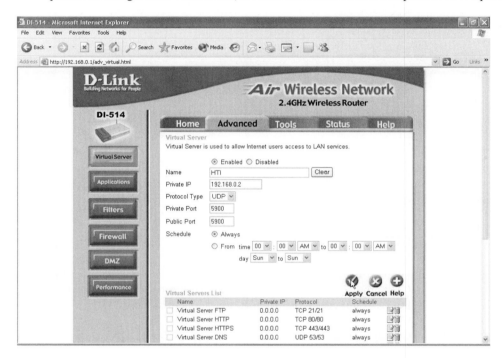

**Figure 34-5:
Port Forwarding**

NOTE: Due to the fact that routers are supplied with software specific to their design, your router software may display port assignments differently than what is shown here. Always refer to the documentation supplied with your equipment for specific information regarding port assignments.

_____d.   Consult the router's user manual for a special application allowing the use of a trigger port, which may be a different number, and even a different protocol than the public port.

_____e.   For the *Trigger* port, enter the value **6112**.

_____f.   Change the protocol to **UDP**.

_____g.   Enter in the *public* port, the value **554**.

_____h.   Change the protocol to **TCP**.

_____i.   If required, change the *private* port to the IP address of **HTI-2**.

TABLES

Table 34-1: MAC Address

Table 34-2: Already Opened Ports

	Port Number	Port Name
1		
2		
3		

Feedback

LAB QUESTIONS

1. You are deciding to use two different applications to act as some sort of data streaming for your home network. One uses the UDP protocol, and the other uses the TCP Protocol. It is important that the data is reliably sent between the two sources. Which application should be used, and why?

2. Describe how DHCP works in a home network.

Network Research

OBJECTIVES

1. Design and configure a PC network for a builder's showroom.
2. Plan, build, and test a new wireless home network.
3. Plan the installation of a home network in an existing home.
4. Decide on a cable type for the project.
5. Decide on a protocol for the new network.
6. Identify a piece of hardware for connecting to the Internet.
7. Select an appropriate range of IP addresses for the new network.
8. Identify a service that will be used to automatically assign IP addresses.
9. Label the IP addresses of the computers and devices connected to the showroom network.
10. Identify a method for hiding private IP addresses on the new showroom network from the Internet.
11. Help with your client's plans to create a Web site.
12. Identify the network type that will fulfil your client's requirements.
13. Describe the building blocks of the new network.
14. Identify the number of wireless access points required.
15. Identify the factors that influence the location of the router.
16. List the elements that need to be configured on the router.
17. Decide on an appropriate mode of operation for the network adapters.
18. Identify a device that may be used to increase signal level across the new network.
19. Identify a suitable networking technology to link computers across the current cabling system.
20. Identify a suitable high-speed Internet service.
21. Configure the router to prevent unauthorized persons on the Internet from gaining access to your client's home network.
22. List methods for using the new home network to connect to an external network.
23. Test connectivity between the computers connected to the new network.
24. Identify a potential cause of degradation in network performance.

Computer Networking

RESOURCES

1. Computer with Internet access
2. Newspapers and magazines
3. Paper and pencil

DISCUSSION

Read the following scenario:

You are a local entrepreneur based in the Bay area who has set up a company that provides quality on-site computer services to small businesses and home offices. A large developer is planning to build a showroom to demonstrate the features and benefits of home technologies. This developer has commissioned your company to design and install a PC network in the showroom.

Figure 35-1 includes specifications and requirements gathered during interviews and written documentation.

Figure 35-1: PC Network Specifications and Requirements

REQUIREMENT CATEGORY	DETAILS
Media type for showroom network	The media selected must be cost-effective, easy to install, and compliant with existing published standards for low-voltage residential wiring.
Internet access	A DSL service is available in the region.
Hardware	Three computers and a laser printer will be networked together.

Computer Networking

PROCEDURE

1. **Design and configure a PC network for a builder's showroom**

    ____a.   Your company has been selected as a wiring subcontractor to install the most economical type of cable in the showroom that will support three computers, a printer, and a router using Ethernet network components. In Table 35-1, record the type of cable would you select that would be responsive to the design requirements described in Figure 35-1.

    ____b.   The builder of the showroom wants potential home buyers to be able to use a web browser to access the Internet. Record the protocol that should be installed on the showroom computers to provide this functionality in Table 35-2

    ____c.   The showroom currently has three computers that are linked together through an Ethernet network. Record the type of hardware required to securely connect the computers to the Internet in Table 35-3.

    ____d.   To access the Internet, you must assign appropriate IP addresses to the three computers and the laser printer connected to the showroom network. Record which of the following IP network addresses are appropriate for use on the new networking Table 35-4.

    a. 170.16.0.0
    b. 10.0.0.0
    c. 192.168.0.0
    d. 172.16.0.0

_____ e.   Your client wants to be able to add computers to the showroom network without manually assigning unique IP addresses to them. Record which of the following services should be running on the gateway to automatically assign IP addresses in Table 35-5.

        a. Routing and Remote Access Services (RRAS)
        b. Dynamic Domain Naming System (DDNS)
        c. Dynamic Host Configuration Protocol (DHCP)

_____ f.   Before the gateway router can assign IP addresses to the computers on the showroom network, you must tell it what range of IP addresses it can safely distribute. In Table 35-6, label the IP addresses of the computers and devices connected to the showroom network using Figure 35-2.

Figure 35-2:
Network Diagram

_____ g.   You need to configure the router to ensure that IP addresses on the showroom computers are not visible to Internet users. Record the service will you enable on the gateway/router to achieve this level of functionality in Table 35-7.

_____ h.   Your client also wants to create a Web site that allows potential home buyers to view all the products available in the showroom over the Internet. Before designing and building the site, record what process should be completed in Table 35-8.

2.   Plan, build, and test a new wireless home network

Read the following scenario:

    You are a home system integrator who provides a full complement of computer services targeted toward small business owners and home office users. You have been called to a two-bedroom apartment (Figure 35-3) to plan, build, and test a wireless home network.

Figure 35-3: Floor Plan of a Two-Bedroom Apartment

Figure 35-4 includes requirements gathered during interviews with the owner of the apartment.

Figure 35-4: Wireless Home Network Requirements

REQUIREMENT CATEGORY	DETAILS
Current network	None.
Hardware details	Desktop computers are available in the kitchen and master bedroom.
Internet connection	Broadband is available via a cable modem.
Functionality	Connectivity to the internal home network is desired while upstairs or downstairs.

___ a.   Your client wants to set up a home network that allows the existing computers in the apartment to share the high-speed cable modem service. Home network access is also required on the balcony and the terrace.

It is not practical to install cable runs from an economic perspective. Drilling through the external walls will be expensive, and local building codes limit the size of the hole required for the cable runs. Record the type of network would you select to fulfill these requirements in Table 35-9. Explain your answer.

___ b.   The building blocks of the new wireless LAN will include network adapters for the computers in the apartment, and an access point or a wireless router. In Table 35-10, match the type of hardware with the corresponding functionality.

- Wireless access point
- Wireless network adapter
- A broadband wireless router

___ c.   Record the minimum number of wireless access points that are required to provide adequate coverage in this design in Table 35-11.

    a. One
    b. Two
    c. Three

___ d.   Record which of the following statements are true with regards to identifying a location for the wireless router in Table 35-12.

    a. It should be installed in a central location.
    b. It should be installed near the incoming telecommunications service.
    c. It should be installed within 3 feet of the microwave oven.

___ e.   Record which of the following must be configured on the wireless router in Table 35-13.

    a. Network name
    b. Wired Equivalent Privacy (WEP) security settings
    c. Firewall features
    d. Active Directory settings

___ f.   The next step involved in the installation of the new WLAN is the insertion of the wireless adapters into the two computers. During the configuration process you are required to choose between two modes of operation — infrastructure and ad-hoc. In Table 35-14, record which mode you will select for this particular configuration and why?.

___ g.   You've finished installing the components, but the WLAN in bedroom 2 isn't functioning correctly. Troubleshooting reveals that the plaster walls are significantly decreasing the signal level in this particular room. In Table 35-15, identify a device that may be used to increase the signal level in bedroom 2.

3. Design a Retrofit Project

Read the following scenario:

> You are a home systems integrator who works for DigitalMentors Ltd. The company has recently been contracted to install a home network in an existing home. The house is a two-story building and the floor plan for the second floor is shown in Figure 35-5.

**Figure 35-5:
Floor Plan for the
Second Story of a
Two-Story House**

Figure 35-6 includes requirements gathered during interviews with the owner of the house.

Figure 35-6: Requirements for a Home Network in an Existing Home

REQUIREMENT CATEGORY	DETAILS
Current hardware	There are three desktop computers that are not networked.
Current cabling system	The house has a daisy-chain phone wiring system that serves four separate outlets.
Internet connection	This is currently not available, but is a required part of the new project.
Functionality	A home network that links three computers together, and to the Internet, using the current cabling system.
In-home networking services	Family e-mail and Internet access is desired. A family member also requires telnet for college projects.

____a. Given the information you have about the current telecommunications cabling system, record whether you think that it is possible to build a home network and why in Table 35-16.

____b. Your client wants fast Internet access so that the rate of receiving data is higher than the sending rate. Record which Internet access method will provide this type of functionality in Table 35-17.

____c. You have installed the network components for the new HomePNA network, you now need to configure the DSL router to prevent unauthorized persons on the Internet from gaining access to your client's home network. The first element of configuring the router is to use port numbers to control traffic flowing in and out of the network.

The home networking services required by your client include Internet, e-mail, and telnet access. In Table 35-18, you are required to match the particular service with the corresponding port number.

- Access to telnet
- Access to e-mail
- Access to the Web

____d. Your client works from home two days a week and needs access to his company's intranet. Record which methods are available to provide this access in Table 35-18.

____e. You have finished installing the new system. You now want to ensure that all the devices can communicate with each other over the new home network. Record which TCP/IP command will enable you to test connectivity between the three computers in Table 35-19.

____f. This retrofit home networking project is based on Ethernet technologies. Record what happens to the performance of this network if your client starts to add more and more digital devices to it in Table 35-20.

TABLES

Table 35-1

Table 35-2

Table 35-3

Table 35-4

Table 35-5

Table 35-6

A.	
B.	
C.	
D.	
E.	

Table 35-7

Table 35-8

Table 35-9

Table 35-10: Hardware Functionality

WLAN NETWORK COMPONENT	FUNCTIONALITY
	Organizes the flow of information between the computer and the network.
	Joins a wireless LAN to a pre-existing wired network.
	Joins a wireless LAN to a pre-existing wired Ethernet network, and support Internet connection sharing.

Table 35-11

Table 35-12

Table 35-13

Table 35-14

Table 35-15

Table 35-16

Table 35-17

Table 35-18: Home Networking Services Port Numbers

PORT NUMBER	HOME NETWORKING SERVICE
80	
25	
23	

Table 35-19

Table 35-20

Designing Residential Networks

OBJECTIVES

1. Provide advice to builders planning to install home electronic systems in their developments.
2. Use the Internet to provide the builder with hardware costs for distributing basic TV, telephone, and Internet services in each two-bedroom apartment.
3. Use the Internet to provide the builder with hardware costs for distributing basic TV, telephone, and Internet services in each penthouse apartment.
4. Identify the different wiring locations associated with wiring a block of apartments.
5. Choose a suitable communication protocol for linking the different home electronic subsystems together.
6. Identify a hardware module for interfacing with the climate control system.
7. Describe how to use a standard touchtone phone to access the system.
8. Describe how to display output from a camera on a standard TV.
9. Match modes of operation with associated descriptions.
10. Update a specific program.

Computer Networking

RESOURCES

1. Computer with Internet access
2. Newspapers and magazines
3. Paper and pencil

DISCUSSION

In this lab, you will deploy and project-manage the integration of a number of different electronic systems into a large development of apartments.

Read the following scenario:

HomeMentors has carried out some of the most impressive developments in Chicago over the last fifteen years, and the company strives to maintain and improve on the standards achieved.

A planning application has just been lodged for an exciting new development of 191 apartments and 9 penthouse suites. It is hoped that development of these new apartments should be completed within a two-year period. HomeMentors has been selected as a prime contractor to work directly with the architectural firm in the design of electronic systems to accommodate this concept of smart living. The various systems and products are to be installed professionally by you, as planned, and within budget.

**Computer
Networking**

PROCEDURE

1. **Cost per Apartment of PC, Telephone, and Internet Connectivity**
    ____a.   The development is a mix of two-bedroom and penthouse suites. Figure 36-1 includes the telephone, computer, and TV requirements for two-bedroom apartments.

Figure 36-1: Two-Bedroom Apartment Requirements

ROOM TYPE AND APPLICATIONS	NUMBER OF OUTLETS PLANNED
Living/Dining/Kitchen Area	
Telephone	1
Computer	1
Cable or Satellite TV	1
Bedroom 1	
Telephone	1
Computer	1
Cable or Satellite TV	1
Bedroom 2	
Telephone	1
Computer	1
Cable or Satellite TV	

___b.   On the quotation form, shown in Figure 36-2, calculate the hardware costs for wall outlets, the distribution box, and the modules required for a typical two-bedroom apartment. Pricing may be obtained from an online supplier of home networking components.

Customer Name: _____

Address: _____

Project ID No: _____

Description of Component	Catalog Number	Number Required	Cost Per Unit	Total Price
CAT5e outlets				
RG-6 outlets				
Faceplates				
Distribution box				
Telephone distribution module				
TV splitter				
CAT5 panels				
Router and hub				
Total Cost of Materials and Components			$	

Figure 36-2:
Quotation Form

_____c.   Figure 36-3 includes the telephone, computer, and TV requirements for penthouse suites.

Figure 36-3: Penthouse Suite Requirements

ROOM TYPE AND APPLICATIONS	NUMBER OF OUTLETS/PORTS PLANNED
Kitchen Area	
Telephone	1
Computer	1
Cable or Satellite TV	1
Bedroom 1	
Telephone	1
Computer	1
Cable or Satellite TV	1
Bedroom 2	
Telephone	1
Computer	1
Cable or Satellite TV	
Bedroom 3	
Telephone	
Computer	1
Cable or Satellite TV	
Living Area	
Telephone	
Computer	1
Cable or Satellite TV	
Main Bathroom	
Telephone	
Computer	1
Cable or Satellite TV	

____d.   On the quotation form, shown in Figure 36-4, calculate the hardware costs for wall outlets, the distribution box, and the modules required for a typical penthouse apartment. Pricing may be obtained from an online supplier of home networking components.

Customer Name: _____

Address: _____

Project ID No: _____

Description of Component	Catalog Number	Number Required	Cost Per Unit	Total Price
CAT5e outlets				
RG-6 outlets				
Faceplates				
Distribution box				
Telephone distribution module				
TV splitter				
CAT5 panels				
Router and hub				
Total Cost of Materials and Components			$	

Choosing a wiring system to distribute incoming services to individual apartments and penthouses is one of the most important decisions of the overall project. After reviewing the design requirements, you have to divide the overall system into three separate distribution locations.

Figure 36-4: Quotation Form

____e.   Match each distribution location with the corresponding description in Table 36-1.

- Local Distribution Point
- Central Distribution Point
- Common Area Distribution Point

2.   Design control and automation features

The hardware architecture of the penthouse automation system is shown in the diagram of Figure 36-5.

Figure 36-5: Penthouse Automation System

_____ a. A hardwired lighting control system is to be installed in all penthouse suites. Each installation will include a central control unit and a number of different types of control interfaces and switch units. The connection of the dimmer units back to a central control unit provides each apartment owner with a number of enhanced lighting features. Record which of the following protocols should you use for integrating the lighting control system into the other apartment electronic subsystems in Table 36-2.

    a. X.25
    b. PPP
    c. H.323
    d. RS-232

_____ b. The builder would like a single controller that will enable residents to control not only the lighting in their apartment, but also the other systems such as HVAC. The controller is configured with a processor, memory, hard disk, control software, and expansion slots. Record what additional hardware module is required to interface with the climate control system in Table 36-3

_____ c. Your client wants to use a standard touchtone phone to access and control the automation system. Record what type of hardware should be installed in the controller to provide this level of functionality in Table 36-4.

_____ d. An increasingly standard security feature in new apartment developments is a video surveillance system. In this project, each apartment's camera output will be assigned to a dedicated security channel. Record what type of device should be installed to convert the baseband output from the camera into a cable channel signal in Table 36-5.

The console for the controller provides the owner of the apartment with an easy-to-use interface for operating the automation system. It comes preprogrammed with five separate modes of operation.

____e.   Match each mode of operation with the corresponding description in Table 36-6.

- DAY
- NIGHT
- OFF
- AWAY

____f.   A powerful feature of the new controller is the ability to create programs based on time schedules and events. Record what you enter into the console to tell the automation system to turn on the porch light when the front door opens in Table 36-7.

> IF Front Door = 1
> Porch Light *Missing Code*

a. 0=OFF
b. 1=ON
c. 2=DIM
d. 3=BRT

____g.   The control unit can interconnect with a variety of different types of interfaces. Identify a user interface that will match the functionality requirements of the particular room in Table 36-8.

- A keypad
- A single ON/OFF switch
- A Web pad or tablet PC
- A touch screen

NOTE: Some of the above user interfaces will be used twice.

TABLES

Table 36-1: Distribution Location Descriptions

DISTRIBUTION LOCATION	DESCRIPTION
	This is located in the basement of the building, or the residential wiring closet, from where all the main electrical and telecommunications services for the building emanate.
	This is located on each floor of the apartment block.
	This is located in the central area within each apartment.

Table 36-2

Table 36-3

Table 36-4

Table 36-5

Table 36-6: Mode of Operation Descriptions

MODE	DESCRIPTION
	The security system is deactivated, fire and emergency alarms are reset, and sirens are silenced.
	The perimeter zones (doors and windows) are protected; however, the sleeping areas of the apartment are not armed.
	This mode arms all doors, windows, and interior motion detectors.
	The perimeter zones are protected; however, there is an entry delay on entry-exit zones.

Table 36-7

Table 36-8: Interface Operation Descriptions

ROOM DESCRIPTION	FUNCTIONALITY REQUIRED	TYPE OF INTERFACE
Kitchen Area	Navigation of the home network management system	
Bedroom 1	The ability to control four separate light fixtures	
Bedroom 2	The ability to turn a single light fixture on and off	
Bedroom 3	The ability to turn a single light fixture on and off	
Living Area	Wirelessly control the home automation and control equipment	
Main Bathroom	The ability to control four separate light fixtures	

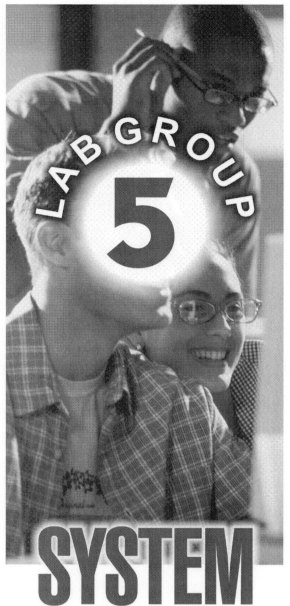

LAB GROUP 5

SYSTEM MAINTENANCE

Working with Task Manager

OBJECTIVES

1. Learn and understand the various functions provided by Task Manager.

Networking

RESOURCES

1. PC-compatible desktop/tower computer system — Customer-supplied desktop/tower hardware system **OR** Marcraft Computer Repair Trainer **OR** suitable PC hardware trainer running Windows XP Professional

DISCUSSION

Task Manager provides information on the programs and processes currently running on the system. Through Task Manager you may monitor items such as currently running applications, system services, CPU usage, memory usage, disk access, and network performance.

PROCEDURE

You may access Task Manager by launching it one of two ways. You may press the CTRL-ALT-DEL combination and clicking on the *Task Manager* button, or you may right-click on a blank area of the tool bar and select *Task Manager* from the pop-up window as we did in the following exercise.

1. **Access Task Manager**
   ____a. Open Task Manager by right-clicking on a blank portion of the task bar and select **Task Manager** from the pop-up window, as shown in Figure 37-1.

Figure 37-1: Selecting Task Manager

Figure 37-2: The Currently Running Applications

_____b. When Task Manager opens it should display the currently running Applications on your system, as shown in Figure 37-2. These are programs that you either started yourself or programs that start automatically when Windows loads. Notice the 3 buttons at the bottom of the screen. Highlighting a running task and clicking the **End Task** button will cause the selected application to be terminated. Any work you have done in that application up to that point will be lost. Highlighting a task and selecting **Switch To** will cause the system to give immediate priority to that application. Clicking on **New Task** opens the *Create New Task* dialog box, as shown in Figure 37-3. You may type in the name of the application you wish to start or you may browse the system for it.

Figure 37-3: The Create New Task Dialog Box

At the very bottom of the you will notice information about the number of processes currently running on the machine, how much CPU time is being used by those processes (all total) and how much of the page file is currently being used.

_____c. Click on the **Processes** tab of Task Manager. A listing of all the currently running processes or services is displayed, as shown in Figure 37-4.

The pane is divided into columns that can display various statistics relative to the system processes. The default columns are Image (or program) Name, User Name, the percentage of CPU use and the amount of memory being occupied by the program or service. Click on **View** at the top of the toolbar and select **Columns** from the drop down menu. The *Select Columns* window opens, as shown in Figure 37-5.

Figure 37-4: Listing of all the Currently Running Processes or Services

Figure 37-5: The Select Columns Window

Placing check marks on the various boxes will add or remove various columns from the displayed information. The information shown under the *Processes* tab can provide valuable information when attempting to troubleshoot system or application errors.

___d.   The *Performance* tab displays a graphical and numerical representation of the current state of your machine, as shown in Figure 37-6.

Figure 37-6: The Performance Tab

Starting at the upper left of the window is a graph representing the current amount of processor time expressed as a percentage and next to it is a graphical representation of the that same information. Below that is numerical representation of the amount of Page File (or swap file) being used and next to that a graphical showing of the same. Beneath that information. The rest of the window is used to display a numerical representation of various system information on physical memory, page file memory, Kernel memory and the number of currently running handles, threads and processes.

___e.   The *Network* tab displays information about the current status of your network connection, as shown in Figure 37-7.

Figure 37-7: The Network Tab

_____f.   Click on **Options** at the top of the toolbar. Figure 37-8 shows the selections available under the *Options* tab. These options can be used to change the way information is displayed.

**Figure 37-8: The
Selections Available**

**Figure 37-9:
Various
Selections
Available**

_____g.   Click on **View** on the toolbar. Figure 37-9 shows the various selections available. Clicking on **Select Columns allows you add or remove items to be displayed**, as shown in Figure 37-10.

Figure 37-10: Select Columns

Feedback

LAB QUESTIONS

1. What are the two ways to access Task Manager?

2. How do you add or remove display items from the Processes tab of Task Manager?

3. What information is displayed in the Performance tab? Be specific.

Creating a User Help Desk Script

OBJECTIVES

1. Research the capabilities of help desk software packages.
2. Examine a help desk script example.
3. Investigate the use of remote assistance programs.
4. Create a user help desk script for setting up a remote assistance program.

Networking

RESOURCES

1. Books
2. Newspapers
3. Magazines
4. Computer with Internet access

DISCUSSION

A service providing information and assistance to computer or network users is called a *help desk*. It's a source of technical support for solving hardware or software problems: a veritable end-user support center. *Help desk management* supports users in maximizing their desktop productivity and in properly operating all enterprise applications. As an internally centralized function of an organization, help desk operations are typically performed by a distinct department within the company, set up to respond to various technical questions by their users.

Large software companies also use help desks to answer questions by users of their products. Questions and answers can be delivered by telephone, e-mail, bulletin board systems, or faxes. Help desk employees often use *help desk software* to answer common questions more quickly. In larger companies, help desks may include a group of topic experts, using software, to help track and analyze user problems. For example, the status of a company's telecommunications network may be in question. In a smaller company, one person at a phone number may constitute the help desk. He or she may have more or less organized ideas about how to handle the problems that come in.

The person who provides technical support for any aspect of an information systems department is called a *help desk analyst*. He or she needs to be knowledgeable about the specified computer hardware, operating systems, applications, and networks. This position requires solid troubleshooting capabilities, and good human communications skills. Because the help desk is the place to ask questions about, or report problems with, network hardware or software, the help desk analyst will either provide help directly, or pass a request on to qualified technical support personnel.

Other names by which help desks are called include:

- Computer support centers
- IT response centers
- Customer support centers
- IT solution centers

- Resource centers
- Information centers
- Technical support centers

A related term is the *call center*, a physical place where customers call to place orders, track shipments, or get help with the company's products. Calls are handled by the company, usually with some amount of computer automation. Call centers have the ability to process many calls simultaneously, screening, logging, and forwarded them to qualified helpers. Large organizations use call centers to handle mail-order catalog sales, telemarketing services, and computer product help desks. These help desks are staffed by people who can solve the problem directly, or forward the problem to someone else.

Call centers often use help desk software, the newest versions of which are Internet based. These software programs improve call center productivity, and manufacturers have learned the value of having a place where customers can call to get help with a problem. Help desk software provides the means to log in problems and track them until they are solved, providing management with information regarding support activities. Web-based help desk services are becoming more automated and relatively inexpensive to operate, providing technical assistance from hardware manufacturers, software publishers, educational institutions, and third-party support companies. Help desk software must be able to effectively support all the possible paths that a service request may follow, from start to finish, as shown in Figure 38-1.

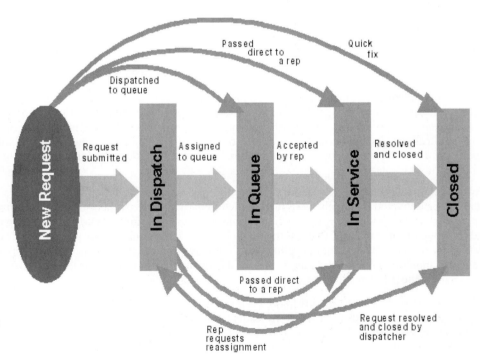

**Figure 38-1: The Basic
Help Desk Process**

Help desk management systems are similar to the trouble-ticket approach taken by equipment maintenance personnel, except for their customer tracking features. In this case, an address book is used to log detailed information about the customer. This permits the support staff to know about past relationships with the customer, and to quickly recognize when a high-priority customer is calling.

Call tracking systems are used to search for related help calls, or to reference a knowledge-based FAQ according to the problem description. Call tracking parameters such as time spent on the phone, time spent solving the problem, and additional billing may also be activated. Workflow and problem escalation capabilities are often included in order to keep track of unresolved tickets, and to direct trouble scenarios directly to those personnel capable of solving them successfully.

Keep these things in mind when either designing a help desk program, or seeking help desk assistance:

- A basic amount of detailed information about the problem must be available.
- For computer problems, the user must be seated at the applicable computer.
- If possible, the suspect application must be running and visible on the screen.
- Applicable error messages must always be reported exactly as displayed, or presented.
- The problem and circumstances must be described in exact detail.
- Both the help desk assistant, and the user must display patience during a help session.
- Realize the difficulty in successfully resolving intermittent problems. Unless the original trouble can be recreated onscreen, the tech support person may not be able to help.

Various formats are used to provide help desk services, including e-mail and telephone calls. While e-mail support is generally free of charge, telephone support may result in a lengthy wait on a long distance circuit. Information about help desk options is usually available on a manufacturer's Website. In general, e-mail responses will take from one to three days, while a telephone inquiry may take several minutes, an hour, several hours, or until one's patience runs out. Premium help desk services are available when paid for in advance: monthly, yearly, or per incident. Some companies will agree to solve a single problem for a flat fee, regardless of how much time is required.

PROCEDURE

1. Various help desk software packages are available to help control, organize, and automate a number of responsibilities related to the function of customer support services. Use your available resources to research these suggested help desk products, as well as those of your own choosing. Compare their capabilities and features, entering the appropriate data in Table 38-1.

Table 38-1: Help Desk Software Packages

Name	Features	Vendor	Cost
Bridge Trak Suite		Kemma Software	
LiveResponse		Kayako Infotech Ltd.	
HelpSpot		UserScape Software, Inc.	
Telemation		Database Systems Corp.	
Polar Help Desk		Polar Electro	
LiveTime Help Desk		LiveTime Software, Inc.	
CISS		Auratech Software	
Eden Help Desk		Eden, Inc.	

2. Scripting is useful for guiding users or customers to resolutions of simple recurring problems, or those of a more complex nature. If a script is written properly, customers may often solve their problems at, or before they reach the help desk. During the initial contact, customers or help desk staff can select from a number of predefined problem categories. They are subsequently led, step-by-step, through a series of questions and answers designed to identify the specific problem. Scripts can feature document and diagram attachments, which in many cases enable the customer to solve his or her problem.

This effort is not wasted, even if the customer is unable to solve the problem using the script, because the help desk system maintains a record of the customer's selections. This information is forwarded through to the help desk for active follow up, giving help desk personnel a head start with the problem scenario.

To get an idea about how automated help desk operations are written and coded, examine the following HTML script fragment. It demonstrates code requesting a customer to input his or her telephone number, and to indicate which department to contact.

```
<tr>
       <td align=center class=lbl>Telephone</td>
       <td align=left><input type=text size=25 name=xTelephone value="(%INPUT_xTelephone%)"></td>
</tr>
<tr>
       <td align=center class=lbl>Department</td>
       <td align=left>
              <select name=xDepartment>
                     <option></option>
                     <option>Sales</option>
                     <option>Helpdesk</option>
                     <option>Service</option>
                     <option>Billing</option>
              </select>
       </td>
</tr>
<script type="text/javascript"><!—
var i;
for (i = 0; i < document.forms['newticket'].xDepartment.options.length; i++) {
  if (document.forms['newticket'].xDepartment.options[i].text == '(%INPUT_xDepartment%)') {
      document.forms['newticket'].xDepartment.options[i].selected = true;
  }
}
//—></script>
```

The corresponding data input page to this script might appear as shown in Figure 38-2.

Telephone		
Telephone:		Ext:
Department		
Sales:		
Helpdesk:		
Service:		
Billing:		

Figure 38-2: A Help Desk Data Input Contact Page

3. Remote assistance programs can be created to monitor customer computer systems, provide help when problems arise, and in some cases, identify potential problems even before the customer notices. This form of assistance often permits help desk technicians to view customer computer screens in real time. Problem sources can be remotely located and identified.

Use your available resources to research the use of various remote assistance programs. Investigate the suggested products, as well as those of your own choosing. Compare their capabilities and features, entering the appropriate data in Table 38-2.

Table 38-2: Remote Assistance Programs

Name	Features	Vendor	Cost
Radmin		Famatech Intl Corporation	
HelpDesk VNC		Your Tech Solutions LLC	
GoToAssist		Citrix Systems, Inc.	
Remote Desktop Control		AQUATRA, Inc.	
Virtual Help Desk		4Star Computer Repair	
Remote Desktop Connection		LabMice.net	

4. When busy help desks are equipped to automatically provide remote assistance, users are presented with scripted formats for making their help requests. For common problems, this approach works very well. In order to avoid customer dissatisfaction, remote assistance programs should, however, provide a means by which more difficult problems can also receive the attention they deserve.

These scripted help desk formats often involve the use of:

- Frequently asked questions (FAQs)
- Phone numbers and contacts
- Documented procedures
- Miscellaneous forms

While *FAQs* are an excellent way of providing important information to customers, they must be kept current, and well organized. This means that the FAQ section must be broken down into various topics that are easy to understand and identify with. A single, cumbersome FAQ that supposedly provides answers to any and all possible questions will simply not do the job. If users are provided with e-mail facilities for submitting additional questions, these inquiries can later be used to expand the FAQ section.

The larger a help desk becomes, the more important it is to provide the *names*, *phone numbers*, and *e-mail addresses* of the people who work the desk. This information should also include any specialties for each person listed. It is not uncommon for help desk workers to have their pictures posted as well.

Many users are technically competent enough to perform the necessary troubleshooting *procedures* themselves, without requiring the step-by-step guidance of the help desk employee. If the required procedures are documented, having them available and online is a valuable time saver. These will be simple "how-to-do-it" documents that provide the identical steps for getting something done, similar to information that the help desk worker would provide over the phone. This type of information would definitely not include any complicated technical repair instructions or procedures.

The bread and butter of remote assistance services are the online data *entry forms* provided to gather specific information about the assistance being asked for. According to how these forms are set up, question can be answered and problems can be solved without having to actually interface with help desk personnel. In addition, much of what users and customers are doing and asking can be tracked for future improvements to the overall service system.

Entry forms can be designed to provide for:

- Making a simple inquiry
- Sending a problem report
- Requesting a procedure document
- Feedback

Questions can be answered directly through e-mail services. Problem reports can be matched to the appropriate FAQ, or submitted to the proper technician for resolution. Requests for documented procedures can be submitted and fulfilled online. Users can be encouraged to provide feedback, not only about how the site is working, but also about how it might be improved.

Keeping in mind the remote assistance services that help desks are capable of providing, create a user help desk script (a general form outline, rather than programmed scripted language) for setting up a remote assistance program. Include provisions for the use of FAQs, contact phone numbers and e-mail addresses, documented procedures, and data entry forms.

Feedback

LAB QUESTIONS

1. What is a help desk?

2. What are two important requirements for FAQs?

3. What is the main reason for the use of scripting within a help desk service?

4. List some of the uses for a remote assistance program.

5. What element constitutes the bread and butter of remote assistance services?

6. When seeking help desk support, why should the suspect application be running and visible on the user's computer screen?

7. During the operation of an automated help desk service, what should happen when an FAQ does not solve a customer's problem?

Windows XP Remote Troubleshooting

Networking

OBJECTIVES

1. Set up MSN Messenger.
2. Add contacts to MSN Messenger.
3. Use Remote Assistance.

RESOURCES

1. Two PC-compatible desktop/tower computer systems — Customer-supplied desktop/tower hardware systems **OR** Marcraft Computer Repair Trainers **OR** suitable PC hardware trainers with Windows XP Professional installed
2. Networked computers
3. Internet connection
4. MSN Messenger installed
5. 2 lab groups (must work together)

DISCUSSION

In Windows XP Microsoft has added a new feature for remote troubleshooting. When you combine the Windows XP operating system with Microsoft's MSN messenger you can now ask for assistance from someone you are chatting with or from Microsoft directly. In this procedure we will show you how to set up MSN Messenger and then how to get assistance while using the program.

PROCEDURE

1. **Set up MSN Messenger (done on both computers)**
   ___a. Boot to the Windows XP desktop.
   ___b. Click on **Start**, **My computer**.
   ___c. Insert the A+ Lab CD into the CD-ROM drive.
   ___d. Double-click on the CD-ROM drive (usually **d:** drive).
   ___e. Double-click on the file **MsnMsgs.Msi**. This will start the installation of MSN Messenger. If the repair or remove screen comes up, as in Figure 39-1, click on **Cancel** and **Yes** to confirm to cancel. Click on **Start**, **Windows Messenger** and continue at Step 2.

Figure 39-1: Repair or Remove

_____f. The Welcome to MSN Messenger Setup screen appears as in Figure 39-2. Click on **Next**.

Figure 39-2: MSN Messenger Setup

_____g. The *End-User License Agreement (EULA)* screen appears as in Figure 39-3. Select that you agree to the terms and click on **Next**.

Figure 39-3: End-User License Agreement (EULA)

_____h. MSN Messenger then installs the components as in Figure 39-4. When it has completed, click on **Finish**.

Figure 39-4: Installing Messenger

2. **Sign in to MSN Messenger**

____a. MSN Messenger then appears as in Figure 39-5. Click on the **Sign In** button.

____b. If it signs in automatically, skip to Step 3. If it asks for a password the password should be your school name. If not, ask your instructor.

____c. If an account is not set up on the computer it will display the .NET Passport wizard as in Figure 39-6. Click on **Next**.

Figure 39-5:
MSN Messenger

Figure 39-6: .NET
Passport Wizard

____d. Select **No, I would like to open a free MSN.com e-mail account now** and click on **Next**.

____e. Enter your Name into the next screen and click on **Next**.

____f. The *Where do you live?* screen will appear as in Figure 39-7. Fill it out for your school's address and click on **Next**.

____g. The *Terms of Use* screen comes up as in Figure 39-8. Select that you agree to the terms and click on **Next**.

Figure 39-7: Where Do You Live?

Figure 39-8: Terms of Use

___h. Fill out the information about yourself as in Figure 39-9.

___i. Create an e-mail address in the next screen. Type in your school name and then your station number with no spaces, as in Figure 39-10, and click on **Next.**

Figure 39-9: Your Information

Figure 39-10: Create an E-Mail Address

___j. Create your password in the next screen that appears. Make the password the city that your school is located in with all the letters being in lowercase. For example, a school in Los Angeles could have the password of losangeles or la.

___k. Notice that when you type the password the screen displays dots instead of the letters; this is normal for password encryption. For the secret question screen, choose **High school name?** as in Figure 39-11.

Figure 39-11: Secret Question

___l. In the *Share your information* dialog box, leave all the boxes blank and click on **Next.**

___m. In the *hotmail member directory* dialog box, deselect *Hotmail member directory* and click on **Next.**

___n. Your done screen appears. Click on **Finish** to exit the .NET Passport Wizard. You should be signed in to MSN Messenger.

3. **Add people to your contact list**

____a. Click on **Add a Contact** under the **I want to…** section, as in Figure 39-12.

____b. When the *How do you want to add the contact* dialog box comes up, make sure **by e-mail address or sign-in name** is selected and click on **Next.**

____c. Get the name of the workstation of the lab group you are working with. It should be the school name and station number. Type it in the blank as shown in Figure 39-13.

Figure 39-12:
MSN Messenger

Figure 39-13:
Add a Contact

____d. You will get a success message stating that the contact has been added. If not, check to make sure it is spelled correctly on both machines. Click on **Finish**.

____e. You will now have a contact in your group. If the contact is green, double-click on the contact. If the contact is red, have the other lab group sign into MSN Messenger and wait until it turns green.

____f. You will get a *conversation* dialog box, as in Figure 39-14. Type **hi** and press the **ENTER** key. This will send the message "hi".

Figure 39-14:
Conversion Dialog Box

4. **Get remote assistance using MSN messenger**

____a. In the *conversation* dialog box, under the *I want to…* section, click on **Ask for Remote Assistance**.

The computer sending the message will get the message stating that you sent an invitation to use remote assistance. The remote computer will get the message asking them to either accept or decline the invitation. These messages are shown in Figure 39-15.

Figure 39-15: Remote Assistance Screens

____b. Click on the **Accept** link to use remote assistance.

____c. The computers then try to connect to each other to use Remote Assistance, as shown in Figure 39-16.

____d. There will be a window asking if you would like to allow the person to view your screen and chat with you. Click on **Yes** to allow this as in Figure 39-17.

Figure 39-16: Attempting to Connect Window

Figure 39-17: Allow Viewing of Screen

____e. Once connected you should get *Remote Assistance* window. Click on **Scale to Window** and now your display should look similar to Figure 39-18.

Figure 39-18: Remote Assistance

___f.   Click on **Take Control** in the upper-left corner to take control of the machine. You should see a screen similar to Figure 39-19 on each machine. The remote user logs onto the machine and shares control.

Figure 39-19: Web Page Dialog Box – Sharing Control

___g.   Click on **Start**, **Control Panel** to bring up Control Panel in the *Remote Assistance* window.

___h.   In Control Panel, click on **Performance and Maintenance** and then click on the **System** icon. You should end up on the *System Properties* screen for the other computer as in Figure 39-20.

Figure 39-20: Remote Assistance – System Properties

___i.   Click on the **Hardware** tab and then **Device Manager** to open Device Manager. This is where you would be able to reinstall all drivers by using Remote Assistance.

___j.   Since everything is working properly, everything in the window appears normal. Click on **Release control** in the upper-left corner.

___k.   Now click on **Disconnect** to stop using Remote Assistance. You should receive a message similar to Figure 39-21 on both machines.

___l.   Close all open windows.

Figure 39-21: Disconnected from Remote Assistance

Feedback

LAB QUESTIONS

1. How do you set up MSN Messenger?

2. How do you add contacts to MSN Messenger?

3. How do you ask for remote assistance using MSN Messenger?

4. Can a remote user take control of your system without your knowledge?

5. Can you change the driver of a modem from a remote connection using Windows XP?

Working with Event Viewer

OBJECTIVES

1. Learn to use Event Viewer to help diagnose system problems.

RESOURCES

1. PC-compatible desktop/tower computer system — Customer-supplied desktop/tower hardware system **OR** Marcraft Computer Repair Trainer **OR** suitable PC hardware trainer running Windows XP Professional

Operating System Technology

DISCUSSION

Knowing how to use Event Viewer to help troubleshoot problems with your system can help cut down on the amount of time spent looking for the source of the problem.

You should review the Event Viewer logs regularly to help prevent small errors from becoming large problems.

PROCEDURE

1. **Open the Event Viewer**

   ___a. Open Control Panel and then double-click on the **Administrative Tools** icon. The *Administrative Tools* window opens as shown in Figure 40-1.

Figure 40-1: The Administrative Tools Window

___b.   Double-click on the **Event Viewer** icon. Event viewer will open as shown in Figure 40-2.

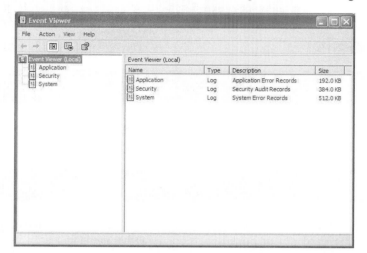

**Figure 40-2: The
Event Viewer**

___c.   Event Viewer is comprised of three categories Application, Security, and System. Click on **Application** to show the events recorded in that category, as shown in Figure 40-3.

**Figure 40-3: The
Events Recorded in
that Category**

**Figure 40-4: More
Information about
the Event**

___d.   To view the details of a particular entry, double-click on an entry. A window with more information about the event opens, as shown in Figure 40-4.

Note the information contained in the details window such as date and time of the event, the type of event, the source of the event, and the user and computer name from where the event originated. Close the details window when you are done examining the information in it.

_____ e.   Click on the **Security** category in the left pane of Event Viewer to display any logged events in that category, as shown in Figure 40-5.

**Figure 40-5:
The Security
Category**

_____ f.   Choose an event entry and double-click on it to display the details, as shown in Figure 40-6.

Notice that the details provided are similar to those shown in the Application details with the exception of the type. The type of event shown in the *Application* entry is listed as Information while the type shown in the *Security* entry denotes Success or Failure of the event. You will also notice an Event ID number displayed. The explanation of the Event ID is normally displayed in the *Description* portion of the event detail.

**Figure 40-6:
Choose an
Event Entry**

_____ g.   Click on the **System** category in the left pane of the Event Viewer to display logged system events as shown in Figure 40-7.

**Figure 40-7:
The System
Category**

PROCEDURE - 40

____h.   Double-click on an event to display its details, as shown in Figure 40-8.

Figure 40-8: Display the Details

Again, notice the information is very similar to that which is displayed in the Application and Security event details.

____i.   Figure 40-9 shows the details for a System event error. System Event errors are denoted by the red "X" symbol followed by the word "Error". The event details for the error displayed refer to a service that failed to start.

Figure 40-9: Details for a System Event Error

2.   Use Find to search for events

Event logs can grow quite large which can make scrolling through them time consuming. If you are attempting to locate certain events, you may find it useful to use the "Find" feature. To use Find to locate particular events perform the following steps:

____a.   From the main *Event Viewer* window, click on **View** then choose **Find** from the drop-down list. The *Find* dialog box opens as shown in Figure 40-10.

Figure 40-10: Details
for a System Event
Error

___b. Enter the information needed to complete the search and click **Find Next** near the bottom of the dialog box. The system will perform the search you specified and return the first item it finds that meets the search specifications. Clicking **Find Next** again will cause the system to search for and display the next entry that meets the search criteria.

3. Use filters to locate event log entries

In addition to the Find Next feature of Event Viewer, you may also use filters to display information about events. To configure Filters, perform the following steps:

___a. Right-click on the category (Application, Security, or System) and choose **Properties**. The *Properties* box for that category opens, as shown in Figure 40-11. For example, we are using the Application category.

Figure 40-11: The
Properties Box

_____b.   Click on the **Filter** tab to access the *Filter* settings, as shown in Figure 40-12.

**Figure 40-12: The
Filter Tab**

_____c.   Configure the filter settings as needed and click **OK** when done. The event log for that particular category will now display only the events you specify.

4.   Change the maximum log file size, archive and clear log files

The default maximum size for a log file is 512 kb. Events kept in the log for more than seven days are automatically overwritten by newer events as they occur. It may be necessary at times to change the size of the log file, archive the log for future reference or to clear the log if it becomes full.

_____a.   Select the event category you wish to change the log size. Right-click on it and choose **Properties** from the pop-up menu. The property page will open displaying the *General* tab, as shown in Figure 40-13.

**Figure 40-13: The
General Tab**

_____ b.   You will notice the General properties page provides much information about the log for that category such as category name, log file name and location, the current size of the file, when it was created and when it was last modified and accessed (usually the same time). The bottom portion of the *General* tab allows you change the default size of the file and make it larger or smaller based on your needs by clicking the up and down arrow next to the size box. You may also make changes to what happens when the log file reaches it maximum size. You may read more about what each selection does in Chapter 4.

_____ c.   It may become necessary to save event log files to aid in troubleshooting a particular problem. If you wish to archive the current log file you may do so by right clicking on the appropriate category and choosing **Save Log File as** from the pop-up menu. The *Save* box opens as shown in Figure 40-14. Choose the location to save the file to and the name you wish to give it and click **Save**. You may also change the file type of the log if needed. You may read more about the various file extensions available in Chapter 4.

Figure 40-14: The Save Box

_____ d.   Should it become necessary to completely clear the log file (often done when trying to troubleshoot a particular error) you may do so by right-clicking on the category and choosing **Clear All Events** from the pop-up menu. Windows will give you a chance to save the log before clearing it.

LAB QUESTIONS

Feedback

1.   What format are Event logs saved as by default?

2.   What is the maximum default Event log file size?

3.   What location are Event logs saved to by default?

4.   Describe how you would set a filter for a particular log event.

Software Updates in Windows XP

OBJECTIVES

1. Upgrade Windows Media Player.
2. Install a Windows XP Service Pack.
3. Upgrade to the latest Internet Explorer.
4. Upgrade DirectX Software.

Software

RESOURCES

1. PC-compatible desktop/tower computer system—Customer-supplied desktop/tower hardware system **OR** Marcraft Computer Repair Trainer **OR** suitable PC hardware trainer with Windows XP Operating System Installation CD and NIC installed
2. Internet access through a network connection

DISCUSSION

Windows XP needs to be updated periodically, just like Windows Me and Windows 2000. This can be done manually by the user, or automatically by the system. Either way, it is important that it be done consistently at least once a month.

An application's internal information display can be helpful in determining its version. Usually, you run the application and select *About* from the *Help* menu to access this feature. This feature may access the Internet and automatically find, download, and install any needed updates.

Upgrades, updates, or patches to the operating system itself are best done through the built-in *Windows Update* feature. Clicking on *Start/Windows Update* can access the Windows Update Web site. If you are connected to the Internet, this will connect you directly to the Microsoft Web site and show you a list of possible downloads for you to access. Once again, you should use this feature at least once a month to make certain that you are not missing any vital patches needed to fix a newly discovered bug or security flaw.

PROCEDURE

NOTE: This lab's time for completion will vary greatly depending on the bandwidth of the user's Internet connection.

1. **Install Internet Explorer through Windows Update**
   ____a.   Boot up the computer.

_____b.   From the Windows XP desktop, click on the **Start** button, **All Programs**, and then select **Windows Update.**

The browser will open and go to *windowsupdate.microsoft.com*. You will see a window similar to Figure 41-1.

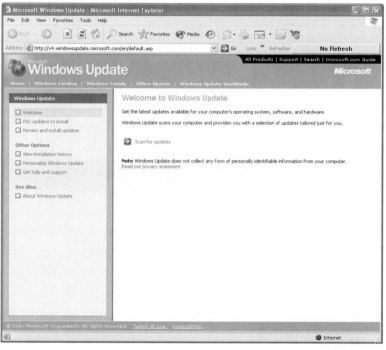

Figure 41-1: Windows Update Web Site

Figure 41-2: Accepting Licensing Agreement

_____c.   On the left side of the screen, click on **Pick updates to install**.

NOTE: The following procedures in this Step may vary over time.

_____d.   If this is the first time the computer has visited the page you will receive a security warning. It asks if you want to install and run "Microsoft Active Setup". Click on the **Yes** button.

_____e.   Click on **Windows XP** in the list on the left side to show the operating system updates that are not critical.

_____f.   Scroll down and look for the latest *Internet Explorer* selection.

_____g.   Click on the **Add** button to add **Internet Explorer** to the selection, if available.

_____h.   Click on **Review and install updates**, as shown in Figure 41-2.

_____i.   Click on the **Install Now** button to begin the installation.

_____j.   Click on the **Accept** button to accept the terms of the License Agreement.

NOTE: You will see a download progress window. After the window has completed you will see the Internet Explorer license agreement once again.

___k.   Click on the radio button next to **I accept the agreement** and click on the **Next** button.
___l.   Click on the **Next** button to begin the download.
___m.   After the program has downloaded and installed, click on the **Yes** button to restart the computer.

NOTE: When Windows restarts, Browsing Services, Internet Tools, and System Services will be set up.

2.   Install the Windows XP Service Pack through Windows Update

NOTE: If the Service Pack is not available, it is already installed. Skip to Step 4.

___a.   Repeat Steps 1a-c to go to the *Windows Update* site.

___b.   Click on **Critical Updates and Service Packs** on the left side of the screen.

___c.   Select the latest Windows XP Service Pack from the list by clicking on the **Add** button, if it isn't already selected.

___d.   Click on **Review and install updates**.

___e.   In the next screen, you will get a warning about installing the Service Pack separately. Click on the **OK** button.

___f.   Click on the **Install Now** button as shown in Figure 41-3.

___g.   Click on the **Accept** button, as shown in Figure 41-4, to accept the licensing agreement.

Figure 41-3: Installing Service Packs

Figure 41-4: Accepting the Manufacturer's Terms

___h. Click on the **Next** button when the *Windows XP Service Pack Setup Wizard* window appears.

___i. Click on the **I Agree** radio button and then click on the **Next** button to accept the license agreement, as shown in Figure 41-5.

Figure 41-5: Accepting Microsoft's Licensing Agreement

___j. Select the default of **Archiving Files** necessary to uninstall this Service Pack at a later time, and then click on the **Next** button.

___k. When the download and install have completed, click on the **Exit** button.

___l. When prompted, click on the **Yes** button to restart the computer.

3.   Install Windows Media Player through Windows Update

___a. Repeat Steps 1a-c to go to the *Windows Update* site.

___b. Click on **Windows XP** on the left side of the window to show the non-critical updates that are available.

___c. Scroll down to the latest *Windows Media Player* update and click on the **Add** button to add it to your selected updates.

___d. Click on the **Yes** button when prompted to install this update by itself.

___e. Record the size and download time for this update in Table 41-1.

___f. Click on **Review and install updates**.

___g. Click on the **Install Now** button.

___h. Click on the **Accept** button to accept the terms of the license agreement.

___i. After the program has finished downloading, the installation process will begin. Click on the **I Accept** button.

___j. Click on the **Next** button, at the *Welcome* screen.

___k. Accept the default settings and click on the **Next** button.

___l. Click on the **Finish** button to complete the installation.

4.   Install the DirectX Software Upgrade

___a. Go to the *Windows Update* Web site again.

___b. Click on **Windows XP** on the left side of the screen.

___c. Click on the **Add** button to select the latest *DirectX* upgrade.

___d. Click on **Review and install all updates**.

___e. Click on the **Install Now** button.

___f. Click on the **Accept** button, and the installation begins.

___g. When the installation is finished, click on the **OK** button to reboot the computer.

TABLES

Table 41-1

Windows Media Player Update	
Update File Size:	
Download Time:	

LAB QUESTIONS

1. Where do most applications display their version number?

2. What Web address does Microsoft use for updating their Windows products?

3. Can the version of IE used in this lab be downloaded and installed simultaneously with other components?

4. What are the three types of updates available on the Windows Update Web site?

Feedback

Installing and Configuring Antivirus and Malware Products

OBJECTIVES

1. Research the capabilities of antivirus and malware programs.
2. Locate and download shareware versions of antivirus and malware products.
3. Install and configure shareware versions of antivirus and malware software.
4. Run the selected antivirus and malware software on the computer.
5. Remove any viruses or malware discovered by this software.
6. Uninstall all antivirus and malware software from the computer.

Software

RESOURCES

1. Books
2. Newspapers
3. Magazines
4. Computer with Internet access

DISCUSSION

Antivirus programs help to protect computers and their related networks from being infested with programs deliberately created to damage them. Companies that produce these programs are good at protecting against viruses they know about. However, the first use of an antivirus program usually occurs following some type of infection. An infection from a previously unknown virus will require a certain amount of time by an antivirus company to come up with a fix.

Once a fix (vaccine) is created, its public distribution can begin. However, this approach is especially problematic for those computers already infected from the initial virus attack. Computers can also be exploited when antivirus users fail to update virus definitions, or keep up with the latest virus alerts. This is why some computers remain infected with viruses that were identified years ago.

Because of these problems, antivirus programs are now capable of monitoring various computer activities for those known to be associated with viruses. When these activities are discovered, they are logged and the user is notified. Antivirus monitoring is effective in preventing the spread of viruses to other computers, as well as disinfecting the host. These programs can be run in automated mode for updating the computer's virus definitions, without requiring user intervention.

In order to achieve the maximum protection possible from an antivirus program, it should be set up to run (scan) every day, automatically. It should also be configured to automatically check for the latest updates and virus definitions.

While viruses make up the main category of damaging software programming, there are many other types of software infections that are generally categorized as *malware*. Malware is any form of programming, or class of files, developed for the express purpose of causing harm or trouble. It includes not only computer viruses, but also worms, Trojan horses, spyware, hijackers, or adware. Examine the following definitions and observe the differences between them.

- *Adware:* These are programs that generate pop-ups on the computer screen of an advertising nature. However, when information is provided up front that the free software being offered includes display ads designed to generate revenue, this is generally not considered to be malware. It is malware when these ads appear out of thin air with no prior warning being given.

- *Backdoor:* This is a program that permits a remote user to execute commands on someone's computer without their permission. Backdoors are typically used to launch attacks on other computers, illegally distribute copyrighted media or software, and otherwise hack into a targeted computer.

- *Dialer:* This is a program that automatically dials a premium rate number charging high per-minute rates. These programs are usually used to gain access to *pornographic materials*.

- *Hijacker:* This is a program that attempts to gain control over various Internet functions. It may redirect the infected computer to the hijacker's start page, or point a search to an unwanted search engine. It may even replace the results from a legitimate search engine with its own information.

- *Spyware:* This is a program that monitors a user's activity or computer data without his or her knowledge. It may even send that information to a remote computer.

- *Trojan:* This is a program designed to appear harmless when actually present to cause some type of malicious activity. It may also be used to provide a backdoor to the infected system.

- *Virus:* This is a program that infects other computer programs and files when it is run. Their effects range from erasing a hard drive to displaying a joke on the screen. Many viruses remain localized to a single computer without the ability to spread. A virus program can include a Trojan, or a worm.

- *Worm:* This is a program having the capability, when run, to spread itself to other computers through the use of mass-mailing techniques. It will spread by using e-mail addresses found on the infected computer, or through the Internet to remote computers through known security weaknesses.

PROCEDURE

Many antivirus and anti-malware programs are available for use on both networks and individual computers. Some of them offer complete protection not only from viruses, but also from worms, Trojan horses, spyware, hijackers, or adware. Some offer protection from only one type of threat. By way of introduction, antivirus software manufacturers often permit their products to be used on a trial basis, before purchase is required. There are other antivirus and anti-malware products that are available online at no charge.

1. In order to differentiate between the capabilities of various antivirus and anti-malware software programs, a certain amount of research is required. Use Table 42-1 to record your research results. In addition to the products suggested, include information about other programs that you have found.

Table 42-1: Antivirus and Anti-Malware Software Packages

Name	Features	Vendor	Cost
McAfee Virusscan		McAfee, Inc.	
Kaspersky Anti-Virus		Kaspersky Lab	
ETrust EZ Antivirus		Computer Associates	
Panda Antivirus		Panda Software	
PC-cillin Internet Security		Trend Micro, Inc.	
Spy Sweeper		Webroot Software, Inc.	
Ad-Aware SE Professional		Lavasoft	
Spybot-Search & Destroy		Patrick M. Kolla	

2. Using the information gathered during the previous step, locate sources for shareware versions of antivirus and/or anti-malware software for download. Then, perform the necessary download(s), placing the files into a temporary directory.

3. From the temporary download directory, take the time necessary to read and understand any readme files included with the shareware antivirus and/or anti-malware programs just downloaded. Then, following all listed precautions and instructions, install and configure this shareware.

4. Look for any help files or instructions for running the antivirus and/or anti-malware programs just installed. Following all listed precautions and instructions, run the installed antivirus and malware software on the selected computer. Note the results of these tests in Table 42-2, including the names of any identified viruses or malware.

Table 42-1: Antivirus and Anti-Malware Software Packages

Program Name	Program Type	Test Results

5. After running the required tests for the installed antivirus and/or anti-malware programs, follow the instructions provided with these programs for removing any viruses or malware infections detected. If no viruses or malware programs were detected, move on to the next procedure.

6. Once all viruses and malware infections have been removed, and/or testing indicates that the selected computer is clean, completely uninstall the antivirus and/or anti-malware programs from the computer. The final condition of the computer should be as it was prior to the installation of the antivirus and/or anti-malware programs. The only exception to this requirement is that any detected viruses or malware have been removed.

Feedback

LAB QUESTIONS

1. Why do some computers remain infected with viruses that were identified and neutralized years ago?

2. List the positive aspects of antivirus monitoring.

3. What should be done to achieve the maximum protection possible from an antivirus program?

4. What type of malware permits a remote user to execute commands on someone's computer without their permission?

5. What do you call a program that secretly monitors user activity or computer data?

Troubleshooting Windows 2000 Faults

OBJECTIVES

1. Delete *boot.ini*.
2. Make a shortcut point to an incorrect location.
3. View automatic restoration of Windows programs.
4. Change a file type association.
5. Edit Registry to run an invalid file at startup.
6. Assign bad drivers to network and video cards.

Troubleshooting

RESOURCES

1. PC-compatible desktop/tower computer system — Customer-supplied desktop/tower hardware system **OR** Marcraft Computer Repair Trainer **OR** suitable PC hardware trainer with Windows 2000 installed
2. Drivers for the Plug and Play network card
3. LAN connection

NOTE: This lab procedure will work properly only if Windows 2000 is the ONLY operating system installed on the Windows 2000 computer.

DISCUSSION

Windows 2000 is the most stable operating system yet. It is harder to "break" than previous Microsoft operating systems such as NT 4.0 or Windows 98. One can delete *arcldr.exe*, *arcsetup.exe*, *autoexec.bat*, *boot.ini*, *config.sys*, *io.sys*, and *msdos.sys* and Windows will still start. If you create a shortcut to a file and then move the file, Windows will search for that file upon execution of the shortcut. If you rename a file, shortcuts pointing to it will be modified so that they still point to it. If you delete files that came with Windows (such as Net Meeting) they will be restored automatically. You cannot rename running Windows files such as Windows Explorer or .dll files. This would cause a fault in Windows.

Some actions can be fatal however. If you delete significant amounts of information from the Registry, you will need to re-install Windows. If you delete ntldr or ntdetect, you will need to run an emergency repair. If you install the wrong driver for an expansion card, you will need to install the correct driver.

PROCEDURE

1. Boot.ini

____a. Boot the computer to Windows 2000 and from the desktop double-click the **My Computer** icon.

____b. Double-click the **C: Drive**.

____c. Click on **Tools/Folder Options**.

____d. Click on the **View** tab.

____e. You need to view all files, so click on the radio button next to **Show hidden files and folders**.

____f. Uncheck *Hide file extensions for known file types* and uncheck *Hide protected operating system files (Recommended)*.

____g. You will get a warning similar to Figure 43-1. Read the warning and click on **Yes**.

**Figure 43-1:
Display Protected
Operating System
Files**

____h. Click on **OK** to close the *Folder Options* windows.

____i. Record your observations about what you can now view in C: in Table 43-1.

____j. Right-click on **boot.ini** and select **Delete**.

____k. Confirm the File Delete by clicking on **Yes**.

____l. Close all windows and restart the computer.

____m. When Windows is restarting record the message that appears at the beginning of startup in Table 43-2.

____n. Once Windows has restarted double-click the **Recycle Bin**.

____o. Right-click on **boot.ini** and click Restore.

____p. Confirm moving the system file by clicking on **Yes**.

____q. Close the Recycle Bin.

2. Shortcut problems

____a. Right-click the desktop and click **New/Text Document**.

____b. Right-click the **New Text Document** and click on **Copy**.

____c. Right-click the desktop and click on **Paste Shortcut**.

____d. Double-click the shortcut and you will see *Notepad* viewing *New Text Document.txt*.

____e. Close the window.

____f. Right-click the **New Text Document** (not the shortcut) and click on **Cut**.

____g. Double-click the **My Computer** icon.

____h. Double-click on **C:**.

____i. Right-click in any blank space and click on **Paste**.

____j. Close the window.

____k. Double-click the shortcut. Record what happens in Table 43-3.

____l. Close all windows.

____m. As before, go through *My Computer*, but this time delete **New Text Document.txt** from (C:).

____n. Double-click the shortcut to **New Text Document.txt**. You will see a window similar to Figure 43-2. Click on **Yes** to delete the shortcut.

Figure 43-2: Delete an Invalid Shortcut

____o.   Right-click the **Recycle Bin** and click on **Empty Recycle Bin**.

____p.   Confirm the file delete by clicking on **Yes**.

3.   Automatic restoration of Windows components

____a.   From the desktop double-click the **My Computer** icon.

____b.   Double-click on **(C:)**.

____c.   Double-click the **PROGRAM FILES** folder.

____d.   If necessary click on **Show Files to view the contents of the folder**.

____e.   Double-click the **NETMEETING** folder.

____f.   Right-click on **conf.exe** (the execution file for Net Meeting) and click on **Rename**.

____g.   Rename the program to **conf.exx** and press **ENTER**.

____h.   You will get a Rename warning similar to Figure 43-3. Click on **Yes**.

**Figure 43-3:
Rename Warning**

____i.   Wait approximately 10 seconds and record your observations about the folder's contents in Table 43-4.

____j.   Delete the file **conf.exx**.

____k.   Right-click on one of the .dll files in the folder and delete it. Use *nmchat.dll*, for example.

____l.   Wait 10 seconds and record your observations about the folder's contents in Table 43-5.

____m.   Close all windows.

4.   File type association

____a.   From the Windows 2000 desktop double-click the **My Documents** icon.

____b.   Click on **File/New/Text Document**.

____c.   Use the default *New Text Document.txt* filename and open the document by double-clicking the icon.

____d.   Type **This is a test** in the document.

____e.   Close the document and click on **Yes** to save the changes.

____f.   From the *My Documents Folder* window click on **Tools/Folder Options**. This menu can be accessed from any folder in the Windows Explorer.

____g.   Click on the **File Types** tab. You will see a window similar to Figure 43-4.

____h.   Look for the extension "TXT" by scrolling down in the *Registered file types* field.

____i.   Click on the **TXT** extension and record its File Type in Table 43-6.

____j.   In the lower portion of the window is a short explanation of the extension. Record the name of the program that TXT "Opens with" in Table 43-7.

____k.   Click on the **Change** button.

Figure 43-4: File Type Associations

Figure 43-5: New File Type Association

_____ l.   You will see a window similar to Figure 43-5. Click on **Imaging** and click on **OK**.

_____ m. Close **Folder Options** by clicking on the **Close** button.

_____ n.   In the *MY DOCUMENTS* folder that is still open double-click the new text document. Record your observations in Table 43-8.

_____ o.   Close all windows.

_____ p.   Open the **MY DOCUMENTS** folder once again and click on **Tools/Folder Options**.

_____ q.   Click on the **File Types** tab. Look for the extension "TXT" by scrolling down in the Registered file types field.

_____ r.   Click on the **TXT** extension and record the name of the program that TXT "Opens with" in Table 43-9.

_____ s.   Click on the **Restore** button in the lower-right portion of the window and record the name of the program that TXT "Opens with" in Table 43-9.

_____ t.   Close Folder Options.

_____ u.   Double-click the new text document and record your observations in Table 43-10.

_____ v.   Close the window that opened and delete **New Text Document.txt**.

5.   Invalid shortcut at startup

_____ a.   Right-click the desktop and click on **New/Bitmap Image**.

_____ b.   Right-drag the new bitmap image through *Start/Programs/Startup* and release the mouse button. Select **Create Shortcut(s) Here** from the window that opens. The screen should look similar to Figure 43-6.

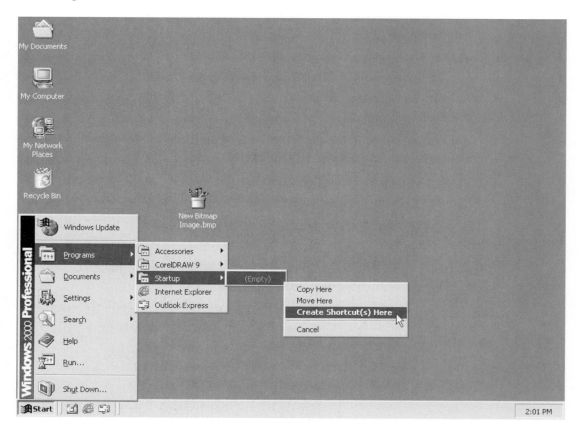

Figure 43-6: Create a Shortcut

_____ c.   You now have a shortcut to open the bitmap image at startup.

_____ d.   From the desktop delete the **New Bitmap Image.bmp**.

_____ e.   Close all windows and restart the computer.

_____ f.   Record your observations when Windows has restarted in Table 43-11.

_____ g.   Close any open windows.

_____ h.   Click on **Start/Programs/Startup**. Right-click on **Shortcut to New Bitmap Image.bmp** and click on **Delete**.

_____ i.   Click on **Yes** to confirm the deletion.

6.   Incorrect network adapter drivers

_____ a.   From the Windows 2000 desktop double-click the **My Network Places** icon.

_____ b.   Double-click on **Computers Near Me**.

_____ c.   Record your observations in Table 43-12.

_____ d.   Close all windows.

_____ e.   Go to Device Manager by navigating the *Start/Settings/Control Panel* path. Double-click the **System** icon.

_____ f.   Click on the **Hardware** tab, and then click on **Device Manager**.

_____ g.   Expand **Network adapters**. Record the name of your adapter in Table 43-13. Right-click on your adapter and click on **Properties**.

_____ h.   Click on the **Driver** tab.

_____ i.   Click on **Update Driver**.

_____ j.   Click on **Next**.

_____ k.   Click on **Display a list of the known drivers for this device...** and click **Next**.

_____ l.   Click on **Show all hardware of this device class**.

_____ m.   Choose a different Manufacturer from the Manufacturers list and choose any Network Adapter. The point is to choose an incorrect driver.

_____ n.   Click on **Next**.

_____ o.   You will see a window similar to Figure 43-7. Click on **Yes**.

Figure 43-7:
Incorrect Driver Warning

_____ p.   Click on **Next** and click on **Finish**.

_____ q.   Close the properties of the adapter and restart as prompted.

_____ r.   When Windows has restarted double-click on **My Network Places** and double-click on **Computers Near Me**.

_____ s.   Record your observations in Table 43-14.

_____ t.   Close all windows. At this point you can install the correct drivers for the network card by using Plug and Play or the drivers provided by the manufacturer.

_____ u.   Repeat Steps e and f. Right-click on your adapter and click on **Uninstall**.

_____ v.   Click on **OK** to confirm the device removal. Right-click the computer name and select **Scan for Hardware changes**.

_____ w.   The following step will vary because Windows may not have the drivers built in. The new drivers will be installed automatically for the Plug and Play network adapter. You may need to follow the Wizard to install the driver provided by the manufacturer. When the correct driver is installed you may close all windows.

_____ x.   Restart the computer and enter *Computers Near Me* as before.

____y.   Record your observations in Table 43-15.

____z.   Close all windows.

7. **Incorrect video adapter drivers**

____a.   Enter into *Device Manager* as in previous steps.

____b.   Expand **Display adapters**.

____c.   Record the name of your adapter in Table 43-16.

____d.   Right-click the adapter and click on **Properties**.

____e.   Click on the **Driver** tab.

____f.   Click on **Update Driver**.

____g.   Click on **Next**.

____h.   Click on **Display a list of the known drivers for this device...** and click on **Next**.

____i.   Click on **Show all hardware of the device class**.

____j.   Choose a different Manufacturer from the Manufacturers list and choose any Network Adapter. Click on **Next**.

____k.   Click on **Yes** to the incorrect driver warning window.

____l.   Click on **Next** and click on **Finish**.

____m.   Close the video adapter's properties and restart as prompted.

____n.   When Windows has restarted record your observations about the desktop in Table 43-17.

____o.   You can now reinstall the correct drivers for the video card. Enter *Device Manager* as before.

____p.   Right-click the video adapter and click on **Properties**.

____q.   From the *General* tab record the Device status in Table 43-18.

____r.   Close the video adapter's properties.

____s.   Right-click the video adapter and click on **Uninstall**.

____t.   Click on **OK** to confirm the device removal. Right-click the computer name and select **Scan for Hardware changes**.

____u.   The new drivers will be installed for the Plug and Play video adapter.

NOTE: The following step will vary because Windows may not have the drivers built in. The new driver will be installed automatically for the Plug and Play video adapter. You may need to follow the Wizard to install the drivers provided by the manufacturer. When the correct driver is installed you may close all windows and restart as prompted.

____v.   When Windows has restarted record your observations about the desktop in Table 43-19.

TABLES

Table 43-1

Observations:	

Table 43-2

New Message at Startup:	

Table 43-3

Observations:	

Table 43-4

Observations:	

Table 43-5

Observations:	

Table 43-6

TXT File Type:	

Table 43-7

TXT File Opens with:	

Table 43-8

Observations:	

Table 43-9

Before Restore TXT File Opens with:	
After Restore TXT File Opens with:	

Table 43-10

Observations:	

Table 43-11

Observations at Startup:	

Table 43-12

Network Observations:	

Table 43-13

Network Adapter Name:	

Table 43-14

Network Observations:	

Table 43-15

Network Observations:	

Table 43-16

Display Adapter Name:	

Table 43-17

Desktop Observations:	

Table 43-18

Video Adapter Device Status:	

Table 43-19

Desktop Changes:	

Feedback

LAB QUESTIONS

1. What happens to the icon in Device Manager when an incorrect driver is installed for the network adapter?

2. What type of mode did Windows enter when you installed an incorrect video driver?

3. How many options were there in the Folder Options/View window?

4. How long did it take for Windows to automatically restore a file that you renamed?

5. What is a possible reason for receiving a Problem with Shortcut window?

Troubleshooting Windows XP Faults

OBJECTIVES

1. Delete *boot.ini*.
2. Make a shortcut point to an incorrect location.
3. View automatic restoration of Windows programs.
4. Change a file type association.
5. Edit Registry to run an invalid file at startup.

Software

RESOURCES

1. PC-compatible desktop/tower computer system—Customer-supplied desktop/tower hardware system **OR** Marcraft Computer Repair Trainer **OR** suitable PC hardware trainer with Windows XP Operating System Installation CD and NIC installed
2. Internet access through a network connection or modem
3. Drivers for the Plug and Play network card

NOTE: This lab procedure will work properly only if Windows XP is the ONLY operating system installed on the Windows XP computer.

DISCUSSION

Windows XP is the most stable operating system yet. It is harder to "break" than previous Microsoft operating systems such as NT 4.0 or Windows Me. One can delete *arcldr.exe, arcsetup.exe, autoexec.bat, boot.ini, config.sys, io.sys,* and *msdos.sys* and Windows will still start. If you create a shortcut to a file and then move the file, Windows will search for that file upon execution of the shortcut. If you rename a file, shortcuts pointing to it will be modified so that they still point to it.

If you delete files that came with Windows (such as Net Meeting) they will be restored automatically. You cannot rename running Windows files such as Windows Explorer or .dll files. This would cause a fault in Windows.

Some actions can be fatal, however. If you delete significant amounts of information from the Registry you will need to re-install Windows. If you delete ntldr or ntdetect you will need to run an emergency repair. If you install the wrong driver for an expansion card you will need to install the correct driver.

PROCEDURE

1. **Boot.ini**
    ____a.   Boot the computer to Windows XP and from the desktop double-click on the **My Computer** icon.
    ____b.   Double-click the **C:** Drive.
    ____c.   Click on the *Tools* menu and select **Folder Options**.
    ____d.   Click on the **View** tab.
    ____e.   You need to view all files, so click on the radio button next to **Show hidden files and folders**.
    ____f.   Uncheck **Hide file extensions for known file types** and uncheck **Hide Protected operating system files (Recommended).**
    ____g.   You will get a warning similar to Figure 44-1. Read the warning and click on the **Yes** button.

Figure 44-1:
Warning Screen

    ____h.   Click on the **OK** button to close the *Folder Options* windows.
    ____i.   Record your observations about what you can now view in C: in Table 44-1.
    ____j.   Right-click on the file named **boot.ini** and select **Copy**.
    ____k.   Right-click on the **Windows** folder and select **Paste**.
    ____l.   Right-click on the file named **boot.ini** in the C:\ drive again, and select **Delete**.
    ____m.   Confirm the File Delete by clicking on the **Yes** button.
    ____n.   Close all windows and restart the computer.
    ____o.   When Windows is restarting record the message that appears at the beginning of startup in Table 44-2.
    ____p.   Once Windows has restarted double-click the **MyComputer** icon.
    ____q.   Double-click on the **C:** drive.
    ____r.   Double-click on the **Windows** folder.
    ____s.   Right-click on the file named **boot.ini** and select **Copy**.
    ____t.   Right-click on the **C:** drive and select **Paste**.
    ____u.   Close all windows.

2. **Shortcut problems**
    ____a.   Right-click the desktop and select **New** and then **Text Document**.
    ____b.   Accept the default name for the file.
    ____c.   Right-click the New Text Document and select **Copy**.
    ____d.   Right-click the desktop and select **Paste Shortcut**.
    ____e.   Double-click the shortcut and you will see *Notepad* viewing *New Text Document.tx*t.
    ____f.   Right-click the **New Text Document** (not the shortcut) and select **Cut**.
    ____g.   Double-click the **My Computer** icon.
    ____h.   Double-click on the **C:** drive.
    ____i.   Right-click in any blank space and select **Paste**.
    ____j.   Close the window.
    ____k.   Double-click the shortcut and record what happens in Table 44-3.
    ____l.   Close the window.
    ____m.   As before, go through **My Computer** and double-click on **C:**.

_____n.   Right-click on **New Text Document** and select **Delete**.
_____o.   Click on **Yes** to send it to the Recycle Bin.
_____p.   Close the window.
_____q.   Double-click the shortcut to **New Text Document. txt**. You will see a window similar to Figure 44-2. Click on the **Delete it** button to delete the shortcut.
_____r.   Right-click the **Recycle Bin** and click on **Empty Recycle Bin**.
_____s.   Confirm the file delete by clicking on the **Yes** button.

Figure 44-2: Problem with Shortcut

3.   Automatic restoration of Windows components
_____a.   From the desktop double-click the **My Computer** icon.
_____b.   Double-click on the **(C:\)** drive.
_____c.   Double-click the **Program Files** folder.
_____d.   If necessary, click on **Show Files** to view the contents of the folder.
_____e.   Double-click the **Netmeeting** folder.
_____f.   Right-click on **conf.exe** (the execution file for Net Meeting) and select **Rename**.
_____g.   Rename the program to **conf.exx** and press the **ENTER** key.
_____h.   You will get a Rename warning similar to Figure 44-3. Click on the **Yes** button.

Figure 44-3: Rename File Extension

_____i.   Wait approximately 10 seconds and record your observations about the folder's content in Table 44-4.

NOTE: The file conf.exe should be re-created at the bottom of the screen.

_____j.   Delete the file **conf.exx**.
_____k.   Right-click on one of the .dll files in the folder and delete it. Use **nmchat.dll**, for example.
_____l.   Wait 10 seconds and record your observations about the folder's content in Table 44-5.
_____m.   Close all windows.

4.   File type association
_____a.   From the Windows XP desktop double-click the **My Documents** icon.
_____b.   Click on the **File** menu and select **New** and then **Text Document**.
_____c.   Use the default _New Text Document.txt_ filename and open the document by double-clicking the icon.
_____d.   Type **This is a test** in the document.
_____e.   Close the document and click on the **Yes** button to save the changes.
_____f.   From the _My Documents Folder_ window, click on the _Tools_ menu and select **Folder Options**.
_____g.   Click on the **File Types** tab. You will see a window similar to Figure 44-4.

Figure 44-4: File Types

____h.　Look for the extension **TXT** by scrolling down in the *Registered file types* field.
____i.　Click on the **TXT** extension and record its File Type in Table 44-6.
____j.　A short explanation of the extension is located in the lower portion of the window. Record the name of the program that opens files with a TXT extension in Table 44-6.
____k.　Click on the **Change** button.
____l.　You will see a window similar to Figure 44-5. Select **Windows Picture and Fax Viewer** and click on the **OK** button.

Figure 44-5:
Open With Dialog Box

____m.　Click on the **Close** button to close the *Folder Options* window.
____n.　Double-click on **New Text Document.txt** in the *My Documents* folder.
____o.　Record your observations in Table 44-7.
____p.　Close all windows.
____q.　Open the **My Documents** folder once again.
____r.　Click on the *Tools* menu and select **Folder Options**.
____s.　Click on the **File Types** tab and look for the extension **TXT** by scrolling down in the *Registered file types* field.
____t.　Click on the **TXT** extension.
____u.　Click on the **Restore** button in the lower-right portion of the window, and the program that opens files with a .txt extension will be changed back to Notepad.
____v.　Close the *Folder Options* window.
____w.　Close the *My Documents* window.

5.　Invalid shortcut at startup
____a.　Right-click the desktop and select **New** and then **Bitmap Image**.
____b.　Right-click and drag the new bitmap image through the **Start** menu, over **Programs**, and down to **Startup**, and release the mouse button.
____c.　Select **Create Shortcut(s) Here** from the pop-up menu.

NOTE: You now have a shortcut to open the bitmap image at startup.

____d.　From the desktop delete the **New Bitmap Image.bmp** file.
____e.　Close all windows and restart the computer.
____f.　Record your observations when Windows has restarted in Table 44-8.
____g.　Close any open windows.

___h.   Click on the **Start** button and go to *Programs* and then *Startup*. Right-click on **Shortcut to New Bitmap Image.bmp** and select **Delete**.

___i.   Click on the **Yes** button to confirm the deletion.

TABLES

Table 44-1

Table 44-2

Table 44-3

Table 44-4

Table 44-5

Table 44-6

Extension	File type	Opens with

Table 44-7

Table 44-8

Feedback

LAB QUESTIONS

1. How many options for hiding files and folders were there in the *Folder Options/View* window?

2. How long did it take for Windows to automatically restore a file that you renamed?

3. What is a possible reason for receiving a *Problem with Shortcut* window?

4. What happens if a file's association somehow gets changed to the wrong program?

Network Diagnostics

OBJECTIVES

1. Add a Network Component.
2. Disable a Network Component.
3. Remove a Network Component.

Software

RESOURCES

1. PC-compatible desktop/tower computer system — Customer-supplied desktop/tower hardware system **OR** Marcraft Computer Repair Trainer **OR** suitable PC hardware trainer running Windows XP Professional
2. Windows XP Professional CD or access to the \SUPPORT\TOOLS directory on the CD

DISCUSSION

This lab covers the installation and use of the *netdiag* tool. We will also explore using the Tracert command, Ping, and ARP.

PROCEDURE

1. **Install and use NETDIAG**

____a. Login in as *administrator* with your password.

____b. Locate the *\SUPPORT\TOOLS* directory on the XP CD. Figure 45-1 illustrates a typical Explorer Window showing the *Tools* folder.

Figure 45-1: The Support/Tools Folder

_____ c.   Double-Click on **Setup** to launch the *Windows Support Tools Setup Wizard*. You will be presented the dialog box, as depicted in Figure 45-2. Click **Next** to begin the setup.

**Figure 45-2:
Windows Support
Tools Setup Wizard
Dialog Box**

Figure 45-3: End User License Agreement

_____ d.   Read the *End User License Agreement*, as shown in Figure 45-3, click **I Agree** and choose **Next** to continue.

_____ e.   Complete the *User Information* screen by entering your **Name** and **Organization**, then click **Next**. Figure 45-4 depicts the *User Information* dialog box.

Figure 45-4: User Information Dialog Box

Figure 45-5: Select An Installation Type

_____ f.   Figure 45-5 shows the *Select An Installation Type* dialog box. Choose **Complete** for the type of installation and click **Next**.

** If you choose *Typical* the network support tools will not be installed.**

____g.   Accept the default installation location, space providing, and click **Install Now**, as shown in Figure 45-6.

Figure 45-6: Destination Directory

____h.   Once the installation is complete, the *Completing the Windows Support Tools Setup Wizard* dialog box will be displayed, as shown in Figure 45-7. Select **Finish,** completing the installation.

Figure 45-7: Completing the Windows Support Tools Setup Wizard

____i.   Navigate the *Start/All Programs/Windows Support Tools/Support Tools Help* path to launch the *Help and Support Center*. This will display a dialog box similar to Figure 45-8.

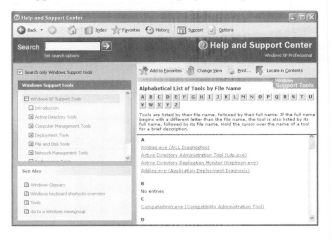

Figure 45-8: Help and Support Center for Windows Support Tools

___ j. Under the *Windows Support Tools* pane expand the options until **Netdiag.exe** is displayed. Double-click it and the right-pane will display information regarding this tool. Figure 45-9 illustrates the *Netdiag.exe Help & Information* screen 2.

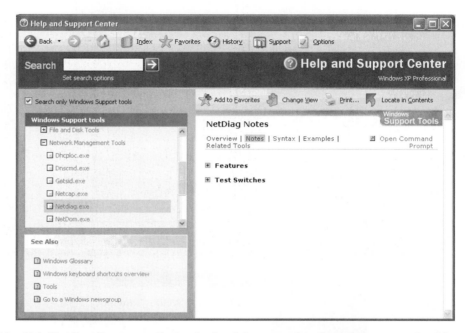

Figure 45-9:
Netdiag.exe Help &
Information Screen

___ k. Double-click **Netdiag Syntax** to display in the right pane what the proper syntax for this command is. Figure 45-10 shows the contents of the Netdiag Syntax pane.

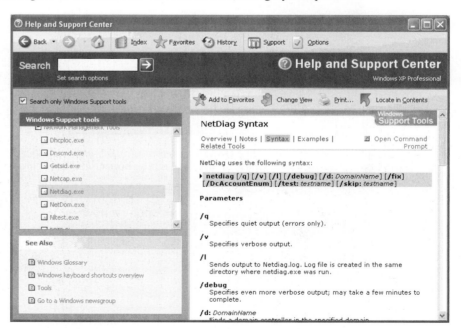

Figure 45-10:
Netdiag Syntax
Pane

___ l.   Locate the **Open Command Prompt** link, it's located in the upper right hand section of the *Netdiag Syntax* window, in red. Double-click it to launch the *CMD* prompt with the Netdiag tool. Figure 45-11 depicts the results of Open Command Prompt.

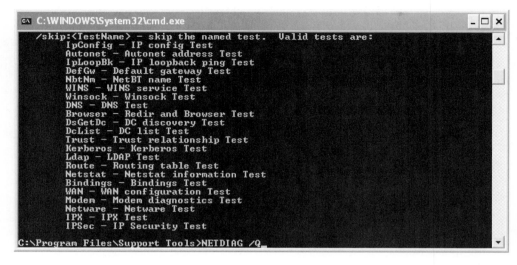

Figure 45-11: Open Command Prompt Results

___ m.   At the *command prompt* type **netdiag /Q**, as shown in Figure 45-12. Record the following settings in Table 45-1.

- IP Address
- Subnet Mask
- Global results
- IP Security test:

Figure 45-12: Netdiag /q Results

2. Use Tracert

____a. From the *command prompt* type **tracert Microsoft.com** and press **ENTER**. If you have a connection to the Internet you should see results similar to Figure 45-13.

Figure 45-13:
Tracert Command

____b. In Table 45-2, record the number of *Hops* it takes to get to Microsoft.com.

____c. In Table 45-3, record the first hop in the trace.

3. Use Ping

____a. From the *command prompt* type **ping** *enter the address of the first hop from step 14* and press **Enter**. Your results should be similar to Figure 45-14.

Figure 45-14:
Ping Command

____b. Record the following values in Table 45-4:

- Packets: Sent, Received, and Lost
- Approximate round trip times: Minimum, Maximum, and Average

4.   Use ARP

____a.   From the *command prompt* type **arp –a** and press **ENTER** to retrieve the information stored in the arp table. Figure 45-15 shows the arp table of our system, record your arp information in Table 45-5.

**Figure 45-15:
ARP Command**

TABLES

Table 45-1

IP Address:	
Subnet Mask:	
Global results:	
IP Security test:	

Table 45-2

Table 45-3

Table 45-4

Packets	
Sent:	
Received:	
Lost:	
Approximate Round Trip Times	
Minimum:	
Maximum:	
Average:	

Table 45-5

Internet Address:	
Physical Address:	
Type:	

Feedback

LAB QUESTIONS

1. What command would be used to display results that combine Ping and Tracert?

2. What is the correct switch to cause the Netdiag command to only display summary information?

3. What command is used to determine the current TCP/IP settings for all network adapters?

CHALLENGE

Using the NETDIAG command, redirect the results of the netdiag /debug command to a file called netdiag.debug. Locate the file and using Notepad, explore the contents of the file.

STAR
WARS

E P I S O D E III

The Making of
Star Wars
Revenge of the Sith

J. W. Rinzler

To Geneviéve, Sarah, & Judith

Photo credits: Keith Hamshere, John Knoll, Derryck Menere, Carl Miller, Tina Mills, Merrick Morton, Ralph Nelson Jr, David Owen, Paul Tiller, and Lisa Tomasetti, along with screen grabs from HD documentary footage by Tippy Bushkin.

Published in the United States by Del Rey Books, an imprint of The Random House Publishing Group, a division of Random House, Inc., New York.

Del Rey is a registered trademark and the Del Rey colophon is a trademark of Random House, Inc.

Library of Congress Cataloging-in-Publication Data
Rinzler, J. W.
Star wars, the making of episode III, revenge of the Sith / J.W. Rinzler.
p.   cm.
ISBN 0-345-43138-3 (hardcover: alk. paper) – ISBN 0-345-43139-1 (pbk.: alk. paper)
1. Star wars, episode III, revenge of the Sith (Motion picture) I. Title: Making of episode III, revenge of the Sith. II. Title: Revenge of the Sith. III. Title.

PN1997.2.S75R56 2005
791.43'72–dc22   2004061810

Printed in the United States of America

www.starwars.com
Del Rey Books website address: www.delreybooks.com

9 8 7 6 5 4 3 2 1

First Edition

I SALUTE YOU, JUN!

LUCAS BOOKS

DEL REY
Ballantine Books

Page 1: The Episode III teaser poster. Page 2: Industrial Light & Magic (ILM) composite image of George Lucas with computer-generated (CG) vehicles, planets, and creatures from Star Wars: Revenge of the Sith *(art directed by concept design supervisor Ryan Church; technical directed by Ryan Jones).* Page 3: A Boga (lizard-creature) animation reference sketch by ILM lead animator Glen McIntosh.
Page 4: (top left) Padmé with dagger by concept artist Iain McCaig; (left) sinkhole battle by concept design supervisor Erik Tiemens; (top right) hapless battle-droid storyboards by concept artist Derek Thompson; (above) Doodle "meeting sketch" of Nien Nunb by concept artist Warren Fu. Page 5: "Chicken-walker" by concept artist T.J. Frame.

Contents

Foreword

The *Star Wars* prequel trilogy has taken up more than my entire life for the last ten years. During the five years before George and I started work on it, during location shooting for *The Young Indiana Jones Chronicles*, I didn't live in the same place for more than two months at a time; in fact, my apartment in Prague had only a photo of a TV set cut out of a magazine taped to a wall. My daughters were playing with fluffy Yoda dolls.

But two things happened. In the extreme cold of a Jackson Hole, Wyoming, winter, George discovered that directing wasn't all bad. During our two-day shoot in December 1992—with Harrison Ford, who was playing a fifty-year-old Indiana Jones for an episode of *Young Indy*—George enjoyed himself so much that he decided he might direct *Star Wars: Episode I*. This decision didn't become final until 1993—the year digital technology came of age—but from that moment on, my life wasn't the same.

From 1995 to 2005, we've spent hundreds of millions of dollars, exposed millions of feet of film, recorded even more high-definition tape, shot over ten thousand setups, ate millions of catered meals, and drank literally thousands of bottles of wine in over a dozen countries. Now I have a permanent home with a genuine television and teenage daughters who lust after the real-life Darth Vader. Yet some things haven't changed: I'm working with essentially the same crew as the one I began with on *Young Indy*. I love working with them and shooting, and I love production. *This* book is a record of Episode III's entire production; *The Making of Star Wars: Revenge of the Sith* chronologically follows our story through its three-year cycle, and we've crammed into it as much as we could. I hope you enjoy it.

Rick McCallum
Skywalker Ranch, October 2004

✳ Introduction

The making of *Star Wars*: Episode III *Revenge of the Sith* really began when George Lucas first touched number 2 pencil to yellow legal pad in 1972. The following year, Lucas showed his treatment for *The Star Wars* to Alan Ladd Jr. at Twentieth Century Fox, who thought its author had potential. When an advanced print of Lucas's second feature, *American Graffiti* (1973), was smuggled onto the lot from Universal for Ladd's viewing–making it a true sneak preview–the deal was sealed. The contract between studio and writer-director was signed on August 20, 1973. The first *Star Wars* (1977) went on to become the phenomenon it still is today. Its sequels, *The Empire Strikes Back* (1980) and *Return of the Jedi* (1983), were also huge successes, and though Lucas directed neither, he was intimately involved with both, from the writing of the stories to the last frame of postproduction.

Following the completion of the trilogy, a period of non–*Star Wars* activity followed for Lucas–until he began the work that culminated with the theatrical release of the *Star Wars Trilogy Special Edition* (1997). The enormous positive reaction that greeted this re-release surprised everyone but the public, which had clearly been waiting to reappreciate these films. *Star Wars*: Episode IV *A New Hope* regained the title of the highest-grossing film ever, surpassing Steven Spielberg's *E.T.: The Extraterrestrial*. To mark the moment, Spielberg took out a page in *Variety* that showed E.T. crowning R2-D2 and the words "Dear George, Congratulations for renewing the most enduring motion picture in cinema history. Your pal, Steven."

Buoyed by his films' continuing popularity–and by the advances made in digital cinema–Lucas embarked in earnest on a vast ten-year project: the making of the *Star Wars* prequel trilogy. These films had actually been forming in his mind for some time, but Lucas had been patiently waiting until the technology was ready. Indeed, many of Lucas's companies–Industrial Light & Magic, the Computer Division, THX, and Skywalker Sound–had been working for years to advance the cause and techniques of digital tools. Nonlinear digital editing was one of his first major achievements. Lucas experimented himself with digital editing and visual effects, first with his TV series *The Young Indiana Jones Chronicles* (1992–94), then on the film *Radioland Murders* (1994), and finally with the *Special Edition*.

Above left: Producer Rick McCallum in the makeup department, Fox Studios, Sydney, Australia. Left: Concept art of Palpatine Leading Clone Troopers (or Rick's First Day of Production) by Church. Above: Hayden Christensen (Anakin Skywalker) in the Alderaan star cruiser (aka "Rebel blockade runner") corridor set in Sydney. Above right: Darth Vader's first complete costume fitting (Christensen, center) and from left: costume props supervisor Ivo Coveney, costume supervisor Nicole Young, author J. W. Rinzler, costume designer Trisha Biggar, CG artist David Weitzberg, and unidentified person. Right: (from left) George Lucas, president of Lucas Licensing Howard Roffman, and Rinzler review image printouts. Far right: "Alien costume 01 (Mustafar)" by concept artist Sang Jun Lee.

In Rick McCallum, whose collaboration with Lucas began on *Young Indy*, the director had found a producer whose independent-film mindset dovetailed perfectly with Lucas's documentarian work habits. McCallum helped recruit a core team of collaborators: production designer Gavin Bocquet, costume designer Trisha Biggar, and director of photography David Tattersall. The result of this confluence of people and technology was *Star Wars*: Episode I *The Phantom Menace* (1999) and Episode II *Attack of the Clones* (2002). The latter was also a historical milestone as it was the first film to be recorded digitally rather than on film.

In spring 2002, although everyone knew that the third prequel and last *Star Wars* film would show how Anakin Skywalker becomes Darth Vader and how the Empire would crush the spirit of the Republic, no one knew exactly how these events would come to pass nor what they'd look like. No one—not even Lucas.

In the following pages, the reader will discover just how organically these events came to be. Not many writers have had the opportunity to witness up close every stage of the making of a film on an almost daily basis. For this, thanks—enormous thanks—go to George Lucas and Rick McCallum. Rick enabled all of it to happen, and George has graciously allowed three years of eavesdropping. During these years, I attended nearly every art department meeting, traveled to Sydney for the filming, attended dailies and animation dailies at ILM, watched George direct in the animatics department, sat in on editing sessions, observed the pickups at Shepperton Studios, and so on. It's been an amazing apprenticeship, and I've met incredible people—all of whom without exception have provided insights that will be found in the following pages. I only hope I've done justice to this great cast and crew.

The point of all this creative witnessing has been to write a book that gives readers the feeling that they were genuinely present in the art department, on the sets, in the dressing rooms, at ILM—and seeing things as they happened. Events, conversations, breakthroughs, and tensions have all been recorded as they occurred in real time, chronologically, with the same lack of future sight that existed at the time the events were recorded.

J. W. Rinzler
Big Rock Ranch, October 2004

Left: Rough color script by Tiemens. Above: Enhanced image of Swiss Alps taken during recce (scouting trip) for possible Alderaan locations. Right: Kit Fisto battle gear by Thompson.

Brad Alexander
Senior Animatics Artist, Skywalker Ranch (SR)

Deborah Antoniou
Second Assistant Director, Australia (Aus)/England (Eng)

Roger Barton
Editor, SR

Trisha Biggar
Costume Designer, Aus/Eng

Colette Birrell
Art Department Coordinator, Aus

Michael Blanchard
Postproduction Technical Supervisor, SR

Gavin Bocquet
Production Designer, Aus

Jill Brooks
Visual Effects Producer, ILM

Ben Burtt
Editor/Sound Designer, SR

Ryan Church
Concept Design Supervisor, SR

Rob Coleman
Animation Director, ILM

Matt Connors
Head Scenic Artist, Aus

Ivo Coveney
Costume Props Supervisor, Aus

Fay David
Art Department Supervisor, SR

Dave Elsey
Creatures Shop Creative Supervisor, Aus/Eng

Colin Fletcher
First Assistant Director, Aus/Eng

Brian Gernand
Model-Shop Supervisor, ILM

Nick Gillard
Stunt Coordinator, Aus/Eng

John Goodson
Concept Model Maker, SR/Digital-Matte Department, ILM

Ian Gracie
Art Director, Aus

Dan Gregoire
Pre-Visualization Supervisor, SR

Roger Guyett
Visual Effects Supervisor, ILM

Greg Hajdu
Construction Manager, Aus

Jonathan Harb
Digital-Matte Painting Department Supervisor, ILM

Simon Harding
"B" Camera Operator, Aus

Phil Harvey
Art Director, Aus

Rebecca Hunt
Creatures Shop Supervisor, Aus/Eng

Alex Jaeger
Concept Artist, SR/Art Director, ILM

Stephen Jones
Production Supervisor, Aus

John Knoll
Visual Effects Supervisor, ILM

Euisung Lee
Senior Animatics Artist, SR

Janet Lewin
Visual Effects Producer, ILM

Jacqui Louez
Assistant to the Producer/Director, Aus

George Lucas
Writer-Director, SR

Aaron McBride
Art Director, ILM

Rick McCallum
Producer, SR

Calum McFarlane
"A" Camera Operator, Aus/Eng

Fred Meyers
High-Definition Supervisor, ILM

Carl Miller
Director of Photography, ILM

Michael Mooney
Assistant Costume Designer, Aus/Eng

Virginia Murray
Production Coordinator, Aus

Chris Neil
Dialogue Coach, Aus

Giles Nutggens
Director of Photography, Eng

Ardees Rabang
Assistant to the Producer, SR

Kathryn Ramos
Production Controller, SR

Denise Ream
Visual Effects Executive Producer, ILM

Richard Roberts
Set Decorator, Aus

Peter Russell
Supervising Art Director, Aus/Eng

David Tattersall
Director of Photography, Aus

Ty Teiger
Property Master, Aus/Eng

Jayne-Ann Tenggren
Script Supervisor, Aus

Erik Tiemens
Concept Design Supervisor, SR

Danny Wagner
Model Maker, ILM

Nicole Young
Costume Supervisor, Aus/Eng

Animatics Artists, SR
Dorian Bustamante
Eric Carney
Chris Edwards
Nathan Frigard
Barry Howell
Nick Markel
Hiroshi Mori
Greg Rizzi
Joshua Wassung

Concept Artists, SR
Robert Barnes
(and Sculptor)
T.J. Frame
Warren Fu
Sang Jun Lee
Stephan Martiniére
Iain McCaig
Michael Patrick Murnane
(and Sculptor)
Derek Thompson
Feng Zhu

Lead Animators, ILM
Scott Benza
Virginie d'Annoville
Tim Harrington
Paul Kavanaugh
Virgil Manning
Glen McIntosh
Jamy Wheless

Note: *For a complete list of cast and crew, and many short biographies of same, go to* **starwars.com.**

PART I

PREPRODUCTION

The Shadow Citadel of Creation

PROLOGUE: The Digital Script

"Cinema started out as a part of vaudeville," says writer-director George Lucas. "They took out the magic act and they put in a film, because it was like a big magic act. 'Look! Right here on our screen— a giant train, moving right toward you!' That was a big event.

"Science fiction also came into its own at the beginning of the twentieth century, as it matured from Jules Verne to George Orwell and other writers, and while the literature of science fiction and fantasy became much more sophisticated, it was extremely difficult to translate those books into cinema.

"So when I did a fantasy film, we were really bumping up against the ceiling of technology all the time, which made it very hard. I'm a strong believer of cinema as cinema—not as a literary medium and not as a musical medium and not as a theatrical medium—but cinema as the moving image. And so I was able to design a fantasy film and push the limits of the medium of the cinematic form just a tiny bit. But what I really wanted to do was much grander and much bigger and much more outrageous—but I knew that I couldn't do that. I could only do so much with the technology I had.

"So I've always been pushing that technology. I've always been thinking, 'Wouldn't it be great if we could do this or we could do that!' But most of the time, you would get stopped. You couldn't do a movie with twenty thousand extras; you wouldn't even think of writing a scene like that. But now you can do it.

"Now you can pretty much do whatever you want. You're in the same arena that writers are in. If you can write it, you can film it."

Puppet Yoda (above) in 1980's *The Empire Strikes Back*; digital Yoda (top) from *Attack of the Clones* in 2002. Opening spread: Duel on Mustafar by Ryan Church.

Seven Planets for Seven Battles

CHOTT EL JERRID, TUNISIA
THURSDAY, SEPTEMBER 7, 2000

George Lucas and crew are on location for *Star Wars:* Episode II *Attack of the Clones.* It is the 53rd day of the shoot. On the list of today's scenes is one described as "PAR-TIAL," which means that some elements will be added later–in this case, five years later, for Lucas and producer Rick McCallum have decided to shoot a part of Episode III now in order to avoid making an expensive return trip later.

Built on the salt flat of Chott el Jerrid, near the towns of Tozeur and Nefta, the set is described as "TATOOINE HOMESTEAD (MOISTURE FARM)," and one of the day's props is listed as a "newborn baby doll," which the Call Sheet refers to as "A.N. Other." So, on a very hot afternoon, actor Joel Edgerton (young Owen Lars) and Breeden Phillip (Obi-Wan Kenobi's body double) are called on to pretend it's three years after the events of Episode II and that it's the moment in which Jedi Knight Ben Kenobi hands farmer Owen an infant Luke Skywalker. Owen is to keep Luke far away from the machina-tions of his corrupted father, Anakin Skywalker–who has become the terrible Sith Lord known as Darth Vader.

According to today's Call Sheet, this scene takes up only one-eighth of a script page–one or two shots in the film. Yet it will take Lucas three years, quite a bit of hard work, and the creative participation of thousands to create a context for this brief but poignant moment.

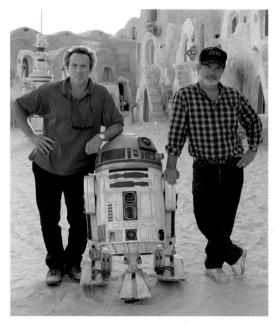

INDUSTRIAL LIGHT & MAGIC (ILM)
SAN RAFAEL, CALIFORNIA–APRIL 2002 (TWO YEARS LATER)

It's about one month before the theatrical release of Episode II. Following this morning's dailies, McCallum–sensing that something is in the air–suggests that concept design supervisors Ryan Church and Erik

From top: Breeden Phillip (Obi-Wan Kenobi's body-double) gives the infant Luke Skywalker to Joel Edgerton (young Owen Lars) for safekeeping in this Episode III sequence recorded during an Episode II location shoot. Producer Rick McCallum (left), director-writer George Lucas, and a familiar droid in Tunisia during a location shoot for The Phantom Menace *in 1997. Theirs is a working relation-ship that has lasted for more than fourteen years.*

Tiemens walk with Lucas among the non-descript buildings that house Industrial Light & Magic. After a few moments of chatting, as Church describes it, "George casually says to us, 'Oh, you guys, I want you to start thinking about seven planets–seven new planets that are completely different from each other–this is where the Clone Wars are happening. I just want you to think about that.' "

Church pauses while telling the story. "Well, this is something I've been thinking about since 1977, when I was kid, so I said to George, 'Oh, I think I've got some planets for you.' "

SKYWALKER RANCH (SR)
MARIN COUNTY, CALIFORNIA
THURSDAY, APRIL 25, 2002

The first Episode III art department meet-ing takes place a few days after Lucas's first instructions. Erik Tiemens, Ryan Church, art department supervisor Fay David, pre-visualization/effects supervisor Dan Gregoire, and producer Rick McCallum gather around a table to hear what Lucas has to say about the next *Star Wars* film–the last of the prequel tril-ogy and the third in the sextet.

Lucas's first story fragments are both embryonic and epic: Episode III will take place approximately three years after Episode II. At that time, the Clone Wars will be wrap-ping up, with seven battles raging on seven new planets. Each planet will have its own species, but the enemy armies will be made up of droids. Jedi Masters Kenobi, Windu, and Yoda are on different planets fighting for the Republic. We may see bounty hunter Boba Fett as a fourteen- or fifteen-year-old. We will visit Princess Leia's home planet of Alderaan; we may visit the Wookiee planet, Kashyyyk. And, Lucas says, because they've been at war for two or three years, vehicles need to be beat up, while clone troopers have added things to their armor to individualize it, based on where they've been fighting, similar to the way American troops did in Vietnam.

By meeting's end, Lucas has divulged just enough to provide the artists material to work on until the next gathering, and, for the next nine months, this will be the pattern. Indeed, for most of preproduction, the concept art department will be working blind–without a script–because

Anakin's Story So Far
A long time ago in a galaxy far, far away....

EPISODE I: THE PHANTOM MENACE

Anakin Skywalker is a nine-year-old slave living with his mother, Shmi, on the remote desert planet of Tatooine. One day while working in Watto's junk shop, Anakin encounters Qui-Gon Jinn, a Jedi Master and a great student of the living Force, who is traveling with Padmé Amidala, the young Queen of Naboo. Qui-Gon becomes convinced that little Annie is the chosen one—the being prophesized to bring balance to the Force. Annie's midi-chlorian count is staggering, and he can see things before they happen, which makes him the only human capable of piloting a Podracer. Consequently, Qui-Gon makes a wager with Watto: If Anakin wins the Boonta Eve Podrace, Watto will give him his freedom. Anakin triumphs and then bids a painful farewell to Shmi. Fortunately, he finds a new friend in Padmé.

Temporarily jubilant after his Podracing victory, little Anakin Skywalker (Jake Lloyd) sits on the shoulder of his would-be Jedi Master, Qui-Gon Jinn (Liam Neeson), and clasps the hand of his mother, Shmi (Pernilla August)...

Anakin's tutelage is tragically cut short, however, when Qui-Gon is killed by a Sith Lord named Darth Maul. The Jedi Master's dying wish is for his Padawan, Obi-Wan Kenobi, to take on Anakin as his apprentice.

EPISODE II: ATTACK OF THE CLONES

Ten years later, Anakin is an accomplished Padawan, though not yet a Jedi Knight. He's also a young man very much in love with Padmé. Because she is now a Senator targeted by unknown assassins, Anakin is assigned as her bodyguard—in part due to the influence of his political mentor, Supreme Chancellor Palpatine.

Hidden away at a Naboo lakeside retreat, Anakin and Padmé grow closer. But the young apprentice is tortured by nightmares in which his mother is suffering greatly. Padmé suggests that she accompany him to Tatooine to investigate. Once there, they discover that Shmi has married Cliegg Lars, a moisture farmer—and has been abducted by Tusken Raiders, the savage nomads who roam the desert wastelands. Anakin heads off alone to save her, but arrives too late: Shmi dies in his arms. Anakin gives in to his rage and slaughters the entire camp of Tusken Raiders, including its women and children. He returns to the Lars homestead and confesses to Padmé.

Shortly thereafter, Anakin receives an urgent message from his Master, Obi-Wan Kenobi, who is in danger on Geonosis. Padmé and Anakin decide to rescue him, but they, too, are taken prisoner by the rogue Jedi Count Dooku, leader of the powerful Separatists, who wish to secede from the Republic. Dooku decides to put them to death in the arena. Our heroes escape, however, and then lead a Jedi counterattack when reinforcements arrive.

Anakin and Obi-Wan pursue Dooku to a secret hangar, where he defeats them easily, cutting off Anakin's hand. But the most powerful of all Jedi—Master Yoda—arrives and saves them, forcing Dooku to flee.

On Coruscant, Dooku reports to his Sith Master, Darth Sidious, that all is going according to plan. Meanwhile, Anakin escorts Padmé back to Naboo, where, because it is against the rules of the Jedi Order, they marry secretly. Back on Coruscant, Obi-Wan, Jedi Mace Windu, and Yoda watch as thousands of clone troopers board Republic assault ships on their way to fight the Separatists in the Clone Wars....

...but a decade later, Anakin (Hayden Christensen) kneels at the grave of his mother, whom he was too late to save, while Qui-Gon's death has deprived him of his surrogate father.

there is no script, no treatment, no outline. "We never truly know what George is doing," explains McCallum, "but it's no different than Episode II, because we didn't know what he was doing on that one, either." Though this style of work begins in a relatively relaxed manner, there is pressure from the get-go. The costume and production design departments will need to begin building soon—the former in November, the latter in January—and that can't happen until Lucas signs off on finished concepts.

"Usually, no one would go off and spend millions of dollars without understanding what the very foundation of the film they're making is," McCallum adds. "But we break that very rule of film production. We do the reverse."

From the audience's point of view, the movies of the *Star Wars* prequel trilogy may seem to have a leisurely schedule, with three years to create each film. The reality is that each movie is enormously complicated. Not only does Lucas push people and technology to their limits, and beyond, but his schooling in the 1960s at the University of Southern California as an avant-garde documentary filmmaker-editor means that he makes his films in an unusual manner. Most filmmakers shoot a specific number of pieces and then turn them over to an editor with instructions on how to put them together. Lucas gathers material as would a documentarian, creating a massive crate filled with tons of pieces. Without instructions, he then slowly sorts through and assembles them with his editors, constantly revising, adding, and taking away as he goes.

This approach has significant practical consequences. One is the liberty of imagination it allows the concept artists, who begin unfettered by words. Another consequence is a more realistic, if longer, production schedule. "I'm shooting next summer for sixty days, and I shoot the following March for ten days, and I shoot that October for five days," Lucas says. "And then when I go to do the looping in London, I may shoot for a couple more

days—and it's in all the actors' contracts. It's in the budget. It's planned for. That's the way I make movies—as opposed to a lot of people who shoot the whole movie in one go and cut it all together, and then the studios say, 'Well what about this, what about that?'

"And so they have to call the actors back and they have to make new deals—but then the film's going over budget and everybody perceives it as being in trouble. And it's just silly. Why not just accept the inevitable at the very beginning? I started out as a documentary filmmaker, so I'm very used to shooting, cutting material together, going out and shooting some more, cutting it together, and creating it out of nothing. You have a vague idea of what your subject is going to be, but the actual story evolves as you deal with real people and real life. You don't quite know what you're going to get."

FRIDAY, JUNE 7, 2002

Light-years away from Hollywood, Skywalker Ranch is located north of San Francisco, on the far side of the Golden Gate Bridge. But from the style of its signage to its remoteness, the ranch has a single-mindedness and late-nineteenth-century aesthetic that align it more with the small towns along the sparsely populated northern California coastline than with the densely populated cities to the south.

Lucas bought the greater part of his property back in 1978, but construction wasn't complete until 1987, and only a very small part of the sixty-five-hundred-acre ranch has been developed. The ranch includes a few large houses, a Technical Center (which houses Skywalker Sound and the three-hundred-seat Stag Theatre), a fitness center, and a guest inn. The Main House was built to resemble a large Victorian manor, with walls of redwood burl, ebony, and rosewood.

The origins of Skywalker Ranch are multiple. Lucas has said that he is a "frustrated architect" and that he simply likes to build. Another motivat-

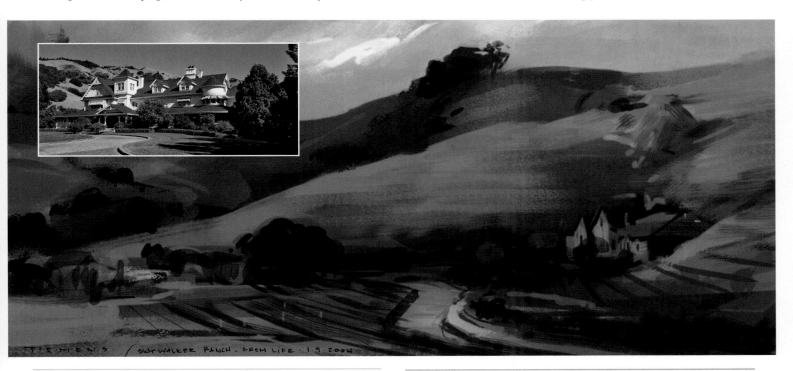

Inset: The Main House on Skywalker Ranch. Below: Episode III concept design supervisor Erik Tiemens painted this view of the Technical Building, where Skywalker Sound is located on the ranch. In order to keep his skills sharp and his vision active, Tiemens often sketches outdoors.

Thursday, May 16: *Star Wars: Episode II Attack of the Clones* is released.
Wednesday, May 29: *Attack of the Clones* passes the $200 million mark.

ing factor was his desire to create a place where filmmakers could work in a suitably relaxing environment—the inspiration for which can be traced back to Lucas's student days at USC and his early years working with Francis Ford Coppola to establish American Zoetrope. In fact, Skywalker Ranch is Lucas's second locale of this sort: the first was his own home, where at one time or another, throughout the 1970s, Walter Murch, Phil Kaufman, Michael Ritchie, and Matthew Robbins had offices. Today Skywalker Ranch is where the likes of Steven Spielberg, Clint Eastwood, James Cameron, and Robert Redford come to hone their films.

This is also where Lucas will work with his Episode III producer, concept artists, sound designers, and editors. As such, though it is a nonspeaking part, the atmosphere and design of Skywalker Ranch will have a major role in the making of the movie.

Within the art department, a trio of concept artists—Church, Tiemens, and Robert Barnes—have begun meeting with Lucas every Friday, a routine that will continue over the next year as they design and perfect the film's characters, cities, vehicles, and costumes. In a *Star Wars* film, nearly everything has to be built from the ground up, from control panels to

gloves to light fixtures, so the number of artists will increase as preproduction continues.

At today's gathering, Lucas examines photographs of exotic locales and interesting architecture, which are auditioning for the role of "planet." On the whole, though, he isn't inspired by anything shown. Church says, "He picked just a few things . . . I think he was saying, 'This has all been seen before.' George really pushed us a lot, but we quickly learned there were no drawbacks to being open with him."

Unused art from previous *Star Wars* films is also dusted off. The idea for a sinkhole planet originated in 1976, when legendary production illustrator Ralph McQuarrie first drew it, and Lucas approves it for this movie. "The idea is to have clone troopers rappel down into it," he explains. Lucas also likes Church's idea for a bridge planet, and says that Kashyyyk, the home planet of the Wookiees, will almost definitely be in the picture. An ice planet and a mining planet are considered, and Lucas proposes a ring planet.

They then examine artwork for "Mufasta," the volcano planet. Joe Johnston—a veteran *Star Wars* trilogy concept artist and now a director—recalls, "When we were doing *Star Wars,* I remember I had done a series of sketches of Vader's home, and there was a sea of lava his house looked out on [. . .]. But before we got too far, George said we would save this for somewhere down the line."

"These are old, old, old. Mufasta's been around a long time," George says. "I've always had this set piece: the end between Obi-Wan and Anakin. I knew that's where this movie was going to end up. It's all this volcanic land, with lava shooting up, so it's almost monochromatic in its red-and-blackness. I've had that image with me for a long time."

Lucas ends the meeting by saying, "The first ten minutes are going to be a huge spectacle. You're not going to know what is going on, other than it's the Clone Wars." He also encourages the artists with what will become the guiding principle of this first conceptual art phase: "Now is the time to go way out there, to be as wild as possible!"

TUESDAY, JUNE 11, 2002

Within Lucasfilm resides the production company that makes the *Star Wars* films: JAK Films, Inc. (The name was formed from the initials of Lucas's three children: Jett, Amanda, and Katie.) The JAK art department is located in a beautiful, if somewhat cramped, attic on the grounds of Skywalker Ranch. The concept artists occupy about a quarter of a space that also houses the animatics department, a small photography studio, shelves filled with art reference books, a kitchenette, one sunny office atop a short flight of stairs, and two bathrooms—one with a bath-shower for those long nights, and another with a sign over the toilet that reads DOOKU'S THRONE ROOM.

A few of the walls are brick, as chimneys from fireplaces below make their way toward the roof. It can be a very light space, but some darker sections are lit only by luminous computer screens. Sculptures of spacecraft and aliens sit on many desks, while drawings, paintings, and photographs of characters and environments are pinned up on nearly all available wall space. At one end of the animatics department sits a great old cast-iron Verona stove manufactured by the Wehrle Company of Newark, Ohio.

Left: Tiemens's sinkhole planet, as inspired by Ralph McQuarrie's Crevasse City (inset). Above left: Superimposed on Church's June 12 Jedi starfighter concept are Lucas's sketched changes to the cockpit, which give it more of TIE fighter look in Church's revised sketch (above right). Right: In the Skywalker Ranch art department are (from left) Lucas, communications director Lynne Hale, McCallum, and production designer Gavin Bocquet.

At today's short meeting, another planet is approved as a concept: crystal world. Art department supervisor Fay David is just back from vacationing in Thailand, where she saw Bangkok's Episode II premiere—projected digitally. "That's good," Lucas says. "Because that means that all over the world, they're getting it." He goes on to say he had a somewhat contentious magazine interview about digital filmmaking. McCallum becomes incensed by what he hears and leaves to take care of a few things. A few minutes later, George asks, "Where did Rick go?" Fay points down the hall and says, "He stormed off that way . . ."

THURSDAY, JUNE 13, 2002

Production designer Gavin Bocquet, at producer McCallum's request, is making a "surprise" visit. When Lucas enters, Bocquet says, "Hello. I'm just passing through." However, Bocquet's voyage here—like many to come—has a twofold purpose: to give him an opportunity to see the design directions the film is already taking, and to remind everyone that production is out there, waiting . . . The meaning of Bocquet's visit, and future head-of-department pop-ins, is always clear to Lucas. As McCallum points out, "The one thing that George does deal with at a certain level is guilt."

Lucas and Bocquet quickly reminisce about how Episode II was supposed to be "smaller" than Episode I, but actually ended up being bigger in terms of the number of sets built. "Well," jokes Lucas, "Episode III will be 'smaller' still." Turning their attention to a Jedi starfighter concept, Lucas explains that the craft is transitional. They talk about its form, how the guns should work, how much they'll have to build, and how much of it will be digital. Rick says he'd like production to have three sets to design by November, but Lucas says that they won't "start these guys till March [2003]—six weeks is plenty." Rick would also like to have concept artist and key costume designer Iain McCaig—a veteran of prequels I and II—join the department by July, but Lucas asks, "What's he going to design—upholstery?"

The tenor of this exchange between Lucas and McCallum is typical of these preshooting months, but they know each other far too well to mistake the intentions of the other. Lucas will take the time he needs to write, and McCallum will continue to push for the time he feels production needs—but Rick is the first to point out that George always responds when he manifests a certain level of need. "With some directors, communication can be a problem because their egos get in the way. But George is more understanding—he understands the process. And he knows that I will never bug him until I really need the information."

As the meeting comes to an end, Lucas again exhorts the artists: "Expand our universe. Expand our weapons—push your imaginations." Turning to Bocquet, he estimates that there will be sixteen hundred visual effects shots for Episode III. Small talk turns to what exactly will push Anakin to the dark side. "It'll be Padmé," George says. "She'll get so angry at him for not picking up his socks."

and English literature. "It was after Vietnam and I didn't have to worry about getting drafted. I was finishing school and didn't know what to do." Although Rick at one time wanted to be a *nez* (nose) in the perfume industry, a summertime job as a part-time office assistant for filmmakers James Ivory and Ismail Merchant offered direction. "There was something immediate about the life of a film."

By the time he'd graduated, McCallum had worked on three Ivory-Merchant movies: *Savages* (1972), *Autobiography of a Princess* (1975), and *The Wild Party* (1975). He then had an opportunity to work for ABC News in Paris, where he discovered another dimension to production. "The assistant cameraman got very sick with food poisoning," Rick says, "so I had to help the cameraman that day—and I saw a whole other aspect of making film. I liked the set. I liked the adrenaline, the long hours, the connections you have with people. There were girls."

He knew now what he wanted to do for a living. Returning to New York City, he enrolled at the American Film Institute, where McCallum discovered that he had other talents. "I realized that my skills putting a short film together were better than my skills working with an actor. I found out that I could actually convince the crew to work for twenty-four hours. I got the locations easy. Then John Frankenheimer and I met. We got along very well and he hired me as an assistant director [on *The French Connection II* (1975), *Black Sunday* (1977), and *Prophecy* (1979)]. Then, when I was twenty-four, I met Dennis Potter."

Already a well-known scribe in his native England, Potter offered McCallum his first position as executive producer, on *Pennies from Heaven* (1981). "It was a huge financial disaster. It was such a disaster, I couldn't get another job." Seeing McCallum's predicament, Potter invited him to the United Kingdom, where

---

Rick McCallum, the producer of the *Star Wars* prequel trilogy, is American but went to school in Europe. He returned to the United States to attend Columbia University, where he studied German, French,

A Tiemens concept painting a gunship (above) and Mufasta (top), the volcano planet, which was originally envisioned by Joe Johnston (above middle). McCallum (top right) during the shooting of a Young Indiana Jones Chronicles *episode. Inspired by a* Star Wars Galaxy *trading card by Al Williamson (right), Lucas requests a lizard-dragon. Robert E. Barnes supplies a concept (above right) with Anakin astride the beast.*

the climate was much more to the expatriate's liking. "The experience was totally different from working in the studio system. And I said to myself, *Wait a second. Here I control my destiny.* In America, you don't. It's too power-centric. If I did a studio film and pissed off the star, I'd be off the picture in a second."

McCallum went on to produce Potter's *DreamChild* (1985) and executive produce his BBC TV series *The Singing Detective* (1986). He also produced director Nicolas Roeg's *Castaway* (1987) and *Track 29* (1988). It was on the set of *DreamChild,* which was being filmed at Elstree Studios, that Rick first met George Lucas, who happened to be visiting the nearby set of Walter Murch's *Return to Oz* (1985), which Lucas was executive producing. According to McCallum, George seemed almost envious of his small crew, because *Oz* was more of a traditional setup, with a relatively large crew.

As the years passed, McCallum became dissatisfied. "I made ten films in England and though they were all good, all of them were unsuccessful. By the time I was thirty-four, it was getting harder and harder to make the movies, to get the money, to get distributed–and that's when I met George again." Lucas was in London looking for a producer for his upcoming TV series *The Young Indiana Jones Chronicles,* and longtime associate Robert Watts reintroduced him to McCallum. "I said I needed someone that could do an American TV series, very fast-paced and difficult," Lucas explains, "and he brought these people in and one of them was Rick. He was just a great find. That's the way it works–it's just like casting." Rick, however, adds a caveat to the story: "I thought *Young Indy* would be an interesting transition from personal filmmaking to making something that was a little more commercial. Little did I know that George wanted to take a very commercial idea and do a very small, independent TV series."

The two went on to do *Radioland Murders* (1994), *Star Wars Trilogy Special Edition* (1997), and the first two prequels. Considering the enormous pressures of the business, theirs is one of the more durable director-producer relationships. "The great thing about Rick is he can do the impossible," George remarks. "If I say I don't want to shoot something tomorrow, or I want to do something else, he'll say, 'Okay,' work all night, move it all around–and it will get done." Rick describes their relationship as "nonverbal" and goes on to say, "Film is a director's medium. Television is a producer's medium. Working with George is a George medium. I have to be able to exhaust all the possibilities in my own imagination, and in everyone else's imagination, to achieve what he wants. And he needs someone like me to enable him to get it in the least dramatic way. Because he wants it easy, he wants it flexible. He wants to be able to do whatever he wants–at a cost that nobody else can compete with–because, at the end of the day, he's paying for it."

FRIDAY, JUNE 21, 2002

As usual, pre-visualization (or "animatics") supervisor Dan Gregoire is at today's meeting to get an idea of what's coming down the pipeline, though his department won't start working on the movie until later in the process. McCallum is in Japan this week for Episode II's premiere, and for talks with Fujinon and Sony on digital cameras and lenses.

Lucas begins by looking at new drawings and digital paintings that have been laid out on the table by Church, Tiemens, and Barnes. The latter is one of only a few to weather the entire prequel trilogy. But despite the long hours and stress, he's not complaining. "I had my own audio business after high school," Barnes says. "The resulting experience was so harrowing that I knew I had to do something that I loved for a living if I was going to be spending so much time doing it–and that's where design came in."

Going through the artwork quickly, Lucas makes comments and approves a half a dozen designs. Looking at one drawing of a round, metallic droid, he says, "Not enough character." He moves on to concept drawings from the previous *Star Wars* films–the last of the old art–and picks twenty-two of them.

Lucas then mentions that he'd like a lizard creature for Anakin to ride in the film. He's thinking of making it into a bronze statue that would be hoisted on top of the big rock that resides alongside the road to Skywalker Ranch B, which is nearing completion (Ranch B will be renamed Big Rock Ranch a few months later).

After the short meeting, Lucas mentions his imminent trip to Japan, where he'll join McCallum. "There's going to be seven hundred and fifty journalists."

"Does each one get a question?" Tiemens asks.

"If they do, I'm never coming back."

Concept design supervisors Erik Tiemens (*Forrest Gump,* 1994; *Star Trek: Voyager,* 1995) and Ryan Church (*War of the Worlds,* 2005) both attended the Art Center in southern California, and both labored at ILM on *Frankenstein*—a computer-generated film that was ultimately canceled—where McCallum saw their "fantastic" work. He consequently recruited them to help finish Episode II, and they've worked at the ranch ever since. Apart from Lucas, McCallum, and a few others, they will labor the longest on Episode III—more than three years. "One's Rembrandt," according to Lucas, "and one's Bierstadt"—Church and Tiemens, respectively.

"I remember on Episode II, when we were first bringing them on," recalls Fay David, "they had worked together on *Frankenstein,* so I think they had already established a rapport. They worked very, very well together. Ryan has a strong industrial design background and Erik brings to the plate a strong fine-art background, and I think the two complement each other."

about giving it up during his first year at Cal State Long Beach. "I had to make a decision," he explains. "Did I want to pursue aviation art or aviation as a pilot? It was winning a scholarship at Art Center that made the decision for me." Nevertheless, he kept up the piloting. "I was about to do my solo cross-country—I was probably weeks from taking my FAA exam—when *Star Wars* came along. One of the things that attracted me to *Star Wars* was the aviation side." Working with Lucas was another plus: "When I first met George, I was impressed with how down-to-earth and informal the meeting was.

"But when he says 'I want this or that'—it happens."

July 1 & 10, 2002

Despite working long days and nights on *Peter Pan* (2003) in Australia, concept artist Iain McCaig (*Terminator 2: Judgment Day,* 1991) is now dedicating his few spare hours to Episode III. He is also talking costumes via telephone with ILM artist Sang Jun Lee (*Men in Black II,* 2002; *The Hulk,* 2003), called Jun, who is, reportedly, thrilled at the prospect of working on Episode III. Jun will do some creature designs as a tryout; if George likes them, he'll be given more to do.

At the next two very short art department meetings, model maker John

Tiemens concurs: "I thrive off art history. Things get stale if you're self-referential. But you can drink from that cup—two thousand years of art . . . When I first met George, he showed me binders of what he likes in landscapes, and that put my imagination at full tilt. I've found that the more I've painted, the more of a rapport we've had. We don't have to talk it out."

Tiemens grew up in Santa Cruz, California. "I've liked drawing since I was a kid. It was just one of those things where the other kids stopped drawing and I didn't. I had a very perceptive mother in that she encouraged my talent. I was also very lucky to get a great art teacher, Katie Harper, at Santa Cruz High. In my senior year, she happened to know someone who was over at Games [Lucas's early video game company], back in 1987. So myself and a couple friends came up to the ranch and had lunch and a little tour. After that, I always thought at the back of my mind, *Wouldn't it be great to work here one day?*"

Ryan Church also started drawing at an early age—but was thinking

Goodson—another prequel veteran—shows Lucas a Jedi starfighter maquette, and freelancer Stephan Martiniére's crystal planet artwork is examined.

Friday, July 19, 2002

The meetings are beginning to have a pattern. Digital paintings of environments and droids are pinned to three-by-five-foot foam core boards and lit by soft lights. Any work that can't be posted—models, artwork in binders, maquettes—is placed on a table directly facing the door through which Lucas always arrives. He reviews the table material first, then the boards.

Top left: Concept design supervisors Ryan Church and Erik Tiemens. The former created a Clone Wars scene on the bridge planet (above), while the latter painted a battle scene on the floor of a sinkhole (top right). The tank is based on a Joe Johnston Star Wars Trilogy concept (middle right), which Lucas has reapproved for Episode III.

Almost always dressed in a plaid shirt under a dark sweater, blue jeans, and white sneakers, Lucas uses two stamps while examining the artwork: OK and FABULOUSO (sic). The former is used to approve a concept for further exploration; the latter is used almost not at all. On *Attack of the Clones,* only a reported four works received FABULOUSOS—Lucas's shorthand for "Don't change a thing; I like it exactly the way it is."

In attendance today are Church, Tiemens, Goodson, David, and first-time attendee Jun. As usual, they are getting last-minute artwork printed and adding final touches to sculptures. Also as usual, there is a bit of tension as the door downstairs is heard to open and shut, the audio cue that Lucas is on his way upstairs. He enters the attic, and the meeting begins.

Goodson, who will be taking a short sabbatical to work on *Terminator 3* (2003), has made a small wooden model of the next-generation Naboo starship. Picking up the model for the new Jedi starfighter, which is looking more and more like a TIE fighter, Lucas gives it the final okay.

A few minutes later, McCallum comes in. "Any okays?" he asks.

"Lots of okays," George responds.

Accompanying Rick is a baseball-capped mystery guest, who draws curious looks from the group. When McCallum spots the approved starfighter, he asks if they'll need to put a real pilot in it. When Lucas answers yes, he asks Goodson to build a model of the cockpit, which will eventually serve as the basis for Gavin Bocquet's full-scale version.

"We're shooting already!" McCallum says.

New paintings include dramatic images of clone troopers rappelling down sinkholes, and after Lucas approves a few more pieces, Rick introduces Jun, who will be working primarily on costume concepts. "I come from South Korea," Jun says. "I drew as a kid, but my parents were not rich. In Asia, you need money if you're going to study art, so people were pushing me to learn computer programming, because you make more money doing that. In South Korea, if you're male, you have to go into the army; so I went into the army for two and a half years and thought about what I wanted to do—and decided to come here. I moved in 1995 when I was twenty-five. When I was a child, *Star Wars* really inspired me. The early *Art of Star Wars* books were very popular. So the first time I met George, I was really nervous, really dry in the mouth."

McCallum's mystery guest turns out to be Ron Fricke, acclaimed documentary filmmaker (*Baraka,* 1992) and cinematographer (*Koyaanisqatsi,* 1983; *Megalopolis*). It's been decided that the kind of material Fricke can gather for Episode III, by traveling to certain key locations and shooting them for use as background plates, will save time and, Rick says, add "the clouds George has always wanted."

The pace of the work is accelerating as the growing number of concept artists continue to work off the ideas Lucas provides. Conceptual researcher David Craig is also employed to unearth esoteric images, books, and films. "He's special, unbelievable—an artist in his own right," McCallum says of Craig.

The artists bounce off these and additional reference material supplied by the Lucasfilm Research Library. Lucas, in turn, is sometimes taken by the artists' designs. Essentially it's a series of inspirational melodies with the director-writer as conductor. Still, the unofficial deadlines are looming. By end of the year, most of the interior design concepts need to be finalized so that Bocquet and his team can start building in Sydney, Australia, where principal photography is scheduled. In addition, this time around Lucas and the concept art team are determined to have environments nailed down so that Director of Photography (DP) David Tattersall will have more to go on cinematographically, and not be stuck lighting for bluescreen without any reference.

Above all, there is a general feeling of excitement. For the artists, this film represents the culmination of all the creativity ever poured into the *Star Wars* galaxy.

FRIDAY, JULY 26, 2002

Lucas is running late. His son, Jett, has had a minor scooter accident. During the wait, conversation turns to the impending transition from Skywalker Ranch A to Skywalker Ranch B, where the business divisions of Lucasfilm will be moving in a month.

When Lucas enters, he explains the accident, saying that someone waved at Jett, who hit a speed bump while waving back. "I did the same thing once on a skateboard," Rick comments. "She was so beautiful, I waved, hit a manhole cover, and broke my arm."

Lucas turns to the business at hand, and approves Goodson's Jedi starfighter cockpit interior. He turns away from another more organic concept, saying, "I've never been a fan of bioships." Next he contemplates a drawing of a floating droid, then turns it upside down. "Now it's okay," he says and stamps it.

While reviewing paintings of planet environments, Lucas advises Tiemens and Church to "stay away from red, except for Mufasta." He also cautions against one rather dark painting. "That's what a regular movie would do. We have to be more careful," he says, going on to explain that most productions would use the shadows to save time (and money), lighting only the center of the set.

Next on the agenda: Jun's costume designs for the tentatively titled "lemur people." Though Lucas would like something "a bit more graceful," he okays a couple. "Two out of three," McCallum says, "not bad!" Lucas

---

Monday, August 19: Except for JAK, all of Lucasfilm moves from Skywalker Ranch into its new facility—Big Rock Ranch: a multistory Frank Lloyd Wright-style building.

FABULOUSO

OK

then turns to the conceptual lizard with Anakin on its back. "Work on the eyes," he suggests. "And add a plume, maybe, or a fan like a peacock's."

Afterward, he returns to the environments and—to everyone's surprise—grabs the FABULOUSO stamp and uses it on two paintings: one of the sinkhole planet and one of the crystal planet.

"When they draw something and George approves it," McCallum observes, "sometimes I have to quickly go to Rob [Coleman, animation director], and ask him, 'Can you do this?' And then—if it's feathers for the lizard—I might have to go back to George and say, 'Can we not make it feathers?'"

As art department supervisor, Fay David has to not only keep the department organized and hire freelancers, but also interface with George and Rick while fielding queries and requests posed by the various production heads. "Fay is the backbone of the department," says Church. She is also the only woman in a predominantly male atmosphere, but says it's not difficult being the "den mom." "It's not just because she's smart," McCallum adds. "It's who she is—she's one of the key musicians in this jazz ensemble."

Fay David grew up in southern California, but because her father was in the navy they moved every couple of years. Her mother had a habit of waking her up in the middle of the night to watch John Wayne movies, like *The Sands of Iwo Jima*. Following her graduation from college, David moved to northern California and applied for a job at ILM. They were starting to ramp up for Episode I and needed production assistants. She was hired, and one of her first brief shows was Clint Eastwood's *Space Cowboys* (2000). A couple of years later, she applied for the art department coordinator position at JAK. After interviewing with McCallum and production controller Kathryn Ramos, David was hired for Episode II.

"You always hear that creative types are difficult to work with, but there were no egos," Fay says. "People were happy to share their ideas, and got along really well—and in very stressful situations. When you're under deadline, it's very easy to lose your temper, but that didn't happen once—instead, there was a lot of laughter coming from the back room."

From top left (counterclockwise): Lucas stamps a painting OK; Tiemens has a late-night discussion with concept researcher David Craig (right). "Nearly every day for ten years, George has been directing the designers," Craig says, "and they do drive the engine. Star Wars *films are returning some of the storytelling to the designers"; art department supervisor Fay David, in addition to many other tasks, keeps McCallum abreast of all art department developments; concept artist Sang Jun Lee at work; a Church painting of the Wookiee planet Kashyyyk, partially inspired by McQuarrie's early work (inset); concept artist Feng Zhu and one of his droid concepts; two lemur creatures by Jun.*

As these weekly meetings accumulate, Tiemens, Church, Jun, et al., are quite conscious of the learning process taking place. "George always goes for distilling the intent of the designer," Church says, "while the designer often becomes too engrossed in the details."

These meetings are also growing in attendance. Apart from the concept artists, there are often animatics artists, a representative from LucasArts (the video game arm of the company), and a documentary crew—between ten and twenty extra people on any given day—in a setting that is already cramped. After jump-starting this particular meeting—the artists thought he was going to arrive later in the day—Lucas explains that, to avoid repetition, the Wookiee environment shouldn't be like that of the Ewoks.

It's the final gathering before George leaves on his first vacation since starting work on Episode II three years earlier. McCallum departed for Croatia and Sarajevo, Bosnia, two days ago. As Lucas goes out the door, on his way to Canada, he turns and says, "This will be my last time off before three years straight on Episode III." In fact, during at least part of his vacation, he'll be working on the script for *Indiana Jones IV* (and he, like McCallum, has been working on

the prequel trilogy nonstop since 1995).

The art department may have a seventh member. For a trial period of two weeks, Feng Zhu has been hired as a freelancer to execute some "hard-core industrial designs." "One day I got the call from Fay to do some test art. Droids," Feng says. "The assignment was to do a bunch of droids from different planets and then put them in front of George to see how he responds."

"Are we ready this time?" Lucas asks as he opens the door. It's 4 P.M. "You came too early last time," Fay says.

"Well, Jane [Bay, his executive assistant of twenty-five years] swears the meeting was for three [o'clock]."

It's a smaller group than last time, and the room is overheated. The first board is of droids; the second is more environments; the third is Kashyyyk, the Wookiee planet. Lucas approves a flying catamaran for the latter. He then recommends that they "try and get Alderaan to look a little more futuristic." As Lucas warms to the subject, he explains that "the environment's buildings should be culturally similar, but not completely unified"—because thousands of architects would've worked on them over the millennia.

The meeting breaks up as McCallum and Lucas sit down for a conference call with costume designer Trisha Biggar, in

London, and Iain McCaig, in Australia. Like Bocquet's earlier visit, this call is somewhat designed to raise the specter of the script. Still, Lucas greets Biggar with, "Well, we can talk about the costumes, but it's hard to discuss the script. I know the story, but . . ."

Later McCallum points out that, while most directors work solely with a production designer, whose concept artists report back to him, Lucas prefers to work directly with the artists before attacking the script in earnest. "These preliminary visuals serve as inspiration for writing, more than anything else," he says. "But the minute George makes a decision in the art department, I relay that information to Trisha, Gavin, and David. The level of commitment to communication is tremendous. Without it, even at this early stage, the process would break down completely."

Although he predicts that the final script won't be completed for a year, McCallum reveals that principal photography is presently scheduled to start on Wednesday, June 25, 2003, at Fox Studios, Sydney, Australia.

FRIDAY, SEPTEMBER 6, 2002

Because a rhythm is developing among the artists and in their relationship with Lucas, the atmosphere is markedly more relaxed than at previous meetings. Individual artists are also developing their own internal rhythms. "Usually I drive back from LA [on Sundays] for five hours on Highway Five," Church says, "just sitting there listening to movie soundtracks, Wagner operas, and inspiring, beautiful music. I have a little tape recorder, and these whole images come into my head and I really get into it. So I just come in Monday morning, play it all back, and draw out ten or twelve ideas. The top six or seven make it to the end of the week. It's a great way to work."

On the table today are about thirty-five binders, labeled CORUSCANT, LEMURS, ALDERAAN, PADMÉ, MUFASTA, CORPORATE ALLIANCE, BRIDGEWORLD, KASHYYYK. Each is filled with art that has been approved for that world, species, or character. However, there are also folders marked MISCELLANEOUS VEHICLE/COSTUME/PLANET. The plan is to ask George to decide where these miscellaneous artworks fit into the movie, which represents another roundabout way of getting him to talk about the script.

When Lucas arrives, there's an initial discussion about the still-nameless ring planet; he says the main planet is made of gas and the ring architecture should be more of a "mishmash"—an international space station that each generation has kept adding to. Alderaan, he says, should be a Switzerland-like setting, but with cities—not villages—nestled among green alps: "An incredible technological event in the middle of the countryside. Very concentrated. Ultramodern."

He looks at a number of Jun's creature sketches and remarks of one, "I don't know what it is, but it looks good." As they sit down to discuss the folders, Lucas asks, "What's this?"

"Well, we were wondering if you'd like to organize these," Fay offers.

"No. We can look at them again, but that's it."

"Nice try," Rick chimes in.

FRIDAY, SEPTEMBER 13, 2002

Outside it's very hot, and in the art department an air conditioner is laboring very hard, making it difficult to hear. John Goodson is back, his stint on *Terminator 3* finished. He's been working at home on a larger-

---

scale Jedi starfighter. It's a beautiful model, about a foot long and eight inches at its widest. Goodson has known since the age of five that he wanted to work in film—ever since watching an episode of *Lost in Space* and being sure that if he could open the back of his TV set, he'd be able to get a hold of the *Jupiter 2*.

Again, there's some confusion as to when the meeting is supposed to start. Depending on whether it was 4 or 4:30 P.M., Lucas arrives either twenty or fifty minutes late. Upon entering, he says, "Sorry," looks at Goodson's model, and quickly says, "That looks nice," then moves to the boards on the easel.

Jun turns off the air conditioner, and everyone's mood seems to improve. Lucas, however, finds the first conceptual interiors of Mufasta, the volcano planet, to be too much like those of the sinkhole planet. Once again, he emphasizes that the societies who build these respective cities would be dramatically different from one another; the architecture should reflect that. On the same track, he turns his attention to Alderaan, reiterating the importance of making the cities at least as big as New York, even though they're in a Swiss-style setting. To illustrate his point, he takes a black Sharpie and draws a huge tower upward over three vertically placed drawings.

Afterward, Tiemens and Church decide that they need to "push it further" and stop thinking too literally. Church says that when he first started working on *Star Wars,* its inconsistencies were often confusing; he couldn't understand how landspeeders still hovered even after being turned off. "Antigravity paint," he was told.

FRIDAY, SEPTEMBER 27, 2002

McCallum has invited Trisha Biggar and Gavin Bocquet to the meeting, as reminders that they're waiting in the wings. When Goodson comes in, Bocquet greets him warmly and remarks, "Every three years I see this man."

The number of artists has again increased, as two former freelancers—T. J. Frame and Feng Zhu (both from Los Angeles)—are now working in-house, the seventh and eighth members of the concept art team. Throughout this and almost every meeting, Feng will wear a baseball cap backward on his head. Frame has been brought in to work on environmental details. "I'd gone to school with T. J.," Church says. "Feng I knew from Art Center as well, and he'd always been really pestering me to get up here."

There's some concern among the artists that things aren't moving fast enough, but Trisha and Gavin aren't worried. The latter says that they got through Episode II and that this one will be fine, too. Bocquet and Biggar

A McQuarrie painting of Alderaan (above) and a Tiemens's version with fall colors (right). Alderaan was first conceived of by Lucas as being home to the Imperial prison, as described in his second draft of Star Wars *(1975): "The towering white oxide clouds pass, revealing the Imperial city of Alderaan. The magnificent domed and gleaming city is perched, mushroom-like, on a tall spire which disappears deep into the misty surface of the planet."*

Monday, September 9: Twentieth Century Fox and Lucasfilm announce that *Attack of the Clones* is coming to IMAX theatres in the U.S. and Canada beginning November 1, 2002.

have worked with Lucas and McCallum for more than a decade, and the mutual confidence of this core group more than offsets any worries about the schedule.

The door opens, Lucas walks in—and does a double take upon seeing Gavin. "I know nothing! Absolutely nothing," he exclaims. Church introduces T. J. and Feng, then talk turns once more to the Jedi starfighter.

McCallum arrives. "Oh, *hi* Rick. We haven't seen these gentlemen in so long," George wryly observes, nodding toward the guests. He then returns to the paintings while Trisha and Gavin sit on the table, the latter swinging his leg slowly back and forth. Once again Lucas is concerned about the similarity between cities. It's the biggest issue—he doesn't want audiences to be confused as to which city they're looking at. Meanwhile, Rick is urgently directing the documentary crew to change angles so that Gavin and Trisha are in the picture. Lucas says the next step is going to be nailing down what kinds of materials these civilizations are using.

"How do we rate their intelligence?" Church asks.

"I'd say they're all fairly sophisticated."

When Lucas gets to Jun's costume drawings, McCallum signals to

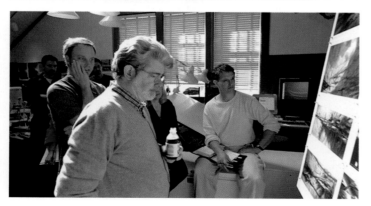

Biggar to move forward just as George, with his back turned to them, calls out, "Trish!" She goes up to the board and they discuss the real-world implications of Jun's sketches. Lucas approves almost all of them.

As the meeting comes to an end, there is some maneuvering as a second, more private meeting with Biggar and Bocquet is hastily convened. "They are observers," Lucas protests to McCallum.

"Just five minutes," Trisha says.

"The three of us," Rick adds, as he signals Fay to get more chairs for her office.

TUESDAY, OCTOBER 1, 2002

Veteran concept artist Iain McCaig arrives at the ranch. Tiemens and Church show him the binders filled with artwork the department has produced so far. "Boy, has the bar been raised this time," he says. "My work is cut out for me!"

While his family stays at home in Victoria, Canada, McCaig takes up temporary residence in Petaluma, a town of fifty-five thousand inhabitants about half an hour's drive through rolling hills from Skywalker Ranch (Petaluma is where Lucas shot nearly all of *American Graffiti*). McCaig first came to work in northern California in 1979. He opened a phone book and started calling production houses in alphabetical order. When he got to K, he called John Korty, one of the original Bay Area filmmaking mavericks and, coincidentally, a longtime friend of Lucas's. Korty hired McCaig, and his first job was to work on the trailer for Korty's *Twice Upon a Time* (1983), which helped persuade Lucas to become the film's executive producer. Eventually Iain went to work for Lucas himself, on Episode I. "George is really shy," McCaig remembers, "so for a year, he seemed uncomfortable around me. And then one day he just starts to relax. After that, he's a different person."

FRIDAY, OCTOBER 4, 2002

Because they work in fairly cramped quarters with no partitions, the artists often listen to music with earphones on to isolate themselves from one another. The result is that on any given day, it's usually quiet and meditative in the art department; craziness is reserved for the late nights.

When Lucas walks in, he remarks that there are a lot of people—and there are: Biggar, Bocquet, the doc team, and the concept art team. McCallum says, "We thought we'd start off slow."

"This is to try and get me to write a script," Lucas says.

"No . . . even I'm shocked," says Rick.

"There are so many people, no one can even hear what I'm saying."

Lucas notices McCaig, welcomes him, and hands him a blank piece of paper with an OK already stamped on it. "You can save it for a rainy day," he says, and Iain laughs.

Jun has created some high-tech costume designs for the people of Alderaan. "I think I'm going to make it a much more futuristic planet, much more elegant," Lucas notes, and gives three FABULOUSOS to Jun's work—startling the attendees and going some way toward finalizing costumes that Biggar can then begin to construct. Lucas says the key word for Alderaan is majestic. They show him a book on Switzerland, and, at the first photo spread, he exclaims, "That's Alderaan right there!" Pause. "Can we go there?" he asks McCallum. "Is it cheap?"

From top left: McCallum, Zhu, Jun, David, Tiemens, and Lucas study a John Goodson model of the Jedi starfighter; costume designer Trisha Biggar, concept artist Iain McCaig, and Lucas discuss Jun's costume designs for Alderaan; Tiemens, Lucas, and McCaig review sinkhole planet concepts. Right: Zhu, McCaig (with earphones), and concept artist Derek Thompson during a late night in the art department. Far right: a Padmé concept by McCaig.

The office of production controller Kathryn Ramos is down the hall from McCallum's. To get to his office, Rick must pass in front of hers. When the two first moved in, as Ramos tells the story, she positioned her desk so she could see when Rick passed by—in order to grab him. She is a fifteen-year veteran of the "Rick Wars," and knows that he can sometimes be difficult to nail down.

From behind her desk, Ramos also has a great view of the sun setting behind the now yellow hills. It casts a warm light over the ranch's grapevines, its red brick Tech Building, and Lake Ewok. In her spacious room hang two paintings: one of a young Tom Sawyer–esque boy who has taken off his shoes and is joyfully walking through the mud, and a second depicting an art deco–style maiden and armored knight. The two paintings are part of Lucas's collection and seem emblematic of his character and films.

Kathryn Ramos began working for McCallum at the BBC, while he was producing Potter's TV miniseries *Blackeyes* (1989). Rick had just fired his assistant, who was an old-timer at the BBC and highly respected. BBC stalwarts closed ranks and refused to provide a replacement—until Kathryn was drafted because she was the newest. During her half-hour interview with McCallum, she vainly tried to convince him that she had neither the necessary knowledge nor the experience for the job. Rick hired her on the spot.

Their first Lucasfilm project was *Young Indy*, which was going to be filmed all over the world. In her apartment, they, together, plotted out the complex location shoot, poring over atlases and almanacs spread over the kitchen table and floor. Their camaraderie continues today, as Rick will often come into her office to talk things over and make calls.

Per Episode III, Ramos says that they're about to open an art department at Elstree Studios, London, where Bocquet and supervising art director Peter Russell (*Indiana Jones and the Last Crusade*, 1989; *Gladiator*, 2000) will set up shop. She also reveals that Fox Studios, Australia, is booked: thirty buildings, all with different start and end dates. The longest-held will be Building 37, where the costume department will be lodged for fifty-one weeks. Without a script, production is obliged to hedge their bets, so some dates are solid, while others are written in pencil.

"We're trying to do this for a price," McCallum explains, "but we're building backward, designing a twenty-five-floor skyscraper without foundations. Do you know what it's like to budget a film without a script? That's what Kathryn goes through every day."

Unintentionally paraphrasing Indiana Jones, Ramos admits, "We're making it up as we go."

2 "Wouldn't It Be Cool If ...?"

"Basically, I would tell them about a scene, an animal, or a character," Lucas explains, "and they would do a bunch of designs. I would okay some or modify or change them, and we build; we go to the next thing. And so, every week, they get more to design. Some of these guys are designing costumes; some of them are designing sets; some of them are designing props or cars. There's just a whole variety of guys up there, and each one does a different thing. And then I'm writing the script."

This is the big conceptual push. From mid-October 2002 to Day One of principal photography, life in the art department will hit its zenith in terms of quality, quantity, and hours. "It's like going to an art gallery opening every Friday," Tiemens says. "Here's ninety-nine new paintings for George to look at."

"It's the most fun I've ever had," Church adds. "Monday or Tuesday, we might go home at seven or eight in the evening; Wednesday, one or two in the morning; Thursday–all night." (Fortunately for these acolytes, the kitchen often sends up its leftovers.) "That was the magic hour," Church continues, "Thursday at 3 A.M.–the three-to-five stretch is the intense, focused work period."

"Here you're working on something you loved as a kid," T. J. says. "Everybody is supertalented and everyone has something to add to the mix."

As of October 18, 2003, three new artists have been added to this mix: Derek Thompson (creatures); Warren Fu (vehicles/environments); and Alexander Jaeger (environments), bringing their number to twelve. "I'd seen these *Art of Star Wars* books, but I'd never made the connection that you could actually make a living doing that kind of work," Fu says. "When I graduated from UC Berkeley, my friends told me about an internship at Lucasfilm. I didn't even know how to make a portfolio, so I just kinda put everything together in a folder and submitted it late. We had to sneak into my friend's office and use his mail machine to backdate it! I was rejected the first time, so this is icing on the cake being up here."

Echoing McCallum's metaphor, McCaig describes the department as a "jazz ensemble" in which each artist instinctively knows when to "step forward and take a solo" and when to merge back into the group, handing off characters and environments the same way musicians would a melody. "This is the biggest art department I've ever worked with," he notes. "And everyone is confident enough in their abilities so that we can jam the way that musicians do–and that's really rare."

"We wanted to make the art department a collective unit–and I wanted the guys to have fun," McCallum says.

Throughout this period, the one common thought voiced by those in the ensemble is: *Wouldn't it be cool if . . . ?* The next few months represents their unique chance to design a character, a weapon, a vehicle, or an environment that sticks– one that leaves a trace on one of filmdom's most celebrated sagas. "For the first part of the design process, it seemed like George was going from what we were drawing, rather than telling us what to do," Jaeger remembers. "A lot of what we did was what we'd really love to see in a *Star Wars* film. We'd draw it, present it, and see if he'd bite."

"George was always appreciative," Church adds, "and might say, 'Wow. Not for my movie, but that's a great idea.' We'd always try something out because–you've got George Lucas's eye, and not many people have that chance."

FRIDAY, OCTOBER 18, 2002
McCaig shows Lucas two paintings on his computer screen: one of Anakin Skywalker emerging from a volcano, burned but still standing, and another of Anakin on the back of a lizardlike mount. The first prompts Lucas to say that Anakin will probably be carried out of the volcano; the second prompts him to say that the lizard can run

---

*Right: A costume and hair style concept for Padmé by Warren Fu (*Artificial Intelligence: A.I.*, 2001; *Attack of the Clones*). "I was five years old when* The Empire Strikes Back *came out, and after I saw it, it was all over."*

up walls and ceilings, which will enable them to create unique fight sequences.

He adds that Anakin won't be scarred till the very end; for most of the movie, he has to be attractive because Padmé is still "madly in love with him." For the first time, it is rumored that Padmé might die in this film. She may be seen last on Alderaan.

FRIDAY, OCTOBER 25, 2002

Lucas has sent the art department a list outlining which planets are important, their spellings (which often change), and their habitats:

```
Episode III Planets (Major)
Coruscant (city)
Naboo (garden)
Alderaan (snowcapped peaks)
Mustafar (volcano)
Dagobah (swamp)
Tatooine (desert)

Episode III Planets (Minor)
Cato Neimoidia (ring city around gas net) [Bad--Trade Federation]
Mygeeto (crystal) [Bad--IG Banking Clan]
Utapo (sinkholes) [Good--lemurs]
Kashyyyk (lake) [Good--Wookiees]
Seleucami (upside-down city/bridgeworld) [Bad--Techno Union]
Felucia (seaweed/coral) [Bad--Commerce Guild]
Polis Mazta (asteroid wasteland) [Good]

Planets (Not in Episode III)
Bespin (gas clouds)
Geonosis (red rock)
Kamino (water)
Hoth (ice)
Yavin Moon (fog/jungle)
Endor Moon (forest)
```

On the table are production photos from the Elstree art department, which is now open for business. Bocquet and his team have already produced a skeletal life-sized construct of the Jedi starfighter.

*Clockwise from top left: Derek Thompson (*Men in Black, *1997;* The Mummy, *1999), also an ILMer, had tried to join the previous concept art teams of Episode I and II–but finally made it on Episode III. Alex Jaeger (*Mission: Impossible, *1996;* The Perfect Storm, *2000) came up from ILM, and says that when Lucas is looking at his artwork, he feels a "little nervous; you can gauge sometimes by what he's been approving, whether yours are going to get picked or not." Concept artist Warren Fu is yet another ILMer. All the concept artists came to regard the heroic Horse Pilot (above, whose specially designed X-wing was created by Alex Jaeger) as their mascot. Actually a character from the* Star Wars Expanded Universe, *"Horse Pilot!" became the battle cry during late nights and inspirational design marathons.*

Coming from the stairway, the assembled hears, "Fee, fi, fo, fum! Ready or not, here I come!" And throughout the meeting, Lucas seems to be in high spirits. He quickly espies the photos of the Elstree starfighter and says, "Already building sets? I may have to start writing the script pretty soon!" After a bit of reflection, he decides to limit how much they'll build of the starfighter, commenting, "For God's sake, I don't need all that–" as he spots pre-viz supervisor Dan Gregoire coming down the hall: "You can do it, can't you?" he calls out, *it* referring to a digital extension of the practical cockpit.

Lucas then addresses the planet list, explaining that, if there are more than seventeen shots for any one environment, they'll need to build a set of some sort for that particular location. They'll need sets for the Jedi Council, Palpatine's office, probably the Senate, and they have a choice: either to return to part of Padmé's Episode II apartment or to create a new one. He also suggests reviewing *Return of the Jedi* and taking a look at Coruscant's plaza/park. Anakin and Padmé might have a love scene somewhere like that–but without greenery.

Suddenly Lucas divulges more of the story–the most since the very first Episode III meeting: At the end of the film, in a thirty-second wrap-up, Yoda will go to Dagobah, Obi-Wan will go with the infant Luke to Tatooine, and Bail Organa–with the infant Leia–will flee to Alderaan. Mustafar–whose name has now been changed from Mufasta–will occupy about twenty to thirty minutes of film time. Lucas is planning a lot of fighting there, about four to five scenes, and one "love scene."

Wednesday, October 23: Lucasfilm lends a copy of *American Graffiti* to a group of Petaluma girl scouts. Lucas shot *Graffiti* almost entirely in Petaluma, which is presently without a movie theater, so these intrepid scouts will be projecting the film onto a parking lot wall to create public support for the construction of a new cinema.

character. For their escapades, he asks the artists to come up with dangerous situations, or what are generally referred to as "gags."

"Turbines?" Tiemens asks.

"Turbines are always good. Anything you don't wanna get near," Lucas says. He then reveals that Anakin and Count Dooku will have a huge duel aboard the ship. The entire opening sequence should last about twenty minutes.

As McCallum wanders around the periphery of the meeting, Fay David brings out a ship binder from which Lucas can select the kind of cruiser he wants. "We're out of our minds," he comments while flipping through the pages. "Making a movie where the bad guys win, and everyone dies, is not destined to be the most successful movie of all time."

After choosing a few vehicle candidates, he turns to Derek Thompson's images of battle-scene key frames, but puts on the brakes, saying, "I haven't gotten that far yet." As they take down one board to show the paintings pinned to the board behind it, there happens to be a completely blank board in-between. "It's a copy of the script!" McCallum says.

When the fully laden board of costume sketches is revealed, Lucas looks at a Photoshopped image of Anakin with a Mohawk, but says he prefers the longer hair worn by Obi-Wan and Qui-Gon. "Anakin's still a Jedi," he points out.

McCaig then mumbles something about Trisha needing to get started, and Lucas's response is similarly indistinct. Rick asks, "Is that a yes?"

"I don't know," George says, "I'm not sure what Iain asked. He's mumbling."

The upshot is that Trisha can start making costumes based on Jun's approved designs. McCallum is "ecstatic," for "production is finally beginning."

"I knew I wasn't going to get a script, but I had to keep them working," he explains. "Without a script, our priority then becomes: We know Padmé's in the film, we know she's going to be in her bedroom, and we know it's going to be night—so can we create a nightgown for her?"

He has also altered the beginning of the film. Instead of starting with seven battles on seven planets, Episode III now opens with a huge space battle. Our heroes crash-land into a "bad guy's ship," perhaps Neimoidian, where there will be lots of "cliffhangers, from one near-death experience to another—*Indiana Jones and the Temple of Doom* aboard a ship." The ship might be breaking apart. He asks the artists to work on a "grand control room and a grand office." The heroes will be trying to rescue a kidnapped

---

October 28-31: Gavin Bocquet goes to Switzerland for a "recce," or location-scouting trip.

Monday, November 4: Production coordinator Virginia Murray opens the Episode III production office at Fox Studios, Sydney.

30

FRIDAY, NOVEMBER 1, 2002

ILM animation director Rob Coleman (*Dragonheart*, 1996; *Men in Black*) is on hand for the first time. Bearded and upbeat, he is the puppet master behind digital Yoda. Coleman is starting three months earlier than he did on Episode II, as he's been told that a few characters are far enough along in the approval process for him to come by and have a look—but he surmises that it's possible Rick is still throwing people at George to get him to write.

Indeed, when Lucas walks in and sees Coleman he does a double take, protesting, "What's he doing here? No animation! You can't come until June 24."

"I'll see you at the film's premiere," Coleman says.

But Lucas quickly offers that he may have to start writing "when reality hits."

"You said you've *been* writing," McCallum protests.

"I've been *thinking* about it."

Lucas does reveal a few more story details, saying that the opening space battle will be fought over Coruscant. Anakin and Obi-Wan in their Jedi starfighters fly into a Separatist cruiser, then split up as the star cruiser slowly breaks in half. Obi-Wan ends up on the bridge after a series of episodic cliffhangers, and manages to land the front half of the ship. Meanwhile, Anakin fights Count Dooku.

Anakin's longer hair is approved. While looking at a costume of a Mustafarian dressed in red, Lucas says, "We have to be careful he doesn't look like the Emperor." Somebody immediately connects the dots and says, "We have an Emperor this time!"

Earlier this week, when Lucas heard the news that Sicily's Mount Etna was erupting, he called McCallum and said that Ron Fricke should get over there and film it. Rick arranged for a local guide and the approval of the Italian government. JAK rented a camera from a company in Milan, and a Sicilian agent organized the hotel arrangements. Fricke flies out today, and will stay as long as necessary.

FRIDAY, NOVEMBER 8, 2002

A new environment is being explored: Polis Mazta, which has been conceptualized in three different ways across six paintings. According to Church, Lucas instructed them to create an asteroid wasteland, to consult 1960s NASA photos, and to include "space-suit guys"—a species that doesn't have much in the way of faces, based on nonutilized Episode II designs for a Kamino species. He hasn't specified yet whether they'll be good guys or bad guys.

Friday, **November 8:** On her return trip from filming *Cold Mountain* (2003) on location in Romania, Natalie Portman (Padmé Amidala) stops in London at Elstree Studios. There, they make a full-body cast of the actress in order to complete a custom-made dressmaker's stand, so Natalie won't have to be present for all of the fittings.

Clockwise from top left: Sketches by Tiemens of possible Naboo meeting places for Anakin and Padmé led to a concept painting; two McCaig conceptualizations of Anakin, one as he emerges from a volcano, and another more samurai-like, but Lucas would opt for longer hair. A Church concept of the asteroid planet, Polis Mazta. Before writing the rough draft, Lucas jotted down some undated notes, divided into three acts. His handwritten pages reveal that many of the final film's set-pieces are already in place.

31

Act I

1 Space
Obi and Annie in dogfight attacking Federation Battle cruiser. Obi maneuver several fighters Obi is hit and crash lands on cruiser - Annie lands after him. General and tyrannos watch them.

2 Federation Battle cruiser Hold and Hallways
Obi and Annie battle droids and fuel leaks to try to find the kidnapped chancellor - Jedi caught in something, Cables etc fighter crashes into them they barly escape. General and tyrannos watch them - told to separate the Jedi

3 Federation Battle cruiser elevator
Obi and Annie struggle to make their way to the Admirals Quarters. Obi is seperated and does not make it to the Admirals Quarters.

4 Admirals Quarters
Annie fights Darth tyrannos and kills him at the urging of Palpatine.

5 Federation Battle cruiser Hallway / Bridge.
Obi-wan fights droids, the Admiral, and the Evil General Grievous - Obi wins the battle but General Grievous escapes in a fighter. Obi struggles to land the damaged ship. Annie and Palpatine join him - Both jedi struggle as a team to land the ship

Lucas examines paintings of Mustafar, a few of which show two Jedi in close proximity to boiling-hot lava. He observes that, "there is a certain reality about toast here–even in fantasy." Then he notices one where Thompson has shown Jedi using the Force to hurl lava at each other. Lucas notes that this represents a "good toast factor."

A series of drawings show Jedi being killed in combat on Mygeeto (crystal world), but Lucas objects–the Jedi will be "betrayed," not cut down in battle.

As conversation flows from one subject to the next, Lucas casually mentions that Episode III's principal villain could be a Separatist droid general–and everyone begins to take notes. McCallum leans against the wall to get a better look.

"I won't limit it at this point to a droid. It could be an alien of some

kind," George clarifies. "I'm not sure if I want him to be human. It's the Darth Maul. It's the Jango Fett, Darth Vader."

"Male, though?" Rick asks.

"I don't care. It's gotta be iconic. It's gotta be pretty evil," Lucas explains.

"Evil. Iconic. Got it," McCaig says.

"It's like, *Uh-oh! This is the bad guy.* Your first reaction is: *Scary.* But it also has to have a lot of personality and be very recognizable. He has to be able to do dialogue scenes."

"This is not a Sith, right?" McCaig asks.

"It's not a Sith."

"Age?" McCallum asks.

Wednesday, November 13: Ian McDiarmid (Supreme Chancellor Palpatine) is fitted for a costume at Elstree.

"Villains are ageless. He can't be young. Old people are scary. You can all get ahold of that and see if you can come up with a new iconic villain."

Rick pulls Iain aside, asking him to keep in mind a great actor or actress while working on designs. "Make that your number-one priority," he says.

"Work on the villain," Lucas reiterates as he leaves. "That's the next real assignment. Now I have to go to a business meeting." He pauses. "In the real world."

FRIDAY, NOVEMBER 15, 2002

George walks in, and Fay David points him toward two Separatist ship models. He likes them both, so he asks, "How many cheers for this one?" Moderate cheers. "And for this one?" Louder cheers. "You see? It's not hard to make decisions around here."

A board is then revealed that features the group's first attempts to create an icon of evil. "We all collaborated on the droid general," Thompson recalls. "It was one of the most exhilarating weeks, because we all got to attack one thing."

It becomes clear, however, that Lucas hasn't received what he wants just yet. He is quiet for about a minute, just looking at the various concepts, then, seemingly careful not to be discouraging, says, "The ones I like the most are . . . ," and stamps two for further research. He doesn't say anything negative, except for "Too ethnic, too *Alien*-ish . . ."

"Do you want to see more?" McCaig asks.

"Some of this is a little too devilish."

A Zhu painting of the duel on Mustafar puts into play Lucas's desire to have the fight and its environments in close proximity to the lava at all times.

"Full figure?" someone asks. "Could it be part droid?" someone else suggests.

"We need to see more articulation, so I know exactly what I'm looking at," Lucas responds. "And we have to be careful not to re-create Darth Vader, since he's showing up at the end of the movie." For those attending, this is a revelation–the first admission from Lucas that Darth Vader will definitely be in Episode III.

FRIDAY, NOVEMBER 22, 2002

This cold morning, anyone arriving at Skywalker Ranch would have noticed problems. A propane leak was discovered during the night, and repair people are everywhere. The artists have been evacuated. To keep warm, some of them are jogging the circuit around the grounds.

By the time the meeting is convened, it's a smaller group than usual: no ILMers and no animartists, except Dan Gregoire. Lucas arrives about half an hour late because of the leak. For the admiral's room, where Dooku confronts Anakin, George is concerned about how they'd actually shoot,

given the design. "This is the place where Dooku meditates on his grand schemes," Lucas points out, so he suggests they take out a column that would block his view of space.

"Could we do something that revolves?" Church asks.

"It's the executive suite. You gotta say to yourself, *If I had an office, this is what it'd look like,*" Lucas says. "Remember: We can't go outside [into space]. Cinematically, it would be inappropriate. We have to stay inside the set."

Felucia (the plant planet) has been rethought based on microphotography. "This is good. Excellent," he remarks. Stamping the paintings, he continues, "If you go five miles, you run into this. This is odd. I like this. This is really odd. This is weird." He combines some landscapes, alters the scale of others, and says that, ultimately, the planet should have two basic areas: jungle and desert.

The next board has the next wave of Separatist general concepts. Warren Fu has conceived of a villain who catches George's eye. "Because my priority was environments, I didn't focus on the droid general until the end of the week–at the last minute," Warren remembers. "The morning of the meeting, I sketched one, which I didn't even like that much. But we put it out there, and George goes right up to it and says, 'That's the one.' I mentioned that the general might have organic eyes–George's eyes lit up and he said, 'Now that's interesting.'"

Monday, November 18: In Sydney, assistant costume designer Michael Mooney and costume supervisor Nicole Young start the costume department in Building 37. The accounting department opens temporary facilities in Building 28.

Left-hand page: Thompson, Zhu, and Church (top) prepare one of the boards featuring November 15's Separatist general concepts; Lucas and McCallum (below) during an art department meeting. Right-hand page: Fu's early sketches (below) for the new icon of evil led to his concept (with clenched fist, above) chosen by Lucas as the model for the droid general on November 22; on December 6, Fu presents the general with his bodyguards (top right), similar to the way Darth Vader arrives flanked by stormtroopers in A New Hope.

DROID GENERAL & HENCHMEN
W.FU 12/06/02
SW3

Moving on to the following concepts, Lucas studies some drawings by McCaig that suggest Padmé is sick while pregnant, and having terrible dreams—and remarks, "That's just because she was spending too much time with you!" But he then adds, "She does have a thing where she gives birth . . ."

"All right. Keep up the good work. The stuff was great, guys," he concludes. "I just have to figure out a movie to go with it."

FRIDAY, DECEMBER 6, 2002

Rick McCallum has returned from Sydney after a three-week trip, and has closed the next few art department meetings to nonessential personnel, knowing that the more intimate atmosphere will result in more decisions from Lucas. This, in turn, will yield more work for the somewhat starved-for-material production departments Down Under.

Sculptor Michael Murnane is here for the first time, the thirteenth member of the group. Eight lemur sculpts, four by Robert Barnes, four by the newcomer, sit on a table. Murnane (*Starship Troopers*, 1997; *Monkeybone*, 2001) worked on *Attack of the Clones* as a sculptor, but early in his career actually wanted to be an architect. "When I found out that architecture involved memorizing wood lengths and that sort of thing, I said 'Forget this,'" he recalls. "So I went to Long Beach State and studied illustration. I took sculpture, too—I took one class and almost changed my major, because I loved it so much. The

things I was trying to learn in two-D, you do it *live* with sculpture!"

When Lucas walks in and sees McCallum, he says, "I haven't seen you for a while—I didn't even know you were alive."

"I'm not," Rick replies.

They then try to show Lucas the same art binders as before, in the hope that he'll start to organize their contents. But Lucas would still prefer not to.

"Until I've started the script, it's hard . . . ," he says.

"Oh, God . . . ," McCallum moans.

"Take some aspirin," Lucas recommends.

"Aspirin? I need to freebase!"

George then looks over the lemur sculpts. He loves them and gives them all FABULOUSOS. Later, Murnane will explain that McCaig is pushing them to do sculpts that are character-driven, not species-driven.

They've added an Egyptian influence to Polis Mazta, the asteroid planet. Lucas muses over it for a while. "Okay. I'll buy that." While reviewing additional environments, he says, "The other film was low-key, twilight. I think we have to raise the sun up and go from sixty watts to a hundred twenty-five." In discussing Palpatine's costumes, he says, "I want to keep him where he was before. This is starting to look a little design-y."

"Working with George is a scary but exhilarating experience," T. J. Frame notes. "He comes up here and asks, 'Is it a good read?' He keeps it pure and honest. He makes sure that design is in service of the story-telling."

Tuesday, November 26: Nicole Young fits Christopher Lee (Count Dooku) for a costume at his home in London.

Lucas notices that he's running out of time: "Should I go for it?" he asks McCallum.

"Go for it," Rick says.

So George looks at another board and approves quite a bit.

"I haven't figured out if there's a correlation between more okays and not enough time," the producer observes, "but you're doing great."

After Lucas leaves, the tension and excitement dissipate—as they usually do—and an analysis ensues. Because of hints thrown out by Lucas that the script may be finished by Christmas, McCaig comments to the others, "We have two more weeks to be as outside the box as possible."

FRIDAY, DECEMBER 13, 2002

It's raining hard, and water is leaking into the art department. Once again, it's a smaller group. Earlier in the week, Lucas actually requested a copy of the infamous binders, so Fay David and her new assistant, Stephanie Lostimolo, made copies and sent them to his home, where he is now reportedly working on the script Mondays through Thursdays.

Lucas arrives ahead of schedule and approves two lizards, one male, one female. The doc team arrives,

and he says to them, "I snuck up here early. You missed the whole thing. A song, a dance . . ." While looking at dress designs for Padmé, he asks the artists to avoid material that won't be good for hugs. "She's a victim in this one, but interacts with Anakin a lot."

Once again, without warning, he volunteers some key story points: "Mace we see more in the Jedi Temple—at this point, we don't see him out in the field, though that's subject to change. We see Bail Organa's wife, the Queen of Alderaan. She gets one baby. On Utapo, I have a big battle now. It's where Obi-Wan kills the [droid] general. So we'll need his henchmen. I'm thinking of doing a droid-dragon chase. I don't know how Obi-Wan is going to possibly win, but we'll figure out how to get out of it later."

Discussion focuses on what kinds of droids can do battle with a lizard-dragon. "Because it's a battle and Obi-Wan is chasing the general, the general will need a vehicle. It's gotta be a big fight. Lasers versus swords; lizards versus droids. Lots of speed, lots of chasing—*lots* of speed—jumping from one vehicle to another. Lizards getting killed, falling off cliffs, things like that."

McCallum then asks Lucas which Padmé costumes Biggar can get started on. "It's too early. I have to get an outline together," Lucas starts, but then adds: "She's in her apartment twice; she's in the Senate; she's on the landing platform." Cursory information—but enough for Rick, who calls Trisha afterward with instructions.

CHRISTMAS 2002

FOX STUDIOS, SYDNEY: After having had knee surgery earlier in December, McCallum arrives in Australia on December 20. Though some departments started weeks before, production begins full-scale operations the day after Christmas. Rick is now hiring an Australian crew, getting buildings organized, negotiating with Fox, purchasing equipment, setting up the wardrobe and art departments, and tackling anything that has a purchase order associated with it. "All of those things need sorting out," Kathryn Ramos says. "He happens to be a really hands-on kind of producer."

"What we're doing is controlling chaos," McCallum says. The way that's accomplished, he explains, is by having key personnel report any and all developments, so that—with Lucas's tacit approval—he can instantly act on that information. Together their communication creates the missing foundation, "because we're not going to find the more apparent foundation until we're well into postproduction—which makes for an interesting paradox."

SKYWALKER RANCH: It's now the ninth month of preproduction. "Back in August, I started writing this," Lucas says, "but the script starts to have its own life. Characters start to tell you what to do—and you end up with problems. By the third film, you have a lot of characters left over from before, and they're all running around yipping and yelling and saying, 'What about me?' And you have to solve these problems, because what you thought was going to happen isn't happening. I got far enough with the outline to realize that the bridge between Episode III and Episode IV still had them about fifty feet apart. So I had to disassemble Episode III and rethink it, to make it line up with Episode IV. When you actually put it down on paper and start doing it scene by scene—when you really start pulling it apart—you say, 'Well, I have to have a through-line. And I have to stick with it.'"

Michael Murnane (above) and one of his lemur sculpts (left). "My mom would always turn off the TV and put drawing paper out for my brother and me"; Lucas's reworking of the film's opening leads to "gags" on a Separatist cruiser by Jaeger (above right), in which the ship breaks in half, and Church (below), with a chase among turbine engines.

3 The Rise and Fall of Darth Vader

As Lucas's writing enters a new phase, work in the art department becomes more closely tied to the emerging script. And though the artists still engage in a great deal of free-flow conceptual creation, they're also very much involved in "detailing out" approved concepts, to the last cornice and control switch.

SKYWALKER RANCH (SR): FRIDAY, JANUARY 10, 2003

Bocquet is stopping by before flying to Sydney. He arrived on Wednesday, after his flight was delayed for nearly seven hours due to snow in London, and he's brought a few maquettes of Padmé's veranda.

Lucas walks in and asks, "Well, is the picture finished yet?"

He surveys a few Mustafarian busts, which he okays—one receives a FABULOUSO. The eyes are too human-like, however, so he requests a tweak. While looking at Mustafar command center interiors, he discusses how they need to be changed so the fight can begin there, then move outside to the volcano. Through the windows, he says, there should be "vistas that say this is bigger than something you see in other movies."

The look of the droid general is now approved; Warren Fu has given him a shield so he can defend himself against Obi-Wan. The next step is to make a sculpture of the villain. As for the Wookiees, Lucas says to keep them slim, so they're not like Ewoks. The Queen of Alderaan is fortyish, and Boba Fett will not be in the film.

He then turns to Bocquet and says, "I hear you have some questions for me. The answers are: 'No, no . . . never, never . . . I don't know.' " In their subsequent meeting, however, Lucas goes through the film scene by scene—with a huge disclaimer: "This is all subject to change."

A partial list of sets and characters include:

- Kashyyyk—Yoda, Wookiees, a 10-year-old Han Solo.
- Blockade runner from Alderaan—conference room and/or hallway—the same as the Vader hallway in Episode IV.
- Coruscant rehabilitation center. This is where Anakin is assembled as Vader.
- Imperial Star Destroyer bridge. This is where the Emperor, Grand Moff Tarkin, and Vader look out into space and see the Death Star under construction.

Lucas approves "version 4" of Padmé's veranda, so now they can build that set in Sydney. As soon as the meeting adjourns, even though it's midnight in Australia, Bocquet phones McCallum with an update. "George always knows when he has to come through for us," Rick would say, while the next day Bocquet would tell starwars.com, "We're in a good position now, but if we're in the same spot in six or seven weeks, we might be a little bit nervous."

FRIDAY, JANUARY 17, 2003

Lucas's rethink of the script is becoming manifest to the artists—though they have yet to actually read it—as more and more links are estab-

Monday, January 6: In Sydney, the art department opens for business in Building 48. The costume department starts in 44B (crowd costume storage), and costume props in 48 (depot). Art director Ian Gracie (*Pitch Black*, 2000; *Moulin Rouge*, 2001) and art department coordinator Colette Birrell (*Mission: Impossible II*, 2000; *The Matrix Reloaded*, 2003) start work today. Supervising art director Peter Russell and costume prop supervisor Ivo Coveney (*The Borrowers*, 1997; *Attack of the Clones*) begin on Wednesday.

Friday, January 10: The art department at Elstree Studios, London, closes its doors.

lished between Episodes III and IV. The bridge between the two is being buttressed, and the difficulty of writing that bridge is evident in many of Lucas's off-the-cuff remarks.

He shows up early, and once again the artists quickly pin the last of the paintings to the boards. Lucas notices that Biggar is present, and she asks, "How are you?" He responds, "Well, I promise you, this is the last time I'm doing this."

As they go through the boards, one of the new sets is unveiled: the rehabilitation center where Anakin becomes the mechanized Darth Vader. After his resuscitation, Vader is handed over to Governor Tarkin, who was played by the late Peter Cushing in Episode IV. Apparently there is some unused footage of the actor that can be cut into the new film. McCaig suggests digitally animating the lips, so Tarkin can be given some new dialogue, but Lucas shelves that issue for later.

He next reviews paintings of Palpatine's anteroom, studying them for a long time and then combining elements of three paintings. Lucas also reveals that Padmé will be pregnant throughout the movie, and, in the last of the Episode IV connections, asks that a peasant outfit be designed for a ten-year-old Han Solo.

"Trisha got maybe forty-five minutes with George," McCallum says in Sydney, "but it was enough to get a little more information and push us along."

FRIDAY, JANUARY 24, 2003

Lucas arrives and swaps the head of a sculpt of the droid general—whom Lucas has named Grievous—with the neck of another general sculpt.

McCaig has done additional illustrations of Padmé pregnant, which Lucas contemplates, slowly stroking his chin. He notes that Padmé has to be pregnant enough so that the audience has no doubt as to her condition, but not so pregnant that it becomes distracting. McCaig has also drawn Han Solo as requested, and Lucas approves the sketch.

The Mustafarian species has now officially been moved to Utapau (final spelling), and the lemur people removed from the film. "I was heartbroken when the lemurs were eliminated," Church recalls, "but that just shows how shortsighted I am. Ultimately, we have enough furry fighting things."

Bocquet and Lucas then retire for a private discussion, during which Lucas approves the building of more sets, including Palpatine's office and anteroom, the Polis Massa (final spelling) conference room, the blockade runner hallway, part of the Star Destroyer bridge, and part of Darth Vader's rehabilitation center. Once again, this information is immediately passed on to McCallum in Australia.

Far left: Darth Vader in the rehabilitation center, by Tiemens. Left: Lucas, flanked by Jun, Biggar, and McCaig. Above: Church's Alderaan starcruiser, aka the Rebel blockade runner (with Grievous's starfighter rising into it), is one of the many links between Episode III and IV.

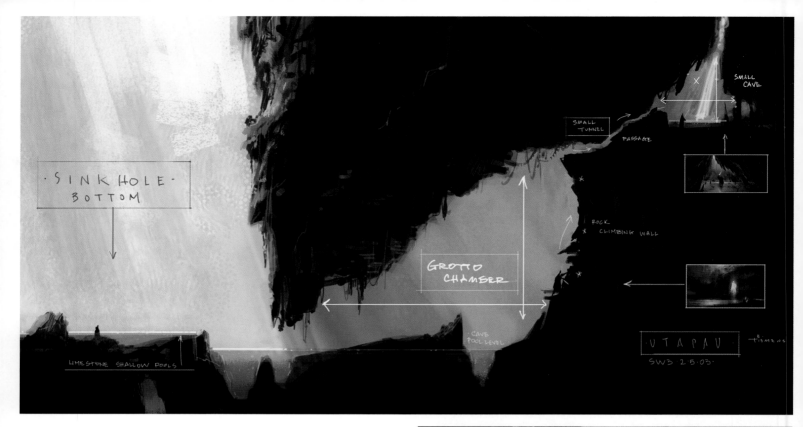

SINKHOLE BOTTOM

SMALL CAVE

SMALL TUNNEL

PASSAGE

ROCK CLIMBING WALL

GROTTO CHAMBER

CAVE POOL LEVEL

LIMESTONE SHALLOW POOLS

UTAPAU

SW3·2·5·03·

Tiemens

FRIDAY, JANUARY 31, 2003

Tiemens has painted an interesting scene for Obi-Wan in an Utapau cave, based on a sketch by McCaig. Drawing on perceived parallels between the cave and the hollow tree in *The Empire Strikes Back*, where Luke confronts an apparition, Tiemens and McCaig have visually hypothesized that Qui-Gon Jinn might appear to Obi-Wan, instructing his former apprentice to go to Mustafar and stop Anakin.

When Lucas gets to the cave illustration, he asks, "What's that?"–indicating Qui-Gon. Before Iain can explain, he adds, "We never see the ghost of Qui-Gon; he's not that accomplished. He's able to retain his personality, but he's not able to become a corporeal ghost."

But the painting does give rise to another key story point: "We have a scene at the end. A funeral on Naboo. A casket is being pulled by horse-ish creatures. You can work on that."

"Where on Naboo?" Tiemens asks.

"Same place as the Episode I parade. This is the only shot on Naboo now."

The same day, Lucas's assistant Anne Merrifield finishes typing up his rough draft, which is shown only to McCallum. "We can't give the script to the department heads yet," Rick says. "Instead, I interpret it for them, because I don't want them to go too far down the line. It has to stay ephemeral at this point. There has to be enough information so they know what's going on and can plan, but not enough information so they lock something down–because everything is going to change."

Having toned down the other characters and the tempting tangents, Lucas can sum up the focus of the revised but still-evolving story in one word: *"Anakin."*

NOTE: This and subsequent summaries contain many scenes and much dialogue that won't be found in the final film. The purpose of these summaries is to show how Lucas assembles the story of Episode III slowly, over a period of years, piece by piece.

It is fifty-five pages and titled:

<u>Star Wars Episode III: Revenge of the Sith</u>

War! Evil is everywhere. There are heroes on both sides. Separatist terrorists have kidnapped Supreme Chancellor Palpatine, leader of the Galactic Senate.
General Grievous, commander of the separatist armies, has attacked Coruscant, the capital of the Republic, and has been driven back by the Jedi Commanders and their army of clones.
In the midst of the battle, two Jedi have discovered the starship where Chancellor Palpatine is being held captive and are attempting a rescue. . . .

ROUGH DRAFT SUMMARY: *The script's opening line belongs to OBI-WAN: "Flying is a job for droids, not Jedi." In their starfighters, OBI-WAN and ANAKIN weave their way among the ships battling above Coruscant. When OBI-WAN's vessel is crippled by buzz droids, he crash-lands into the Federation cruiser where PALPATINE is being held. ANAKIN follows. They fight off droids but are cornered by GENERAL GRIEVOUS, who greets ANAKIN as "the young hero of Bakura." ANAKIN and OBI-WAN communicate through hand signals, then whip out their lightsabers, cut a hole through the floor, and escape. However, they fall into fuel tanks, where they're surrounded by lethal, stinging jellyfish called "nitro fobos." ANAKIN and OBI-WAN escape through a vent and take an elevator to where they believe the CHANCELLOR is being held.*

LUCAS: "Obi-Wan always had a suspicion about Anakin. In the beginning, he didn't want Anakin to become a Jedi. He thought what Qui-Gon was doing was wrong. But the Jedi Council let Anakin in and they made him Obi-Wan's Padawan. Then, over the years, he lived with this kid–they fought together and they worked together, so they have a very strong bond now. So Obi-Wan is supporting Anakin because they're friends. He's been seduced by his closeness to the situation."

When the elevator door opens, droids capture OBI-WAN while ANAKIN escapes through the ceiling of the lift. OBI-WAN is brought to GRIEVOUS, and they fight on the ship's bridge. ANAKIN finds the CHANCELLOR, but is surrounded by droids. COUNT DOOKU arrives–or as he is now known, DARTH TYRANUS. They fight, cutting down the hapless droids and exchanging verbal slights:

DARTH TYRANUS
I can feel your anger. Your hatred tells me you
are not unfamiliar with the dark side.

PALPATINE
Anakin, he was bragging earlier about how he
arranged to have your mother killed by the
Tusken Raiders.

ANAKIN
You!

DARTH TYRANUS
Yes, and now there is no escape for you,
my young Jedi.

ANAKIN cuts off DOOKU's hand. PALPATINE orders him to kill TYRANUS, and ANAKIN slices off his head.

LUCAS: "Palpatine has told Dooku, 'I have somebody who I think will become a great Sith Lord and I think we can get him to join us. But we need to test him. So we're going to set up a situation where you fight him. If he gets the best of you, then I'll stop the fight and he'll have passed the test. If you get the best of him, then we'll let him go, and we'll let him stew for a few more years until he's ready.' But behind it, obviously, is Palpatine's real intention: If Anakin is good enough, Anakin can kill Dooku and become Palpatine's new apprentice. But he didn't tell Dooku that."

As the cruiser falls out of orbit, GRIEVOUS abandons ship in an escape pod. ANAKIN and PALPATINE join OBI-WAN and the former succeeds in landing what's left of the broken ship on Coruscant.

There, they are met by BAIL ORGANA, MACE WINDU, JAR JAR BINKS, and other Senators. When the main group moves off PADMÉ appears; she tells ANAKIN that she is pregnant and they embrace.

GENERAL GRIEVOUS retreats to the sinkhole planet called Utapau. He orders NUTE GUNRAY and the rest of the Separatist Council to Mustafar; he then speaks with DARTH SIDIOUS via hologram. GRIEVOUS questions his strategy but SIDIOUS councils patience.

On Coruscant, ANAKIN is awakened by a nightmare in which PADMÉ is consumed by flames. PADMÉ comforts him but ANAKIN worries her by stating: "My ability to use the Force is becoming greater than any Jedi. Soon I will control it . . . Maybe I wasn't destined to become a mere Jedi."

PALPATINE announces a reorganization: he would like ANAKIN to act as liaison between the Jedi Council and the Chancellor's office. The Council eventually accepts, with YODA speaking as a hologram.

When the meeting is over, YODA, who is on Kashyyyk, speaks with the spirit of QUI-GON JINN. YODA would like to know how the Jedi will be destroyed, but QUI-GON can't say because the Force is out of balance. Ten-year-old HAN SOLO then joins YODA.

HAN SOLO
I found part of a transmitter droid near the
east bay . . . I think it's still sending and
receiving signals.

YODA
Good. Good. Track this we can back to the
source. Find General Grievous, we might . . .

HAN SOLO and YODA track the signal to Utapau. YODA informs the Jedi Council, and MACE decides to send OBI-WAN, along with thousands of clone troopers, to capture GENERAL GRIEVOUS.

On Utapau, GRIEVOUS and OBI-WAN fight; droids attack, and clone troopers weigh in. GRIEVOUS flees on his wheel scooter; OBI-WAN pursues on his lizard. After a breakneck chase, GRIEVOUS shoots the lizard from under the Jedi–but OBI-WAN cuts down the GENERAL.

OBI-WAN informs the Jedi Council of his victory, and MACE WINDU goes to see PALPATINE to negotiate a peace now that GRIEVOUS is dead. PALPATINE refuses. When MACE insists that the Senate decide whether or not to halt the war, PALPATINE attacks with "electric bolts" that emanate from his fingers. At PALPATINE's urging, ANAKIN cuts off MACE's sword hand. "MACE crumples, the blue rays engulfing his body. Finally, the Jedi leader falls silent."

The tremendous effort needed to generate the sustained lightning has transformed PALPATINE's face into that of DARTH SIDIOUS. With ANAKIN standing by, he orders the clone troopers to execute "Order Sixty-Six." On Mygeeto, KI-ADI-MUNDI is killed. KIT FISTO is killed on Saleucami (final spelling), PLO KOON on Cato Neimoidia, and AAYLA SECURA on Felucia. YODA is meditating and forewarned by the Force; he defeats the troopers sent to assassinate him.

On Utapau, OBI-WAN is shot off his lizard and falls hundreds of meters into a sinkhole. He swims underwater and emerges in a hidden cave. Two seeker drones emerge from the

---

Above left: Tiemens schematic of a hidden grotto within an Utapau sinkhole traces Obi-Wan's path to a possible meeting with his former Master, Qui-Gon Jinn (lower inset). Like Alderaan, Utapau existed long ago in Lucas's second draft of Star Wars. At that time, it was a stand-in for what became Tatooine on the script's opening page: "A vast sea of stars is broken as the warm amber surface of the planet Utapau emerges from a total eclipse . . . A tiny silver spacecraft races from behind one of the lifeless Utapau moons." Left, middle: Church's painting offers a close-up view of Obi-Wan's trek. Far left: One of the seeker droids that pursues Obi-Wan in the cave, by Thompson. Above: McCaig's Han Solo concept hypothesizes that the younger scoundrel may have been a slob.

water looking for him. OBI-WAN climbs into a hole and presses against the wall; a quick-moving nos monster streaks by OBI-WAN, swallows one of the droids, and pursues the other. OBI-WAN makes his way to a landing platform, where he commandeers a starfighter.

On Coruscant, PALPATINE completes his seduction of ANAKIN, who at first refuses to go over to the dark side—until the Chancellor makes a startling confession:

```
                    DARTH SIDIOUS
I have waited all these years for you to fulfill your des-
tiny [. . .] I arranged for your conception. I used the
power of the Force to will the midichlorians to start the
             cell divisions that created you.

                      ANAKIN
                I don't believe you.

                    DARTH SIDIOUS
Ahhh, but you know it's true. When you clear your mind,
you will sense the truth. You could almost think of me as
                   your father.

                      ANAKIN
                That's impossible!

                    DARTH SIDIOUS
          Nevertheless, you must decide . . .
```

Thanks to promises of powers that would save PADMÉ from death, ANAKIN gives in to temptation. OBI-WAN and YODA return to Coruscant and the Jedi Temple, where they find a hologram that shows ANAKIN slaughtering the younglings. In the hologram, DARTH SIDIOUS enters, and ANAKIN kneels before him:

```
                    DARTH SIDIOUS
You are a Jedi no more, Anakin Skywalker. That life is no
more. Today you begin your new life as Darth Vader, Lord of
the Sith and bringer of peace and justice to the galaxy.
```

BAIL ORGANA arrives and informs YODA and OBI-WAN that PALPATINE has announced the formation of the First Galactic Empire. OBI-WAN wants to go after ANAKIN, but YODA counsels patience. BAIL and YODA flee to Polis Massa, while OBI-WAN makes an excuse to join them later. He goes to see PADMÉ and tries to persuade her to tell him where ANAKIN is, but she refuses,

Above left: Church concept painting of Palpatine and Anakin in the former's office. Above middle: T.J. Frame and animation director Rob Coleman waiting for Lucas's arrival. Above right: David, Coleman, and Lucas review very early CG animation on Coleman's laptop.

and he departs. PADMÉ then boards her ship with CAPTAIN TYPHO and her HANDMAIDENS.

On Mustafar, ANAKIN obeys SIDIOUS's orders and slaughters NUTE GUNRAY, POGGLE THE LESSER, and the rest of the Separatists.

PADMÉ arrives—but her entourage is gunned down by clones. As they close in on her, ANAKIN appears and calls them off. She pleads with ANAKIN, but he says she is either with him or against him. Just then OBI-WAN reveals himself—having sneaked aboard her ship. ANAKIN is enraged and, believing PADMÉ has betrayed him, Force-chokes her and then throws her against a wall. OBI-WAN and ANAKIN fight.

The old friends battle through Mustafar interiors and exteriors until,

```
    Just as ANAKIN looks as if he has beaten OBI-WAN,
    the Jedi makes a quick move, cutting off ANAKIN's legs,
  and he tumbles down an embankment and stops near the edge of
    the lava. Suddenly, the Sith Lord bursts into flames
                  and starts screaming.
```

OBI-WAN picks up ANAKIN's lightsaber and walks away. There is no dialogue. OBI-WAN rescues PADMÉ and takes her to Polis Massa. DARTH SIDIOUS rescues ANAKIN and takes him to Coruscant, where ANAKIN is operated on and made into the mechanical DARTH VADER.

On Polis Massa, OBI-WAN informs YODA and BAIL that PADMÉ is pregnant with twins. During the subsequent operation, the twins are saved but PADMÉ dies on the operating table. YODA tells them to send her body to Naboo. BAIL volunteers to care for the girl. OBI-WAN says he knows of a family on Tatooine who will take care of the boy while he watches from afar. YODA tells OBI-WAN that in his solitude he has training for him with "one who has studied with the Ancient Order of the Whills . . . Your old Master, Qui-Gon Jinn."

On Naboo, there is a funeral for PADMÉ. On Dagobah, a pod arrives, hurtling through the mist; after it lands, YODA emerges. As his ship nears Alderaan, BAIL ORGANA gives C-3PO and R2-D2 to CAPTAIN ANTILLES, telling him "to clean them up. Have the protocol droid mindwiped." "Oh, dear," C-3PO says.

On Alderaan, the QUEEN is presented with a baby girl. On Tatooine, OBI-WAN gives a baby boy to UNCLE OWEN.

On the bridge of an Imperial Star Destroyer, the EMPEROR, GOVERNOR TARKIN, and DARTH VADER look out into space, where they see the construction of the Death Star.

WEDNESDAY, FEBRUARY 5, 2003

Now permanently ensconced in Sydney (Oz), Rick McCallum, Gavin Bocquet, Trisha Biggar, and other production heads have set up regular communications with Lucas at his home via a videoconference link.

Tuesday, February 4: At a JAK-OZ videoconference, Isola Bella, Italy, is suggested as a location for the Theed funeral. Lucas says he'd need only a crowd there, no principals.

Wednesday, February 5: At the 2003 Empire Movie Awards in London, the Sony Ericsson Award for best scene of the year goes to Episode II's lightsaber duel between Yoda and Count Dooku. Christopher Lee accepts the award on behalf of himself and the Jedi Master, saying, "To you, his regards he sends."

They usually talk on Mondays and Wednesdays. Before each meeting, Bocquet e-mails production department artwork and costume photos to Fay David, who prints them out. Ryan Church then takes them to Parkway, Lucas's home, where the video call is placed to McCallum, Biggar, Bocquet, and whoever else is necessary, and the material is discussed.

"I would go down to his place two times a week with detailed artwork, presenting it to him, because he was working very hard on the script," Church recalls. "He's got a side nook, a writing room. It's lined with books, and he's got a writing desk. He has a cool teleconferencing system, so it was really like sitting in the same room with the guys from Australia. You could hold up an image to them. And George's kids are running around; he's extremely relaxed, shoes off. I learned a lot about making movies. He'd talk about how important it is to see the light on people's eyes."

Saturday, February 8: In the Presidio Park of San Francisco, California, ground is officially broken for the Letterman Digital Arts Center, future home of Lucasfilm Entertainment (Lucasfilm, ILM, and LucasArts).

Monday, February 10: Oscar nominees are announced. Rob Coleman, Pablo Helman, John Knoll, and Ben Snow are nominated for Best Visual Effects for *Star Wars*: Episode II *Attack of the Clones*. Gary Rydstrom and Richard Hymns at Skywalker Sound are nominated for Best Sound Editing for Steven Spielberg's *Minority Report*.

Above: Short Polis Massan scultps by Murnane. Top and bottom right: Utapau cave dragon revisions by McCaig dated February 20, after Lucas found the February 7 concepts too rancor-like.

FRIDAY, FEBRUARY 7, 2003

Several artists have passed the night in the attic. Lucas arrives. "Well, hello, hello. Nothing today?"

"Polis Massa," McCaig replies, indicating a sculpt of an alien.

"It's good that he's short."

"You like?"

"I like."

They move on to the horses that will be pulling Padmé's coffin. "Horse things," Church says.

"Too horsey."

"Too horsey?"

"A horse is a thing that pulls a wagon . . . Sorry about that. I sent you in the wrong direction."

Looking at the Utapau cave dragon, Lucas says, "It reeks of rancor. Let's open up those imagination vaults."

Church suggests that Grievous might be able to breathe in space, which would give him an advantage over Obi-Wan, and Lucas thinks it's a good idea. Grievous could crawl out onto the hull of the space cruiser, then re-enter and escape in a pod.

At this meeting, for the first time and perhaps because he's reached a more comfortable place in his writing, Lucas starts directing within the art. He talks about what he's going to do with the camera and where he's going to pan. He goes into details, requesting visual bridges or combinations of images that will enable him to do what he wants with the camera. He designates exactly which paintings will be used for establishing shots, then consults a list, which he reads from: "Crystal world: Ki-Adi-Mundi. Field headquarters and a battle . . ." He stops and thinks. "You pan around, you end up here [pointing to a spot on a painting of the crystal world]. This would be damaged; as you pan in, this wouldn't be damaged . . ." Fay puts Post-its on paintings noting his directions.

Because there's an impending two-week lull without a meeting, Lucas gives them projects to work on, reading further from his list. "You might want to play with the ship pulling apart. Maybe do something upside down on the bridge . . .

Heavier tail fin

Current Design

Larger docking bay

Surface bombardment blasters

More aggressive nose

When the ship crashes, there can be fireships pouring foam on it. We need a taxi ship for Bail . . ."

"All right, so have a good weekend. I gave you a few things to do."

"Dagobah?" Rob Coleman asks.

Lucas consults his paper. "It's not in here. A mistake. I'll have to put it in here." He confirms that there will be one shot of Dagobah, the same swamp as in *Empire*, and adds that we'll see a meteorite hit Polis Massa. It opens up, and Yoda walks out of it.

George leaves. Looking at the others, Coleman says, "That was a good one."

FRIDAY, FEBRUARY 21, 2003–DAY ONE MINUS 19 WEEKS

The countdown to Day One of principal photography has begun. Although there remain ninteen weeks, art department activity has begun to function very much with that one day in mind. The artists are now focusing even more on refining, and less on conceptualizing. Two more prequel film veterans are here today, perhaps to spur things on: ILM visual effects supervisor John Knoll and sound designer-digital editor Ben Burtt. Lucas hired Burtt way back in 1975 to create the original sounds for *Star Wars*. Burtt's work for *Revenge of the Sith* begins with his creation of videomatics, which will help Lucas visualize the movie's action scenes (Burtt will tackle editing and sound design in postproduction).

Rob Coleman is here, too, along with the others–and John Goodson, who says he's "glad to be alive" after surviving a car accident in which he broke his sternum. Lucas walks in and looks at some drawings of Jar Jar Binks. Someone asks, "Is Jar Jar in this film?"

"Does he have a tragic death scene?" Knoll asks.

"In this film, he's battle-hardened," Coleman points out.

Given a choice of Jar Jar costumes, George picks one that would cover most of the Gungan's body.

"You chose wisely," Coleman says, as that one will make animation easier.

Next are 3-D representations of the Separatist ship, which prompt Lucas to say: "I've redesigned the ship. It has more armaments on it, so it's clearly the most powerful ship out there . . . I've got a sequence where the elevator shaft is turned on its side–and [Obi-Wan and Anakin] run through it with the elevator chasing them. There's a sequence where the bridge turns over. Droids have magnetized shoes, but Obi-Wan doesn't. So he's running along the ceiling chasing them."

Top: Lucas's sketch stuck onto Frame's cruiser concept indicates where the general's quarters should be (inset, Church). Right: Thompson (left) and McCaig launch into several weeks of intense sequential storytelling. Top right: Thompson's storyboards show an early version of the Dooku/Anakin battle, with the Jedi using the Force. Far right: Obi-Wan takes on Grievous's bodyguards–who have a nasty tendency to fight on even without key body parts.

February 13: JAK-OZ videoconference–Attendees learn that the Kashyyyk meeting hall is "tricky." It will have Han Solo and Wookiees, and it will be almost completely digital.

Thursday, February 20: Lucasfilm and the Cartoon Network announce the creation of 20 three-minute-long animated shorts called *Star Wars: Clone Wars*, to be broadcast in late 2003 and early 2004. Helming this new series is Genndy Tartakovsky, the creator of *Samurai Jack* and *Dexter's Laboratory*.

Lucas is going out the door when he notices Burtt: "Well hi, Ben! You lurking in the back?"

"Rick told us to come and lurk," Burtt says.

"Well, it's on again," Lucas says. "No script, but a lot of interesting ideas."

FRIDAY, FEBRUARY 28, 2003—DAY ONE MINUS 18 WEEKS

For the first time, McCaig, Jun, and Thompson—who has returned after a brief layoff—have been storyboarding, drawing out action sequences in panel-by-panel format.

After Lucas arrives, the storyboards are unveiled. "Without anything more than a few hints, we took a stab at it," McCaig says. In the drawings, the cliffhangers of the script's first twenty pages are laid out, interpreted, expanded. After studying one sequence, Lucas suggests that the Jedi lock a

door, then, in the ensuing explosion on the other side of the door, many droids could be blown up. As the concept artists and Lucas begin discussing in detail the storyboards, as story points are discarded and new ideas inserted, you can hear the film being made.

In the storyboards, Anakin finds Palpatine imprisoned in what looks like a Puritan stock that immobilizes his hands and head. Dooku arrives via elevator and advances upon Anakin. While dueling, Anakin acquires

Dooku's lightsaber, and Dooku uses dark side lightning. Palpatine tells Anakin that he must cut off Dooku's hands—he does so. Then he cuts off Dooku's head with a "full swing."

"Can he use Dooku's blade?" McCaig asks.

"Yes," Lucas says—which is followed by a collective "Oh yeah!" from the group.

But Lucas warns them not to get too detailed. "All we need is assemblages, then Dan [Gregoire] can get in there [with animatics]—otherwise these sequences are too cinematic for boards." In parting, he suggests, "I'd focus on the air battle first. We need to keep it edge-of-your-seat."

FRIDAY, MARCH 7, 2003—DAY ONE MINUS 17 WEEKS

Earlier this week, the pre-viz, or animatics, department officially started work. Led by Dan Gregoire, they are building assets—computer elements and models used in animations—and getting ready to tackle sequences.

Wednesday, March 5: JAK-OZ videoconference—Lucas advises that the Trade Federation cruiser generator room will have to be filmed in a tank of water. He confirms that C-3PO will have a gold finish throughout Episode III.

Friday, March 7: Production begins discussions with ILM on what will be needed on the sets to facilitate the computer-generated effects that will be added in post-production. JAK art director Ian Gracie asks visual effects supervisor John Knoll a variety of questions: what shade of white the rebel blockade runner should be, whether Jedi starfighters need windscreens, and so forth.

for generating two to three shots per day. As shots are finished, they're sent down to editorial, where Lucas approves, modifies, or disapproves them. Ben Burtt then works the approved shots into his videomatics, which use everything from concept art to photography to give the director an idea of how the scenes are developing.

At today's art department meeting, a model of a clone trooper starfighter, tentatively called a V-wing, sits on the table. There's also a sinkhole environment sculpt by Danny Wagner, who's here for the first time, making him the fourteenth member. Wagner started his career at a small effects studio in San Francisco. "The first movie we worked on was *Look Who's Talking* [1989] and my first job was making sperm, trying to

the two Jedi head down the hallway followed by the little astro droid R2. the Jedi stop and turn around. artoo stops

Anakin

artoo, go back and stay with the ships.

they start forward and R2 starts forward, they all stop.

Anakin

artoo back!: Back to the ship now!

the little droid lets out a little sigh, and turns around and heads back to the ship.

"I forgot my glasses," Lucas says upon arriving. "I can't see anything. Give me a stamp! I'll deny everything afterward." Looking over the new paintings of Mustafar, he thinks it might be funny if Obi-Wan and Anakin "jump and ride on the backs of some droids. I don't know if we want to get humorous in the middle of their fight, but we can go for it."

There is a new height chart for Wookiees, but Lucas finds that these Wookiees are too short, reminding everyone, "Chewbacca is seven foot four—but he's a *small* Wookiee. And in this film, their only companion is Yoda! All we'll see is feet. Yoda will be surrounded by feet."

FRIDAY, MARCH 14, 2003—DAY ONE MINUS 16 WEEKS

Heretofore static concept paintings and models are beginning to move, to take on life. The animatics department is designing shots using the art department's approved concepts, creating low-resolution animated three-dimensional sequences, or "digital storyboards." Their first assignment is the aerial battle above Coruscant. Each shot designer is responsible

Tuesday, March 18: Jimmy Smits (Bail Organa) is fitted for a costume in Los Angeles, California.

make them look goofy and funny. My first job at ILM was as a slime wrangler on *Ghostbusters II* [1989]. Hmmm . . ."

Top: Lucas, Tiemens, David (taking notes), and Jun. Middle: Handwritten evidence of Lucas's efforts to write R2-D2 into the script. His notes indicate dialogue between Anakin and the droid after the Jedi have crash-landed in the cruiser hangar. Bottom: At the request of property master Ty Teiger, set decorating coordinator Helena Donohue asks the archives department at Skywalker Ranch to send to the props department in Australia Vader's lightsaber and Luke's lightsaber from Episode IV for reference.

Command Room

McCaig is eating a salad. He says he's "exhausted" from doing storyboards, because it's like acting, creating a performance. When Lucas arrives, everyone seems to freeze for some reason. "What do we do now?" he jokes. As they review the V-wing model, someone asks, "Do the clones have Artoo units?"

"They're everywhere," Lucas responds. "Don't you have one in the back of your car?" Looking at the sinkhole sculpt, he says, "Make it big. Obi-Wan could climb out of there in two minutes. Don't be afraid."

He next studies Robert Barnes's in-progress sculpt of droid general Grievous. He observes that the only biological parts of Grievous are his eyes, brain, spinal cord—and that, perhaps, he has "a plastic sac for all of his organs." There is talk about how his earpieces could move to show emotion. During all this conversation, Barnes is in acute pain, which he explains later: "Generally, Thursday nights, everyone works late or all night. And I was on that pattern. One of those nights, my shoulder was cramping up until around two A.M.—when it stopped me in my tracks. It turned out I had two herniated disks in my neck. General Grievous just about killed me."

A moment later, in a rare instance, Lucas expresses mild frustration, as some paintings diverge from previously approved concepts. He emphasizes once again that clone troopers should look more beat-up and sport customized outfits—even to the extent, he says, of having written on their helmets the words FORCE YOU.

In Australia, McCallum says, "I'm a man without a script. Usually you get a script a year before production begins, and it's broken down, and

storyboarded, and costumes and sets are broken out; the actors are locked in to dates—but we don't have that. So everybody's taking the leap and focusing on what little information we get each week, which happens to be enough for us right now.

"We started set construction about two weeks ago, costumes have been pumping up, and the creature shop is just being set up. Everything is moving. We're heading for a destination, but we're not sure where we're gonna end up."

FRIDAY, MARCH 21, 2003—DAY ONE MINUS 15 WEEKS

Sitting with others in his office, Lucas delivers a short "state-of-the-script" report: "Well, I wrote a rough draft. It's really crude, but it basically gets the essence of the story down and the main beats of the film. I've also written about half of the first draft. Now I am going through, filling out and being more articulate. I still have elements, like Artoo-Detoo and Threepio, which I haven't really fit in everywhere. They're in one scene, but I haven't actually filled in their reality yet, because the film doesn't center on them. So I'm hoping to have the first draft done in two weeks. Then I'll start working on the second draft, and I'm hoping to get a third draft in before I have to go to Sydney—which means I'm going through a

---

Above: In a process used for various interiors, in order to give Lucas a more solid idea of what a set will look like and what camera angles he might have, T.J. Frame has digitally pieced together several conceptual artworks of Mustafar into 3-D artworks. Mustafar interiors consist of a command (war) room, conference room, landing platform, collection arms, and so on—but, thanks to these ensembles, draftspeople and model-makers in Australia are able to plan set construction (above left). Their early 3-D renderings of the "Mustafa" war room show several "set-build proposals"; the orange portions represent digital set extensions that would eventually be created by ILM.

KEY

COLOUR 2
AS PER
APPROVED
SAMPLE

COLOUR 3
AS PER
APPROVED
SAMPLE

COLOUR 1
AS PER
APPROVED
SAMPLE

COLOUR 4
AS PER
APPROVED
SAMPLE

draft about every six weeks. Then I'll have it as best as I can—but I'm looking at the shooting very much as another draft."

When someone asks what his biggest challenge is going from rough draft to first draft, he responds, "What challenges me is what always challenges me."

"Which is?"

"Inertia. [laughter] Procrastination. I sit there with that page in front of me . . . I am very diligent about going to work at eight thirty every morning and leaving at six o'clock every night. But I can be chained to my desk and I still can't write it. I do it, you know, I do get it done; I actually write five pages a day. But left to my own reality, I would probably write a page a day. I force myself. It becomes agonizing to get those other four pages, otherwise—"

"You can't have dinner?"

"Well, I can't leave [laughter], so if I do four pages and I get onto the fifth page, I rationalize it: I've done my five pages."

Above: In March, the art department in Sydney begins working out the details of Padmé's veranda, from column styles and statue concepts (by Gert Stevens) to detailed blueprints with floor patterns. During videoconference calls, computer-generated representations enable Lucas and McCallum to decide how much of the set should be practical and how much digital. Church (right) and Tiemens (inset) created concepts of the Utapau windmills that McCaig had envisioned while sitting in a Vancouver airport.

FRIDAY, MARCH 28, 2003–DAY ONE MINUS 14 WEEKS

Everyone seems tired. Once again, many were up all Thursday night. Earlier this week, Fay David received a call from Lucas asking the art department to work on the windmill concept, as conceived by McCaig the week before, in which Obi-Wan and Grievous pursue each other through giant whirling blades. So McCaig, Tiemens, and Church have done passes on that idea, while Goodson has done a model for an Utapau vessel, which might become Grievous's starfighter.

"I like it," Lucas says, as soon as he arrives. "Should we put some guns on it?"

"We have some that pop up," Church points out.

When he comes to the windmills, Lucas says, "I actually gave this chase scene to Anne [Merrifield] to type up today. Obi-Wan loses his sword—he actually uses a pistol [against Grievous]—we haven't seen that before!"

After approving a few of the windmill paintings, he goes on to the next drawing. "What's this?" he asks.

"The glowing fungus room," McCaig replies, drawing the words out, knowing that this drawing is perhaps pushing Lucas's limits.

"I say, 'Nice try.' What's this one?"

"Glowing tube-worm room!" McCaig admits, and everyone laughs.

"Again, I say, 'Nice try.' "

FRIDAY, APRIL 4, 2003–DAY ONE MINUS 13 WEEKS

Another prequel veteran is visiting: stunt coordinator–sword master Nick Gillard. Wearing an *Indiana Jones and the Temple of Doom* dungaree crew jacket, the diminutive but steel-framed fight expert is accompanying Lucas on his rounds. "When Nick came here, he was waiting for four days," McCallum says, "before it was the right time for him to see George."

Lucas gives Danny Wagner's revised, much deeper sculpture of the Utapau sinkhole a FABULOUSO. To Gillard, Lucas explains, "This is where Obi-Wan and Grievous fight." He puts pins in the clay to show where action sequences are going to take place. Nick has already worked out on

paper much of the fight sequences, but he's here to learn more about the various fight locales that have yet to be built.

Indicating an Utapau interior, Lucas asks, "What is this signage for?"

"Restaurant?" Church offers.

"Where is the restaurant? Show me more—how does the restaurant fit in here?"

"We can be a little more literal."

"Yeah, because eventually we have to say where they eat and shop," Lucas says and then goes into more detail for an unusually long time—it's clearly important the artists get this right for next week. He pokes holes in the ceiling of an Utapau interior to allow for shafts of light. "We have to figure out how the city falls together. It's slightly organic, but they have cars."

Tuesday, April 7: In Sydney, Nick Gillard starts the stunt department in Stage 4.

Saturday, April 12: DP David Tattersall and high-definition supervisor Fred Meyers conduct digital camera tests at ILM.

Lucas ends the meeting by saying that he wants Nick to speak with Dan Gregoire in animatics. "Have fun," he tells Gillard.

THURSDAY, APRIL 10, 2003–DAY ONE MINUS 12 WEEKS

As they have several times before, McCaig and Thompson are going to Lucas's home for a storyboard discussion. "We drove up to a big white house surrounded by cypress trees," McCaig remembers. "We drove through the double gates, past the main house, to an annex off to the right side. It's all beautiful redwood. You open the door and Lucas's office is like the deck of a ship, with what looks like a captain's poop deck at the end of a long room. That's his writing area. And today when Derek and I walked in with our boards, George was at the end of the room. His pencil was down and he was just sitting there with his head bowed. Then, looking calm and drained, he came down and said, 'I just wrote the end.' He had just finished the first draft."

FRIDAY, APRIL 11, 2003

Another longtime Lucas-McCallum collaborator from the *Young Indy* days, director of photography (DP) David Tattersall, is present. When Lucas arrives, he greets David warmly, "How ya doing!" and shows him various environments that he'll have to light.

Following last week's precise directions, the artists have created lots of Utapau interiors. "Utapau's starting to turn into a city," Lucas says. "I like this."

"David has to know what's going on," McCallum explains. "There's no way you can walk into this world unless you're constantly kept a part of it."

Above: Lucas's request for more Utapau-interior details results in Church's view of Obi-Wan's headlong pursuit through the sinkhole city of the droid general—whose vehicle began as a stand-alone monoped droid, but which was adapted for the general when the script required a vehicle as agile as the Jedi's steed.

grab GRIEVOUS's fallen blaster and discharges it into the droid's guts. GRIEV-OUS explodes from the inside out.

LUCAS: "I wanted it to be an alien who is mostly a droid, which is an echo of what Anakin is going to become. That was his job in the movie, and he needed to be designed in a way that was very compelling and very interesting to watch. Because he was the main action villain, we needed to create a special talent for him. So we gave him two arms that turn into four arms, which is a neat trick and visually very arresting."

The MACE/PALPATINE dialogue and fight are much more complex than in the rough draft. They fight and MACE knocks PALPATINE's lightsaber away.

```
                    MACE
        You are well versed in the ways
        of the Jedi, yet you are no Jedi!
```

PALPATINE unleashes his lightning bolts. Both MACE and PALPATINE ask ANAKIN for help.

```
                  PALPATINE
        I offer you knowledge, Anakin.
        Don't join their rebellion . . .
        I am your pathway to power.
```

Sunday, April 13, 2003

Anne Merrifield has typed up the first draft, which bears today's date. A few artists are allowed to read it. "It's very dark—darker than you would think," Tiemens comments. Apart from being fifty-six pages longer than the rough draft, this version has the following changes and developments:

As they fly in their Jedi starfighters, R2-D2 now acts as ANAKIN's astromech; R4-G8 is OBI's. The two Jedi are also guided to the cruiser holding a kidnapped CHANCELLOR PALPATINE by the locator of Jedi Knight SHAAK TI.

The fuel tanks no longer have poisonous creatures; on the other hand, after they seal the hatch, a spark hits the fuel and the resultant massive explosion takes out the pursuing droids. Now it is R2-D2 who makes the elevator descend, separating the Jedi. OBI-WAN is captured by droids and led to GRIEVOUS—who kills a captive SHAAK TI before his eyes.

GRIEVOUS and OBI-WAN fight as the ship falls out of orbit, but now the droids magnetize so they can walk along the ceiling. GRIEVOUS escapes by breaking a window and crawling along the ship's hull into an escape pod. While fighting ANAKIN, DOOKU no longer claims responsibility for the death of ANAKIN's mother.

HAN SOLO has been eliminated from the film. It is now the CHANCELLOR who tells ANAKIN where to find GENERAL GRIEVOUS. PALPATINE also tells him more about the power of the dark side and the Sith Lord DARTH PLAGUEIS—who could keep life-forms from dying and who could communicate with midi-chlorians, influencing their creations.

On Utapau, GRIEVOUS reveals that he knows how to use lightsabers—and that he has four arms. OBI-WAN eventually rips off GRIEVOUS's stomach plate, revealing "the alien life-form's guts encased in a bag." OBI-WAN uses the Force to

```
                STAR WARS EPISODE III
                 REVENGE OF THE SITH

                         by

                    GEORGE LUCAS
```

```
LUCASFILM LTD.
                                        first
                                    April  13, 2003
                                    Revised April 13, 2003
                                    90 Pages

THIS MATERIAL IS THE PROPERTY OF LUCASFILM LTD. AND IS INTENDED AND
RESTRICTED SOLELY FOR USE BY LUCASFILM LTD PERSONNEL.  DISTRIBUTION OR
DISCLOSURE OF THIS MATERIAL TO UNAUTHORIZED PERSONS IS PROHIBITED.  THE
SALE, COPYING, OR REPRODUCTION OF THIS MATERIAL IN ANY FORM IS STRICTLY
PROHIBITED.
```

LUCAS: "This is the point where Anakin has to make a decision. His rationalization is: 'Everybody is after power. Even the Jedi are after power.' Therefore, he thinks, 'They're all equally corrupt now. So which side am I going to be on? Do I align myself with Palpatine, who is a Sith Lord and who can possibly help me save Padmé? Or do I side with the Jedi and maybe lose Padmé?' "

MACE is winning, pushing the Sith Lord toward the window and his death. Just as MACE is going to force PALPATINE off the ledge, ANAKIN cuts off MACE's lightsaber hand. PALPATINE then blasts MACE with lightning that flings him out of the window to his death.

ANAKIN kneels at the feet of DARTH SIDIOUS.

```
                   ANAKIN
        I want the power to stop death.
```

From this point on, the script refers to ANAKIN as "DARTH VADER." PALPATINE then explains that he has a plan to wipe out the Jedi.

The first to receive Order 66 is CLONE COMMANDER BACARA (1138), and, this time, the list of Jedi who meet their end is more extensive. On Mygeeto, clones blast KI-ADI-MUNDI and SAESEE TIIN. On Saleucami, they kill KIT FISTO, BARRISS OFFEE, and ADI GALLIA. On Kashyyyk, MINA PODIA is gunned down—but YODA saves himself. On Cato Neimoidia, PLO KOON is blasted out of the sky, while an unnamed Jedi lies dead on the planet surface. On Felucia, AAYLA SECURA and QUINLAN VOS are silenced forever.

Sunday, April 27: Hayden Christensen (Anakin Skywalker) arrives in Sydney to start training.

Above middle: The typed title page of an interim draft. This version, with Lucas's handwritten corrections, would become his first draft dated April 13. Top left: Thompson's early storyboards show how Grievous, with his four arms brandishing four lightsabers, might take on Obi-Wan aboard the Separatist cruiser.

And this time, after seeing the hologram of ANAKIN in the Jedi Temple killing the younglings, YODA announces that he will kill PALPATINE and that OBI-WAN must kill ANAKIN—and OBI-WAN objects. But YODA tells him it must be done: "The boy who was your apprentice, he is not."

YODA confronts DARTH SIDIOUS below the Senate. On Mustafar, PADMÉ and her entourage are attacked, but this time by droids, which ANAKIN destroys. PADMÉ confronts ANAKIN with what OBI-WAN told her—that he has gone over to the dark side—but ANAKIN claims to "have brought peace to the galaxy."

```
                  PADMÉ
     Obi-Wan was right. You've changed.

                  ANAKIN
        For the better. I have become
         more powerful than any Jedi
          ever dreamed of being [. . .]
       Together we will rule the galaxy.
```

LUCAS: "The thing that breaks Padmé's heart in the end is the fact that Anakin says to her, 'Come and join me. I have all the power now. I can rule the universe and you can do it with me.' So the idea of saving her life has become a minor issue. And that's when she says, 'Wait a minute. This is not what I want and you're not the guy I fell in love with!' "

Back on Coruscant, PALPATINE easily deflects YODA's attacks, and the latter barely escapes with the help of BAIL ORGANA.

PADMÉ dies on the operating table saying, this time, "He's not evil . . ." On Coruscant, after ANAKIN has become the mechanical DARTH VADER, he asks where PADMÉ is, and PALPATINE's line is new: "I'm afraid she was killed by a Jedi . . . she is no longer our concern."

"As I write the next drafts," explains Lucas, "there'll be a lot more cutting and pasting. Certain sequences will be right, and I'll just jump through them. The last thing that will be dealt with is the dialogue, because that you can change on the set or even afterward—you know, I'm not known for my dialogue. [laughs] I think of it as a sound effect, a

Diplomatic Cruiser
Sample Wall Section

Ref Image.

Ref. Image

1.

2.

3.

4.

rhythm, a vocal chorus in the overall soundtrack. Mostly, everything is visual.

"What drove me to make these movies is that this is a really interesting story about how people go bad. In this particular case, the premise is: Nobody thinks they're bad. They simply have different points of view. This is about a kid that's really wonderful. He has some flaws—and those flaws ultimately do him in.

"The core issue, ultimately, is greed, possessiveness—the inability to let go. Not only to hold on to material things, which is greed, but to hold on to life, to the people you love—to not accept the reality of life's passages and changes, which is to say things come, things go. Everything changes. Anakin becomes emotionally attached to things, his mother, his wife. That's why he falls—because he does not have the ability to let go."

Left: Sheets like these are put together by the Sydney art department to show Lucas how early set construction of the Alderaan cruiser corridor replicates its appearance in the 1977 Star Wars. *Dated April 8, panel 2 of the sheet shows, for scale, art director Ian Gracie next to Darth Vader. Above: Thompson's storyboards illustrate an early conceptualization of Obi-Wan's usage of a blaster against the insidious droid general.*

OBI-WAN struggles to maintain control of his ship.

                         OBI-WAN
~~Split.~~ *I want you to split off and take them from behind. I'll stay here as bait.*
                         ANAKIN
          Are you sure?

                         OBI-WAN
          ~~Yes, I'm sure.   Don't worry~~.   I
          can hold them off for a bit.

                         ANAKIN
          A very little bit.   ~~I'm fast, but
          not that fas~~t.

                         OBI-WAN
          Tower coming up...~~split~~! *take off*

As they race toward a control tower on one of the Federation
Battleships, they fire at it until it EXPLODES.   OBI-WAN
makes an abrupt turn to avoid the tower.   ANAKIN accelerates
right into the explosion.   The Droid Ships follow OBI-WAN,
blasting him with intense laser fire.   He deftly maneuvers
around a large ship's superstructure, but the two Droid
Fighters stay on his tail.

                         OBI-WAN   *R 4*
          I'm running out of tricks ~~here~~!

WEDNESDAY, APRIL 23, 2003–DAY ONE MINUS 10 WEEKS

Starwars.com announces that Anthony Daniels (C-3PO), Kenny Baker (R2-D2)–and Peter Mayhew (Chewbacca)–will be reprising their respective roles in *Revenge of the Sith*. Mayhew hasn't appeared in a *Star Wars* film since *Return of the Jedi* (1983), so his return makes headlines worldwide. "I'm delighted to return as Chewbacca," he says. "I think his reappearance in this film is a fitting way to tie the whole saga together."

THURSDAY, MAY 1, 2003–DAY ONE MINUS 9 WEEKS

Lucas has requested an impromptu art department meeting. It's scheduled for 9 A.M., but he's late. At this point, the artists are under a fair amount of pressure. They're working now not only on general designs, but also on myriad design details for the Sydney art department, which is in the process of physically creating heretofore conceptual work. Many aspects of relatively sketchy paintings, such as columns, control panels, and chairs, now must become highly precise.

Lucas walks in, close to an hour late. "Here you go!" he says, tossing the first draft on the table. "There's a lot of cheating in there," he adds.

Friday, May 2: JAK-OZ videoconference–It's decided that the Polis Massa observatory where Yoda speaks with Qui-Gon will be completely computer generated.

" 'They fight,' things like that. It's a hundred and one pages. I was aiming for a hundred. I overshot by a half a page, but I'll fix that."

Fay David gets a call from Jane Bay. Frank Darabont, who is working on the script for *Indiana Jones IV*, is on hold. George leaves, saying, "Frank is a hard man to get on the line."

Taking advantage of the lull, a few peek at the pages Lucas has left on the table. "Oh, 'Obi-Wan passionately kisses Padmé!' " Feng jokes.

"The beast returns!" Lucas says upon reentering. "I think we need to add a face to the droid tri-fighter. So put a face on that turkey." As for Padmé's funeral procession on Naboo, he flattens her coffin.

"What's the time of day?" Tiemens asks.

"I think we could make it a twilight. I would avoid sunset. We could do it at dawn. We can also expose for the shadows, so they can walk into the beams of light."

After George has looked at the last piece of art, there is a pause. "Next week, I'll be back . . . ," he says, scanning the group. "I'm bringing in a guest director so I don't have to do this anymore."

Everyone is silent for a moment or two.

"Can you say who, or is it a secret?" Fay asks.

Sunday, May 18: The Academy of Science Fiction, Fantasy, and Horror Films honors *Attack of the Clones* with two Saturn Awards in the categories of Best Costume (Trisha Biggar) and Best Special Effects (John Knoll, Ben Snow, Pablo Helman, and Rob Coleman).

JEDI CRUISER FRONT
RYAN CHURCH
3-APRIL-03
SW3

"Well, you'll see 'cause he's going to be here next week."

"All right . . . Wow!"

"Well, the fun part's over . . . ," Church says.

"I've done my part, so I'm bringing in a guest director. And all I have to do is sit back and watch it on television. [much laughter] It's easier than actually having to work for a living." Pushing his glasses up, Lucas adds, "I'll just see what he can come up with."

"Nice," McCaig says.

"Awesome," Church says.

"I've done pretty much everything I can do. All the sets are designed. All the people are cast. All the sequences are set up. It's up to Rick and the sword master," Lucas sums up, suddenly looking tired. "The director's coming in on Thursday, so I want to go through all this and show him everything that's here."

"Okay, we'll have a presentation ready," Fay promises.

"All right, I'm off to editorial," he says, leaving.

Church would later describe how he and the others spent the whole weekend wondering what Lucas was talking about, wondering if he needed to move back south—it was, he says, a "huge bombshell."

MONDAY, MAY 5, 2003—DAY ONE MINUS 8 WEEKS

In a basement suite of offices, Ben Burtt is at work on the videomatics: a hodgepodge of old film clips, temporary soundtracks, storyboards, stunt footage, and whatever else will work to create pre-principal-photography action scenes. Burtt's bureau is decorated with movie posters for *Sagebrush Trail*, starring John Wayne, and *Lo Sparviero del Mare (The Sea Hawk)*, starring Errol Flynn. On one wall are images from reels one through five of *THX 1138*.

Top left: Lucas's revisions to page two describe how the Jedi in their starfighters maneuver around a control tower. (Obi-Wan's astromech is here given the number R4-P17, which Lucas would later revise to R4-G8.) Top right: Church's painting of the battle over Coruscant has directional arrows to aid the animatics department. Church's Jedi cruiser (above), dated April 3, will be part of the opening space battle (OSB).

4.   7ft vertical opening

Today Ben is having a brief videomatics/animatics meeting with Dan Gregoire and senior animatics artist Euisung Lee. Gregoire starts by saying that the word from McCallum in Sydney is "more quantity, less quality." They then watch the opening space battle videomatics. Some shots aren't long enough, so Burtt has them add frames. When the cruiser crash-lands, Gregoire suggests that instead of Mace standing there waiting, he could arrive in a gunship. "Yeah, I'd entertain that," Ben says. "That way, Mace doesn't look like he was just going for a walk."

Lucas Licensing president Howard Roffman arrives and Burtt shows him the first ten minutes of videomatics—complete with music, sound effects, and voices (all provided by Burtt)—titled *Who Framed Binks?*

THURSDAY, MAY 8, 2003

The mystery guest-director turns out to be none other than Steven Spielberg. "Spielberg came to be involved in the animatics because we had new technology and I was talking to him about it," Lucas explains. "I said how great it was and I showed it to him. And his film had fallen out over the summer, so I said, 'We'll give you a laptop and we'll give you the program and I'll give you some scenes—and you can direct the scenes while you're just sitting by the pool.' He loves to do that stuff."

Spielberg tours the art department with Lucas, and they go over the script together. Though it initially sounded much more dramatic, what Lucas and Spielberg are doing is something they often do—collaborate—albeit, in this case, in a limited manner. "We have very, very similar sensibilities," George says.

FRIDAY, MAY 16, 2003–DAY ONE MINUS 7 WEEKS

Rob Coleman is here, along with the usual group, minus one: Iain McCaig's last day was May 9. Warren Fu and Alex Jaeger left some time before that. Today is John Goodson's last day. As the need for con-

---

Monday, May 19: In Sydney, drafting starts for the Alderaan cruiser conference room and other sets. Prefab construction begins on Stage 7 for the Mustafar conference room and the admiral's quarters. These two sets, among the largest, will take thirteen weeks to construct. On Stage 1, five weeks of construction on Padmé's veranda begins .

---

ceptual art dwindles, the inevitable downsizing of the art department has begun. On the table is a six-by-nine-inch birthday card reading, "Happy Birthday George! From the JAK Films art department."

Lucas shows up early. He conjures up the spirit of Spielberg by saying, "Our director's come up with a really good idea," which is for the battle on Mustafar: Obi-Wan and Anakin would end up on a large, burning piece of masonry on a lava flow, he explains. They'd have to stop fighting and, without speaking, start hacking off pieces with their lightsabers to create a path on which to jump to shore.

MONDAY, MAY 19, 2003–DAY ONE MINUS 6 WEEKS
ILM: ILM has been on the show now for about three weeks. Located in an industrial zone, its facility is a "rabbit warren," according to Coleman, who has been at ILM for ten years and who admits to still becoming disoriented "when they start punching new holes in walls." Made up of constantly reorganized interiors, lackluster cubes, temporary buildings, trailers, and makeshift work areas, ILM is all seemingly held together by the almost permanent squawking of a public-address system.

In the structure housing what will be the Episode III department, a big whiteboard posts projected schedules for the computer construction of characters and vehicles. The schedule is light for now, as most of the

"heavy lifting" won't begin till winter, when the department is fully staffed. As Coleman explains, the first stage is to build the skin, so the artists are divided into soft-surface/creature builders and hard-surface/vehicle builders. The next step is to create the "bones" or "chains" that move the asset. Then comes paint, and so on. It takes around six to eight weeks to fully realize a character or vehicle. ILM's first sequence, he says, will probably be the opening space battle. Theoretically, they should finish earlier this time—January 2005 for a May 2005 theatrical release.

Top: Dated April 9, the Sydney art department cyclorama of Palpatine's office complex reveals his office, waiting room, and antechamber. It also shows how Mace Windu and Palpatine measure up in the window where the two will have their showdown. Above: As of May 16, Palpatine's office set on Stage 7, after a couple weeks of construction. Above right: Coleman, Lucas, David, Wagner, Murnane, and Barnes examine the latter's lizard-head sculpt. Right: As of June 13, Padmé's veranda set on Stage 2 after several weeks of construction.

Rob's abode is small and dark; a bulletin board is covered with post-cards, including one of John Lennon. Coleman reveals that he's having a hard time working up enough enthusiasm. On Episode I, he "just wanted to survive"; on Episode II, there was the creation of a digital Yoda to inspire him. But Rob describes Episode III as "having to climb Mount Everest—again."

FRIDAY, MAY 23, 2003
SR: In the art department, Burtt introduces to the artists editor Roger Barton, who's preparing for his long stint by studying the editing techniques Lucas used in Episodes I and II.

Lucas arrives, but, before he can start, the cell phone rings. Fay David says Jane Bay has Spielberg on the line. Lucas takes the phone and begins to discuss the DVD release of the *Indiana Jones* trilogy and *Indy IV*: "Hello. Sure. You're the boss. Uh-huh. I don't think we touched that or anything . . . No. We have a different point of view: you're more of a traditionalist; I'm more of an out-there kinda guy . . . That would be fine . . . I have to work all weekend . . . [Lucas begins okaying paintings while talking.] I like that

idea. Well, that'll be the week before we start shooting—or how about the week after. Let me read it first. We have to agree, so we can be a united front . . . If anyone should know, you should know. . . . Well, I look forward to it. I'm excited about it. Okay. Bye-bye."

While they next study Mustafar fight story-boards, Thompson asks if it's okay for the duel between Anakin and Obi-Wan to shift back and forth in terms of who's aggressing whom. "They should reverse back and forth a couple times," Lucas agrees, "but Obi-Wan is the one who's come to kill him."

FRIDAY, MAY 30, 2003—DAY ONE MINUS 5 WEEKS
SR: Looking at a lizard sculpt, Lucas objects to the way the jaw closes. "If it doesn't look real, people don't buy it. Make yourself the dragon—become one with the dragon." Looking at some new takes on General Grievous, he rejects the new cape style with epaulets. He refers them back to Warren Fu's original, approved drawing, saying, "I really like this. This is moody, weird.

"That's it for me," he says, turning to Gregoire. "Did you have fun in LA?"

Gregoire has been traveling down south every so often to help Spielberg do his animatics for the Mustafar combat. "The first time I went down, I went with certain assets," Gregoire says. "I worked with Steven in the morning at his office at Amblin, and then George showed up. I showed Steven what we could do, and then those two kinda did their thing while I worked on the stuff that Steven had drawn out for me. The best approach we found was that I would 'drive,' instead of him actually moving the mouse around. Steven would draw umpteen sketches and then I would frame the shots and try to move the cameras around."

FRIDAY, JUNE 6, 2003—DAY ONE MINUS 4 WEEKS

SR: Lucas says to Coleman, "You did a great job with Yoda on MTV last night."

"Thanks. It was an incredible rush job."

"If you can do that, then you can do the whole film just as fast."

"That's what I was afraid of," Rob sighs. "I fell into your trap."

"You fell into it and now you can't get out of it," Lucas jokes. Turning to the others, he says, "We've got a new scene with Yoda and the Wookiees, with an AT-ST going through the water at night. I have a new ship, too. A Yoda escape pod for leaving Kashyyyk. The Wookiees pull the limb of a tree, and it comes out of the ground."

"We'll get on that," David says.

Looking at a strange vehicle, Lucas seems perplexed, so Church says, "It's really weird, built for droids."

"The only problem is, humans have to watch it," Lucas counters.

"That's it. We're back on schedule," he says as the meeting concludes. "And pretty soon, it'll start to make sense. Anne is typing [the second draft] now."

Saturday, June 1: At the Shrine Auditorium, Yoda receives an MTV Movie Award for Best Fight Scene for *Attack of the Clones*. In his acceptance speech—as created by animation director Rob Coleman, lead animator Jamy Wheless, cloth simulator Aaron Ferguson, and technical director Jean-Paul Beaulieu, and voiced by Frank Oz—Yoda says, "Hmmm... grateful am I this award to receive. To win, I did not expect. Promised myself, cry I would not." He then thanks George Lucas, Chewbacca, and others—but becomes angry when music cuts him off.

FRIDAY, JUNE 13, 2003—DAY ONE MINUS 3 WEEKS

SR: Today is the last art department meeting before principal photography begins. Present are Tiemens, Church, Jun, David, Thompson, Zhu, Frame, Gregoire, Wagner, Lee, Coleman, Barnes, Murnane, and Lostimolo. For Tiemens, Church, and David, it's been more than a year of intense activity. Although the three of them will continue to act as the art department, today marks the end of the major conceptual push. The remainder of the team will be broken up during the next few weeks, never to reconvene in such inspiring circumstances. "It was bittersweet," Tiemens recalls, while Church remembers, "My emotions were with the guys who were leaving."

Lucas arrives and starts by looking at Murnane's sculpts of the nos monster, asking, "Are we going to work on an eye for this guy?"

"The color for the eyes is this see-through, almost glaucoma eye...," Murnane responds, and Coleman adds, "They're reflective—he's gonna be in the cave and the lights from the droids will hit him."

"But it's good to get irises or something that give you a sense of direction," Lucas says. "Otherwise, it just becomes dead. It's hard to get him to act if you don't have eyes."

While studying Thompson's drawings of Yoda on a flying insect creature, Lucas hesitates, so the artist offers, "We were thinking on Kashyyyk that Yoda might have a local steed or something to bring his eye line up to the Wookiees."

"It's a possibility—but only during the escape," Lucas agrees. A few of the artists exchange pleased glances.

After reviewing the last piece of artwork at this last meeting, George asks, "That's it?"

"That's it. The last meeting," Fay says.

"All right, everybody happy?"

"Yeah, we're happy—are you happy?" a few answer simultaneously.

"Well, I'm done with my second draft—that makes me happy. Now I have to go write the third and fourth drafts—and get it done in two weeks!"

"Well, it's a long flight to Australia," Church jokes.

Lucas pauses before leaving.

"Have fun, guys. I'll come back with a movie," he says, adding to Coleman, "You'll come back with a headache."

Wednesday, June 4–Saturday, June 7: HD supervisor Fred Meyers conducts camera prep at Plus8digital in Burbank, California. Together they create a digital package that includes six lenses for production, a compact Cine Zoom lens for miniatures, tripods, matte boxes, HD monitors—in short, everything they'll need in Sydney except the cameras, which will be provided by Sony.

Saturday, June 7: Ewan McGregor (Obi-Wan Kenobi) arrives in Sydney; he starts stunt training the following Monday.
Wednesday, June 11: JAK-OZ videoconference—Lucas advises production that there's a new wet Wookiee scene, but says it may be difficult to accomplish. He'll discuss how to accomplish best with John Knoll, who has been counseling the use of a few "real" Wookiees.
Friday, June 13: The final JAK-OZ videoconference—In her notes to this last meeting, Sydney art department coordinator Colette Birrell writes, "Fay . . . that's it for teleconferences with George. SEE YOU SOMETIME IN THE NOT TOO DISTANT FUTURE! (Yeah baby!!!!)"

Top left: Six images of the last art department meeting, on June 13—Lucas exits the attic, traveling shortly thereafter to Australia. Far left: Yoda animation in preparation for his appearance on MTV. The artists worked in a "locked" room for six hours preparing the Jedi's acceptance speech, which consisted of about 3,500 CG frames. Above: On June 18, the Trade Federation cruiser bridge on Stage 1 after about five weeks of construction. Top: A Sydney art department CG shot shows how the set might look when battle droids walk on the ceiling—which scenario is further explored in a concept painting (inset).

"I'm starting to get one already," Rob says. "It's looking more and more like an animated movie."

"Well, that's what this is: Malleable film is called animation," Lucas says. "See you in September."

"Have a great time," Church says. "It was the best year of our lives."

"Well, the best is yet to come," Lucas says and closes the door behind him.

The 135-page revised second draft is dated June 13, 2003. In general, scenes have been refined; in preparation for shooting, they have been numbered. The major differences between this and the first draft are:

When OBI-WAN is hit by buzz droids, the emotional content is greater—ANAKIN insists on saving OBI-WAN, who is ordering ANAKIN to go on without him.

OBI-WAN and ANAKIN now both end up in the GENERAL's quarters. "This time we do it together," OBI-WAN says when COUNT DOOKU appears. However, COUNT DOOKU kicks OBI-WAN, who falls to the ground, unconscious. After killing COUNT DOOKU, ANAKIN insists on carrying the still-unconscious

OBI-WAN to safety, ignoring PALPATINE's orders to leave him behind.

Whereas in the earlier drafts ANAKIN dreamed that PADMÉ was falling into a pit of flame, in the second draft he sees her suffering in childbirth. She dies screaming, "Help me! Help, ANAKIN! ANAKIN, I love you. I love you."

A new scene with OBI-WAN, YODA, and MACE WINDU makes it clear that the Force is realigning and that a dark shadow surrounds the CHANCELLOR. Another new scene has MACE and OBI-WAN in a gunship accompanying YODA to a waiting Republic assault ship, which will take him to Kashyyyk. They discuss ANAKIN. OBI-WAN is confident and YODA says, "The chosen one, he is. Balance to the Force, he will bring." But MACE is skeptical and questions ANAKIN's loyalty to the Jedi Order.

In another new scene, PALPATINE insinuates to ANAKIN that OBI-WAN is meeting clandestinely with PADMÉ. The dialogue indicating that PALPATINE is responsible for ANAKIN's creation has been cut.

A new wordless shot has MACE, EETH KOTH, KIT FISTO, and SAESEE TIIN arriving at the Senate to arrest PALPATINE, "like gunfighters out of the Old West." ANAKIN enables PALPATINE to kill MACE and then bows before the Sith.

When YODA confronts the EMPEROR, he has the upper hand at first and quips, "If anything I have to say about it, at an end your rule is, and short it was, I must say."

During his duel with OBI-WAN, ANAKIN says, "This is the end for you, my friend. I wish it were otherwise. This is your last chance to join me." After OBI-WAN cuts off ANAKIN's legs, his tune changes:

ANAKIN
Help me, Master.

Left: On June 18, Palpatine's office takes form on Stage 7, with recognizable details like the window that were worked out conceptually months before. Above: A Church painting of the duel on Mustafar, for which, Hayden Christensen (Anakin) and Ewan McGregor (Obi-Wan) prepare in Sydney, continuing to learn complex moves under the supervision of Nick Gillard on June 26 (inset). Right: Thompson's storyboards illustrate Jedi Master Shaak Ti's death at the hands of General Grievous aboard the Separatist cruiser.

OBI-WAN
Don't ask me, Anakin . . . you're evil.
You bring nothing but pain and
suffering. I can't help you.

ANAKIN
I hate you!

Later, it is clear that PADMÉ is dying of a broken heart.

MEDICAL DROID
Medically, she is completely healthy.
For reasons we can't explain, we
are losing her [. . .] She has lost the will
to live.

*And another key
exchange has been added:*

OBI-WAN
Do you think
Anakin's children
will be able to
defeat Darth Sidious?

YODA
Strong the Force runs, in the
Skywalker line.

*PADMÉ stays alive long enough to see
both children being born, and they're held
up for her to see. But she can "offer up
only a faint smile"–the smile Leia will
recall in Episode VI.*

*On Coruscant, when Darth Vader
regains consciousness, he asks:*

DARTH VADER
Where is PADMÉ? Is she all
right?

DARTH SIDIOUS
I'm afraid she died. . . .
It seems in your anger, you
killed her.

A low groan emanates from
VADER'S mask. Suddenly everything in the room begins to
implode, including some of the
droids. VADER screams, breaks
his bonds to the table, and
steps forward [. . .] VADER's
painful screams echo throughout
the center.

*The order of the end scenes has been
switched so that the last shot is now on
Tatooine: "OBI-WAN leaves OWEN and
the BABY, watching the twin suns set."*

SYDNEY, AUSTRALIA: MONDAY, JUNE
16, 2003–DAY ONE MINUS 2 WEEKS
On the lot of Twentieth Century
Fox Studios, housed within
Building 28's oval interior, the
Episode III production office is a
scene of concentrated action. Beneath
a ceiling that resembles a series of

inverted tepees, several assistants, drivers, technicians, and crew are tele-
phoning, faxing, e-mailing, walkie-talking, and just plain shouting. A *Return
of the Jedi* poster decorates one wall, and a *Phantom Menace* pinball machine–
its setting on UNLIMITED PLAY–resides next to the receptionist's desk.

The northern wall of the office
area is divided into very plain, func-
tional work spaces that look out onto
a football field–sized quad. One of
these cubicles is McCallum's; another,
Lucas's. Their assistant, Jacqui Louez,
sits at a desk facing their work
spaces–essentially in
production's heart of
hearts.

Having arrived the
day before with his
family, Lucas is talk-
ing with script super-
visor Jayne-Ann
Tenggren about the
creation of a fourth
draft when Ewan
McGregor arrives.

"I know you!"
Lucas exclaims. "You're that suave
guy."

Before long, Lucas begins his
first extensive walkthrough of the
lot's seven stages and their work-
in-progress sets. With McCallum
and other department heads, he
arrives on Stage 7 to examine the
set of Palpatine's office. He looks
around, sips his coffee, and says,
"Home, sweet home."

He then talks things over, as
he will for each set, with Gavin
Bocquet. Much of their conversation is almost shouted as they
compete with the sometimes
enormous din of hammering,
sawing, and welding. McCallum
mentions that they have, this
time, a four-by-four-by-four
recording device, which gives
them higher resolution. Lucas
decides that they'll shoot a blank

plate, or "control take," of each set before shooting the actors, so they can digitally alter, or reproduce, each one in postproduction.

They then enter the set of the Alderaan space cruiser interior—an exact reproduction of the white corridor Lucas filmed back in 1976. "I love it," he says. "Maybe I could reshoot some of Episode IV. This particular set was where there was a lot of drama," he adds, referring to that film's last-minute, studio-decreed multiunit shooting. "The hardest part of these movies is that you get these great sets and you shoot on 'em for half a day—and then you have to destroy them and move on to something else."

Back in Building 28, Lucas goes over the shooting schedule with first assistant director (1st AD) Colin Fletcher. There are presently seventy shooting days scheduled, "but I'm sure there are things we can cut out," Fletcher notes. The two of them attack the schedule as if it were a riddle, puzzling out which set moves and costume changes they can eliminate to save time. "It's the hairdos that kill you," Lucas points out.

Next, he goes through binders of actors and actresses with casting director Christine King. Lucas is looking for handmaidens and other tertiary characters. He mentions that Keisha Castle-Hughes was incredible in *Whale Rider* (2002), but King says she's currently unavailable.

THURSDAY, JUNE 26, 2003—DAY ONE MINUS 4 DAYS

Lucas's fourth draft comes in at 129 pages typed. The differences between it and previous drafts are:

After ANAKIN kills COUNT DOOKU, PALPATINE says, "It's not the first time, Anakin. Remember what you told me about your mother and the Sand People."
The story of DARTH PLAGUEIS has been augmented:

```
            PALPATINE
He became so powerful . . . the only thing
    he was afraid of was losing his power,
   which eventually he did, of course . . .
```

```
Unfortunately, he taught his
   apprentice everything he knew,
 then his apprentice killed him in
             his sleep.
              (smiles)
  Plagueis never saw it coming.
It's ironic he could save others from
       death, but not himself.
    According to the legend,
   it was a power his apprentice
    found no value in. So the ability
     to save loved ones was lost
       with Plagueis "the wise."
```

As PADMÉ prepares to leave for Mustafar, she now forbids CAPTAIN TYPHO and her HANDMAIDENS from accompanying her, so their deaths on the Mustafar landing platform have also been cut.

And when ANAKIN lies dying, OBI-WAN's final words are new:

```
             OBI-WAN
You were the chosen one! It was said
      you would destroy the Sith,
    not join them. It was you who
   would bring balance to the Force,
    not leave it in darkness. You've
       become my brother, Anakin.
  I love you, but I won't help you.
```

"It's a downer," Lucas acknowledges. "The saving grace is that if you watch the other three movies, then you know everything ends happily ever after. Nevertheless, I now have to make a movie that works by itself, but which also works with this six-hour movie and this overall twelve-hour movie. I'll have two six-hour trilogies, and the two will beat against each other: One's the fall, one's the redemption. They have different tonalities, but it's meant to be one experience of twelve hours."

The last year has seen the written and visual creation of numerous and entire planets and civilizations, one iconic villain, one dragon-lizard, several Wookiees, and dozens of sleek starships. They've come into existence through numerous written drafts and thousands of images conveyed in drawings, paintings, sculpts, and storyboards. When principal photography begins, Lucas will move on to the real world of sets, a production crew, and actors, where much of this will be tested—and another draft of the script will be written.

From top down: Lucas with his key collaborators during the last days of preproduction at Fox Studios, Sydney, Australia: with McCallum; in the make-up department with Christensen (Anakin); in the art department with Gracie, Peter Russell, and Bocquet; in the creatures department with Rebecca Hunt and Dave Elsey; in the costume department with Biggar.

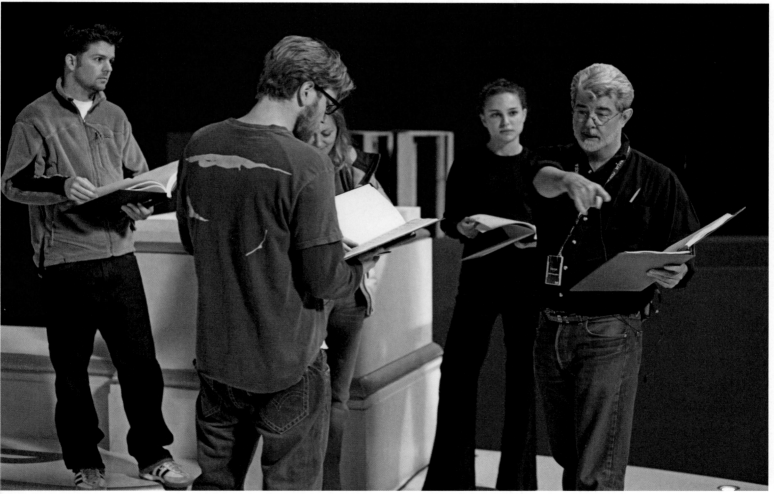

Top: (from left) First assistant director Colin Fletcher, DP David Tattersall, Lucas, and key gaffer Eddie Knight, in Sydney. Above: (from left) Dialogue coach Chris Neil, McGregor (Obi-Wan), script supervisor Jayne-Ann Tenggren, Natalie Portman (Padmé), and Lucas, during rehearsals.

Monday, June 23 to Friday, June 27: The veranda set is dressed and rigged.

PART II

PRINCIPAL PHOTOGRAPHY

The Moviemakers
of OZ

PROLOGUE: The Crew

Twenty-seven years separates these two photos, the first (right) taken on the set at EMI Studios in 1976 (Mark Hamill as Luke, Lucas, Carrie Fisher as Leia, and Harrison Ford as Han) and the second—designed to mirror it—in 2003 on the set in Sydney (Christensen, McCallum, Lucas, Portman, and McGregor).

"When I did the first *Star Wars*," Lucas remembers, "I was confident primarily because of my inexperience. Now I'm confident because of my experience. When I did the first *Star Wars*, I was on my own in England, with a crew that was partly hostile, partly supportive. I made very close friends with the supportive part, and a lot of those guys went on to do the next two films. On these last three *Star Wars* films, I've been working with a group that I started with on *Young Indy*. So I have a lot of people who I've worked with for a long time—a talented, professional, experienced group—which makes everything easier, because even under the most stressful of times, this group is very good at working together."

The members of this core group are: producer Rick McCallum, production designer Gavin Bocquet, director of photography David Tattersall, costume designer Trisha Biggar, and financial controller Kathryn Ramos. Tattersall remembers that, way back in 1992, while shooting a scene for *Young Indy* on the grounds of a chateau in France, Lucas and McCallum were already talking of assembling essential personnel for the next *Star Wars* film.

This group would come to include those who began on either the *Star Wars Trilogy Special Edition* (1997) or *The Phantom Menace* (1999): animation director Rob Coleman, stunt coordinator Nick Gillard, visual effects supervisor John Knoll, supervising art director Peter Russell, property master Ty Teiger, script supervisor Jayne-Ann Tenggren, and others. "I really invest a lot of time trying to create the best atmosphere that I possibly can," McCallum says, "especially in my relationship with the people I work with. We've spent almost a lifetime together. Kathryn and I just celebrated fifteen years working together—to me, our lives are intertwined."

"The most sublime state of filmmaking is where everyone is interdependent," he adds. "No one person on the film can let anyone else down, because it has a ripple effect on the whole picture. It's incredibly collaborative—most people don't realize how collaborative it is, how intensely personal, how emotionally draining. You wake up at four-thirty A.M. and you finish around ten P.M. If you're not in the right physical and mental shape, you can go into a downward spiral."

4 Shooting a Foundation

As the plane banks, travelers get their first glimpse of Sydney. "It's like San Francisco on steroids," Lucas would say. After weaving their way through customs and the tourist shops selling koala T-shirts, kangaroo dolls, and Aboriginal art, visitors to the Episode III set are usually met by a driver, who whisks them to Fox Studios, Australia.

During the twenty-minute trip on the left side of the road, travelers pass a variety of pubs, streets, residences, and a general decor reminiscent of London. Sydney was founded in 1778 as an English penal colony, but today it has the energy and optimism of a country not overwhelmed by its past.

Fox Studios is located on the city outskirts, adjacent to Sydney's soccer stadium and across from a large park. It has two arched entrances, one for the public and one for the crew. The former leads to a shopping area, playground, and multiplex. The latter leads to a kiosk staffed with good-natured guards. A hundred yards farther along, a second kiosk admits visitors into the heart of the studio: seven stages that will house Episode III's seventy-one sets, and about a dozen buildings that will house the supporting construction, props, costume, art, and creatures workshops.

Originally used for grazing cattle, and then as a fairground, these premises were converted to a studio in 1998. Yet the first film shot here—*A Daughter of Australia*—was back in 1922, and the studio's stages and streets bear the names of Australian film-industry luminaries: Chips Rafferty Lane, the Hector Crawford Stage, the Ken G. Hall Stage. But nothing ever hit these premises like *Star Wars*. A quick look around today reveals massive and continuous movement: trucks making deliveries, sets being painted, golf carts ferrying people. There are pylons, sacks of pebbles, metal girders, tents, cars, scissor lifts, props, and bicycles. The center of the studio is a tree-lined, hundred-yard-long grass quad, with wooden benches and many ibises—the Australian equivalent to the pigeon—on the lookout for crumbs.

"At the time Fox was considering starting a studio, I flew over to Sydney and met with the head of Fox, Kim Williams," McCallum says. "I was very reticent at first to shoot in a studio. I'd rather not have to worry about the film that's already in being late, or the film coming in behind you. It forces you into a situation that I didn't want our movie or George ever to be in. But after spending a week with Kim, I knew that he could deliver the studio—that it would be ready for us on time and that it was going to be a great place to work. He was such a decent man that I knew we'd have enough time on each side of our booking to be safe."

Lucas, McCallum, Hayden Christensen (*The Virgin Suicides*, 2000; *Life as a House*, 2001), Ewan McGregor (*Trainspotting*, 1996; *Big Fish*, 2003), Natalie Portman (*Cold Mountain*, 2003; *Garden State*, 2004), and many key cast and crew personnel arrived months, weeks, or days ago. "I've been here since the beginning of May," Christensen says, "getting in shape and learning the lightsaber fights."

"Hayden was here much earlier than I was," McGregor says, "but I had about three weeks of fighting, five days a week, for half-a-day at a time. It's much harder work now. On Episode I, I'd fight all day long, whereas now I'm like, 'Okay, guys, I think I've reached my limit.' It's repetition, repetition—but it's got to become fluid."

"I closed some of the actors' deals just days before we started shooting," McCallum admits. "I just didn't know how long we'd need them, until the script was done and the schedule set."

Indeed, the cornerstone of principal photography is the shooting schedule, which will be constantly revised as production gets ahead or falls behind. The keepers of this document are Lucas, McCallum, and 1st assistant director Colin Fletcher. Any changes they make have a butterfly effect on the whole production. Modifications are therefore immediately commu-

Previous spread: Padmé (Portman) and Anakin (Christensen) are the star-crossed lovers. Above: On June 25, gathered round Lucas are Mousy McCallum, assistant to the producer and director Jacqui Louez, Rick McCallum, and 2nd assistant director Deborah Antoniou. Below: The skyline of Sydney, Australia.

nicated to the 2nd and 3rd ADs, who create the Call Sheets that the actors and crew live by—as these list when and where everyone needs to be at any time of day.

Lucas and Fletcher have been poring over the schedule for the last two weeks. "George answered all my questions," Fletcher says. "We had about an hour a day. A lot of directors hate going through the schedule because it means facing reality, but George would just go through it as many times as I wanted."

Fletcher is not the only one with questions, and so, a few days ahead of Day One, a technical read-through of the entire script takes place in the cafeteria, with all the department heads and key technicians present. As each scene is discussed, every foreseeable problem is tackled from a logistical point of view.

The evening before Day One, thousands of details are finally in place, and a giant machine is about to go into motion. Consisting of nearly a thousand crew members, many of whom just finished working on the two *Matrix* sequels, and literally tons of supplies, the machine's successful navigation of a projected sixty-three-day shoot will depend on the ability of its director and producer to keep the system moving, and to keep up morale while overcoming a variety of obstacles. With that in mind, McCallum is clear as to production's overriding priority: "There should be no hierarchy on the film, except that you have a writer-director who has an idea—and everything we do has to enable him to get to the purest state of realizing that idea. At the end of the day, that's what filmmaking is."

SHOOT DAY 1: MONDAY, JUNE 30, 2003

On today's Call Sheet, there is a note to the crew from McCallum and production supervisor Stephen Jones:

Dear Dudes and Dudettes,
Thank you for your hard work during preproduction.
We hope you know how much we appreciate everything you have done for the film. Have a great shoot.
Rick & Stephen

Top: Christensen and McGregor arrived early in Sydney for their lightsaber boot camp: weeks of intensive training for the film's multiple duels, often with fencing double Kyle Rowling (middle). Above: During the technical read-through of the script in the cafeteria, Gillard, Knoll, Coleman, and Bocquet.

The Call Sheet also sets the stage for today, as it will for every day. The term *pt* indicates that only part of a scene will be recorded; the rest of that scene will be shot either another day or completed by ILM. Not every scene shot is listed.

NO. OF SCHEDULED DAYS: 63   SCHEDULED FINISH: Sept. 24
CREW CALL: 7:00
LOCATION: Stage 2
SET: INT. Elevator hallway—Federation cruiser
SCHEDULED SCENES SHOT: 5B (R2-D2 is ordered back to the ship), 11 (the Jedi squeeze through and seal the hatch in a main hallway), 14 (the seal holds when the explosion hits), 15 (they are attacked by wheel droids), 23 (Anakin & Obi-Wan step from the elevator), 16pt (battle takes place in the elevator), 27pt (Anakin with Obi-Wan over shoulder waits for elevator)

Though Day One Call sheet indicates that "crew call" is for 7:00 A.M., many of the crew and cast have arrived at 6:00 A.M. or well before, which will be the case for the duration of the shoot. In the cafeteria, a copious breakfast buffet is available starting at six, and many will fill up, since working days here are on average fourteen to fifteen hours long.

Lucas and McCallum arrive on the minimal set housed in Stage 2 just as daylight breaks outside. "I always love the first day—the energy, the excitement," the latter exclaims. It is June Down Under—the beginning of winter—but still fairly warm. Lucas talks with visual effects supervisor John Knoll, who arrived about a week ago, and then spies a heater next to a chair with his name on it. "You'll need one in the next three months," a PA says, explaining that it will become colder and colder in these hugely empty stages.

As the crew prepares for the first setup, "sides"–bite-sized script pages for the day's relevant scenes—are distributed to Lucas, script supervisor Jayne-Ann Tenggren, and dialogue coach Chris Neil. Lucas asks that in the future they be delivered arranged in order of the scenes to be shot. He explains to Fletcher that he intends to cross out each scene as they finish it: "Believe me, it's very therapeutic."

Today's seven scenes are simple ones. For scene 23, all that Christensen and McGregor are required to do is exit an elevator, say a couple of lines, and walk off camera. When they arrive for rehearsal, Christensen is in his dressing gown and McGregor wears a sports jacket. They greet Lucas and prepare to block out the scene.

Note: A "take" refers to a single run-through of a scene or shot, which may be completed in one "take" or fifty "takes."

"The actors are on the set," Lucas announces to the crew, and the two shake hands with Fletcher. "Stand by to rehearse," Fletcher says. A bell rings, announcing that all extraneous work should cease and that no one can either enter or exit the sound stage. The bell also triggers a siren-like warning light on the stage's exterior wall.

"And . . . action!" Lucas calls out.

He then watches on a monitor as they rehearse. Immediately afterward, stand-ins Tom Maynard (Obi-Wan) and Peter Jackson (Anakin) take the actors' places.

"Basically, you rehearse with the actors so everyone can see what's going on," Fletcher explains. "The stand-ins watch what happens. The actors then get set up and complete their makeup while we start lighting the shot. We might get the stand-ins to go through the moves while we're lighting, so the cameras can rehearse. And when the lighting is complete and the actors are back on set, generally then we just shoot it."

At 8 A.M., they're ready for the control take. In a tradition dating back to the *Young Indy* days, McCallum operates the clapboard for the first shot of the film. The bell sounds. "Here we go," Fletcher says. "Camera, speed, please."

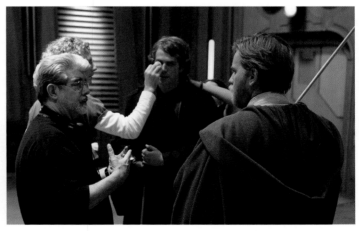

"Okay, Rick, ready?" Lucas asks.

"V23," McCallum reads off the board. "Take one. 'A' camera . . ."

"And . . . action!" Lucas calls out.

"Good luck, everybody," Rick adds. "Kick some ass! Let's do this in sixty days!" And begun, this shoot has.

"Beautiful," Lucas says after the control take. "Now let's try one with people."

The actors return from makeup in Jedi garb attended by Trisha Biggar, who is overseeing a couple of last-minute adjustments. At 8:26 A.M., they're ready for the first live-action take.

"Roll camera, roll sound," Fletcher requests. "And . . . action!" Lucas yells out.

After the take, McGregor informs Lucas that because he was situated behind the elevator door, he couldn't hear the word *action*. While crew fix that problem, Lucas reviews the scene with the actors, explaining that the Jedi are on the Separatist cruiser trying to find a kidnapped Chancellor—but

Above left: The ubiquitous heater always placed next to the director's chair. Above right: One of the flashing warning lights posted over stage doors. Left: McCallum performs his traditional clapboard duty. Above: Makeup artist Shane Thomas touches up Christensen as Lucas discusses scene 23 with McGregor.

they're aware that Count Dooku has baited a trap. "The trick part is the attitude," he says. "You don't have to be quite so serious about it. You *say*, 'It's a trap.' But your *attitude* is, *Noooo problem.*"

On the next take, Hayden's cloak gets caught in the door. On the following one, it is caught again. "Very good. Very good for the outtakes," Lucas says to Christensen. "Let's try one more—and lighten it up even

more." Take. Lucas walks onto the set. "I think we can go even lighter," he says to the actors.

The next take works. They're about to go tighter for close-ups, but Ewan's hair won't stay in continuity. Lucas asks Tenggren to intervene, but at that moment the actor gets his hair to obey. "All right! Nobody move!" he says, and they run through the scene without a hitch.

Later in the day, R2-D2 makes his first appearance. Cast and crew react visibly to his arrival, for the little astromech droid provides a physical link to the overall saga, and he reminds many here of their childhood experiences watching *Star Wars.* George remarks to Rob Coleman that the story of *Star Wars* is actually recounted by R2-D2 to the Keeper of the Whills, one hundred years after *Return of the Jedi. Journal of the Whills* is what Lucas titled his first outline of *Star Wars* back in 1972.

CAMERA WRAP: 19:10 SETUPS: 48 SCRIPT SHOT TODAY: 2m 28s
CATERING: Breakfast (140); lunch off-set crew (330); lunch on-set crew (351); afternoon tea (110).

SHOOT DAY 2: TUESDAY, JULY 1, 2003
LOCATION: Stage 2
SET: Federation cruiser interiors
SCHEDULED SCENES SHOT: 18B (Anakin climbs though hole in the ceiling); 21 (Obi-Wan fights droids)

Previous spread: Shooting on the Trade Federation cruiser hallway and elevator set. Top: 1st AD Fletcher with Lucas. Early versions of scene 16 called for the elevator door to be damaged in a Jedi battle with droids. Above: With droid wrangler Don Bies at the controls, R2-D2 prepares to make his entrance.

Outside, it's raining off and on. Inside, Lucas walks through the cool, dark stage interior until he arrives at the bright lights of the hot set. "I have a tendency to be a quiet person on the set," he explains. "I don't do a lot of yelling. I try to keep everybody happy and focused on what it is they're supposed to be doing, which is a challenge because there's always a lot of raw emotions on a movie set. But I've been doing this for so long that I've seen just about every crisis you can possibly imagine—and gotten through it.

"In working with the actors, I basically go over the scene with them and suggest what to do," he adds. "They know beforehand where we're going and what we're shooting. It's just a matter of getting that on tape. It's the same thing with the cameramen. I just assume we won't shoot till nine A.M., and then, after lunch, until three P.M., with forty-five minutes per setup. You have your wish list, then you have the realities."

His relaxed demeanor doesn't mean Lucas is unaware of the constant need for speed, as Fletcher remarks: "George sets himself challenges every day. What he's going to do, where he's going to be by lunchtime. He's like . . . incredible."

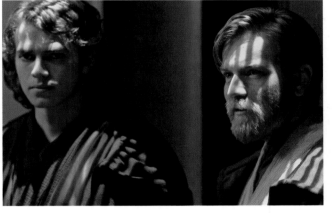

Today's scenes are again fairly straightforward. As the setups and the decors change, one thing about a set remains constant: the "video village"—a mobile command center that follows production everywhere. It's where Lucas watches two Panasonic TH-42PHD5 high-definition plasma wide-screen monitors that display in real time everything the two HDC-F950 Sony digital cameras record through their custom-built Fujinon lenses.

Seated beside him are Jayne-Ann Tenggren, Chris Neil, John Knoll, Rob Coleman, and ILM matchmove supervisor Jason Snell. All the village's equipment—monitors, tables, chairs, wiring—can be broken down and reassembled in a matter of minutes. The village is also where the most interesting conversations usually take place, and where McCallum comes to check on things. (He and his assistants remain in constant touch with on-set action via walkie-talkie).

"I was recommended by Francis Coppola, with whom I've worked on a number of movies," says Neil (*The Rainmaker*, 1997; *The Virgin Suicides*).

"The most challenging thing for me is coming in and trying to fit myself into the mix, to fill a role that hadn't been created on the other two films. It's a daunting task because you're dealing with the abstract and emotional world of artists and relationships."

"I'm advising George when questions come up [per visual effects]," Knoll says, "and answering questions that the [Sydney] art department may have. Jason Snell is getting measurements of camera positions and set measurements.

"But directing a movie is this really intense thing," he adds. "It's been described as being nibbled to death by ducks—and I don't want to be one of the ducks."

"The most important reason for *me* to be on set is to build a relationship with George," Coleman says. "We've collaborated before, so there's a history and a working relationship there—but a whole year goes by between Episode II and Episode III where I don't see him that much.

"It's also important for me to understand what George is thinking in terms of the interaction between an animated character and, say, Ewan McGregor. If I wasn't on set to hear a key piece of information, it could easily be a year before that little tidbit reaches me."

English-born Tenggren (*Sleepy Hollow*, 1999; *Road to Perdition*, 2002) has been at Lucas's side since *The Phantom Menace*: "The day that I flew up from LA to SF [to interview with Lucas], there was a terrific rainstorm and the plane was delayed for about three hours. Then there was a problem renting the car, so I arrived at Skywalker Ranch four hours late and was a complete wreck. I went in to see George, who looked a bit puzzled, because I really did look like a drowned rat. I said, 'Sorry, I was thwarted by the weather.' And he said, 'Well, what are you doing in this country anyway?' And we just hit it off. It was great. But it's only a good story because I got the job!

Top left: While shooting the June 30 elevator scenes, Lucas ("side" in hand) talks things over with McGregor and Christensen. Top right: The two Panasonic HD screens are plain to see in the video village. Middle top: McGregor (Obi-Wan) emerges from the ventilator shaft in scene 11. Middle bottom: Christensen (Anakin) and McGregor (Obi-Wan) are brothers-in-arms soon to fall prey to the dark side.

"I always feel that no matter what happens, George will always take the problem on board and come up with a solution," she continues. "There's never that fear element that the director will freak out. Whatever it is, good or bad, I always know I'm going to get a practical response—that doesn't always mean he's going to be pleased, but it means he's a real problem solver."

LOCATION WRAP: 19:57   SETUPS: 38   SCRIPT SHOT TODAY: 1m 25s

SHOOT DAY 3: WEDNESDAY, JULY 2, 2003
LOCATION: Stage 1
SET: INT. Padmé's apartment
SCENES SHOT: 69 (Obi-Wan and Padmé discuss Anakin),
71pt (Padmé tries to get the Senators on her side)

Today McGregor and Portman are doing their first scene together. As they wait, McGregor jokes to Portman about her character's amorous relationship with Anakin: "Yoda has become fiercely jealous," he says, and she laughs.

"Okay, here we go," Fletcher announces. "Roll cameras, please."

"It was so exciting to do substantive scenes with Ewan this time, because I respect him so much as an actor," Portman recalls. "He's really serious about the work, but he also lightens up the set."

"Get ready for rehearsal—as soon as we can, folks," Fletcher says, urging the crew on to the next setup. The following scene, in which Padmé rallies fellow Senators against Palpatine, is the first to include Anthony Daniels (C-3PO). In full costume, Daniels walks onto the set in his unmistakable manner. Seeing him, Lucas announces, "*Star Wars* has arrived." The two shake hands.

As the first few setups are completed, however, it is nearly impossible to hear the actors' voices, for the grating sound generated by C-3PO's costume whenever he moves drowns them out. Consequently, some takes are recorded without him. "I worry sometimes," Daniels admits. "People are in this really beautiful scene and I'm clanking through it, and I know they're going to have to replace everything they say."

LOCATION WRAP: 19:10   SETUPS: 38   SCRIPT SHOT TODAY: 2m 37s

SHOOT DAY 4: THURSDAY, JULY 3
LOCATION: Stage 1
SET: Int. Padmé's apartment
SCENES SHOT: 75 (Anakin questions Padmé about Obi-Wan's visit),
54pt (Anakin awakens in a panic and weeps)

Every set is attended to by dozens of technicians: grips, gaffers, makeup artists, and many more. Despite their number, which is relatively small for a film of this size, they make very little noise—which doesn't mean there isn't a lot of talking. It's just that everyone is whispering into their headsets. At any given time, there may in fact be at least twenty conversations going on without any two people actually standing next to each other.

One ongoing conversation has "A" camera operator Calum McFarlane giving directions to his crew, who operate the Techno crane on which is perched one of the two digital cameras. McFarlane always sits in or near the video village and is in fairly constant communication with Lucas. The director's desires to tighten up or pan are transmitted by McFarlane to his crew and into his own deft movements with the mechanisms that control the camera. "I don't think about the pedals and wheels," he says. "If you think about it, you're dead."

McFarlane's deadpan wit and calm will complement Lucas's, creating a nucleus of humor throughout the shoot. A second-generation Australian, McFarlane (*Moulin Rouge*, 2001; *The Last Samurai*, 2003) was given a camera when he was fifteen. His father said he'd pay for the developing if the teenager wrote down the exposures and shutter speeds. "I try and make the director and everyone look good," he says. "And there are people below me who are helping me out. The last thing I want is some poor bugger at ILM to have my face up on a dartboard, saying, 'My God, I've just

spent the last few months cleaning up stuff he could've fixed in five minutes on the set.' "

Whatever McFarlane records is also being captured from another angle by Simon Harding's "B" camera, because Lucas uses two cameras on nearly every shot. Harding had been laid off in the United Kingdom some years before, so he took a Steadicam course and emigrated to Australia, where his talents were welcomed by its nascent film industry. He describes working with Lucas as "fantastic" and wishes it would never end.

In the video village, while waiting, Lucas is describing his experiences during the making of Coppola's *The Rain People* (1969) to Chris Neil. A few yards away, they're putting on Anthony Daniel's C-3PO face. Droid supervisor Don Bies fastens together the two headplates that conceal him. "Don Bies did re-create the neck in a way that doesn't choke me," Daniels says, gratefully. "It used to be that I felt like Darth Vader was gripping me in every scene."

Bottom left: A typical formation in the video village—"A" camera operator Calum McFarlane talks with McCallum, Knoll, match move supervisor Jason Snell, and Lucas, as Neil studies the script. Top left: Another typical snapshot has Tenggren, Neil, Lucas, and Fletcher studying a scene on the monitors. Top right: While waiting to shoot scene 69 in Padmé's apartment, Portman and McGregor talk. Above left: "Star Wars has arrived"—Anthony Daniels (C-3PO) meets Lucas on the set (electrician Alex Laguna is in background), prepared for scene 71. Above right: Droid technician Justin Dix and Bies help Daniels get into costume.

McGregor is next to arrive on set. "I've had a couple of moments on Episode III that have taken me back to when I was a child watching *Star Wars*," he says. "And they've been both with Anthony Daniels, with See-Threepio. I don't think I was in a scene with him in the other two. When I was on set with See-Threepio, I really remembered what it was like to be six or seven and watching these films. And I felt the excitement of being in them, you know–now."

Later that afternoon, McCallum and Lucas are discussing the last scene of the day, a shot that has Anakin and Padmé in bed. The audience will

When Christensen arrives, Lucas shows him where on the bed he'd like him to sit when he awakes from his nightmare: "You pop up and throw the sheets back." To Portman, he says, "It's like when you were sleeping with the bugs crawling all over you [in Episode II]. But now you've got a big bug sitting next to you."

LOCATION WRAP: 20:15   SETUPS: 37   SCRIPT SHOT TODAY: 3m 10s

see only the back of her head, but Hayden has asked for Natalie to be present–it's an emotional moment for Anakin, who's having terrible nightmares, and the actor feels her presence will add to his performance.

It becomes a race against time to get the last shot: "I have forty minutes left. I have to shoot the scene. It's going to be very tight," George says to Tenggren.

Top: McGregor and Daniels share a scene together on Padmé's veranda. Above left: Back in June, costume props supervisor Ivo Coveney working on Darth Vader's helmet and breastplate–acoutrements that Anakin Skywalker will soon be needing, as his dreams (in scene 54) push him toward evil (above right). Above middle: Lucas discusses a scene with Portman and McGregor. Above, far right: Bocquet in the Sydney art department, and with art director Phil Harvey and Russell on the set. Right: Lucas frames a shot for "B" camera operator Simon Harding and McFarlane.

SHOOT DAY 5: FRIDAY, JULY 4, 2003
LOCATION: Stage 2
SET: Int. Padmé's veranda—Coruscant
SCENES SHOT: 66 (Padmé wants Anakin to ask the Chancellor to stop the fighting)

This is the fourth day on the veranda. "The Padmé set was like the kind made for MGM musicals," Jay Laga'aia (Captain Typho) recalls. Of course, beautiful sets like this one were conceptually born back in the art department of Skywalker Ranch, but they've been brought into three-dimensional form with the aid of multiple disciplines in Sydney: set decorating, props, construction, paint, fiberglass, and others. All of these departments—about four hundred people strong—are overseen by the head of the JAK Australia art department: production designer Gavin Bocquet.

"In theory, being the head of the department, I supervise everything—*in theory*," Gavin says. "But of course, there's a whole hierarchy of delegation and so many good people on the ground. I'm very interested in the technical drawings, so I'm very much in-hand with all the draftsmen, but when it starts to be the building side of it—particularly on a film of this size—then the art directors who are looking after those sets will be the ones on the ground checking on a daily basis that the details are right."

The art department is located in Building 48 at the far eastern end of the lot. It's a hangar-like locale, where a Jedi starfighter, airspeeder, and couches sit downstairs. One room is entirely dedicated to blueprints, hundreds of which hang from racks. Upstairs, in a U-shaped series of rooms, are the draftspeople, CAD technicians, model builders, and art directors.

"Production designers and art directors all have this blind faith that everybody is doing their job properly," Bocquet says, "but to write a textbook about it would be hard. Our scheduling and budgeting amounts to hundreds of thousands of dollars—and yet there is no book on film budgeting. Generally, you have a ballpark figure, say sixty thousand dollars. And then the construction manager and Ian [Gracie] and Peter [Russell] will break that down into how many carpenters and how many painters and how many nails. And it's amazing how close very often the ballpark figure is to the final one. I suppose that justifies experience. But I find it fascinating—and frightening—if you step back from it."

The son of a bank manager, Bocquet says that his "benchmark film" was *2001: A Space Odyssey* (1968), which he saw thirteen times. Another big influence was Gerry Anderson's work (*Thunderbirds Are GO*, 1966). After studying product design at the Royal College of Arts in London, he was put in touch with production designer Norman Reynolds, who was working on *Return of the Jedi*. Gavin was hired and helped on Jabba's skiff, among other things.

Years later—after working on many films, including Steven Spielberg's *Empire of the Sun* (1987)—he returned to the Lucas fold when McCallum needed someone for *Young Indy* who, in addition to being a top-notch production designer, was also familiar with Czechoslovakia. Lucas and McCallum had opted to film much of the TV series there, and Bocquet's employment was sealed thanks to his experience in Prague working on Steven Soderbergh's 1991 film, *Kafka*.

"Basically the global control of all of the art department is down to Gavin," Peter Russell says. "Directly below Gavin is the main art department, set decoration, and props. Gavin takes concepts and works them up into viable set proposals, which are then handed down through myself or the other art directors [Ian Gracie and Phil Harvey]

every little thing. And it goes on for three years solid, nearly every day of the week, hundreds of questions every single day. It never lets up. A friend of mine once said in every shot of a movie, there's a thousand ideas—and that's true actually."

"It is a very big machine," Ian Gracie agrees. "We have in excess of sixty-seven sets, which is a lot to rotate through seven sound stages. And George and Rick are very much aware of how much it takes to make a movie, so we have to be frugal. We try to double up on sets and re-use pieces just to make life a little easier and cheaper. Half the job of the art department is to not only make it look good, but to make it fiscally viable."

"Most films are road movies: They're on location, they're contemporary," McCallum sums up. "Or if they're period films, they use period locations. But everything in the *Star Wars* universe has to be built. There's no place you can go and rent a *Star Wars* prop—it's just a different kind of filmmaking."

Back on Stage 2, "B" camera operator Harding is using a Steadicam for a scene that starts out with talk about Anakin and Padmé's unborn child. "I'm having a hard time shifting from the baby to the politics of the scene," Portman says, but Lucas assures her it's okay.

Later, Lucas, McCallum, and Fletcher go over the shooting schedule. McCallum still thinks they can finish in less than sixty days. In the darkness behind them, only C-3PO's luminous eyes are visible.

LOCATION WRAP: 20:03   SETUPS: 20   SCRIPT SHOT TODAY: 2m 55s

SHOOT DAY 6: MONDAY, JULY 7, 2003
LOCATION: Stage 2
SET: Int. Padmé's veranda—Coruscant
SCENES SHOT: 116 (Anakin tells Padmé of the rebellion and leaves for Mustafar)

Over the weekend, Samuel L. Jackson (Mace Windu), Peter Mayhew (Chewbacca), and Ian McDiarmid (Palpatine) arrived in Sydney. On set, Jackson greets Lucas, who gives him a hug. "It's good to be here," Jackson says.

to our eight draftsmen—and they're the backbone of the department; they're the guys who actually do the mileage. Up until then, it's all sketches; from then on, it can be measured, priced, budgeted, and painted. Next, you do an overall assembly drawing and up to twenty subsequent drawings for detail."

Of course, the director is consulted at each stage. "I guess I've been accused of being a micromanager," Lucas says, "but as far as I'm concerned, that's what making a movie is all about. I'm really responsible for every single detail on the picture. I work with a lot of very talented and creative people, but I have to make sure that it's exactly what I want it to be, because it's so critical that it look natural and fit into the environment. So I have to spend a lot of my time answering questions and making decisions about

Top left: Coleman, Knoll, Bocquet, and Russell in the Sydney art department. Middle left: Lucas and Bocquet study a maquette. Above left: A concept painting of Padmé's veranda by Tiemens—this painting is part of the visual script, whose purpose is to act as a lighting and reference guide throughout production; it contains paintings by the Skywalker Ranch art department for every scene in the movie (for more information, see page 222). Above: A tender moment in Padmé's apartment. Right: Portman (Padmé) in the green cut-velvet robe.

"Welcome home," Lucas replies.

While Christensen and Portman rehearse, Lucas and Jackson talk. "Did you get in this morning or last night?"

"Saturday. I've played two rounds of golf already!"

"Well, we're at it again," Lucas says.

"To be back at Fox Studios, among the army of people that create what all the fans know as *Star Wars* is pretty wonderful," Jackson would later add. "For many, this will be the height of my career—the one thing that people will never forget—because it'll be part of something way bigger than anything else I've done. I actually tend to forget how really enormous this process is and what a gigantic family feeling it is. When you come together at lunchtime, everybody knows everybody. You look outside and there's a football game going on, and there are people standing around talking, and there are people riding on bicycles, and there are people gathered together who have known each other for a very long time."

On the set, Christensen and Lucas are discussing Anakin's temperament when he returns to Padmé's apartment after slaughtering Jedi at the Temple.

"Do you think there's more or less a sense of urgency?" Christensen asks.

"You're full of adrenaline because, one, you've spent the whole night killing people, and, two, the situation is not good: The Jedi Council has tried to overthrow the Republic," Lucas replies. "That's news to everybody. Take a little bit of time with that. When you say, 'I will not betray the Republic'—that's your rationalization. So you're very strong on that."

Lucas then talks to Portman about Padmé's thoughts: "You're saying, *This is* not *the guy I married*."

Speaking of Anakin's warning to Padmé, George suggests, "When you get to 'You need to distance yourself,' I'd take that a little slower."

"So it's almost threatening," Hayden agrees.

"Yeah—and the slower you take it, the more threatening it becomes."

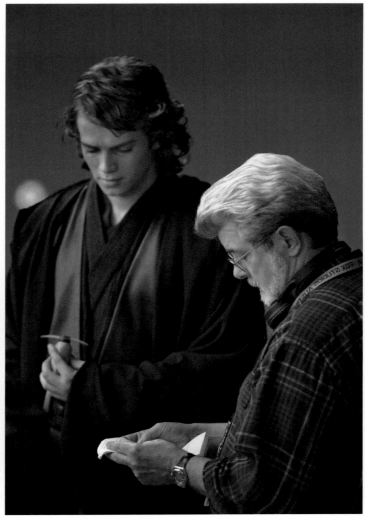

Back in the video village, Knoll tells Lucas that on-set personnel have assured him that an impending set change will take only a few moments. Ian McDiarmid joins them. "Hi, Ian. How are you doing?" Lucas says. "Welcome to the picturesque veranda." He then walks to the set and says to Christensen, "Make sure it's personal. It goes up and down. Take a few beats [pauses] in there."

"You understand where my instincts are coming from," Christensen says. "I'm trying to give it sort of a monotone."

"Yeah, but a monotone isn't right. You're emotional here. You've made a decision—but you don't know if it's the right decision . . . There's always this good in you, and this little part is always asking, *What am I doing?* Even at the very end. That's what makes you turn and kill the Emperor."

Christensen nods in agreement.

"At this point, you're not completely cold. The point where you become numb and flat is when you say, 'I hate you' to your best friend," Lucas continues, adding, "That last take was really good."

"Sure."

"I spent the whole weekend rewriting the scene with you and Palpatine, where you turn. I've added some more to that. I've stretched it out and given you a little more to go on in terms of him pulling you in."

"Nice."

"Anyway, I know we can do this."

Returning from the set, Lucas tells McDiarmid about the rewrite, noting that Jayne-Ann will give him the new dialogue. He explains that the scene now has more justifications for Palpatine's behavior. "You're just misunderstood," George says.

"Of course," Ian smiles.

LOCATION WRAP: 19:10   SETUPS: 35
SCRIPT SHOT TODAY: 3m 21s

SHOOT DAY 7: TUESDAY, JULY 8, 2003
LOCATION: Stage 2
SET: Int. Padmé's veranda—Coruscant
SCENES SHOT: 140 (Obi-Wan tells Padmé that Anakin has gone to the dark side)

On the veranda set, the actors are having difficulty. "Oh, I just want to get through it," Lucas says mostly to himself, after the third mistake. McGregor asks if they could stop a moment so he can collect himself. After the next take, the scene is finished without error and Natalie gives Ewan a hug.

Meanwhile on Stage 4, Jackson is rehearsing his lightsaber battle with Nick Gillard and the swordsmen. They go back and forth repeating the moves on a wide, long red carpet marked with masking tape. Dressed in a

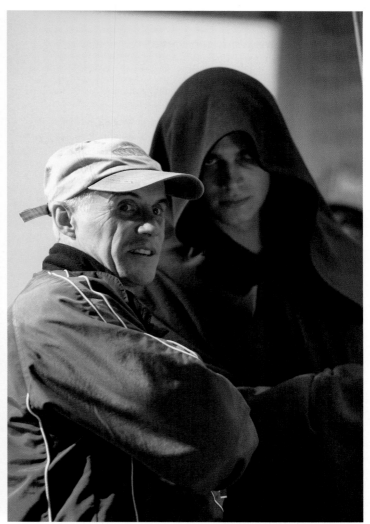

black T-shirt, dark blue sweatpants, and a baseball cap, Jackson goes through the moves in slow motion. "Even your defensive moves are attacking," fencing double Kyle Rowling says to Jackson.

"Nick and I have been talking about this for a couple of years," Jackson says. "And he has graciously been trying to figure out a really spectacular [light]saber battle for me to do. He's combined a lot of different styles, so that it looks very good and it travels well. The fight actually makes me dominant, it makes me vulnerable, it makes me sneaky. Nick is always trying to find things that make Mace at ease yet lethal. The fight that I'm doing here, I had to learn pretty quickly. I had to learn some ninety-seven moves in two to three days, and then learn to speed them up *and* learn to move."

Stunt coordinator-sword master Nick Gillard was born, grew up, and still lives in Brighton, England. "My father was in the navy, so I was sent to military school when I was twelve," he says. "They dropped me off but I quit that school. There was an advert in the newspaper for riders for a circus, so I went along. I did trick riding and we also ran a medieval jousting tournament. My parents came to take me out, but my mum realized I was

having a good time, and it was keeping me off the streets. I was there from twelve to probably twenty, but I went into the stunt business when I was eighteen. We got called at the circus to go and work on a film, *The Thief of Baghdad* [1978]. That was it for me. We got good food. It wasn't money or anything—it was the food.

"I was on the set of *Jedi*; I had just become a stuntman," Gillard recalls. "Mark Hamill actually wanted me to double him, but it didn't happen. In England, to be a stuntman or -woman, you have to be an instructor in six sports just to get on the register. You have to have a fighting one, a gymnastic one, a trampoline one, a water one, and a horse-riding one. You have to be category ten in skydiving. And then you do five years probation where you can only work under a stunt coordinator, a full member. And then you do another three to five years where you can coordinate yourself but not others. It all goes before a committee each time, and they work out when you've gained enough experience."

Back on set, Ewan and Natalie continue. Portman is becoming appropriately emotional as Obi-Wan tells her character that her husband has done terrible things. After one take, she immediately asks, "Can we go again?" in an effort not to lose the moment.

After subsequent takes, Lucas says, "I'm happy. I got two different good takes. Our work here is done."

Previous spread: A panoramic view of the veranda courtesy of John Knoll. Above left and middle: Lucas discusses with Portman and Christensen an emotional scene. Concept artist McCaig has this to say about Padmé's tragedy: "You have a person who began so naive and idealistic. And here she is at the end of her life still idealistic. She believes her love can redeem Anakin—even at the end, she believes it." Above right: Christensen (Anakin) with his friend and fight instructor Nick Gillard.

LOCATION WRAP: 19:45   SETUPS: 24   SCRIPT SHOT TODAY: 2m 42s

SHOOT DAY 8: WEDNESDAY, JULY 9, 2003
    LOCATION: Stage 2, Stage 3
    SET: Int. Padmé's veranda
    SCENES SHOT: 55 (Anakin tells Padmé about his dream)

After this scene wraps, the veranda will be destroyed, decimated in a few hours, whereas it took the construction department more than seven weeks to make it.

"The veranda was tricky," construction manager Greg Hadju says. "Nothing's straight and square on *Star Wars*. It really stretches the carpenters, particularly. A couple of the foremen are good mathematicians and really understand practical geometry and the development of arcs. We've managed to track down some books and have them republished for us, too. After Episode II, they said, 'When's the next one happening, 'cause we've never done such a complicated job and we've never had our skills stretched like this.' They all live for *Star Wars* basically."

In the creatures department building, Peter Mayhew is having his first fitting in the new Chewbacca costume. Under the care of creatures shop creative supervisor Dave Elsey and supervisor Rebecca Hunt, it's here that all eight Wookiee costumes are being made, averaging twelve weeks each. Indeed, it takes a week of ten-hour days for one person to add the black hair to one particular Wookiee suit. The twenty or so craftspeople working here also fabricate Neimoidians, Mon Calamari, casts of Darth Sidious, and

so on. Tacked to one board are dozens of ears to choose from. In a box rests baby Luke Skywalker, whose seams are clearly visible.

"When I was a kid, all I used to do was watch horror movies," Dave Elsey recalls, "which made me what I am now: a maker of monsters. It was only my parents pointing out that it's actually not doctors that make monsters, but the makeup people. So I said, 'Great. Now I know what I want to do for the rest of my life.'

"So I'm in charge of the actual creating of the things—making them, sculpting them, painting them, sticking them on, and implementing things—and Becky [Rebecca Hunt] makes sure that I do that on time and on budget."

After they finish putting his head on, Mayhew does his characteristic head tilt and stands up, towering over the technicians. "We're going to need a stepladder for on-set checks, aren't we?" one technician notes. Mayhew flexes his biceps and says, "The Wookiee is back."

In the video village, Lucas is saying, "If I'd taken the prequel trilogy to a marketing company, Episode I would have started here [with Episode III]—and Episodes II and III would've been about Darth Vader killing people. But in the end, I wouldn't be able to write movies like that."

On this occasion, because there's ample time, Lucas continues with his perspective on the *Star Wars* saga: "If you see them in order, it completely twists things about. A lot of the tricks of IV, V, and VI no longer exist. The real struggle of the twins to save their father becomes very apparent, whereas it didn't exist at all the first time [audiences saw Episodes IV, V, and VI]. Now Darth Vader is a tragic character who's lost everything. He's basically a bitter old man in a suit. 'I am your father' was a real shock. Now it's a real reward. Finally, the son knows what we already know.

"It's a very different suspense structure. Part of the fun for me was completely flipping upside down the dramatic track of the original movies. If you watch it the way it was released, IV, V, VI, I, II, III—you get one kind of movie. If you watch I through VI, you get a completely different movie. One or two generations have seen it one way, and the next generations will see it a completely different way.

"It's extremely modern, almost interactive moviemaking. You take blocks and move them around, and you come out with different emotional states."

LOCATION WRAP: 19:45   SETUPS: 21   SCRIPT SHOT TODAY: 2m 49s

SHOOT DAY 9: THURSDAY, JULY 10, 2003
LOCATION: Stage 5
SET: Int. Jedi Temple—council chambers
SCENES SHOT: 62 (Anakin is approved as the Chancellor's representative)

Left: Peter Mayhew returns as the Wookiee Chewbacca; prosthetic make-up/fabrication technician Kristelle Gardiner (right inset) checks on things in the creatures department in building 48. On July 9, as word spreads throughout the studio that Mayhew is in full costume for the first time, many visitors come to pay their respects—including a familiar astromech droid. Alas, the two will have to wait nineteen "story years" to meet again on film, as Episode III has no scenes with them both. Above right: Lucas studies the Jedi Council layout.

The Jedi Council set, which seems at once familiar and larger than it appears on screen, has been built on a raised platform. In fact, many of the sets are built that way, which allows for more things to happen around and under the construct, and for the bluescreen to be evenly lighted.

Alien Jedi arrive and take their places for rehearsals. Lucas walks from one to the other, greeting the Council. "You found your old chair," Lucas says to Jackson.

"Everyone quiet, please!" says Fletcher, who, at one time, with all these aliens about, might have felt bewildered. "At first I didn't know the *Star Wars* language," he admits. "People were talking about 'Neimoidians'—and I just didn't know what they were. So I went out and got some of the *Star Wars* books, and went through them to understand."

Lucas looks over the composition of the Council members and has one alien change chairs. Jackson asks whether, when Anakin arrives in the room, he can point Anakin to a seat. Lucas agrees that it'd be a good idea.

"Is there someone I'd be addressing in particular?" Hayden asks.

"Yoda, Ki-Adi-Mundi, or Mace—the senior triumvirate," Lucas answers.

During the first rehearsal, Christensen paces to show Anakin's displeasure with the Council. But Lucas explains, "You can't really wander around while you're arguing with them. It's more West Point."

LOCATION WRAP: 20:30   SETUPS: 44   SCRIPT SHOT TODAY: 3m 59s
TRAVEL: Christopher Lee (Count Dooku/Darth Tyranus) flew Auckland-Sydney.

SHOOT DAY 10: FRIDAY, JULY 11, 2003

LOCATION: Stage 7
SET: Int. Palpatine's private office
SCENES SHOT: 59 (Palpatine and Anakin discuss the Jedi Council)

Anthony Daniels has walked over to the makeshift editing suite on the second floor of Stage 2. In a bare room with standard office furniture and a few computers, editor Roger Barton has called up C-3PO's scenes on the Avid for Daniels to study and then overdub. "Pardon me, my ladyship, is there any way I might be of service?" he intones. For each line, Daniels does a few readings till both he and Roger are satisfied. Sometimes, they add a joke. "George will kill me!" Anthony predicts.

"George occasionally lets me fiddle with the lines, because every actor becomes an expert in their own role," Daniels explains. "But I wouldn't want the responsibility he has on these movies. I've realized that if he walks by and doesn't acknowledge you, it's not that he's being rude, it's just that his head is full of a whole universe—some of which is about to crash."

Meanwhile on the cavernous Stage 7, Christensen and McDiarmid are rehearsing the scene in which Palpatine appoints Anakin to represent him on the Jedi Council. Lucas reflects out loud that he could've filmed the rehearsal: "I could have done it all in one shot this morning and we could've saved a day."

"Well, you're keeping people employed," McFarlane says.

Scene 59 is long on dialogue, and, at the end of a long day, they do another take. "That was brilliant," Lucas says. "I'd say we got it."

There's applause, and Lucas walks over to Christensen and McDiarmid. "There were shades of different performances that I like. Two takes were very good," he says. "I'll see you guys tomorrow to figure out next week's work. The marathon week." Lucas and Christensen hug goodbye. The cast and crew seem happy with the way the second week of principal photography has gone—a level of comfort has been established.

Lucas shakes David Tattersall's hand. "You did a good job."

"Are we rehearsing tomorrow [Saturday]?" David asks.

"Yes, probably ten to one."

LOCATION WRAP: 19:45   SETUPS: 29   SCRIPT SHOT TODAY: 2m 55s

LOCATION: Stage 7
SET: Int. Palpatine's private office
SCENES SHOT: 94 (Palpatine revealed as a Sith Lord)

"Let's hold the work." Fletcher requests. The warning bell sounds. "This is a long scene, everybody, so find a place that's comfortable. No movement on the stage," he adds.

"And . . . action!" Lucas calls out.

McDiarmid and Christensen, Emperor and Jedi, circle each other as they converse. Cut. Lucas reviews with the two how he wants the scene blocked. Take. The director asks for more surprise and more energy from Christensen—more incredulity—as he discovers that the Supreme Chancellor is in reality a Sith Lord. Looking off the set, Lucas spots McCallum and Bocquet, who is waiting to ask how many chairs he wants in the opera box.

"George suddenly invented an opera scene," Bocquet says. "So we needed a theater box, and we literally had a day. So we took three of the chairs out of Palpatine's red office and did a quick repaint job, changed the back, and added fabric—all the things we could do in, like, four hours.

Even in the world of multimillion-dollar filmmaking—thanks to the early days of dressings, greeblies, and old aircraft parts—George loves the idea that if you stick a few things on and paint them silver with care and attention, they'll look great."

Take. "That smile at the end worked," Lucas says to McDiarmid. As the crew prepares another setup, he and McCallum talk about the impending Mace-Palpatine fight. "If I can get through that fight in one day, I'm home free," Lucas says.

After lunch, on Stage 7, the cameras roll, and Ian flubs his lines. During the next take, Hayden says his line, "I should kill you," but Ian responds, "Yes, you should—except for the fact that I'm standing on your cloak."

While waiting for a new setup, Lucas consults with two makeup artists, who are showing him photos of Senators for approval. "We've never really done eye shadow," he explains. "It's not part of our universe."

Going from choreography chores, to makeup and costume decisions, to camera setups, to answering a dozen rapid-fire questions, Lucas moves swiftly from subject to subject. "It's like cooking," he says, "which is like chaos. But if you're really good, you can make sure that everything comes

Left: The hallway leading to Palpatine's antechamber is the locale for the intense scene 59 between Sith and Jedi during which Anakin is tempted (insets). Above: The rigging is plainly visible above the set of Palpatine's office. Top: Technical supervisor

Michael Blanchard (standing) and assistant editor Jett Sally in the editing suite on the second floor of Stage 2.

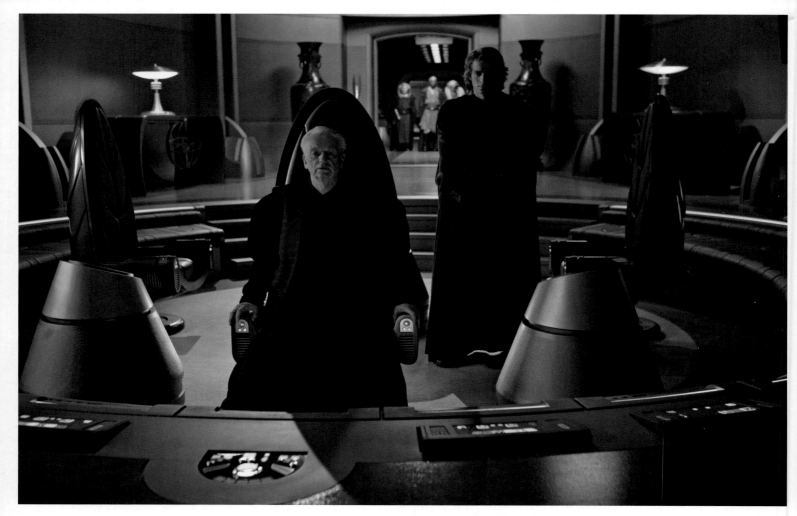

off at exactly the same moment. When I go to film schools, sometimes I get asked, 'When you're doing a movie, I see that you're always asked a lot of different questions. How do you know what the right answer is?' And I say, 'If you don't know what the right answer is, then you're not a director.' The director has to take in what everybody else is doing, which takes training—but the way you know is in your gut."

"One of the things that can go wrong, if you don't have a strong leader," McCallum agrees, "is that you end up with a production designer making his own film, a director of photography making his own film, a costume designer making her own film—all of them making their own best interpretation of what they think the movie is. That's why I've always loved working with a writer-director. There are fewer misunderstandings."

On set, Lucas says to the actors, "You can slow it down a little bit. If we try and keep it as slow as we can, we'll be there."

Tracks are added for a dolly shot that will enable the camera to circle the actors as they circle each other. McDiarmid is now very much into character, as is Christensen. Multiple takes later, they're done. McDiarmid sits down next to Lucas in the video village. "I'm beginning to believe it!" Ian says of the scene.

Group discussion then turns to the next day. "Tomorrow's just three and one-eighth pages," Lucas says to McCallum. "And I talked to David already—he's got it lit—we're ready to roll."

"Beautiful," Rick responds.

LOCATION WRAP: 20:00   SETUPS: 31   SCRIPT SHOT TODAY: 3m 52s

SHOOT DAY 12: TUESDAY, JULY 15, 2003
LOCATION: Stage 7
SET: Int. Palpatine's office
SCENES SHOT: 89 (delegation of Senators meet Palpatine); 99pt (Palpatine cuts down Kit Fisto, Eeth Koth, Saesee Tiin, and fights Mace Windu)

The next shot begins what will be a series of scenes pitting Mace Windu against Chancellor Palpatine, first verbally—then physically. On a fairly large set, flanked by three fellow Jedi, Mace walks through the hallway to Palpatine's antechamber. "When Mace grabs his sword, you guys grab your swords, too," Lucas instructs them. But he then notices that the supporting Jedi are wearing awkward gloves made of rubber, and says, "Uh-oh. This is going to be tough."

A tentative solution is found, and they do a take. Fletcher cues McDiarmid, who is seated in a proto-Emperor chair, so he can spin around to confront the Jedi. Take. Jayne-Ann calls their attention to a dialogue error. Take. "Are you guys happy?" George asks the cameramen. "Yeah, that was good," McFarlane replies.

Above left: Anakin stands with Palpatine as Mace Windu and three Jedi arrive to inform the Chancellor of Grievous's defeat. McCallum watches the shoot (below), which can also be seen on the monitor. Right: Between setups, Lucas talks things over with Jackson (Windu), while Tux Akendoyeni (Eeth Koth) looks on.

"Okay, we're going to try the fight now while we're in position," Lucas decides rather suddenly. "I'm curious to see how this will work." Gillard walks over. "We're going to rehearse it once," Lucas tells him, "then shoot it once and see how it looks. Okay, this is it, Nick."

Gillard organizes the actors and Michael Byrne (Palaptine's fencing double) while Lucas observes from the video village. Stuntman Ben Cooke (Kit Fisto) is still having problems holding his lightsaber with his gloves. "This Kit Fisto holds it by the blade. You can tell he's not a real Jedi," Lucas jokes, watching the monitor.

"He's tough—he doesn't feel the pain," Knoll says.

Take. The spontaneous shot of the fight isn't working. "You can't win if you don't take risks," Lucas shrugs. "Well, that was interesting. I think we've exhausted that idea."

LOCATION WRAP: 20:00   SETUPS: 58
SCRIPT SHOT TODAY: 2m 52s

SHOOT DAY 13: WEDNESDAY, JULY 16, 2003
   LOCATION: Stage 7
   SET: Int. Palpatine's office
   SCENES SHOT: 99pt
   VFX [visual effects] NOTES: Sc. 99—Anakin's lightsaber goes flying, chair is zapped out of the way, lightsaber flies into Anakin's hand, lightsaber flies into Palpatine's hand.

Gillard is talking logistics with Lucas and Coleman. Today is going to be one of the more difficult days of the shoot, as the Mace-Palpatine fight is one of the trickiest in terms of preparation and choreography. Fletcher asks whether the three Jedi Masters, whom Palpatine has struck down, can leave the stage. "We can lose everybody; they're all dead," Lucas responds. "We'll turn around and do Mace now."

Lucas and Gillard talk things over again. "I have to get the movie done," the director is saying. "Regardless, I have to have something on the screen that works."

"One of the first assignments for me when I got here was to spend two weeks with Nick Gillard," Coleman explains. "So Nick and I are collaborating quite a bit right now, as I try and figure out what fight elements we can achieve with animation. As fights are taken from the rehearsal room, with no set pieces, to the actual sets, sometimes the fights have to change a little bit because George will either have time constraints or set constraints, or need to change an element. And then Nick has to react right away, so I'm there as he turns around and asks, 'Can you animate that backflip? Because it would take us X amount of time—which we don't have—to do it.'"

The bell rings. "Quiet, please," third assistant director Samantha Smith says. Take. Makeup artists pat down Jackson's head for glare. He and McDiarmid are in close quarters with

Top left: Lucas stands between Palpatine (McDiarmid) and Windu (Jackson). Top right: The fight continues. Above left: McCallum and Coleman. Right: Mayhew (Chewbacca) arrives for Lucas's final costume approval, flanked by Rebecca Hunt, Kristelle Gardiner, Hamish Roxburgh, and Lou and Dave Elsey.

their lightsabers; the Steadicam is practically on top of them, so Harding is wearing a helmet. Ian performs some lightsaber moves only just learned. Lucas asks him to keep his hands together on the saber handle.

Several takes later, Jackson and McDiarmid clash and freeze, staring into each other's eyes.

"Okay, cut!" Lucas calls out. The two almost collapse in laughter. "We're going to be here all day," the director says.

After the crew breaks for lunch and leaves the set, silhouetted against a greenscreen by the remaining lights, Lucas, McCallum, Knoll, and Coleman discuss the fight.

"I need a close-up of Ian," Lucas is saying. "We're not going to be able to do a shot like this off a digital character. We can try—and if we do it, I will applaud you tremendously. But nobody told me I couldn't shoot close-ups."

"What I think the misunderstanding is, 'cause I wasn't there—" McCallum starts.

"Nobody said anything to me till this morning," Lucas injects.

"I think there was a misunderstanding—"

Gillard arrives and suggests alterations to the fight. "There's always time," he says.

"You saw what I did. I want to see Ian's expression," Lucas says to him.

"I misunderstood. I thought it was going to be face replacement," Gillard explains.

"But I have to have some close-ups. I can't shoot the whole thing in a wide shot."

"There are places in there where they're not fighting—you could move in there," Gillard suggests, but Lucas reiterates that he doesn't want to switch too often from wide shots to close-ups, and he has doubts about digital face replacement.

"I think we can push the face replacement closer than we did last time," Knoll says.

"If the reference is really good," Coleman agrees.

"Well, that's lunch anyway," Lucas concludes.

Later that day, Mayhew, in full costume, climbs into a station wagon—seated in the copilot's seat, of course—on his way to Stage 7 for Lucas's final approval. With staff from the creatures department in tow, he arrives on the set of Palpatine's office. George walks over and says, "Looks good. Excellent. How do you feel?"

"Great," Mayhew says from within his Wookiee mask.

"Back home," Lucas says, and then beckons to Samuel Jackson, who strolls over and says, "Oh, you're dressed today—and combed." The two actors then talk "Wookiee" together, making appropriately seal-like barking sounds and laughing.

"We walked onto the set—and I heard afterward that it was actually quite a tense time—and you could hear people suddenly gasp," Rebecca Hunt recalls. "And the noise grew, saying, 'Wow.' I was absolutely blown away. People love Artoo and they love Chewie. And he was great. When we finally took the head off, you could see Peter was just pumped up with excitement."

Between takes, Rick comes over and congratulates the creatures team. "Thank you, guys," he says.

LOCATION WRAP: 20:15   SETUPS: 62   SCRIPT SHOT TODAY: 1m 03s
TRAVEL: Jimmy Smits [Bail Organa] arrives in Sydney.

SHOOT DAY 14: THURSDAY, JULY 17, 2003
LOCATION: Stage 7
SET: Int. Palpatine's office
SCENES SHOT: 99pt (Anakin becomes Darth Vader)
VFX NOTES: Anakin cuts off Mace's hand.

Dave Elsey is putting the final touches on Ian McDiarmid as Darth Sidious, doing his face and nails. The actor then lies on the ground, blue lights flashing in his face to simulate the blue lightning coming from his fingers, which will be added in postproduction. For each take, Jackson, wearing glasses, yells his lines from off camera over the noise of a wind machine.

The next setup has Anakin in close-up as he watches Palpatine and Windu slug it out. "The thing to remember is there's a huge display of craziness going on here," Lucas reminds Christensen.

"As much as I'm watching what's going on, I think I'm really searching myself to see what I'm going to do here," Christensen says.

"Right."

"I'm listening to them but I'm also in my own head at the same time."

Lucas agrees, but adds, "We still have to get the audience into what you're thinking. When you get into these scenes, you have to be visually reacting, too."

They then shoot the moment in which Palpatine implores Anakin to help him. "At the point when Palpatine begs for Anakin's help," Jackson points out, "I'm bending those lightning bolts right back on him. I mean, that's why he's begging—because I got him. I'm like, 'Yeeeeah! Who's your daddy now?!'"

In the next scene, Anakin becomes Darth Vader. Christensen kneels before McDiarmid, rehearsing his dialogue to himself.

"Anakin's relationship with Palpatine eclipses his relationship with Obi-Wan," Christensen remarks. "But he doesn't really have a clear devotion to one or the other. Anakin as he will be played is—I don't want to say naïve, but his belief system is still open. He still isn't exactly set in his devotion to the Jedi or to Palpatine. He is looking to see how he can get more power, but his ideas of good and evil are not black and white."

"And . . . action!" Lucas calls out. After a few takes, with Hayden kneeling among a dozen crew, Anakin's transition to the dark side is complete.

LOCATION WRAP: 20:30   SETUPS: 42   SCRIPT SHOT TODAY: 4m 31s
NOTES: On wrap, it was discovered that Ian McDiarmid had suffered a considerable amount of discomfort with his contact lenses. As a result, contact lens nurse Helen Johnstone gave him an eye bath and checked for any damage.

SHOOT DAY 15: FRIDAY, JULY 18, 2003
LOCATION: Stages 7 & 4
SET: Int. Palpatine's private office; Int. Coruscant ballet
SCENES SHOT: 99 (Palpatine fights with Mace Windu), 67pt (Palpatine tells Anakin the Jedi Council wants to control the Republic)

"If we can get through this day, we'll be okay," Lucas predicts to Fletcher on the third day of shooting the Mace-Palpatine fight. The stunt crew attaches wires to Jackson so they can violently pull him backward to simulate Windu being pummeled by a particularly vicious blast of dark side lightning. Lucas describes the scene to the actor: "Your first reaction is surprise—your hand's been cut off—and then you're blasted away."

They do a rehearsal and suddenly Sam is floating above the set, pulled there by wires yanked by stuntmen jumping off a ladder to create the necessary force. "It's almost like I've practiced for this death all my life," Jackson says. "Last summer, when I was in San Francisco doing another film [*Twisted*, 2004], George and I had lunch and discussed what was going to happen in this film. And he said, 'Well you're pretty much the only important character that I can actually kill off, so it has to be a pretty spectacular death.'"

As they prepare to shoot close-ups of Anakin cutting off Mace's hand, Lucas suggests to Christensen, "It's good if it's a clean move," and then explains how the scene will go quiet afterward, with "low strings and scary music."

The next scene on the schedule is at the opera, where Palpatine continues his seduction of Anakin, recounting the story of Darth Plagueis. "A little political plotting at the ballet is just the thing after a hard day's swordfighting," Lucas says to McDiarmid.

Makeup artists touch up Sandi Finlay (Sly Moore), David Bowers (Mas Amedda), and McDiarmid, who are seated, staring out at a performance that doesn't yet exist. "It'll take us six months to figure out what they're watching," Lucas says. Ian then recounts to Anakin the story of Plagueis

Left and insets: Lucas directs the principals as Anakin intervenes—fatally—in the Windu/Palpatine conflict. Above right: Elsey applies finishing touches to McDiarmid's Darth Sidious makeup/prosthetic. "I love the Emperor," Elsey says. "Re-creating that makeup was both a challenge and an honor."

several times in several setups, each delivery flawless and chilling.

"Scenes where Ian did most of the talking, I just had to sit there and listen," Christensen reveals. "I literally just sort of nod my head and agree with the story he's telling me—and those scenes were my favorites, because he's an amazing storyteller. I was so in awe of what he was doing in each scene, I'd find myself at times almost breaking out of character."

"I come from a tiny town called Dundee," McDiarmid remembers. "When I was four years old, I was taken by my parents to see a variety show, which completely fascinated me. It was rather scary and, at the same time, seductive. And every now and again a kind of magic seemed to happen. All those people up there doing strange things—and they wore lots of makeup in those days. Afterward, I got to meet a couple of the performers, who were charming—but they were terrifying to a small boy. Taller and in lots of makeup smiling down at me. I can still see their faces."

"That's a wrap," Lucas says. Joining McDiarmid on the set, he adds, "That was amazing, absolutely amazing. Everyone was glued to the monitors."

Just then, Anthony Daniels, in costume, arrives pushing a birthday cake on a tray for Colin Fletcher. "I'm blown over," Fletcher says.

As people break up into groups, chatting and eating cake, George says to Ian: "You've got one more fight with a little green frog, but that shouldn't be too hard."

LOCATION WRAP: 20:45   SETUPS: 40   SCRIPT SHOT TODAY: 6m 45s
NOTES: A splinter unit headed by Rick McCallum did pickup shots this morning on the "private office" set. They completed Palpatine's wire work for Sc. 99.

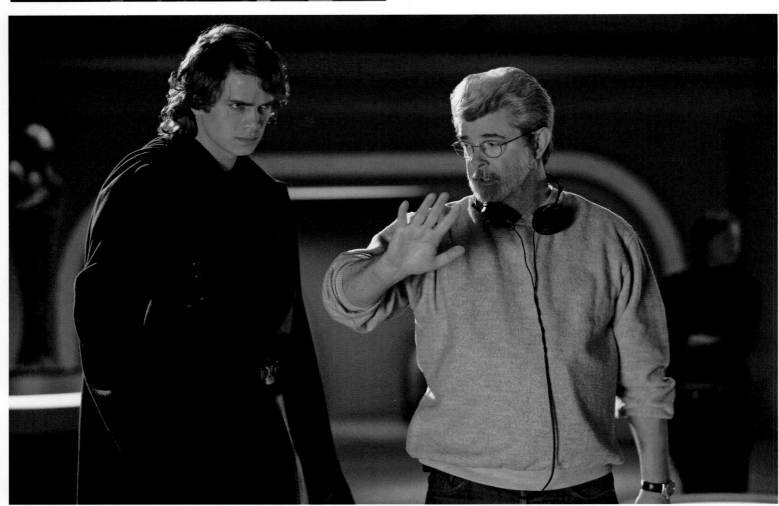

Top: At the opera, McDiarmid continues his performance as the insidiously proactive Palpatine. The veteran stage performer likens the Chancellor to Shakespeare's Prospero in The Tempest. *"I've played other monsters, too,"* he notes. *"Count Cenci is almost as monstrous as Palpatine. He's diabolical in every sense . . . his daughter kills him by driving nails through his eyes." Above: Lucas directs Christensen, whose fearful Anakin is no match for McDiarmid's monster.*

⑤ Return of the Emperor

REHEARSAL DAY: SATURDAY, JULY 19, 2003

Within a nearly empty Stage 3, Lucas is talking story with Jimmy Smits. Christensen arrives, and the two actors shake hands. Everyone is in street clothes. While leaning on the makeshift staircase leading up to the set, Lucas posits the political question *Revenge of the Sith* answers: "How do you turn over democracy to a tyrant with applause? Not with a coup, but with applause? That is the story of Caesar, Napoleon, and Hitler." He adds, "Idiocy is the controlling factor of life–particularly when you get into politics."

Bocquet, Russell, Tenggren, and dialogue coach Chris Neil are present. Portman arrives, and after they consult the visual script to learn what the scene will eventually look like, she, Smits, McGregor, and Christensen begin rehearsals on an otherwise empty set.

"Rick brought in Chris," Natalie Portman says, "who was, I would say, a rehearsal arbiter. [laughs] We did end up rehearsing a lot more, which is really, really helpful, and we had a lot of conversations. This time, Anakin and I are supposed to have been married for several years. We've supposedly been living together and made a baby together, so you have to fill in those blanks."

"One of the things we focused on in rehearsals was this sense of history between Anakin and Padmé," Neil says. "I looked out for the little touches, certain adjustments that might lighten the moment–an embrace, a line reading, or an unspoken moment that might give the audience a chance to invest emotionally in the characters.

"George's approach is to play Anakin as not consumed by the dark side from the very get-go," he adds, "but over the course of the movie. So my notes to George concerning Christensen and Natalie–Natalie especially–were to try to figure out the marker points for his progression toward the dark side."

Top: Lucas and Jimmy Smits (Bail Organa) go over the script. Above: Fletcher, Lucas, McCallum, and Matt Sloan (Plo Koon).

SHOOT DAY 16: MONDAY, JULY 21, 2003
LOCATION: Stage 4
SET: Int. Coruscant ballet
SCENES SHOT: 67

Producer Rick McCallum starts his day at 4:00 A.M. By 4:50 A.M., he's at his desk in the production office where a small mountain of faxes awaits him, accumulated during the night thanks to the time difference between Australia and the States.

Today's material–which includes ILM planning documents and animatics reports–also contains the UK payroll, so McCallum gives longtime *Star Wars* accountant Raj Patel a call in England to confirm its details. At 5:30 A.M., Rick meets with Jones and Fletcher to go over the day's work. Next is a visit to makeup and then the assistant directors' office, where 2nd AD Deborah Antoniou (known as Deb) fills him in on the actors' status. After checking out Stage 4 to make sure it's ready, McCallum joins Lucas, Jones, and Fletcher for breakfast at 7 A.M.

"The breakfasts are really big deals for us," he explains, "because George goes through the schedule for the day and we play a very crucial game. As we eat, he bounces ideas off of us–pushing us to the limit by testing out different scenarios–what happens if he finishes a certain scene at three instead of five?–which forces us to understand why we've made judgments. He's testing the assumptions of what the schedule is and conceptualizing the milestones he has to achieve in order to finish each scene–so he can guarantee we'll finish that day's work. George is one of the few directors to do that."

The rapid pace of the early morning continues as McCallum visits with Tattersall, to check on the lighting; Bocquet, to discuss the sets; Russell and Gracie, to talk over the set-building schedule; the riggers, about tonight's stage work; then back to makeup, to touch base with the actors.

By 8:50 A.M., McCallum is talking with production accountant Kevin Plummer and going through the week's budget and any possible cost overruns. The rest of the morning is filled with e-mail, return calls–and constant status reports from Deb and Colin Fletcher on anything out of the ordinary.

"Deb tells me, for example, if an actor is late," Rick says. "Colin will call and tell me that George has added another six shots. So I'll go over and talk with George about how that's going to affect the schedule. It's a wired world."

Every hour of the day, consequently, has McCallum spending ten to fifteen minutes on the set. At 11:15 A.M. today, he checks in with the construction department—a vast hangar filled with hundreds of crew. "We had a situation where we found out an outside construction company was ripping us off," Rick says. "So we got the documentary crew to tape all the arrivals of the trucks delivering the materials over a three-day period. We were ordering X feet of lumber, and they were delivering hundreds of feet less. They thought we'd be too rushed to check how much they actually sent—but we check *everything*. So I sent the tapes to the construction company and said, 'We're not going to pay your outstanding bill.' "

Meanwhile, on the set, a gum-chewing Finlay is helped into the opera box, the end of her robe carried as if she were arriving for a wedding. McDiarmid and Bowers take their seats.

"It was very interesting, the scene we did in the theater," Ian remembers. "There seemed to be lots of guests on the set that day, which could have been a distraction. On that day, it was a help. I found it was rather like playing to an audience."

Lucas explains that, following a Saturday run-through of the scene, he switched it from Palpatine's office to an opera box. "During rehearsal, I said, 'My God, this is a four-page scene—I've had five scenes in this office already—how am I going to do this?' So I put it in an opera house, watching a ballet—*Squid Lake*—which worked out great."

After the scene is finished, Lucas joins McCallum, Fletcher, and Jones for lunch. The cafeteria at Fox Studios is a temporary structure made of wood, canvas walls, see-through plastic windows, and a corrugated metal roof. If the weather is hot, the walls can be removed. Cast and on-set crew file past two long tables stacked with main courses, which are generally very good. There is an additional table with salads, and another with desserts. Some of the crew eat outside, while others sit inside on fold-up chairs at long fold-up tables.

"Lunch is about what we accomplished," Rick says, "compared to what we thought we'd do—why didn't we get it done, what we're still trying to do, and where we can make up time."

At 2 P.M., he calls Ramos, back at the ranch, for more budget talks, particularly questions about postproduction, the groundwork for which is being laid now. "Ours is a dialogue," he notes, "that goes all the way through the filmmaking process. There's a constant juggling of assets, and Kathryn is production's alter ego—she keeps us honest. Someone once said that it doesn't matter what it costs, if you get it right. But the truth is, it does matter how much it costs, it does matter how you do it–that's the fun part."

Today's discussion is cut short, however, as a problem is reported over the walkie-talkie. Due to a sick cast member, one scene will be pushed back and another will leap forward–so McCallum makes an emergency trip to the costume department. He and Biggar quickly go over what kind of additional staffing she might need to create the suddenly due robes. Rick then hightails it over to the art department where, with Bocquet and Gracie, he discusses what kind of overtime they'll need to finish building a set whose production just accelerated.

"It's like a miniature village," McCallum explains, "and every day there is drama."

Rick revisits the set and Lucas, and checks in with the ADs. He then meets with Fox personnel to go over what stages they might sublet from JAK. It turns out that a small independent film can shoot on a stage that is temporarily available during the weekend.

At 5:30 P.M., McCallum walks over to the second floor of Stage 2 for a review of the previous day's tape with Roger Barton, which is followed by a walk-through of all the sets and an inspection of assets that can be wrapped, shipped, or sold. Back in the production office at 6 P.M., Jacqui debriefs Rick on anything he missed, and loose ends are tied up by 7 P.M.– when it's time to meet again with Lucas and Fletcher to go over the cast-

ing of tertiary characters and tomorrow's schedule.

Production coordinator Virginia Murray then bombards McCallum with questions concerning travel, equipment, insurance, accident reports, and actor contracts. These last items will take him about two hours to read. "Film has about ten thousand separate tasks, which are highly visible and interdependent," Rick remarks, "and which have to be finished before you can deliver the movie. Each one of those has to be checked off, legal clearances have to be obtained, there are lawyers, contracts, and billing rights."

"The first real film I worked on was *101 Dalmations* [1996]," Murray says, "which included a team that were all Rick McCallum protégés from the *Young Indy* days–and that was my big break. Most of his old first and second ADs, and production coordinators, are all top-class production managers and executive producers on *Harry Potter* and goodness knows what else.

"It's the best office ever," she adds. "It *is* a bit all-or-nothing, so Rick likes everybody to have a good time."

At 10 P.M., pizza is ordered and Deb arrives to give McCallum a roundup of the cast–any problems that arose and what the general feel of the day has been. By 11 P.M., he's out the door.

LOCATION WRAP: 20:30   SETUPS: 44   SCRIPT SHOT TODAY: 1m 42s

SHOOT DAY 17: Tuesday, July 22, 2003

LOCATION: Stage 3
SET: Ext. Coruscant industrial landing platform; Int. Coruscant—Jedi gunship
SCENES SHOT: 65 (Obi-Wan and Mace Windu travel with Yoda to the landing platform), 73 (Anakin waits as Palpatine emerges from his transport)

"I came in this morning and said, 'Wrong ship, guys,'" Lucas remarks to McGregor, because instead of the needed gunship, another vessel had found its way to the set. "Fortunately, we're fast on our feet here," he adds. They then stand for a few moments without speaking, Lucas sipping coffee from a Styrofoam cup.

Jackson joins them, and rehearsals begin. Yoda is, of course, invisible, so his lines are spoken by offline reader Duncan Young, a well-known Australian TV and stage actor who will voice many CG and otherwise unavailable characters during the shoot (all of whom will be overdubbed in postproduction).

Previous spread, top: The spontaneously created opera box, with Anakin (Christensen), Palpatine (McDiarmid), and Sly Moore (Sandi Finlay). Below: Another of John Knoll's panoramic photos shows the enormous makeshift cafeteria, which every day serves breakfast, three lunch shifts, and constant snacks—all generated by the kitchen-in-a-truck next door. Left: Lucas directs scene 73, with red guards, Mas Amedda (David Bowers) and Palpatine (McDiarmid). Top-left: Saesee Tiin (Kenji Oates) and production coordinator Virginia Murray. Above: Lucas and Jar Jar Binks (Ahmed Best). Top right: Cast and crew on the Senate landing platform.

This scene, in which Senators and dignitaries come to greet Palpatine following his dramatic rescue, is the first to include many extras. Among them are a few recognizable characters, such as Bail Organa and Jar Jar, as well as new faces, such as Malé-Dee (Kee Chan) and Giddean Danu (Chris Kirby). As he disembarks from his transport, the group will escort the Chancellor through a massive colonnaded area. Except for some partially built columns, this zone is mostly greenscreen, so Lucas instructs the actors and extras where to walk to avoid digital columns or ships.

Katie Lucas (Chi Eekway) and Amanda Lucas (Terr Taneel) are also among the Senators, as is Rena Owens (Nee Alavar), the voice of Taun We in *Attack of the Clones*. "Are Senators allowed to smile?" Owens asks. Lucas says yes. Smits asks if greeting the Chancellor with a nod conforms with Republic etiquette. Lucas says yes again.

After a rehearsal, Lucas walks over to the edge of the set, which is on a raised platform surrounded by many onlookers. "Do you think we should put some boxes here in case someone falls?" he asks Smith. "Some of these people can't see in their costumes." Boxes, which act as cushions, are added. Between takes, a handheld blower is used to gust air into the mouth of an overheated Mon Calamari (Paul Davies).

Director Rob Cohen (*XXX*, 2002) arrives at the video village, and Lucas explains to him that the brightness level of the plasma HD screens is tuned not so he can check the on-set lighting, but to be bright enough so he can assess the actors' performances. He also notes that he's using filters, because they're actually getting too much definition from the digital cameras. "It's a whole different way of making movies," he says. "It's painting now; it's not photography anymore."

The next shot is a close-up of C-3PO and R2-D2. The take is fine, and Daniels walks off camera—but can't see that he's heading straight toward some black knee-high borders. He continues right through the edge of the set but, luckily, not off the ledge. He goes down on his knees, then falls forward on his chest. Don Bies and others immediately run over to help him up. Lucas arrives, but Daniels appears to be okay, and shooting soon recommences.

"I walk forward—and the world changes!" Daniels exclaims, noting that he got his foot caught. "Because I'm top-heavy, I tumbled—and it made a terrible sound in the suit. I heard George call out, 'Tony, are you all right?!' because he saw my golden butt staring up."

LOCATION WRAP: 20:00   SETUPS: 56   SCRIPT SHOT TODAY: 4m 05s

SHOOT DAY 18: WEDNESDAY, JULY 23, 2003
LOCATION: Stage 5
SET: Int. Senate office building—main hall
SCENES SHOT: 50 (Padmé tells Anakin she's pregnant)

While Padmé secretly meets with Anakin in the shadows, many aliens are again on stage today, and many of Trisha Biggar and her team's costumes are evident. "*Star Wars* is a fictitious environment that has to have some reality to it," Lucas says, "but it shouldn't look like it was shot in 1968 or 1980. The most important part of that are the costumes, and Trisha's been great. She's the one that has the job of taking a rough sketch and turning it into something real. She takes the fantasies and turns them into a reality that actors can actually live in, which works in the shooting environment. And that's a very hard job."

"We bought fabrics in New York, San Francisco, Los Angeles, and London," Biggar says. "I sourced a lot of fabrics through a big biannual trade show in Paris, which features manufacturers from all over the world. So through Paris, and then through their agents in London, we bought fabrics from Japan, China, and India. I also like to use a lot of vintage fabrics, so I source them in different places: Scotland, America, France—all over the place."

Biggar grew up in Glasgow, Scotland. One summer, toward the end of her schooling, a friend of her mother's suggested she work in the theater— and Biggar wound up in that medium for more that ten years. "It was fantastic fun," she recalls. "There was a great social life. Parties all the time. It just seemed like the job you wanted to have." Years later, fellow Scot David Brown, who was *Young Indy*'s production supervisor, asked Biggar if she was interested in doing the costumes for the series' third season. She met with McCallum, who sealed the deal.

LOCATION WRAP: 20:30   SETUPS: 34   SCRIPT SHOT TODAY: 4m 40s
NOTES: Annie Leibovitz and her team did publicity stills all day.

SHOOT DAY 19: THURSDAY, JULY 24, 2003
  LOCATION: Stage 7
  SET: Int. Alderaan starcruiser—hallway
  SCENES SHOT: 118 (Bail Organa wants to warn the Jedi),
  173 (R2-D2 and C-3PO are given a new master)

One particular set on Stage 7 has been attracting visitors since the day its construction began back in early May. Today it's revealed in all its iconic glory: the hallway from *Star Wars*' Rebel blockade runner—the hallway into which Darth Vader strode twenty-six years ago.

"We get the same fan fascination ourselves," Gavin admits. "The tricky thing about building this set was that the first film wasn't really archived very well, because nobody knew it was going to be successful. So we had to rely much more on photographs; we only had a few drawings to work from."

Standing among those familiar walls of projecting rectangles, Lucas and Smits discuss how Bail Organa should deliver his line, "Have the protocol droid's mind wiped." As they attempt different readings, they both flub the line, which is somewhat of a tongue twister. "I can't even say it," Lucas jokes.

Above left: One camera is put on dolly tracks to follow the Chancellor (McDiarmid) and his soon-to-be-Sith apprentice (Christensen); although the columns are only partially built, the visual script (inset) reveals how the scene might look in post. Top right: Bocquet and Biggar. "It's nice to work for a director who's actually interested in the costumes," she says. Above: Senior cutter Anthony Phillips at work on one of those fabrics in Building 37, the costume department.

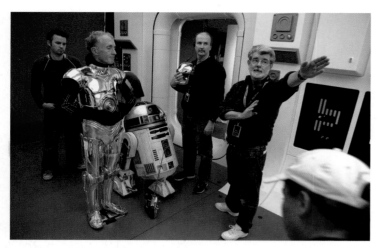

"What is truly remarkable—and this shows George's true understanding of the relationship between man and machine—is that it's done in the most callous, offhand manner," Daniels observes. "Jimmy Smits asked me, 'Should he not be upset at saying this?' And I said, 'No. I'm about as important to you as a trash can that needs emptying. You must think of me as a robot; I'm just an object.' And that's why it's very cleverly written as a throwaway line."

As droid wranglers Zeynup Selcuk and Justin Dix dress Daniels, layering his C-3PO persona over his black bodysuit, Lucas says to him, "This is almost the last dialogue in the picture: you saying, 'Oh, dear.' And you have the first dialogue in the next picture: 'Did you hear that?'"

"Let's roll cameras, please," Fletcher says, and a piece of C-3PO falls off, which is somehow appropriate. The droid is hastily reassembled and they do a take. Jimmy delivers the "mindwipe" line. Take.

"This is it, the end of the movie," George says to Anthony upon completion of the scene. "Not the exact end, but the end for you for another twenty years. When you return, you're a little battered, but still charming."

LOCATION WRAP: 20:30   SETUPS: 50   SCRIPT SHOT TODAY: 2m 46s

SHOOT DAY 20: FRIDAY, JULY 25, 2003

LOCATION: Stage 7
SET: Polis Massa—medical center observation dome
SCENES SHOT: 53 (Dream: Padmé dies giving birth),
169 (the twins are delivered)

"I know within a couple of weeks if a picture's going to work," McCallum says. "It's just a dynamic—something happens, it's magic. About three or four weeks into production, I got a sense that Episode III is going to work. But it's going to take a lot of effort to get there, because there are a lot of problems inherent in the story: It's the most adult of the six; it's the darkest—it's the most interesting."

It is perhaps this darkness—and a healthy workload—that explains the warning on the door to the props department: *Sheer Hell*. Behind this portal, however, is genial series veteran Ty Teiger (*White Hunter, Black Heart*, 1990; *Die Another Day*, 2002). "All the wall dressing, all the consoles, all the tables, the door controls on the walls—everything apart from your hand props is built into the set," he says of his team's contribution. "Every bit of pipe, every light switch—we do all that, and that's why I end up with eighty or ninety people working for me.

"On most films, you would farm things out," Teiger continues. "But because nobody's supposed to know about what we're up to, we have to make literally everything in-house, from your molding to your engineering to carpentry to model-making to vac forming. My job is basically to get the sets ready, and then supply the hand props to my standby prop men, who look after the set. Obviously if I'm on the floor all day long, I can't be back here orginizing and making sure everything's ready and built for the next day. So you'll see me on the set the morning of a handover, and that's it. I don't like to be on the set too much—I make too much noise," he concludes with a laugh.

LOCATION WRAP: 19:45   SETUPS: 32   SCRIPT SHOT TODAY: 2m 34s

Top left: Justin Dix, Daniels in costume, Bies, and Lucas. Left: Back to the past in the Alderaan starcruiser corridor go McFarlane, Fletcher, Harding, Lucas, "B" camera clapper loader Lee Mariano, and stand-by props Robert Moxham. Above left: Property master Ty Teiger and dozens of Naboo military costume props (above right). Top: Crew prepare a camera setup for a scene in the Polis Massa medical center, which is then shot with McGregor and Portman (inset).

SHOOT DAY 21: Monday, July 28, 2003

LOCATION: Stages 1 & 5
SET: Int. Alderaan starcruiser—conference room; Ext. Jedi Temple—landing platform
SCENES SHOT: 171 (Bail, Yoda, and Obi-Wan make plans for the babies); 113 (Bail Organa escapes on the side of his airspeeder); 71 (Padmé tries to get Senators on her side—Bail Organa only on camera)

This morning's scene takes place in the Alderaan cruiser's meeting room. Because Yoda will be added in post, his chair has a string attached to it, which is pulled by one of the crew to simulate his movements (one of the film's more low-tech moments). Smits and McGregor rehearse with the empty chair, while Duncan Young reads Yoda's lines off camera. "Good chair acting," McCallum says after the first take.

In order to give Coleman and his team some Yoda to animate as early as possible, Lucas has asked editor Roger Barton to cut together this scene as soon as they wrap.

"I start with a few animators, five or ten, then go up to forty-five," Coleman says. "Right now, I'm expecting about eighty minutes of animation, but I don't think that I'm going to need the sixty animators I had on Episode II, because I have a more experienced team; a lot of the same animators are coming back; we know these characters a lot better than we did on Episode I; the technology has increased in terms of the speed; and I've learned a lot through my relationship with George over these last six years. When I see a piece of animation, I'm pretty clear on what his take will be."

In the cafeteria during lunch, George sits at a table with his kids. Christopher Lee, who came to Sydney straight from New Zealand where he was filming *The Return of the King* (2003), is eating and chatting with crew. In order to save him a return trip to Australia from his home in England, his scenes will be shot against bluescreen—before the general's quarters set is actually ready. He'll then be composited into the completed set later in post.

After lunch, on Stage 5, Jett Lucas plays a Jedi Padawan (Zett Jukassa) who is gunned down by clone troopers outside the Jedi Temple. Bail Organa arrives and witnesses the short and deadly battle on a raised set where everything is bluescreen except the landing platform and Bail's "Ferrari" (built on the chassis of Anakin's yellow airspeeder from Episode II). Biggar and Katie and Amanda Lucas watch from the floor. Nick speaks to Jett, who has to execute lightsaber moves and a somersault.

Take. "That was so cute. Too cute for words," Katie says.

"Very good, Jett. That was really good," his father adds.

"I said to myself, *What happened?*" Amanda remembers. "*You're not a little boy anymore!* I was very proud just to watch him do it."

After Jett and Jimmy complete the scene, production moves to Stage 5, where Smits completes pickup shots for a scene recorded earlier. Because the set was torn down weeks ago, it's all blue-screen. Having arrived a few days ago, Ahmed Best (Jar Jar Binks) watches from the video village. He asks Lucas if today has been a long day.

"Every day is a long day," Lucas replies.

LOCATION WRAP: 19:45   SETUPS: 46   SCRIPT SHOT TODAY: 3m 12s
NOTES: Hayden Christensen/burned Anakin makeup test (Stage 2). Christopher Lee (Darth Tyranus) performed some low-impact stunt rehearsals.

SHOOT DAY 22: Tuesday, July 29, 2003

LOCATION: Stage 4
SET: Int. Coruscant—Senate chamber
SCENES SHOT: 137 (Palpatine announces that the Jedi rebellion has been foiled)

A painter is adding some last touches to a Senate pod that will hold Portman, Smits, and Best. With Lucas, they discuss the scene, calling Biggar into the pod for consultation. Lucas talks to the actors for a good

Previous spread: A Knoll panorama of the medical center. Above left: Smits (Bail Organa) prepares for a scene in the Alderaan cruiser conference room. Above: Lucas prepares his son, Jett, for his scene. Top: Crew prepare Bail's speeder on the Jedi Temple landing platform. Above right: Handmaiden Motée (Kristy Wright), Organa (Smits), and Senator Amidala (Portman) listen to the Emperor announce the end of the Republic. Right: Amanda and Katie Lucas with their father.

The second floor of Stage 2 is where ILM maintains its command post: a number of portable computers clustered together on four desks. This afternoon, it is where a departing Ahmed Best says good-bye to Rob Coleman, as two of the co-creators of the much-maligned Binks part ways.

"Whether you think Jar Jar is cool or not is completely subjective," Best observes. "There are people out there who try to justify their ideas of Jar Jar, but it's an opinion developed in the constructs of the prejudice they have in themselves. It has absolutely nothing to do with reality. By the same token, there are people who just didn't like Jar Jar as a character. And that's completely valid. But as far as Jar Jar being a negative creature, no, he wasn't."

Back on Stage 4, Ian, Sandi, and David are readied for their turn in the Senate pod. In one of those filmic sleight of hands, this scene is shot in the same pod where the others stood this morning.

"Ian, look out, all around, look up," Lucas instructs. "But at some point, look here [indicating a spot near the camera]: That's where Padmé is going to be."

Lucas tweaks the dialogue and suggests a royal wave. But McDiarmid asks, "Is everyone happy with the inside of my hands?" drawing attention to the fact that the wave will expose his palm, which hasn't been made up. The makeup team goes to work, but takes a bit long. "As soon as you can, guys, please," Fletcher urges. They depart, Emperor Palpatine's palm now white and eerie.

With each take, McDiarmid purrs the lines, "A new beginning . . ."

Between takes, Knoll points out that the Emperor has "a little shine on the end of his nose." Ian drinks water through a straw. Then, as cameras roll take after take, he never flubs a word. The scene finished, it takes a team to help the three actors down the stairs from the elevated pod, as none of them can see or walk very well in their costumes.

While waiting for the next scene to be shot, Coleman says, "In the scene tomorrow, George has decided to add a droid." Something elegant serving drinks. "You can have a year to design

ten minutes—this is an important scene, during which Palpatine dissolves the Republic and inaugurates the Empire. Smits stands outside the pod, nodding as he listens. Portman asks where she should look, where the other Senators are. Lucas tells her, adding that when she hears Palpatine's line about the Empire lasting "ten thousand years," she should look shocked and dismayed. Returning to the video village, Lucas says to "A" camera operator McFarlane, "A little lower. I need something dramatic here."

Young reads Palpatine's lines off camera, and claps when applause is called for in the script. Take. Smits paces as they set up for another angle. Portman stretches, raising her hands in the air. Jay Laga'aia watches, with a stiff leg he broke doing pickups for *The Return of the King*. Coleman is explaining to a visitor how Lucas taught him that things are either 49 or 51 percent—they either work or they don't.

Monday, July 28: Drafting begins in the art department for Darth Vader's rehabilitation chamber set.

something, or—boom—the next day it's needed." An hour later, he is showing potential designs to Lucas of sexy droid females. "I'm guessing this is the kind of stuff See-Threepio would have on his wall," Rob jokes.

Next on the schedule is a surprise: a scene for *Star Wars*: Episode V *The Empire Strikes Back*. "We're replacing the other actor with Ian so we have the same actor in all the films—so we have continuity," Lucas explains. The one scene featuring Darth Vader and the Emperor in that 1980 film is being reshot with McDiarmid, who took on the role in *Return of the Jedi*. The new footage will be cut into the DVD and all subsequent versions of *Empire*. The dialogue has also been altered so that it makes more sense with the continuity established in the prequel trilogy.

> DARTH VADER
> I have felt it.
>
> EMPEROR
> We have a new enemy. The young Rebel who destroyed the Death Star. I have no doubt this boy is the offspring of Anakin Skywalker.
>
> DARTH VADER
> How is that possible?
>
> EMPEROR
> Search your feelings, Lord Vader. You will know it to be true. He could destroy us.
>
> DARTH VADER
> He's just a boy. Obi-Wan can no longer help him.
>
> EMPEROR
> The Force is strong with him. The son of Skywalker must not become a Jedi.

Lucas instructs McDiarmid to "relish" the idea of turning the boy to the dark side—to take a deep breath before responding, savoring its repercussions. "Let's try it once more," he says. "Make the 'yes, yes' a little louder—and close your eyes before you say it."

Take. "Great. Cut. Now we can do a side view," Lucas says as he climbs the stairs to the pod.

"I think it's a case of tidying up," McDiarmid observes. "It was perfectly well done before, but it just makes sense. George has only slightly tweaked the words, now that we all know the history of Anakin Skywalker."

LOCATION WRAP: 20:15   SETUPS: 42   SCRIPT SHOT TODAY: 2m 45s

SHOOT DAY 23: WEDNESDAY, JULY 30, 2003

LOCATION: Stages 6 & 3
SET: Int. Bail Organa's office; Alderaan palace balcony; Bail's speeder
SCENES SHOT: 60 (Senators meet in secret), 153 (Bail rescues Yoda), 179 (Bail brings a small baby to the Queen)

Like many of the sets, Organa's office is enclosed on all four sides by blue fabric, which creates a corridor between the other side of its hanging blue "walls" and the real walls of the stage. Crew can thus circle the set through this circular corridor to reach makeup stations, sound and video technicians, food, and a tiny slit that accesses the set.

Portman, Genevieve O'Reilly (Mon Mothma), and other Senators walk

Left: Because they'll be shooting Christopher Lee against bluescreen, Lucas plots out the camera angles he'll need ahead of time on a maquette provided by Bocquet's team (above right), as inspired by earlier concept art of the general's quarters (aka "throne room"). Right: Jaeger's waitress droid concept for the scene in Bail's office.

General Layout Showing Possible Moves
*Note: Very loose direction not based on latest script developments

onto the set. Smits requests that they run the lines while their makeup is touched up. The lights cast long shadows on the set, which gives this early morning a twilight feel.

"Let's clear the eye lines, please," Fletcher asks.

"What's that noise?" Portman asks.

The origin can't be located, so Lucas decides, "This is a wide take, let's go with it."

The servant, who will eventually be replaced by an animated CG droid, walks in and out of the scene wearing a blue bodysuit.

While Lucas is on the set talking with the actors, McCallum tells a story in the video village. On location for *Young Indy*, he and Ben Burtt were out in Kenya's vast Masai Mara. Having followed the dust of their trucks for hours, a figure appeared on the horizon and very slowly approached from a great distance. As he neared, they could tell he was a local. When he finally joined the two, there was a moment of silence. Then the local asked what they were doing there. Rick explained in the simplest terms that they were making a television show. "Ah, television!" the man said, and whipped out a laminated card with location rates. "You must pay. It's $150 for TV, $500 for film."

George comes over and confides in his producer, "This is one of those terrible 'dinner' scenes, but it should be all right . . . I'm getting too old for this."

After lunch, in one of the sadder scenes of the film, Bail gives the infant Leia to his wife, the Queen of Alderaan. While prep continues, Gillard shows Lucas some test footage of the revolving set, and Bocquet shows him fab-

ric samples for approval. Lucas examines the creatures department's baby Leia while Biggar makes last-minute adjustments to the Queen's robes.

"Trisha was great," Rebecca Jackson Mendoza (the Queen of Alderaan) recalls. "The whole team was great. Just very patient. My costume actually changed: I believe it was going to be a lilac color, and then they decided to go more with the color of Alderaan, which was a nature green. My hair was almost like a crown, so I was a queen for a day."

During prep for the Bail speeder scene, Christopher Lee arrives, wearing an off-white raincoat with a red scarf, and talks with Lucas, McCallum, and Gillard. He has large hands, which he moves expressively while speaking. Lucas explains to him that the dialogue scenes will be first. "That's where I'll need your help, in terms of my reactions," Lee says. Next are the action scenes. "But I mustn't do it too fast," Lee comments.

As Smits sits down in the airspeeder, where a digital Yoda will join him, Lucas instructs, "You look up and then down as Yoda goes *plunk*."

Behind Lucas, Lee is chatting with some visitors, discussing how films are made, telling them that the director must have a "tremendous amount of stamina—the ability to deal with endless disappointments.

"Some relatives of mine who live here came to the set," Lee says.

Top left: Bail's airspeeder on July 30—Smits's last day. "I was just getting to know everybody," he says. Left: Organa (Smits) and the Queen of Alderaan (Rebecca Jackson Mendoza). Top right: A panorama of the video village during the Lee shoot. Above left: Lucas directs Lee (Count Dooku), as Rowling and Michael Byrne (Palpatine's stunt double) look on. Above right: Fletcher and Lee, who has appeared in more than 200 films.

"They were completely bowled over. I told them that the man sitting there in front of the monitor is unique, because he decided at a certain point: no studio control. 'I will have total and complete control over my work; nobody will interfere with it; nobody will tell me what to do.' *He's* done it."

LOCATION WRAP: 20:30   SETUPS: 46   SCRIPT SHOT TODAY: 3m 27s

SHOOT DAY 24: THURSDAY, JULY 31, 2003
LOCATION: Stage 1
SET: Bluescreen; general's elevator lobby—revolve "A"
SCENES SHOT: 24pt (Count Dooku close-ups for dialogue and fight)

It's a brisk, sunny, cold morning. As technicians and craftspeople walk quickly to their various jobs, many carry Styrofoam cups with hot tea or coffee to dispel the chill. Within Stage 1, Lucas warms his hands on the portable heater by his chair, which is now quite useful.

With pulleys, the crew raises a circular bluescreen curtain, creating another enclosed area within the stage. They touch up the wooden floor with blue paint. Coleman barely slept the night before, worrying about today's shoot: It represents, potentially, an enormous amount of work for him and his department down the road. He says he won't know how it'll all work out till December, when Lucas cuts the sequence together.

The eighty-one-year-old Lee arrives on set in costume, and Lucas walks him through the shots, referring repeatedly to a miniature maquette of the future set. Christensen arrives in street clothes, as he will be off camera feeding lines to Lee. Rick confers with George. Lucas wants to be close to the actor as they shoot, so they set up a small monitor next to the "A" camera.

111

Soon everyone is ready to shoot Lee's dialogue for Count Dooku's violent confrontation with Obi-Wan and Anakin. Take. "We'll try one more. Excellent," Lucas says. "What we might do at the end of this one is . . . *anger!*"

For the next take, Christensen sits on a box for Lee's eye line. "Christopher, can you look to your right and left to see if there are any other Jedi?" Lucas asks.

"With my hands in my belt?" Lee asks.

"Yeah. Now you see them . . . and . . . cut! Great. That was perfect."

The day takes an optimistic turn when Lee grabs hold of a lightsaber for a shot with Christensen and McGregor, who has joined them on set. The next setup, Count Dooku's death scene, requires Lee to be on his knees for quite a long time. After the first take, Lucas instructs Lee to space out his words, and tells "B" camera operator Harding to move in.

Between takes, Lee suggests that it is out of character for Dooku to ask Palpatine for help. Lucas agrees, and Jayne-Ann cuts the word *help* from the script. For nearly twenty minutes more, the actor is still on his knees, until he is finally able to recline. "Okay. I think we got that," Lucas says.

The next scene has Dooku advancing on the Jedi. Lee walks forward, re-creating the menace of his earlier incarnations, and whips out his lightsaber.

"Not many people realize that *dooku* is Japanese for 'poison,'" Lee says. "Which is very appropriate, really, because he's lethal."

LOCATION WRAP: 20:00   SETUPS: 62   SCRIPT SHOT TODAY: 1m 35s

SHOOT DAY 25: FRIDAY, AUGUST 1, 2003

LOCATION: Stage 1
SET: Bluescreen; Int. Trade Federation cruiser bridge
SCENES SHOT: 43pt (Obi-Wan yanks his lightsaber from
the general)

"Waiting . . . waiting . . . and more waiting. "Four or five minutes," Fletcher says.

"Four or five?" Lucas asks, and Colin comes over to explain.

"The way most movies are made," Lucas would observe, "you have to have a very good ability to delay gratification. You have to be able to say, 'This will come . . . in time.' "

Gillard, with fencing doubles Michael Byrne and Kyle Rowling, rehearses a few lightsaber moves for Lee's benefit, then the actor goes through the moves himself. Riding the crest of yesterday's success, Lee is emboldened and will execute a spin. Take.

"We'll do it once more," Lucas says.

But Lee holds his head and says he's "quite dizzy." During the next take, Byrne and Rowling flank Lee, ready to catch him if he stumbles.

Andrew Lesnie, director of photography for *Lord of the Rings*, joins Lucas in the video village. Indicating the monitors showing bluescreen, Lucas says to him, "You've been shooting some of these same locations, I believe," and Lesnie laughs.

Since he knows the fight choreography intimately, Rowling tells Lee where to look during the next take, "Left, right, left, low, little turn," and gives him hand signals. Lee falters, and they leap up to grab him.

"Perfectly all right," Lee protests, pointing to the blue carpet. "It's just that I'm trying to spin on this material."

"I want to do another one," Lucas says to Lee, "with real anger in your face." Take. "That was good. I think we'll try one where you're not swinging the lightsaber as you walk." Take.

"I think we got it. You did great," Lucas says.

Lee exits the bluescreen set and pats the director on the shoulder.

Fletcher calls out, "Attention, folks. That was Christopher Lee's last shot." There is a round of applause, while McCallum and Coleman congratulate the legendary actor.

LOCATION WRAP: 19:45   SETUPS: 66   SCRIPT SHOT TODAY: 1m 10s

REHEARSAL DAY: SATURDAY, AUGUST 2, 2003

At 9 A.M., Lucas, McCallum, and Jett Lucas ride one of the studio's electric golf carts to the editorial suite on Stage 2 for a videoconference with Skywalker Ranch, where it is still Friday afternoon. Editor Roger Barton joins them, and, after a few attempts, a link is established with Burtt, Church, Gregoire, and other artists.

United by technology, both groups watch an animatics sequence of the film's opening space battle. Jett applauds as the *Star Wars* crawl scrolls by. McCallum taps his fingers to the music. At the end of the ten-minute sequence, cliffhanger text reads, "To be continued next week: *Jedi Death Plunge!*"

"It's starting to fill in the [visual] blanks," Gregoire says.

"But we need to clarify what's going on," Lucas notes, and, during the discussion that follows, they attempt to sort out what's missing.

"Do you want a long shot all the way into Obi-Wan's cockpit?" someone asks.

"Do you want him to try it?" McCallum seconds.

"Let's just wait till I get back," Lucas says, sounding tired. "It's a few weeks more. Seven to be exact—"

"—and three days," McCallum adds.

"We've got about a dozen Jedi getting killed," Burtt says of another sequence.

"Hopefully, in slow motion," Rick says. "With just the same Jedi getting shot over and over." Jedi death jokes follow.

The connection is severed, and Lucas says to McCallum, "When it gets down to four minutes, it'll all start making sense. We need to reboard it. The shots never show the bad guys."

Top far left: Unidentified costume personnel, costume supervisor Nicole Young, and Coveney work on Christensen's first complete Darth Vader costume fitting. Top left: Assistant costume designer Michael Mooney checks on a Neimoidian, whose hat conceals servos and intricate mechanics (above). Left: The bridge, which took several weeks to construct, and whose lighting reference is once again a page from the visual script (top right) by Tiemens.

This Saturday morning is a key rehearsal, as Christensen, McGregor, and Portman will be running through the scene in which Anakin essentially kills Padmé by breaking her heart. In an empty, cold Stage 3, Lucas and McCallum stand on what will be a Mustafar landing platform. A maquette showing the whole of the complex Mustafar layout sits on a table, for everyone's reference. McGregor arrives, wearing black-rimmed glasses, and studies it with Lucas.

Christensen and Portman are next to climb up to the set, and the three of them run through the scene a few times, with Neil and Tenggren observing. George explains to Hayden that Anakin doesn't need to be angry when he first greets Padmé—that, in fact, he should be happy. "Everything is great for Anakin," Lucas explains, also asking Christensen to sound more like the Emperor: confident and self-assured. Continuing that thought, Lucas comes up with the idea that Christensen should leave his back turned toward McGregor: Anakin is so confident in his new powers that he doesn't need to face his former Master.

McGregor and Christensen then quickly run through part of their lightsaber battle—beautiful, quick moves—while Lucas tells Gillard that he now needs a new beginning to the fight, with Anakin jumping then flipping toward Obi-Wan from his backward position.

SHOOT DAY 26: MONDAY, AUGUST 4, 2003
LOCATION: Stage 1
SET: Int. Federation cruiser bridge
SCENES SHOT: 43pt (General Grievous escapes by smashing a window)

At dawn, Lucas, McCallum, Bocquet, Fletcher, Russell, and others meet, as they do most mornings, for a walkthrough of the sets in progress. Their quest is to identify problems, approve works in progress, and generally troubleshoot. On the Mustafar landing platform, they discuss the changes made during Saturday's rehearsal; McCallum thinks it looks "cooler" now. "It's all one scene—one shot, one take," he explains to Fletcher, who reminds them that they'll have McGregor only until 5 P.M. that day. After that, he must leave to attend the Australian premiere of his film *Down with Love* at 7:45 P.M.

Fletcher then goes down his list of shots. "We can do Padmé being thrown against the wall—"

"We can do the whole thing," Lucas says. "I'll get into the fight. And

when Ewan leaves, I'll do a little bit of Artoo and Threepio—"

"But you have to be at the premiere, too," Rick says.

"The next day, we'll finish the fight; we'll do the odds and ends—no problem," George assures.

Peter Russell, dressed in gym clothes, then goes off to inspect another set, while Ian Gracie returns to the art department to check the advance schedule. Gavin Bocquet takes off on his bicycle, as he has the most ground to cover, pedaling over to the Jedi Temple briefing room. In a gray sweatshirt and jeans, there Bocquet consults with head scenic painter Matt Connors, choosing colors for the set. As he makes each rapid-fire decision, an assistant places a piece of masking tape on the appropriate surface with the correct color code: gray 1 or 2, silver 3, etc.

Connors left school at fifteen and was looking at "a lifetime of laboring jobs," but discovered that "film was something I could get into without qualifications." He began as a set builder on *Mad Max Beyond Thunderdome* (1985) but "met the painter on that who was doing great [faux] rock faces—and it was fascinating." Sporting consistently disheveled hair and perpetually stained hands, he says that his department paints everything and can imitate any surface—metal, leather, marble—using various techniques and an arsenal of about thirteen hundred colors. He notes that a *Star Wars* film, particularly now that they're digital, demands a high level of finish.

"The sets are built primarily out of wood," Russell explains. "It's only when that last two and a half millimeters of paint goes on that it actually becomes what it is: steel, glass, stone."

At 2 P.M., on the bridge set, McGregor and Christensen are battling CG droids and a blue-suited Rowling, who duels as a physical placeholder for CG Grievous. As crew set up the next shot, Lucas and Knoll discuss

where the sun should be in relation to the bridge. The space exteriors and sun will be added later, but the lighting on set must be established now. In the next shot, McGregor and Christensen have to grab on to a banister to prevent themselves from being sucked into space as Grievous breaks a window and flees.

To cue them, Lucas calls out, "Window!" during each take. A wind machine is placed on the bridge, so Lucas's "Action!" becomes necessarily louder, electrifying them into movement as the on-set combat intensifies.

LOCATION WRAP: 20:00   SETUPS: 37   SCRIPT SHOT TODAY: 32s

Monday, August 4: After five days of drafting, prefab construction begins on Stage 4 for the Darth Vader rehabilitation chamber set.

Above left: Head scenic artist Matt Connors, Tattersall, set decorator Richard Roberts, and Bocquet make their rounds on Stage 2. On Stage 7 (above right), construction of the general's quarters as of August 6. Right: Christensen, Lucas, and McGregor study a "side" on the bridge.

SHOOT DAY 27: TUESDAY, AUGUST 5, 2003

LOCATION: Stage 1

SET: Int. Bridge Federation cruiser

SCENES SHOT: 47 (Obi-Wan and Anakin cut down the droids; Anakin pilots the cruiser to a landing platform)

"Okay, let's find us a shot," Lucas says as he arrives on set. "To me, the script is just a sketchbook," he adds, "just a list of notes, and, sometimes, I prefer the documentary feel of free flow, so I let my instincts tell me where to go. I like to create cinematically; I don't like to have a plan. I like to have a rough idea of what I'm going to do—certain themes, certain issues I'm going to deal with—and then I try to do so. At first, I shoot *around* the

side to let others pass. Because some of the technical jargon defies memorization, McGregor has taped his lines to a viewscreen.

"How manic should I be with this?" Hayden asks, indicating the vessel's controls.

"I would keep it reasonably calm and steady, as this is a pretty big ship," George replies. As the cruiser is supposed to be splitting in half, Lucas adds, "Why don't we say 'boom' or 'crash,' so everybody knows when to jerk forward."

After lunch, Jayne-Ann points out that Ewan's hair is once again out of continuity. Lucas goes over the scene's lighthearted tone with McGregor, who improvises, "Nothing to worry about, gentlemen, but we're only flying half a ship."

movie—and then [in the editing room], I figure out where the movie is in the middle of all this."

Huge lights are switched on to simulate Coruscant's sun, bathing everyone in a soothing orange glow. The actors take their places in seats aboard the bridge. While climbing the narrow staircase to the set, in costume as the Supreme Chancellor—ruler of the galaxy—Ian has to squeeze to one

More takes. "You happy with that?" Lucas asks McFarlane.

"Yeah, I'm very happy. It had a good feel."

LOCATION WRAP: 20:00   SETUPS: 44   SCRIPT SHOT TODAY: 2m 15s

---

Above: Lucas and Christensen. "There's this ongoing theme," the actor points out, "this undertone to the whole film concerning Anakin's suspicions of Padmé's relationship with Obi-Wan." The set was closed to all nonessential personnel while Portman and Christensen (above right) play out Anakin and Padmé's tragic end.

LOCATION: Stage 3
SET: Mustafar landing platform
SCENES SHOT: 145pt (Padmé confronts Anakin on Mustafar and
Obi-Wan arrives)

Dry ice is being used to generate jets of steam, which rise on either side of the stairs that Christensen climbs. Lucas walks back and forth, talking on a cell phone outside the stage. McCallum arrives, checks on a number of details, and exits. A cushion is given to "A" camera clapper Simon Williams, who will be astride a ladder for most of the morning. Because this scene promises to be emotional, extra care is being taken so that no

After a few takes, Lucas has a fairly long talk with Christensen, McGregor, and Portman. McCallum returns. Makeup artists walk past him on another of their endless to-and-fro journeys to touch up the actors. "What a team," he remarks. Their discussion finished, Natalie performs dance steps on stage while waiting. George watches the proceedings with his hands folded behind his head. "We'll get there—even if it breaks my heart," he says to Rick.

Multiple takes follow. "That was good," Lucas says after the most emotional one. "I think we got that—and just in time . . . for lunch."

The lunch break, however, is taken up with a design meeting in the cafeteria with Bocquet, Russell, Gracie, and others. Lucas gets up for dessert just as Knoll passes by and is sucked into the conversation. As he

one is in the actors' eye lines. Crew erect a black felt curtain to mask even the video village from their view.

"Final checks, please," Fletcher calls out. "This is a pivotal scene. No one who doesn't have to be on set should be watching."

Over the roar of the wind machines, however, it's hard to hear any of the drama without headsets. McGregor can't hear, either: "It might be a nice idea to cue me," he says, after a quick rehearsal. "I can't hear Hayden."

attempts to leave, George returns with a bowl of ice cream and deadpans, "You can't get away. You're trapped in the art department."

At 2:45, they're ready for close-ups of Hayden. Lucas discusses the tone with him. "This is Anakin's greatest moment; he's got all these new powers—everything is fine."

"Anakin's just gone and killed his family, more or less, so I've done a deed that I thought would've weighed on me," Christensen would say the

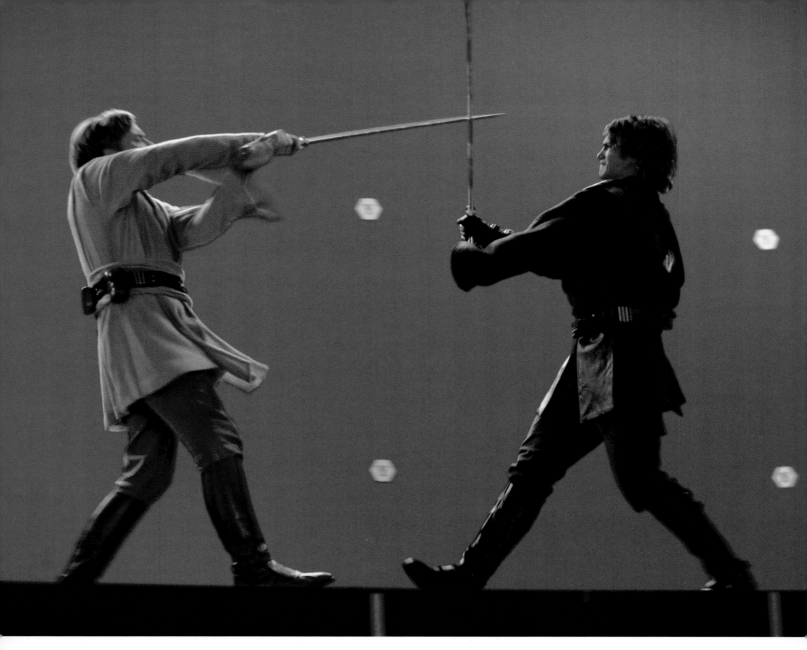

following day. "But George sees it as an outburst of almost accidental anger that Anakin then has to suffer the repercussions of for the rest of his life. Anakin thinks he's done the right thing in killing all the Jedi, so George wanted me to come to the scene with enthusiasm. Things are good. I'm the most powerful man in the universe and I'm going to be able to save Padmé."

The process continues late into the afternoon, until Lucas says to Christensen, "I think we got it."

In a matter of minutes, crew break down one setup to create another on the opposite end of the Mustafar landing platform. Lights, tables, portable screens, wires, cameras, wind machines, costumes on hangers, and more are moved quickly to the next position. Lucas leads the advance—but then stops, chin on hand for a few moments as he reflects.

During the next take, Christensen's voice cuts through the sound of the wind machine as Anakin rails about his wife's betrayal: "*Liar!* You're with *him*. You brought him here to *kill* me." He then makes a fist, choking Padmé with the dark side of the Force: "You will not take her from me!" he screams at Obi-Wan.

Between takes, Christensen stays in character, muttering his lines to himself, head bowed.

LOCATION WRAP: 20:00   SETUPS: 22   SCRIPT SHOT TODAY: 3m 30s
NOTES: Company wrapped Ewan McGregor early today to be available for the premiere of his new film *Down with Love*.

SHOOT DAY 29: THURSDAY, AUGUST 7, 2003
LOCATION: Stage 3
SET: Mustafar landing platform
SCENES SHOT: 149 (R2-D2 tries to drag Padmé back onto the skiff), 145pt (Obi-Wan walks toward Anakin and the ferocious swordfight begins)

Above: McGregor and Christensen begin their characters' climactic duel. Top right: McCaig's death-head concept for Padmé is realized on the set (below). Far right: Jun's concept for a funeral attendee. Following spread: The greed and anger of Anakin (Christensen) results in his wife's death. Key hairdresser Miles, assistant hairdresser Hellingman, set dresser Kodicek, Mooney, Biggar, and costume standby Hassan work on Portman (Padmé).

Ewan McGregor's attendance of the *Down with Love* premiere has made the morning news in Sydney. So has Lucas, who also attended the gala and whose response to a question about Episode III—"Everyone dies and the bad guys win"—has been picked up by the media Down Under.

On the quad, a golf cart drives by with a Mon Calamari head in the passenger's seat; a hairdresser runs by; a garbage truck makes its rounds. On the set, a crane lifts Anakin's starfighter into the air, the closest it will ever come to flying. Although someone could theoretically be crushed if something were to go wrong, a grip remarks that most injuries on set are due to utility knives.

The epic duel between Anakin and Obi-Wan now begins—the climax of the prequel trilogy—but their encounter starts out humorously, with nearly every take ending with Christensen and McGregor joking, fake fighting, or fake dying.

"The saber fights are like being six-year-old kids again," Christensen remarks. "Buying the best toy in the store and getting to go home and play with it for two weeks with your best friend. Nick was there every day during rehearsals, correcting us and making sure that every single minute detail was right. Even if we were making mistakes, we had him there on the sidelines saying it was still good. It's his fight, so he deserves all the credit."

During the next few takes, Christensen and McGregor make mistakes three times in a row. "They're getting in trouble there at the end," George says to Nick, who goes over to talk with the actors. They get it right, and Hayden walks to the monitors. "That was the fastest we've ever done it," he says to Lucas.

"I'm very happy with all the fighting scenes," McGregor notes. "They're incredibly exhausting to do, and it's such an intense burst of energy, but Hayden and I have gotten them to such a pitch that they're incredibly fast. We do those fight scenes fantastically well—I think it's all right to say that—because after you've done them and you look at the playback, it looks extraordinary. I'll be very proud of them when it's all put together."

LOCATION WRAP: 20:15   SETUPS: 72   SCRIPT SHOT TODAY: 2m 49s

SHOOT DAY 30: Friday, August 8, 2003

LOCATION: Stages 2 & 4
SET: Jedi Temple briefing room; Naboo main square; Plo Koon's cockpit
SCENES SHOT: 58 (Obi-Wan tells Anakin that the Chancellor has requested his presence), 108 (clone pilots blast Plo Koon out of the sky), 175 (Padmé in coffin)

After lunch, Fay David arrives on set for a visit, after being shown around the studio by her art department counterpart Colette Birrell. "I work with this small group of artists," Fay recalls, "but to go there and see this entire network of people who take this stuff and turn it into something larger than life, in a very short period of time, was . . . overwhelming."

David is just in time for close-ups of Portman in Padmé's coffin, surrounded by bluescreen. As specified in the script, Padmé, as she lies in state, still looks pregnant and is holding the japor snippet that Anakin gave her in *The Phantom Menace*. Visitors to the set begin to multiply, as do jokes about what the gossip on Naboo might be.

"Everyone's talking about it there," Lucas says. "The tabloids say Jar Jar is the father."

Biggar arranges Portman's hair and the flowers in the coffin. Set decorator Richard Roberts (*Titanic*, 1997; *The World Is Not Enough*, 1999) and others help out, and about twenty minutes is spent at that task. More than fifty people are now on hand to watch this emotional scene. To help McFarlane gauge the speed at which he needs to pan, Lucas tells him that horse-like creatures will be pulling the coffin.

He then notices the surplus of spectators and remarks, "Oh my God, it's a real funeral."

As the setups multiply, Natalie has to remain perfectly still, both during and between takes. Biggar is asked how much she can move, just as Portman rubs her eye. "Not much," she responds, and goes to touch up the arrangement.

"I want to get the camera where I can see the snippet . . . ," Lucas is saying to McFarlane. "That's it. Perfect."

"George, you could see her breathing," Knoll observes.

"You can stop pulses, right?" Lucas asks.

After several takes from several angles, while all the assembled remain very quiet, the scene is finished.

"I think they call it the 'End Dress,' " Portman remembers, speaking of her costume. "It's really, really beautiful. I think Trisha wanted to get an ocean sense. Someone said to me that it was very 'Ophelia.' With the flowers and the hair, it does look like I'm drowning."

Above: The visual script illustrates the death of Plo Koon (Matt Sloan), who consults with Lucas (far right). Right: The Sydney art department's floor plan has been faithfully reproduced in the Jedi Temple briefing room, as captured by Knoll (below). While not being being used as a set, this locale serves as the site for a marriage proposal (see starwars.com for the complete story).

Drinks and champagne have been announced for 6 P.M., so most of the production crew has gathered on Stage 4 to see Jedi Master Plo Koon (aka Matt Sloan, droid mechanic) meet his demise. This celebration marks the halfway point of principal photography and the completion of one thousand setups. As spectators mingle, Lucas directs Sloan, who is sitting in a starfighter cockpit: "Flying along. Look right. Look left. Okay . . . Light!"

On Lucas's cue, a mobile light representing an enemy fighter travels quickly along a steel monorail, arcing over the rear of the cockpit.

"Now!" Lucas calls out—and a special effects explosion goes off on the back of the starfighter. Sloan slumps forward and everyone applauds.

It's a wrap and the atmosphere is genial as champagne is poured, toasts are made, and people relax.

"It's midpoint," Lucas says. "We're on schedule and it looks good."

LOCATION WRAP: 19:15   SETUPS: 36   SCRIPT SHOT TODAY: 2m 18s

The Last Setup

SHOOT DAY 31: Monday, August 11, 2003
LOCATION: Stage 4
SET: Anakin's starfighter cockpit; Obi-Wan's starfighter cockpit
SCENES SHOT: 2 (Obi-Wan bounces through the flak), 3 (Anakin blasts Federation droid fighters)

Following Sloan, it's Christensen's turn to sit in the cockpit of the gimbal-mounted Jedi starfighter. Indeed, there is only one, which is redressed for each occupant. A bank of red-gelled lights indicates enemy fire, and Young stands off camera to read the lines of other pilots, verbal descriptions of the action, and even R2-D2's beeps and whistles. Lucas is recording all of the aerial dialogue at one go, along with ad-libs and wild lines.

"Are we ready?" he asks.

"I don't think so," Christensen responds, noting that the lighting is still being tweaked by David Tattersall's team.

Tattersall was born just south of the Scottish border. After studying fine art for three years, he was attending the National Film School in London when MTV started up. He began moonlighting and shot more than two hundred music videos. The first bluescreen he lit was for Boy George. An admirer of Vermeer and Caravaggio, Tattersall created the paintings for a low-budget film he shot called *The Bridge* (1992), about American impressionist Philip Wilson Steer. After seeing that film, McCallum hired him as DP on *Young Indy*.

"It's not just that we're shooting on digital that makes this movie so unusual and the procedure so different," says Tattersall, who, most days, is dressed in jeans and black sneakers. "It's the colossal number of digital effects shots that will be dealt with in the course of postproduction, and the number of virtual sets, partial or total, green- or bluescreen. Really for us—for the shooting crew—we're just making a foundation that ILM will build on over the next eighteen months. To be honest, Episode III is more than fifty percent animated."

LOCATION WRAP: 20:00   SETUPS: 31   SCRIPT SHOT TODAY: 5m 30s

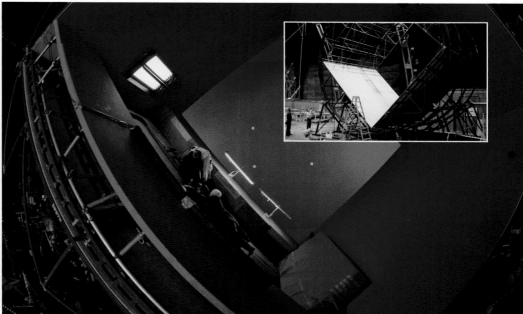

SHOOT DAY 32: TUESDAY, AUGUST 12, 2003

LOCATION: Stages 3 & 5

SET: Coruscant landing platform—Naboo skiff; hangar bay—Federation cruiser

SCENES SHOT: 143 (Padmé refuses to let Captain Typho join her, and Obi-Wan slips on board), 143A (Padmé & C-3PO pilot the Naboo skiff)

Today is the last work day for Anthony Daniels, Natalie Portman, and Jay Laga'aia. "We've accomplished all the heavy dialogue scenes, so now what we have left is all the action scenes," Jayne-Ann says.

Sitting on green crates, the three actors chat as they wait for the first setup. "Natalie's a young woman now," Laga'aia would say, "whereas before, she played a young woman, but she was really still a teenager. Every time we'd cut, she'd have her friends from school there and they'd just turn into teenagers again, which was lovely to see. But this time around, she seems to be a lot more grounded."

George approaches Natalie to tell her about a new scene aboard the Naboo skiff as it flies toward Mustafar. Padmé is distraught, he explains, because Obi-Wan has told her about Anakin's turn to the dark side. "This is you sitting there thinking about the news," Lucas says, adding that they're going to shoot the new scene two ways: with C-3PO talking to her while she's crying, and with C-3PO not talking to her as she's crying.

Ewan arrives and gives Natalie a hug. He'd like to find her before she departs, he says. Laga'aia bids farewell to Lucas, Portman, and others as he leaves the set.

Lucas then talks Daniels through the scene and lets the actor know that he can ad-lib: "You can talk about how you're not really a combat droid . . . and we'll put the dialogue in later."

"This is the climax of the movie, I can tell," Daniels says, laconically.

Seated on a box, Lucas watches the scene intently. Take. "Can we get more extreme?" he asks.

Portman asks for a cut. "We're going to do one more with a chattering Threepio, which will probably make you cry even more," Lucas jokes. Take.

"We'll do one more. Give me as much as you've got." Natalie takes a deep breath. As they're rolling, Lucas calls out instructions: "Push the autopilot button and lean back." On the monitors, a tear can be seen rolling down Portman's face.

"Folks, that was Natalie's and Anthony's last shot with us," Fletcher says shortly afterward, and there is much applause. George walks over to them. "Thank you, Tony." He hugs Natalie.

"I got a Styrofoam cup of champagne," Portman says, laughing. "The usual in the glamorous movie world."

As she leaves, Anthony autographs marker tape for crew. A few moments later, Daniels is alone. "I guess this is show business. An empty stage and already I've turned to drink," he says and takes a sip from his cup. "It's been fun. I think we can say, 'Cut.' "

LOCATION WRAP: 20:15   SETUPS: 40

SCRIPT SHOT TODAY: 2m 14s

EDITING: Anthony Daniels to do ADR [additional dialogue recording] with Jett Sally [assistant editor] on completion of sc. 143 & Naboo skiff scene.

Far left: Christensen (Anakin) and McGregor (Obi-Wan, inset) take turns in production's sole starfighter cockpit. Top left: DP Tattersall and Lucas. "George likes to shoot fast and loose," Tattersall says. "He likes to shoot with zoom lenses, and one of his phrases is, 'It's better to have more slates than takes.' " Top right: Stuntmen on the revolving set (insert), this time made up as the elevator shaft. Above: R2-D2 and Daniels.

125

SHOOT DAY 33: WEDNESDAY, AUGUST 13, 2003

LOCATION: Stages 1 & 2

SET: Elevator door—revolve "B"; elevator shaft—Federation cruiser

SCENES SHOT: 22 (droids find Anakin, who flips himself up), 31pt (the elevator shaft turns; Anakin, Obi-Wan, and Palpatine hang from wires)

Ewan and Ian are sitting with George in the video village, watching the stuntmen on the revolving set. Lucas explains to the actors what's happening. Turning to McDiarmid, he says, "And then I have to place you on the spinning wall."

"I can't wait for that," Ian says, not entirely enthusiastic.

Later, Lucas does an advance inspection of the Mustafar conference room on Stage 7. Drawn up conceptually many months ago, honed and made practical by the Australia art department, the construction department actually built it. "Really, we have several different departments," construction manager Hadju explains. "Carpentry is the biggest one, followed by set finishing, the plaster department, stagehands, and riggers (who also look after lighting), then steelworkers and sculptors—three hundred forty-five crew members.

"My guys feel like they're the unsung heroes, if ya like," he adds. "I expect we'll spend around one million dollars on timber and plywood and board product. Paint, we basically run out of because the manufacturers run out. And the same with timber and plywood and MDF [medium-density fiberboard]—they pretty much run out. They don't have enough in the country to supply us. Huge amounts. Huge quantities. Just in liquid sili-

cone, which we use for taking molds, we've used nearly two tons. It's quite unlike any other show that we've ever done, or will ever get to do."

LOCATION WRAP: 19:45   SETUPS: 36   SCRIPT SHOT TODAY: 1m 11s

Top left: Preparations are made for the cruiser generator room scene. Above: Fay David visits Lucas on the set. Top right: In the video village, animatics of the scene are reviewed. Above right: McCallum and Fletcher, who, as a younger man, traveled in Europe and North America for four years, working in an English pub and on a Canadian cattle ranch. When he returned home, he got a job in television, as a studio cameraman, then a floor manager. Fletcher broke into the film business and, among many other projects, was 1st AD on Phillip Noyce's Dead Calm *(1989) and with Carroll Ballard, one of Lucas's old friends, on* Wind *(1992).*

SHOOT DAY 34: THURSDAY, AUGUST 14, 2003

LOCATION: Stage 2

SET: Underwater—generator room; underwater Utapau sinkhole/cave

SCENES SHOT: 105 & 120pt (Obi-Wan dives in, fits breathing device, swims to rock wall), 7pt (Obi-Wan in hand-to-hand combat with droid)

The permanent tub located on Stage 2 has been filled with tons of water. A protective barrier runs around it, and throughout the shoot here, the hum of generators will be heard. Of the divers in the pool, some are stuntpeople; others, camera operators.

"The stunt guys have to grab Obi-Wan just as he gets to the camera," Lucas is saying to Gillard. "It'll be fine," he adds to Fay David, "but it's going to be painful to get."

Also in the water is McGregor, who—despite swimming around in his specially-designed-for-water Jedi garb—says, "It's quite different now. When I did Episode I, I didn't really have any idea what to expect. I remember being shown around the sets by George; they were building a big submarine and I asked George whether we would be filming underwater in it. And he looked at me like I was mad, and just said that none of it's real, you know, it's not real. So nearing the end of Episode III, I'm quite well practiced in the arts of making the magic."

Between takes, actors and divers float with the aid of life preservers. "It's a good shot even if it's not a perfect shot," Lucas says to McGregor.

"I didn't really get dragged back," the actor says.

"Can you really yank him back?" Lucas asks the stuntmen, who will be

replaced by CG super battle droids intent on drowning Obi-Wan. They can, so they do one more.

"That completes that scene, folks. Moving onto the wall then," Fletcher announces, and a cave wall is lowered in to the water.

"Very good?" McCallum asks Lucas.

"Yep. There are a bunch of scenes, so it's tricky," he replies.

But by end of day, Lucas can say to Knoll, "I didn't think we were going to get this far. I thought this was going to be a total disaster, but we can do it."

LOCATION WRAP: 20:15 SETUPS: 46 SCRIPT SHOT TODAY: 1m 18s

DIVE SUPERVISOR: Rick MacClure

SHOOT DAY 35: FRIDAY, AUGUST 15, 2003

LOCATION: Stage 2
SET: Utapaun rock wall; Federation cruiser—vent shaft
SCENES SHOT: 8 (Obi-Wan and Anakin reach the hatch and get out)

Many crew are feeling the strain of constant twelve-to-sixteen hour days. On-set nurse Marguerite O'Sullivan, who used to be a Club Med nurse, sees about a hundred people per week. Neck and shoulder pain are the most common ailments, though she mostly distributes vitamins and Band-Aids. Bigger problems can include the strain of barely seeing your family for weeks or months on end.

"I explain it to my kids," McCallum says. "You don't get to go to their baseball games, their basketball games, and homecoming things. You miss out on their life and their development. But you talk every day. You keep the connection.

"And I'm not the only one. Really, you have a bunch of people who are just trying to make a living. They're all freelance, their hours are horrendous, and they, too, have to sacrifice their kids' birthdays and their wedding anniversaries. The truth is you give up an enormous amount to be in the film business."

One of the business's riskier crafts is that involving stunts. During the Mace-Palpatine fight, "Rob and I ended up doing second unit," McCallum says, "and there was a pretty complicated shot. The stuntman had rehearsed it for days and the first take was fine. But when we did a second, safety take, he hit his leg on the stairs and broke it. Rob and I were all over him, saying we were sorry, and he said, 'That's what I do.' I turned to Nick, and, without missing a beat, he said, 'Bring in the next stuntman.' That's the business they're in; those are the additional sacrifices they make."

Back at Skywalker Ranch, Ben Burtt and Dan Gregoire are in the middle of a conference call with Steven Spielberg, who is in Los Angeles. Together they're reviewing animatics of the Mustafar duel between Obi-Wan and Anakin.

Over the speakerphone, Spielberg says, "I want these guys pouring, dripping sweat. Their hair should at some point be smoking." He asks Burtt about a sequence in which Anakin seems to be hurling lava at his former Master.

"The idea is that Anakin is using the Force," Burtt explains.

"That's a great idea," Spielberg says.

In the next shot, Obi-Wan parts a wave of lava.

"The Moses effect," Spielberg comments. "I like all this because it's biblical and mythological—but it feels slow to me." So work continues.

LOCATION WRAP: 19:45   SETUPS: 60   SCRIPT SHOT TODAY: 1m 57s

SHOOT DAY 36: MONDAY, AUGUST 18, 2003

LOCATION: Stage 5
SET: Jedi Temple—hallway and alcove
SCENES SHOT: 132 (Yoda fights clone troopers), 133 (Obi-Wan and Yoda find bodies of young Jedi students)

Jayne-Ann asks Lucas if Obi-Wan should be wearing a cloak as he makes his way clandestinely through the Jedi Temple. McGregor is of the opinion that if Obi-Wan has lost it on Utapau, he should not have a new one. Lucas thinks he could've picked one up on the Alderaan cruiser.

"I wouldn't have gone to get a cloak, would I?" McGregor wonders.

"I don't think anyone's going to ask that question," Lucas predicts. "And if you're creeping around, wearing a cloak makes it feel sneakier."

Meanwhile, the Jedi younglings are in the makeup room getting prepared for their big scene. "My dad does filming on *Star Wars*," says one. "My father's a grip," says another. Among the little Padawans are Ian Gracie's son Will, and Ty Teiger's son Joel.

To the pleased looks of family and well-wishers, the younglings lie down on the set for their big scene, pretending to be Anakin's victims. After the last take, the children are all happy. "Very good, kids," Lucas says. "Nobody moved."

LOCATION WRAP: 20:30   SETUPS: 46   SCRIPT SHOT TODAY: 3m 36s

SHOOT DAY 37: TUESDAY, AUGUST 19, 2003

LOCATION: Stage 1
SET: Hallway—Federation cruiser
SCENES SHOT: 6 (Obi-Wan & Anakin meet General Grievous; Shaak Ti is killed), 42 (they are trapped in a ray shield box)

"This is Artoo's last shot," Lucas says, after discussing the blocking with droid wrangler Don Bies. "Artoo is the unsung hero of the two trilogies," he adds. "He's the only one who knows the whole story."

Following crew photo ops with R2-D2, Don Bies and Justin Dix carry away the iconic droid.

"I was in Artoo's last scene and it was quite weird," McGregor remembers. "I find myself quite choked up about it, about this robot, you know."

LOCATION WRAP: 19:45   SETUPS: 52   SCRIPT SHOT TODAY: 4m 27s
NOTES: Denise Ream & Samir Moon (ILM) arrived in Sydney.

SHOOT DAY 38: WEDNESDAY, AUGUST 20, 2003

LOCATION: Stage 1
SET: Utapau—landing platform
SCENES SHOT: 80 (Tion Medon is questioned about the visitor)

The note "SWF" on a Call Sheet next to an actor's name means it's not only his or her first day of work, but also the last, which is the case for many cast in tertiary roles. "For these sorts of characters, there's very little time to rehearse," Bruce Spence (Tion Medon) explains. "You just walk out

---

Above: The vent shaft under construction on July 29. One side of the wall is removable to enable the cameras to get in close and maneuver. "The camera will be 8 or 10 inches from the actor's head," assistant art director Clive Memmott explains. "So the drawings specified what every centimeter is for and assigned it a paint color and a texture." As of August 18, construction continues on the general's quarters (above right) and the Mustafar war room (right), both housed in immense Stage 7.

and do your scene on the day, so you really have to bring a lot of information to help you open up those little moments. But we did a lot of makeup tests and a lot of work on the costume, so, as we started to actually make the face move, little mannerisms, little elements, and little twitches of that character started to develop."

On a platform surrounded by greenscreen, multiple takes are quickly shot with Spense (*The Road Warrior*, 1981) and McGregor.

"Cut. Great," Lucas says. Fletcher announces that it was Bruce's last shot as the director climbs the stairs to shake the actor's hand.

LOCATION WRAP: 20:15   SETUPS: 57   SCRIPT SHOT TODAY: 2m 13s

SHOOT DAY 39: THURSDAY, AUGUST 21, 2003
LOCATION: Stage 1
SET: Utapau—secret landing platform
SCENES SHOT: 125 (Obi-Wan makes contact with Bail Organa)

Atypical *Star Wars* set involves frequently being blinded, as cast and crew walk in and out of very intense lights. While struggling to see, it's best to stand still, rather than trip over any number of wires, cables, and electrical cords that snake endlessly along the ground. All the fiber-optic cables have one destination: the mobile "mother ship," which is the black-tented abode of high-definition supervisor Fred Meyers.

This is where the HD footage and "meta data" is vetted and monitored as it's transferred to Roger Barton and Jett Sally in the editorial suite. Here

Meyers sits day after day, never far from the set, overseeing banks of computers, electronic units with blinking lights, and keyboards glowing blue in the obscurity.

LOCATION WRAP: 20:15   SETUPS: 56   SCRIPT SHOT TODAY: 1m 36s
NOTES: Hayden Christensen had his final Darth Vader costume fitting.

SHOOT DAY 40: FRIDAY, AUGUST 22, 2003
LOCATION: Stage 1
SET: Hangar bay on side
SCENES SHOT: 40 (Obi-Wan and Anakin struggle on pipes; Palpatine falls)

During a second day of fairly noneventful filming, Lucas is free to step back and take a look at the big picture: "You have to make sure that you're being diligent about telling the story of the movie. Because once the film gets on the screen, it's really unforgiving. Any little tangent can become boring. If you screw up five minutes, it affects the next ten or fifteen minutes. If your first half hour isn't that great, your last half hour better be really spectacular. If it isn't, then you're building up a lot of bad will."

Top: McFarlane behind the HD camera; Bruce Spense (Tion Medon), a denizen of the planet Utapau, with Lucas. Above: HD supervisor Fred Meyers in the "mother ship." Above right: Including the death of Nute Gunray, Anakin's rampage through the Mustafar conference and war rooms is portrayed for reference in the visual script.

"Over the last thirty years, the sophistication of the audience's cinema knowledge and cinema psychology has really grown. Back when I was shortcutting, it was unusual. I shortcut by not holding long shots, not doing establishing shots, and by making large leaps forward in the editing. When I was doing the first *Star Wars*, I was reasonably avant garde. Now it's completely accepted, because people's skill at reading images in motion is much better. Younger audiences can pretty much follow everything, because they see a commercial; they see MTV videos; they do it in video games. Their ability to see things and follow them is much more acute, and that's just a matter of the culture learning."

LOCATION WRAP: 19:45   SETUPS: 42   SCRIPT SHOT TODAY: 1m 49s

SHOOT DAY 41: Monday, August 25, 2003
LOCATION: Stage 2
SET: Mustafar main conference room
SCENES SHOT: 135pt (Anakin destroys the rest of the Separatists), 150pt (Obi-Wan and Anakin fight in the conference room)

"Everything was great—except obviously the door didn't open," Lucas says to Silas Carson, who plays two characters in two different death scenes. Today he is being killed as Neimoidian viceroy Nute Gunray; later he'll be blasted to death as Jedi Ki-Adi-Mundi.

In Nute's case, Anakin Skywalker does the honors. As they rehearse, Christensen walks through the set, methodically killing additional CG characters. During the first take, Fletcher calls out "droids" to cue the arrival of droidekas. Lights flash to simulate their CG blasts.

"It looked good," Lucas says to Christensen. "I'm just going to show you a picture of Wat Tambor," he adds, indicating a spot where the actor can pretend to grasp the CG Separatist—as he stabs him. "This is Shu Mai,

who you kill on the table," Lucas continues, showing him another photo. "It's always nice to get to know the people you're killing."

"Final checks, please," Fletcher calls out.

As they roll cameras and Christensen moves about the room, all that can be heard are his breathing and footsteps as he cuts an imaginary swath of death. Despite some problems with cues, which create some unexpected results, Lucas remarks, "Hmm . . . That's not bad, in its own weird way."

LOCATION WRAP: 20:15   SETUPS: 33   SCRIPT SHOT TODAY: 1m 48s

SHOOT DAY 42: Tuesday, August 26, 2003
LOCATION: Stage 4
SET: Mustafar main collection plant
SCENES SHOT: 157 (Anakin and Obi-Wan fight)

"I decided to have the actors focus on their acting for the first part of the film, and then have them focus on their swordfighting," Lucas explains. "To mix those up is harder for an actor to cope with, in terms of what he has to learn. Ewan had to learn a thousand moves—and you really have to memorize them well, or you get hit in the head. It's also much more tedious shooting action scenes, because they get broken down into little pieces. So it's difficult and dangerous, and people wear out.

"Toward the end of the movie, we have one of the longest continuous swordfights ever filmed," he adds. "Days and days and weeks and weeks of shooting, of these guys coming in at seven in the morning and fighting till seven at night, with not very much rest. It is physically exhausting for them."

As they prepare for the second half of the Obi-Wan–Anakin duel, the director goes over the schedule with Fletcher. Trisha then asks George what will be staining the Jedi robes on Mustafar: soot, dust, or lava by-product? Lucas then talks with makeup supervisor Nikki Gooley about the sweat progression for a multiday fight shot out of continuity, for the Jedi can't be dripping sweat in one scene and dry the next.

Christensen arrives on set, as does McCallum. Within a large rectangle draped in blue, McGregor and Christensen shake hands and exchange a

few warm-up parries. Lucas goes in tight and then wide: "That way, we'll save ourselves a move," he says.

Hayden then performs his own stunt, falling two yards backward onto a blue mattress. "I want to try one with more struggle," Lucas tells him. Take.

"Too much?" Hayden asks.

"No. It was good. You just have to tilt your head up." Take. "Great. That was excellent."

LOCATION WRAP: 20:00   SETUPS: 63   SCRIPT SHOT TODAY: 1m 07s

---

Wednesday, August 27: After nineteen days of prefab materials prep, construction begins on the Darth Vader rehab chamber.

Top panels: Amid a sea of green, the Jedi fight in the collection plant. The tower collection-arm battle continues on the video village monitors (above) and on the set (inset right). Above right: McGregor and Christensen stand on what will eventually be platforms floating along a lava river; director and crew look on, including "A" camera clapper loader Williams, Harding, dolly grip Brett McDowell, and Gillard.

SHOOT DAY 43: WEDNESDAY, AUGUST 27, 2003
 LOCATION: Stage 3
 SET: Mustafar collection tower arm, floating platforms
 SCENES SHOT: 160pt (Obi-Wan and Anakin fight continues)

McGregor is standing on a small rectangular platform that's resting on springs, while Christensen is on another rectangular platform that circles Ewan's, riding on tracks.

"Ewan has always been a great swordfighter," Lucas says. "He and Ray Park [Darth Maul] were very good. Christensen is very athletic, and he's also very good at it. The difference in this particular film is they have to fight each other. As actors, there's a little bit of competitiveness about who's going to be the better swordfighter. So we got some very, very good performances."

As they approach the end of the climactic battle between Obi-Wan and Anakin, Gillard explains how he's rated the various *Star Wars* swordsmen: "On *Attack of the Clones*, I had to give them levels," he says. "Sidious is a level nine [out of ten]. On this film, Obi is eight—he's moved up—Anakin is a nine; Mace is a nine, Yoda is a nine. They're up with Sidious. Once you get to eight, you have a Pandora's box. You could go any way with it. The way not to go is the dark side. But it would tempt you, because that would jump you right past the others. So you need to arrive at level eight at the right age—not as young as Anakin. That young, the dark side is just too tempting."

LOCATION WRAP: 20:00   SETUPS: 58   SCRIPT SHOT TODAY: 1m 02s
NOTE: Hayden Christensen hurt his knee during filming today due to a lightsaber hitting him.

SHOOT DAY 44: THURSDAY, AUGUST 28, 2003
 LOCATION: Stage 3
 SET: Mustafar collection tower arm, floating platforms
 SCENES SHOT: 158pt, 160pt

On what looks like a miniature Leaning Tower of Pisa, the battle continues—shot by the digital cameras that have performed flawlessly.

"As we do each picture, we're learning more and more how to shoot with digital technology," Lucas says. "On *Phantom Menace*, we did just a few shots, because we were really in the experimental stage. On *Attack of the Clones*, we were able to shoot the whole film digitally. But the cameras we had were the very first off the production line, so there was still a lot of experimentation going on. For the crew and myself, there was a lot of learning about how to use this new technology. On Episode III, the cameras and lenses have been improved, and we really know what we're doing.

"Digital is democratizing film," Lucas continues, "because it cuts the cost enormously—especially for lower budget films—and eventually it will cut the cost of distributing films. Ultimately, digital is the equivalent of going from frescoes to oil painting, in terms of the flexibility and the freedom it gives the artist."

"We don't believe that HD is the foundation of digital," McCallum adds. "It's just the first step. We believe there are going to be hard-disk systems where this issue of resolution will completely disappear—where the resolution will be two, three, four times that of film. That's in the future. And it's no different than what happened with color or sound or nonlinear editing. You have to go through a nascent period during which you've got people who are becoming facile with the tools. You have to learn what the differences are, the pros and the cons. But I don't think the next generation has a single problem using digital cinematography. They're already there."

LOCATION WRAP: 20:15   SETUPS: 80   SCRIPT SHOT TODAY: 1m 43s

SHOOT DAY 45: FRIDAY, AUGUST 29, 2003
LOCATION: Stage 1
SET: Control room balcony; pipe across the lava
SCENES SHOT: 155 (Anakin is forced to tightrope walk over the lava)

A rare bit of Episode III casting news is that Keisha Castle-Hughes, whom Lucas had wanted to hire so many weeks ago, has actually been cast as the Queen of Naboo. On Friday, Biggar flies to New Zealand to take the young actress's measurements.

On the more mundane side, Nurse O'Sullivan reports that the second wave of flu is taking its toll on the crew (the first bout was back in July). With only a little more than two weeks of principal photography left, McCallum comments that this part of the shoot, for nearly all the crew, is dominated by the question: *Where is my next job coming from?*

After today's fighting wraps, in honor of the movie's two thousandth setup, production has its second champagne celebration.

LOCATION WRAP: 19:15   SETUPS: 65   SCRIPT SHOT TODAY: 0m 53s

Friday, August 29: Darth Vader rehab chamber set is dressed and rigged, after three days of construction.

SHOOT DAY 46: MONDAY, SEPTEMBER 1, 2003

LOCATION: Stages 1 & 4
SET: Mustafar volcano edge; Imperial rehab center
SCENES SHOT: 156 (Anakin and Obi-Wan fight), 174 (Darth Vader lives)

Many of the Australian crew have remarked that yesterday was the first day of spring. The second will see the rebirth of Darth Vader, the Dark Lord who has lain dormant these last twenty years.

But first, on Stage 1, production prepares to record the fall of Anakin Skywalker, just prior to his underworld renaissance. The set is a large triangle with one side placed on the floor, and the volcano cliff as the hypotenuse.

While fluorescent red is painted onto rocks to make them more lava-like, Lucas shows Biggar where Anakin is injured—"He gets cut right across the knee"—so they put blue stockings on Hayden's shins and another one on his left forearm, which will also be cut off. Anakin receives his near-fatal injury when he jumps at Obi-Wan, who, in one swipe, deprives him of his three remaining limbs. Anakin rolls down the side of the volcano, stopping perilously close to the lava.

Top right: The mask goes on, and Christensen is reborn, "more machine than man," as Darth Vader—who takes his place next to Darth Sidious (McDiarmid); the two are then recorded on the rehab center set (inset) by Harding's "B" camera with Brett McDowell astride a ladder holding the boom mike (above left). Left: Christensen (Vader) talks things over with Lucas and Tenggren.

McGregor joins Christensen on set. During the first take, McGregor stops in the middle. "Everyone in here has to be still," he says. "It's a very important moment."

After the first complete take, Lucas and McGregor discuss where he should say each line: "As you watch Anakin slide down, how about if you take one step forward," Lucas suggests. "For a moment, you think about it. Your first impulse is to save him—but then you realize you can't."

As the takes multiply and the actors find their rhythm and emotions, the scene becomes more and more powerful. Christensen yells, "I hate you!"

McGregor says, "I love you. But I will not help you." Lucas explains that what Obi-Wan's really saying to Anakin is: "*You were our only hope—and you blew it. Now we don't have any hope.*"

Take. After Anakin implores Obi-Wan to save him, George asks Ewan to say "I will not . . ." softer, almost to himself. Take. "After he bursts into flames," Lucas directs, "it's as if you're talking to a dead person. To a piece of toast." He suggests, to drive home this point, that McGregor change the words in the script to the past tense, "I *loved* you."

The actor acquiesces, but points out that his subsequent line would have to change to "But I *could* not help you." Lucas agrees, and Tenggren alters the script accordingly.

Christensen groans to get into character, and then gives an emotional delivery of the two lines, "Help me, Master," and "I hate you!"

"That was fantastic," George says.

As he leaves the set for lunch, Hayden says, "Just another day playing in the dirt." And Lucas replies, referring to the afternoon scenes, "Go become Darth Vader."

A crowd is gathering late in the afternoon on Stage 4. The set is minimal: a raised platform and a table. Christensen isn't yet in costume as he discusses the action with Lucas.

"Is it really going to be that hard to get out of the restraints?" he asks.

"No," Lucas responds, "but I need you to build up the anger in yourself."

The lights are dimmed in the middle of the rehearsal, creating a somber mood and casting long shadows. Because Christensen in his Vader costume can't walk very far, a makeshift dressing room has been constructed near the set. From behind its white curtains, laughter can be heard as Hayden

Right: Prosthetic-makeup artist Kerrin Jackson works on Christensen in his "burnt Anakin" suit. "My favorite prosthetic makeup is 'Burnt Anakin,'" Dave Elsey says, "because, in many ways I feel like I've been researching this makeup since I was a kid and first saw Return of the Jedi. *To me this was a chance to do something fresh, in every sense of the word, for* Star Wars. *Although we'd seen Vader without his helmet at the tail end of the first trilogy, I always wanted to know how he'd got so badly scarred and the reason he had to wear the Vader suit. I had read that he had fallen into volcanic lava, and had always, in my mind, been creating a prosthetic makeup that demonstrated these devastating injuries. In other words, I feel like I've been designing this since I was fifteen. And Hayden was fantastic in the makeup. He embraced it, brought it to life. He added a sense of dark evil." Left: On-set nurse Marguerite O'Sullivan cares for a crew member in the shadow of Vader. Top left: The visual script shows the moment where "burnt" Anakin is rescued by the Emperor—whose gesture echoes that of Obi-Wan touching Luke's forehead in* Episode IV.

changes. The number of spectators grows as word spreads that Darth Vader is about to appear, and those usually occupied in far-flung departments come to witness a bit of film history.

All is going according to plan when Lucas asks, "This may be a stupid question, but did anyone make ankle cuffs?" A flurry of eleventh-hour work ensues, as the answer is, plainly, no. Fortunately, it takes only twenty minutes to fabricate the cuffs from bits of a sprinkling system discovered by costume props supervisor Ivo Coveney.

Another few minutes later, Fletcher walks over to the dressing shack and asks Biggar through the curtains, "Is it working? Because there's no point in continuing if it isn't working."

"He has them on," Coveney responds. Colin then laughs to himself as he realizes that Vader doesn't need a makeup check, and so they have a bit more time than he'd thought. McDiarmid, already made up as Darth Sidious, sits on a stool waiting for his apprentice to appear.

"Okay. Cast on set, please," Fletcher announces—and the crowd applauds as Christensen, in full Darth Vader regalia, emerges. He greets McDiarmid, and they pat each other on the back.

Studio lights are turned down even lower, and the floor lights are turned up, creating a sinister ambience. Christensen inserts himself into the shackles, and the table is moved into a horizontal position to start the scene in which Vader breaks the bonds holding him to his operating table, screaming in pain.

"Action!" Lucas yells, and the table is slowly rotated to its vertical position. The leather of the Vader costume creaks as Hayden turns his head toward the Emperor, who informs him that Padmé is dead. Vader bursts his bonds and struggles forward. Upon "Cut," there is applause again.

Between takes, cool air is pumped through a ventilation system in the Vader costume. "Hayden, that was good," Lucas says, "except when you say, 'Where is Padmé? Is she all right?' Don't tilt your head back; tilt forward toward Sidious."

"I'm of the school where you don't really draw from your own experience," Christensen says. "I just try to use my imagination and what is motivating my character. I try to make that real for me as best as I can."

"The most special day of the shoot was when Hayden got into the Darth Vader suit," McCallum enthuses. "Every single person in the studio was waiting outside the stage doors—I'd told them they could get a glimpse of Hayden as Darth Vader. After he walked by, we had champagne and the party lasted for hours."

"It was thrilling," Christensen adds. "It was something I'd been looking forward to since I found out I got the part, hoping I'd get to don the dark helm. And I hope that my performance as Vader doesn't feel disjointed, that it has a linear connection, so that when people watch the original trilogy, they see my face under the mask. I hope it feels like one single character."

"Hayden is very good at doing the dark side, and always has been," Lucas says. "Having him finally make it into the suit completes the circle

Above: An aerial view of burnt Anakin on the operating table, with the Vader helmet suspended on a rod so it can be lowered onto Christensen's face. Above right: Immolated Anakin (Christensen) on the side of the volcano. Right: One of the hundreds of Polaroids snapped by technicians as continuity reference. The note reads "Blue screen glove; CGI dots," which refers to the computer graphics that will replace the actor's lower arm with a mechanical one.

of the movies. There was this key missing piece, which everybody's always wanted to see—and that's the return of Anakin Skywalker as Darth Vader."

Seen on the monitors in the video village, the close-ups of Vader are working, as a PA remarks that you can somehow feel his emotions through the helmet.

"Very good, Hayden," Lucas says. "Excellent."

"That's a wrap," Fletcher announces.

LOCATION WRAP: 20:30   SETUPS: 70   SCRIPT
SHOT TODAY: 1m 55s
NOTES: Company did 20 mins overtime today due to the nature of the Darth Vader costume.

SHOOT DAY 47: TUESDAY, SEPTEMBER 2, 2003

LOCATION: Stages 4 & 1
SET: Coruscant—Imperial rehab center; Mustafar—volcano edge
SCENES SHOT: 160 (Anakin slides down the embankment and bursts into flames), 164 (Darth Sidious finds Anakin still alive)

Christensen will spend nearly all of today in his burned-to-a-cinder prosthetic, or "toasty Anakin" costume. The suit is impressive, with exposed veins and pieces of charred flesh, but he describes wearing it as "being in a wet suit filled with gooey stuff." As he smokes a cigarette in his fried-flesh outfit, Hayden couldn't be more of an anti-tobacco public service announcement.

In this rehab center scene, burned Anakin is fitted with the Vader mask, which has been attached to a pole so it can be lowered onto Christensen's face. "I'll probably do two takes: one with your eyes open, one with your eyes closed," Lucas explains.

"The one with my eyes open, would you say I'm really unhappy with what's going on?" Hayden asks.

"No. You really don't know what's happening to you."

As the crew sets up, there's talk about Vader in the video village. "This puts a new perspective on Darth," McFarlane says. "He's a pathetic character, a sad character. I mean, he gets a nice new suit . . ."

"He gives up everything he loves for power," Lucas elaborates. "He makes a pact with the devil. But he kills the devil at the end, for love of his children."

Take. "Hayden," George calls up to the platform. "I'd like to try one where you keep your eyes open—and then open them real wide just as the mask comes down."

"I was thinking I could close my eyes just as the mask comes down."

"Well, the takes with your eyes open looked really good."

"Okay."

Back in the morning twilight of Stage 1, they shoot additional footage for yesterday's partially completed scene on the volcano, with

Christensen in his prosthetic. He walks over to the monitors and claps Rick's hand. "That was good," Rick says, "really moving."

The next take is just coverage, so Christensen lies on the ground, moaning for about a minute, till he cracks a smile and says he can't do anymore.

"Eyes in?" Lucas asks, and orange-yellow contacts are added to Christensen's eyes.

"Do you want me to just yell?" Hayden inquires.

"Yeah, start with your head down; look up–wait a beat–then yell, 'I hate you.' A couple of screams wouldn't hurt," Lucas answers. Take. "Great," Lucas says. "So that's lunch and then we'll do Sidious."

After lunch, Sidious's scene is quickly but poignantly completed. "There is a moment–just one moment," McDiarmid remembers. "It's just after Anakin's been almost destroyed and he's got a little life in him. Palpatine has sent for the medical team and he's waiting for them to arrive–and he just very gently touches Anakin's forehead. Sidious doesn't have any of the qualities we normally associate with humanity, except he does have a master-servant relationship with Anakin. *Anakin* means something to him."

LOCATION WRAP: 19:45   SETUPS: 62   SCRIPT SHOT TODAY: 2m 24s

SHOOT DAY 48: WEDNESDAY, SEPTEMBER 3, 2003
LOCATION: Stage 7
SET: General's quarters–Trade Federation cruiser
SCENES SHOT: 24pt (Anakin & Obi-Wan fight Count Dooku)

Ahead of schedule, the production has moved to the spectacular general's quarters. This work of art has taken more than two months to create and dress. It stretches more than fifty yards and recalls–as Lucas directed way back at the concept art stage–the Emperor's lair in *Return of the Jedi*, from its thronelike chair to its tuliped control areas.

More of the crew seem to be whistling *Star Wars* music today, perhaps because this set is so reminiscent of the first trilogy. "I remember doing *Return of the Jedi*," McDiarmid recalls. "And the Emperor was in that big set and George said, 'It's like Richard Nixon in the oval office.'

"I think it's very witty of George," he adds, "because Palpatine's first appearance in this film is in a chair that turns 'round to reveal an apparently kidnapped man strapped to it–but of course he's no less powerful than he's ever been."

What is recorded today of Kyle Rowling doubling for Dooku in his fight with Anakin will be cut together with Christopher Lee's performance, shot back in August. Wearing a T-shirt that reads MR. HORSEPOWER–given to him by his daughter Amanda in recognition of how much energy directing requires—Lucas watches footage of Lee on a monitor and discusses with Knoll how they'll match it.

"Somehow we'll make it work," Lucas says, "and nobody will be able to tell the difference."

Moments later, he is working out the shot sequence with Fletcher, and adds, "If this goes together, it'll be a miracle."

He then goes over blocking with the principals, explaining that droids will file in as the two Jedi fight Dooku. After the first take, Lucas walks onto the set. He'd like Obi-Wan and Anakin to add a salutation to their meeting with the Chancellor: "Greetings, Chancellor," McGregor ad-libs, "today you are being rescued by Jedi Obi-Wan Kenobi and Anakin Skywalker."

McCallum arrives at that moment and Lucas says to him, "We're struggling, but we'll be okay."

But following the first rehearsal, there are more delays as lights are put in place.

"Let's just try one without dialogue before lunch or we're never going to get one in here," Lucas says, and McCallum adds, "We have to break the scene's back—if we don't, it's demoralizing for everyone."

Following lunch, during a take, someone accidentally lets a door bang close and Fletcher threatens to throw workers off the set if they can't be quiet. Rehearsals continue until Lucas says, "I say we shoot."

The drama increases, however, as Christensen's knee—injured a week ago—begins to act up, particularly when he needs to duel going upstairs.

Some of the tension dissipates after two exciting sword-slashing takes. There is some applause, too, as the crew becomes aware that Christensen is fighting through a fair amount of pain. But tension builds again as cuing problems arise, which creates more waiting. In the video village, they calculate that it's costing roughly $333 a minute to make this movie. "So if it takes three minutes to move a cable, it's one thousand dollars," Chris Neil says.

"I would've done it for twenty," McFarlane volunteers.

LOCATION WRAP: 20:00   SETUPS: 45   SCRIPT SHOT TODAY: 1m 31s

Above left: Lucas in the shirt given to him by his daughter Amanda. While (above) McCallum's daughter Mousey (Bene) poses with Nick Gillard (Cin Drallig) and Coinneach Alexander (Whie). Left and top right: McDiarmid, Christensen, and McGregor in the general's quarters. "Sometimes an actor will say, 'Gee, I feel I want to do this,' and we'll discuss it," Lucas says. "I do have to keep an open mind. So then I have to assess the change without getting led astray." Above middle: Christensen and Lucas.

Because of his knee, Christensen is out for the first part of this morning, and his fencing double Ben Cooke fills in. "Hayden was really in pain," McCallum says. "But I was honest with him. I said we'd be in big trouble if we couldn't shoot, but that I didn't recommend cortisone because it would affect him for the rest of his life. So I said, 'Look. What I want is for you to do some physical therapy; we'll have a doctor here, and between each take we'll take a look at it'—and that helped him through the day."

In the village, Lucas discusses with Knoll a new computer program that uses "subsurface scattering" to better imitate how light reflects off different levels beneath the skin. About an hour later, Hayden arrives and takes a seat next to Knoll, putting his leg on a chair in front of him. McGregor walks over between takes. Looking at Hayden's leg, he jokes that now Obi-Wan will be the one killing Dooku. As the morning progresses, however, Christensen recuperates rapidly.

"What do you think, Hayden?" Lucas asks.

"I'm good to go."

"Okay. It's a real wide shot, so don't overdo it."

"All of this is deconstruction," Gillard says of the film's increasingly complex lightsaber battles. "They [the duelists] are always in check. If you get in check, you have to move out of it, which makes the moves much more complicated. It means that if you want to arrive at an end move, it might take you fifteen moves prior to that to get there. Just like chess. You start feinting and offering up parts of your body to try and tempt them. Anakin is offering his sword arm to Dooku, and he falls for it—and he knows as soon as Anakin draws his hand back, that it's all over. It's much more than a swordfight. The mental game that's going on is just as important as the moves. Dooku's weakness is that he's already beaten Anakin—and he's pretty sure he can do it again."

That afternoon, as they prepare to shoot Dooku's execution, Lucas says to McDiarmid and Christensen, "The thing to do is slow it down a bit. Pause before each line."

Christensen does push-ups to warm up, then they do a take.

"Try and struggle the next time on 'I shouldn't,'" Lucas suggests. Take.

"That was great," he says. "There was more struggle going on within you."

While waiting for the next setup, Ian and George talk about how

Palpatine will ultimately be disappointed with Anakin, after he's been permanently maimed by Obi-Wan: "He's less than what you bargained for," Lucas says. "By the end of the film, he's just a man in a shell. So when this young kid [Luke] comes along . . ." Lucas also explains that Darth Vader can't generate Sith lightning because he doesn't have real hands or arms.

During the next and final takes, Lucas watches a monitor on the set, with Tenggren sitting at his side. "I think that's it," he observes. "We made it."

LOCATION WRAP: 19:45　SETUPS: 63　SCRIPT SHOT TODAY: 1m 16s

SHOOT DAY 50: FRIDAY, SEPTEMBER 5, 2003
LOCATION: Stages 1 & 6
SET: Bridge—revolve; Jedi Temple—computer room
SCENES SHOT: 43 (the fight rages on as the ship rolls over), 138A (Yoda shows Obi-Wan a hologram of Anakin kneeling before Darth Sidious)

What had been scheduled for next Wednesday has been moved up to today because Christensen's knee won't permit him to do the scheduled fight scenes. As they prepare to shoot on the revolving set, McCallum arrives with questions ILM has posed about scenes to be shot next week, which will involve the lizard now known as Boga. "Originally the gimbal footage was going to be shot after the animation was done," McCallum says, "and it would've been controlled by the computer based on the animation. Rob was already back in the States when George changed his mind. I said,

'George, this is not what we discussed.' But he said, 'I want to get it over with; I don't want to be sitting six months from now on a stage with a gimbal. So let's try and make it work now.' And I said 'Okay, let's do it.' "

After reviewing ILM's inquiries, Lucas says the questions are too detailed, given the nature of what he'll be shooting. "It doesn't need to be perfect," he says to Rick. "My understanding is that I'm going to do the best I can. Anything that isn't right, we'll reshoot in March. All they have to do—all I need to know—is the lizard's gait."

After lunch, on Stage 6, Lucas goes over next week's shooting schedule with Jayne-Ann. Looking at his sides, he reads, " 'They fight . . . they fight . . . [turns page] . . . they fight.' "

LOCATION WRAP: 19:15　SETUPS: 55　SCRIPT SHOT TODAY: 4m 46s
NOTES: Governor Tarkin had an approval fitting by GWL today.

SHOOT DAY 51: MONDAY, SEPTEMBER 8, 2003
LOCATION: Stage 7
SET: Mustafar—main control room
SCENES SHOT: 130 (Anakin cuts down the rest of the Separatists)

The Mustafar control room is on the other end of Stage 7, about thirty yards from the general's quarters, which now resides in darkness. The extras playing Passel Argente, Nute Gunray, and assorted Neimoidian guards are getting into costume. The control room is another of the larger

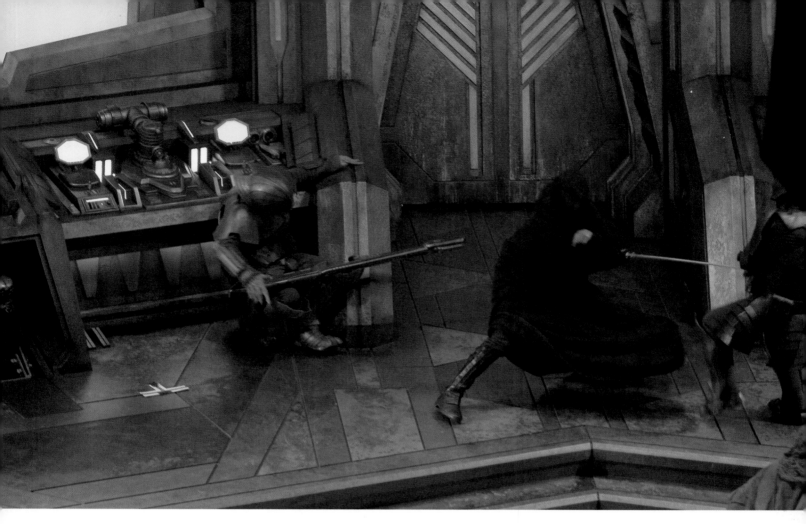

sets. With glass vacuum tubes on control panels and copper-like fixtures, its decor is reminiscent of the golden age of horror films.

Gillard walks each of the thirteen or so Separatists through his or her death scene, as Hayden, whose knee has improved, rehearses his rampage route through the room. While waiting, Silas Carson (Nute Gunray) exercises his Neimoidian mouth, which triggers gears in his exposed animatronic head that move in sync.

"They shouldn't turn around to look at Anakin till that blast door shuts," Lucas says to Fletcher, who repeats the director's instruction to the assembled cast over the PA. After the first take, Lucas asks one Separatist to run to the blast doors. He tells another to "run back and forth, so you're basically going in circles." Colin once again clarifies through the PA: "When the hologram ends, you're all chatting; you'll hear me cue Anakin; you ignore that. The next cue you have to react to is: 'Door.' "

On "Action," Christensen goes through his choreography, with each Separatist falling as he "kills" them. As he prepares to exit the set, however, he spies a lone Neimoidian he's forgotten to kill—who gives him a cheerful wave. Hayden breaks into a large grin.

"That definitely goes on the DVD," McCallum says.

During the next take, the "A" camera goes wildly askance. Lucas asks what went wrong.

"The camera was hit by a Neimoidian," McFarlane says.

"The camera was hit by a Neimoidian?!"

"Yeah, he just ran—smack—into it."

"Those Neimoidians, always causing trouble . . ."

LOCATION WRAP: 20:00   SETUPS: 56   SCRIPT SHOT TODAY: 2m 34s
TRAVEL: Roger Barton (editor) and Jett Sally (assistant editor) flew SYD/LA.

Left: Obi-Wan (McGregor) watches a hologram of Vader killing Jedi, which will be added more than a year later in post. Above: Darth Vader (Christensen) cuts down two Neimoidian gunners (Dean Gould and Chris Mitchell) in the Mustafar war room. Right: A Neimoidian gets some air in the only way possible given his mask.

SHOOT DAY 52: TUESDAY, SEPTEMBER 9, 2003

    LOCATION: Stage 7

    SET: Mustafar—main control room

    SCENES SHOT: 148 (Anakin and Obi-Wan fight moves toward the control center)

One of the more intense moments of the Anakin–Obi-Wan lightsaber duel takes place toe-to-toe. "That toe-to-toe thing shows that they can't get through each other's defenses," Gillard explains, "because they know each other's moves so intimately. I think it's something like forty moves; I did the first eight and then I let them go with it."

During this action, the rhythmic *clack-clack-clack* of the steel lightsabers cracking against each other in rapid-fire succession can be heard. After one remarkable take, Christensen and McGregor repair to the village to watch the playback.

"Perfect," Lucas says, and there is applause. "That was really maybe the fastest we've ever done it," Ewan says to Hayden, and they shake hands.

"Hey, folks," Fletcher announces, "that completes the Anakin–Obi-Wan fight!"

LOCATION WRAP: 20:00   SETUPS: 51   SCRIPT SHOT TODAY: 29s

TRAVEL: Gavin Bocquet (production designer) flew Sydney-LA.

SHOOT DAY 53: WEDNESDAY, SEPTEMBER 10, 2003

    LOCATION: Stage 3

    SET: Blue elevator shaft

    SCENES SHOT: 31 (they run along elevator shaft)

With the departure of Bocquet, the editors, and many others, much of production is winding down. But for Christensen, work goes on as before.

At 6:20 A.M., after a 5:30 wake-up call and a 6:00 pick-up at his apartment on Bondi Beach, he walks, or shuffles, into the makeup room on the ground floor of Stage 2. Opera music is playing softly as hardly awake makeup artists begin their routines. Bare, uncomfortably bright lightbulbs run around the perimeters of large wood-framed mirrors clearly reflecting everyone's general fatigue. Second AD Deb sits nearby in the ADs' office. Originally from Adelaide, she fell in love with cinema watching Hitchcock classics.

Wearing a bathrobe over nondescript clothes and black sneakers, coffee in one hand, Hayden shaves himself with the other while sitting in what looks like a barber's chair. Makeup artist Shane Thomas heats up a towel in a microwave oven. Hairdresser Pip Lund and makeup artist Bliss MacGillicuddy arrive. Each actor is assigned one or more makeup people, and Shane has been assigned to Hayden. "He's making me look tan and

rested," Christensen mutters, whereas in reality he says he feels "tired and pale." Ian McDiarmid arrives at 6:30 A.M. Colin Fletcher pops in at 6:40 to verify that everyone is on schedule.

A fake scar is applied to Christensen's face with a material called Rigid Collodion, which is also used to heal cuts during boxing matches. Another scar, on his eyebrow, is real and resulted from a childhood accident on a slide. Two more scars on the left side of his chest came from a Portuguese man-of-war during a family vacation in Florida. At 7 A.M., key hairdresser Annette Miles takes over, working on Christensen's hair, and the music switches to something more contemporary.

Left: In Stage 2's hair and makeup department, makeup supervisor Nikki Gooley and makeup artist Shane Thomas prepare Christensen (Anakin) for another day on the set. "The first professional production I was in was The Member of the Wedding *by Carson McCullers," Christensen says, "I was nine or ten years old." Above and right: Weeks of training are put into action, as days and days of dueling take their toll on Christensen and McGregor.*

144

At 7:30 A.M., Christensen goes to his studio apartment in Stage 4, which consists of one room with a bed for naps, and another equipped with a couch, a beanbag chair, and a TV connected to a PlayStation 2 that he's never turned on. After breakfast–eggs and toast–medic Rob McMinn arrives to do what he can with Hayden's still-fragile knee, while the actor talks about a production company he's formed with his brother. Their film–*Shattered Glass*, starring Christensen and Hank Azaria–has just opened at the Toronto Film Festival.

"I definitely feel more acclimated this time around," Christensen says of his second *Star Wars* film. "Last time, I had the fish-out-of-water syndrome and was very much in awe of everything around me. It was a big change for me: I went from performing in high school plays and trying to make sure I made it on time to my tennis lessons, to playing a central role in one of the biggest films in popular culture."

"Amazed" is how he describes his reaction to seeing the finished *Attack of the Clones*. "You get to enjoy it on the same level as the public, because it's fresh and new when you see it because you haven't seen any of those sets," he says, adding, "George has amazing control, and his ability to manipulate the medium is unbelievable."

Christensen puts on his precostume clothes: two pairs of black pants, boots, and a T-shirt. By 7:50 A.M., he completes his transformation in Stage 4's changing room, which is nothing more than a closet big enough for

softened by the mats below. "Ian, are you up for another one?" Lucas asks.

"Yeah, go on," he replies.

Everyone breaks for lunch at 12:45. At two o'clock, Christensen is back in makeup for refurbishing, and, at 2:15 P.M., he's back on set. After a few more setups, Lucas happily remarks, "Well, we just do that and we're done." But Fletcher reminds him that they have an additional scene to do.

four people standing. Ian is here in the cramped quarters, too, getting dressed on the other side of a plywood wall.

"Is Palpatine here?" 2nd AD Paul Sullivan asks, poking his head in.

"Mind your own business," a voice comes from the other side.

"You see what I have to put up with?" Paul says. "Put that in your book."

By 8 A.M., Hayden is on stage. Whereas some might feel at least a twang of apprehension performing in one of the most anticipated films of all time, he feels a "rush" whenever he arrives on set–which is one of the things that attracted him to acting. Talking in a relaxed, almost subdued manner, he outlines once again how a theatrical agent spotted him when he was a kid, which led to commercials, stage acting, drama school, TV, and film.

Hayden's individual course now merges with life on the set. He and Ian must lie down on an approximately thirty-yard-long board that can be angled into the air to become a giant slide, which will in turn become an elevator shaft in postproduction. On one take, the angle is increased. Christensen grabs on to the side, but McDiarmid shoots by him, his fall

"Oh, that's right," Lucas says, less happily. "My God, why do I keep doing this to myself?"

Production moves on to the scenes pitting General Grievous against Obi-Wan, which means Christensen is done for the day. He says good-bye to Ewan and Ian. By 4:55 P.M., he's back in makeup for its removal, and Bob Marley is on the radio. McMinn comes in to go over the physical therapy plan for the next day. At 5:25 P.M., Christensen poses with McDiarmid for a public relations photo. At 5:30, Annette Miles fits him for a wig for the March reshoot (if Christensen has to change his hairstyle for any reason, they'll have an Anakin wig in reserve). At 5:40 P.M., an unusually early wrap for Christensen, he is driven the twenty minutes back to Bondi Beach.

"Doing Episode III is an immense learning experience," Hayden says in the car.

LOCATION WRAP: 20:00   SETUPS: 84   SCRIPT SHOT TODAY: 1m 11s

SHOOT DAY 54: THURSDAY, SEPTEMBER 11, 2003
LOCATION: Stages 3 & 6
SET: Utapau—Boga
SCENES SHOT: 83 (mount Boga), 87 (Obi-Wan fights General Grievous)

"What a handsome crew," communications director Lynne Hale remarks as the official on-set crew photo is snapped. Afterward, it's Obi-Wan versus Grievous and his bodyguards in another sea of green.

"Young lady, I've been doing this since before you were born," Lucas is saying to 3rd AD Samantha Smith. "I started this thirty years ago."

"Do you get time off for good behavior?" McFarlane asks.

"I got fifteen years off and raised my kids."

The fight with the bodyguards is quickly finished, and the crew applauds fencing double Michael Byrne and stuntman Dean Gould, who have finished their work on this fight.

"Is that it?" McGregor asks.

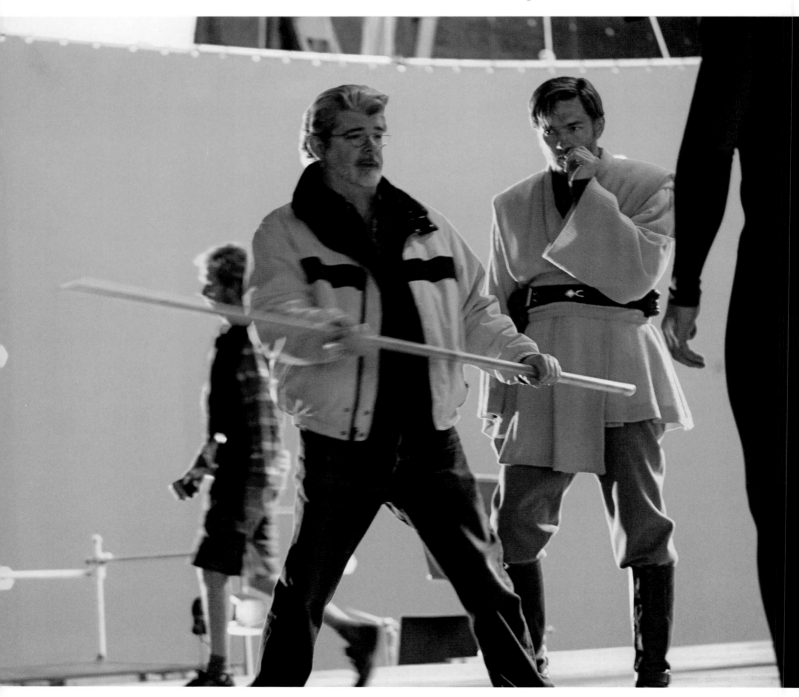

"All you have to do is fight Grievous, ride Boga, give the baby away, and you're done," Lucas says.

After lunch, McGregor continues with Rowling doubling for Grievous, who will be added later as a CG character.

"Grievous has got four arms," Gillard says of the combat. "We do a really complicated fight with two arms, but there are moves in there where Ewan is moving to the second two arms that obviously we don't have yet. We dispatch those two arms as quickly as possible. When he fights Grievous's four bodyguards, it's totally different—that's quarterstaff, the same as with Darth Maul, but at another level now. If that comes off, it should be phenomenal. Ewan's done really well and is still in tip-top form."

Multiple takes and setups are quickly completed. "Very good," Lucas concludes. "I'd say we're on the wrong set."

"Guys, that completes the Obi-Grievous fight," Fletcher announces, and production moves to the next stage.

Later in the day, McGregor is astride Boga, sitting on a saddle placed on what looks like a bucking bronco machine, whose engine makes a whirring sound. A revolving six-sided mirror in the rafters reflects light onto the lizard, creating the illusion of movement. Knoll feels that the beast's motions are jerky and that it stops too suddenly. As late afternoon becomes early evening, he remarks, "Maybe it's a robot lizard."

LOCATION WRAP: 20:00   SETUPS: 64   SCRIPT SHOT TODAY: 2m 41s

SHOOT DAY 55: FRIDAY, SEPTEMBER 12, 2003
LOCATION: Stage 6
SET: Utapau—Boga
SCENES SHOT: 100 (Commander Cody returns Obi-Wan's lightsaber)

Wearing a blue bodysuit, actor Temuera Morrison is back—not as Jango Fett, whom he played in Episode II, but as Commander Cody, a Jango clone. From astride the mechanical lizard, whose move-

ments will be smoothed out in post, McGregor asks, "Is Grievous chasing me or am I behind him?"

"You're chasing him," Lucas replies. "So you can whip the lizard hard to catch up."

As the scenes change but the set stays the same, McGregor asks, "So I'm not chasing Grievous anymore?"

"You've killed Grievous and you're just going along."

After a few more takes and angles, they switch to Obi-Wan fighting droids while still seated on Boga. "Remember, the droids are about this high," Lucas says, indicating a level near the actor's feet. "So it's more like playing polo."

With these last few days of the shoot, crew are moving on to other projects, such as *Mask 2*, the next film scheduled at Fox Studios Australia. Today is the last day for most of the construction department. At 5:45 P.M., Lucas wraps, the earliest wrap ever for the on-set crew.

LOCATION WRAP: 20:00   SETUPS: 66   SCRIPT SHOT TODAY: 1m 15s

SHOOT DAY 56: MONDAY, SEPTEMBER 15, 2003
LOCATION: Stages 6 & 3
SET: Utapau—Boga; Tatooine
SCENES SHOT: 106 (Ki-Adi-Mundi is cut down by clone commanders), 180 (Obi-Wan hands baby to Owen Lars)

At long last, Lucas is adding to the scene he began shooting three years ago in Tunisia: Obi-Wan's gentle delivery of Luke Skywalker to the Lars family. Lucas carries the prop baby to McGregor, who, this time, will be handing Luke to Beru, not Owen. "I just felt it would be better if Luke were handed over to a woman," Lucas explains.

On "Action," McGregor gives the baby to Bonnie Maree Piesse (Aunt Beru), as followed by cameraman Harding, who pans right. Piesse then hands the baby to Owen Lars, whose part is being temporarily handled by on-set PA Hamish Roxburgh, because Joel Edgerton (young Owen) is unavailable.

Left: Holding a quarterstaff favored by Grievous and his bodyguards, Lucas demonstrates what he'd like McGregor (Obi-Wan) to do. Top: Temuera Morrison (Commander Cody), who will also play various clones, and McGregor. Middle: Silas Carson is made up as Ki-Adi-Mundi by prosthetic makeup and hair techni- *cians Katherine Brown and Sophie Fleming. Above: The "handsome" on-set production crew photo taken September 11. Sitting in the front row is McCallum, of whom art department coordinator Collette Birrell says, "He makes everyone feel they have an important role; he's generous."*

Between takes, a crew member carefully cradles the prop baby to make sure the folds in its blanket remain the same for each take.

The last shot of the day belongs to Silas Carson, who is prepared for his second death scene, this time as Ki-Adi-Mundi. "You turn and look at the clones," Lucas says to him, "they pull out their guns, and—blam, blam, blam!"

LOCATION WRAP: 20:30   SETUPS: 88   SCRIPT SHOT TODAY: 1m 05s
NOTES: Ewan McGregor wrapped picture today.

SHOOT DAY 57: TUESDAY, SEPTEMBER 16, 2003
LOCATION: Stages 3 & 5
SET: Naboo main square; Chancellor's holding office
SCENES SHOT: 175pt (Padmé's funeral), 146pt (Palpatine and Yoda fight)

Taking part in Padmé's funeral procession is the Queen of Naboo, as played by Keisha Castle-Hughes. Resplendently mournful in her costume and headdress, she is followed by hooded dignitaries, blue guards, and about two dozen others. Leading them is Padmé's coffin (sans Portman) on a metal table with wheels. "There's one girl who's not following the way she should," Lucas remarks. The group walks in circles, and the only audible effect is the sound of their footsteps.

Ivo Coveney works on thirteen-year-old Keisha's headdress between takes. "It was about a month ago they first said something about *Star Wars*," she says. "I discussed it with my agent and my mom, then we decid-

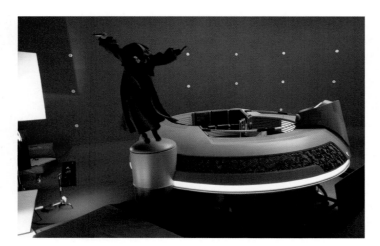

ed like only a week and a half ago that I would come over and play the part. It was pretty tight; we came to Australia in the day before filming. I only just met George today, and I was really excited."

In keeping with *Star Wars* crowd-scene tradition, many of the crew have been cast in background parts, among them assistant publicist Lisa Shaunessy (a female Senator) and Jacqui Louez (Senator Jacquito)—George Lucas's and Rick McCallum's assistant.

"I officially have the best job on the film," Louez says, "which is to protect them and to make their lives easier."

LOCATION WRAP: 20:15   SETUPS: 58   SCRIPT SHOT TODAY: 3m 05s

SHOOT DAY 58—END OF PRINCIPAL PHOTOGRAPHY: WEDNESDAY, SEPTEMBER 17, 2003
LOCATION: Stages 4 & 2
SET: Imperial Star Destroyer
SCENES SHOT: 177 (the Emperor, Tarkin, and Darth Vader watch the construction of the Death Star)

Star Wars has returned to the bridge of a Star Destroyer. Imperial uniforms like those seen in *A New Hope* are making their first prequel trilogy appearance, worn by "pit" officers. The tension and joy are palpable among the crew and the crowd who have come to witness the end of the shoot. "The last day was very moving," McCallum says "It was a special, wacky day, because we shot on seven different sets—we were running constantly."

Lucas stands on the ramparts above the pit, giving directions to McDiarmid, Christensen, and Wayne Pygram (Tarkin): "It's your average Star Destroyer. Tarkin and the Emperor look at each other. Then Anakin steps up; Tarkin turns, looks at Anakin, and leaves. Then Anakin and the Emperor both turn and look out the window to contemplate the Death Star."

"Final checks, please," Fletcher calls out. Coveney puts Vader's helmet on Christensen.

"I hope he can see," Lucas says, as once again the actors are perched fairly high above the ground.

"And . . . action!" he calls out.

Left: Michael Byrne (Darth Sidious double) leaps from a Senate pod during the Sith's battle with Yoda. Above left: Keisha Castle-Hughes (Queen of Naboo) is touched up between takes, and then takes part in the funeral flanked by handmaidens and a Sio Bibble picture double. Right: Crew prepare the "pit" of the Star Destroyer. Above right: An aerial view of set; McCallum handles the slate for the last shot of the film (above, far right).

Darth Vader strides forward, taking his place next to the Emperor. Looks are exchanged. Tarkin exits, and the two Sith turn to look out into space.

"And . . . cut!" Lucas says.

He sets up another angle. "We need to do one more with highlights," the director says, referring to the lighting. During the next take, he instructs, "And you look at each other and . . . you look back. A little more to the right . . . okay, cut. I have to do one more."

As he did the first, McCallum prepares the last slate. "You got speed?" he asks. "V 177 G, Take One."

"And . . . action!" Lucas calls out—for the last time.

Vader crosses his arms.

"Take a half step forward, Ian . . . right there!" George says, and Ian stops.

"Cut. That's it. Done. Finished. All done!" Lucas announces—and many people applaud, as Rick hugs Hayden and everyone celebrates.

"You were fantastic," Lucas says to the two actors.

"Thank you for the opportunity," Christensen says.

"I can't wait to put it all together," Lucas says. "I think we have some great stuff." He then finds David Tattersall and informs him excitedly, "A hundred setups we did today! You can put *that* on a T-shirt."

"A hundred setups?!" Tattersall asks, genuinely surprised.

"A hundred. That's why I did that last one again."

"Just don't let the word out, or everyone will want to do it," McFarlane chimes in.

"Get those drinks going," Rick says.

Gillard and Lucas shake hands. Lucas then locates Knoll and says, "I've been working on it for eighteen months and I have exactly eighteen months to go."

"I feel like my vacation just ended," Knoll remarks, for, as of this moment, the burden of production has shifted to ILM.

As drinks are poured and tremendous relief is felt, bystanders and crew form a long semicircle facing McCallum, who, with mike in one hand and drink in another, says to the assembled: "This is a very emotional moment for me. But I do want to tell you, you have been the most fantastic group of people to work with. And definitely the nicest, the most fun–you've made it such an easy thing for us–I can't thank you all enough . . . and here's George."

Taking the mike offered by McCallum, Lucas says, "What Rick says goes for me, too. I must say this is actually the most fun film I've ever worked on. It's been really easy, and it's been very swift. And at the same time, everyone's worked in harmony, and that's extremely important. And there hasn't been a lot of crazy politics and ego and all the other things one finds on movie sets. This has definitely been the best crew I've ever worked with. I really enjoyed being with all of you. And I think we've made a great movie. I'm really looking forward to going in and cutting it and seeing what happens. Thank you–thank you very much–to all of you."

They all drink a toast. Someone from the back yells, "Thank you, George!" Everyone then watches a highlight reel of the shoot, which finishes with Fletcher saying, "And that's a wrap, everybody."

LOCATION WRAP: 21:00   SETUPS: 100   SCRIPT SHOT TODAY: 1m 57s
NOTES: End of principal photography–production wrapped five days ahead of schedule.

TOTALS:
PAGES SHOT TO DATE: 121 [OUT OF 130]
TOTAL SETUPS: 2883
TOTAL SCENES: 144
TOTAL SCENES TO COMPLETE: 41
TOTAL HOURS WORKED (FROM FIRST SHOT TO CAMERA WRAP): 709 hours 25 minutes
TOTAL SCRIPT TIMING SHOT: 144 minutes 46 seconds
[APPROXIMATE TIME SPENT PER SCRIPT-MINUTE FILMED: 4.9 hours]

NOTE ON LAST CALL SHEET:

> To Everyone on the Crew,
> Just a short note to tell you how truly fantastic you have been to work with—your professionalism, energy, humor, and lightning speed have allowed you to be unemployed 5 days earlier than originally scheduled!!! Seriously, though, it has been an honor and a truly great experience for us, and I hope you know how much both George and I appreciate all the hard work you have done. We are very grateful and indebted to all of you. You have made it so easy!
>
> Australia Rules!!!
>
> All Love, Rick.

EPILOGUE

On Day One, Trisha remembers Gavin saying to her, "Isn't it sad? This is our last start day for a *Star Wars* film."

About twenty-five hundred people attend the wrap party a few days after the end of principal photography. Many promise to work together again, but the atmosphere is slightly melancholy. Additional shooting for *Revenge* is scheduled, but no one knows for certain if they'll be involved. The greatest of their creative efforts is over, and an epoch has come to an end.

"I was happy; I was relieved," Jayne-Ann says. "It was a great shoot. It was fast and intense, and it was a lot of work, but it was civilized."

"It's amazing how it all comes together," Ty Teiger notes. "Because at the beginning, you get the script and think, *How are we going to get through it?* The trilogy has been a long part of my life. Both of my children have been born while I've been on these films. It's not often in your lifetime, as a film technician, that you can have the joy of working on such an amazing thing."

"It's always devastating to end a shoot," McCallum admits, "because you've really connected with people–no matter how many films you've done. But you've got to shut it off; you can't carry it with you. And then I get excited about postproduction."

"You're all friends, you know each other," Lucas says. "But I have a tendency to not let my private life and my professional life mix–and once the movie finishes, everybody goes their own way. When you're together, you're together, and when you're not, you're not."

Far left: Darth Vader (Christensen) arrives on the Star Destroyer bridge and gazes at the construction of the Death Star (inset, visual script). Left: Stills photographer Keith Hamshere and Lynne Hale; Murray and Birrell. Above: Lucas, McCallum, and Jacqui Louez with Christensen.

PART III

DIGITAL SHOT PRODUCTION

A Symphony Is Born

PROLOGUE: Editing

Previous spread: Like huge naval vessels, a Jedi cruiser and a Separatist flag ship exchange withering blaster-cannon exchanges in this final frame. Above: Lucas works with editor Roger Barton on the Avid. Right: McCallum, Tattersall, and Lucas. Below: In Sydney, dressed as stormtroopers and a Jedi are: assistant editor Jett Sally, Barton, apprentice editor John Briggs, and assistant editor Jason Ballantine.

"The auteur theory is very abstract and intellectual until you get to know filmmakers," Lucas says. "But when you know them personally and you know how they make their decisions, then you realize these people *are* their movies. Marty [Scorcese] *is* Marty's movies; Francis [Ford Coppola] *is* Francis's movies; Steven [Spielberg] *is* Steven's movies. You can actually see their sensibilities in their films.

"I come out of abstract filmmaking. I like the idea of cutting together contrasting images and ideas so they flow one after the other. If you watch a silent movie, you can see how a story is told; if you watch abstract films, you can see that by juxtaposing images, you also tell stories, and, in doing so, the issue of cutting on one frame rather than on another becomes very important.

"On the editorial level, which is the cinematic level, movies are a mass of objects moving across a large surface. You're watching these little details, which are the ones that make the cut work, as they move through the back of the frame. You're orchestrating how these things flow, by deciding how you cut from one shot to another. The subtlety of the medium demands that a star break the frame at the right moment, because what reaction you get has a lot to do with spatial relationships: where things are in the frame, what color things are, where the bright objects are--and where your eye is going to be.

"When the movie cuts to a different shot, if your eye has to move a great distance to follow an object, it becomes a rough cut; if your eye stays in the same place, then it's a smooth cut. If your eye has to move too much, you're usually lost for two frames on a cut. You don't understand what you're seeing because you can't register it that fast. If you're just cutting dialogue, it doesn't matter; it's just talking heads and the emphasis is *all* on the dialogue. But in my films, the dialogue is not where the movie is. My films are basically in the graphics. The emotional impact comes from the music—and from juxtaposing one image with the next.

"Cinema is about moving images. But it's moving from one image to the next that creates the emotional impact."

7 Directing on Three Fronts

Following the completion of principal photography, for most of the Australian crew, work on the film is over. As of October 2003, however, Lucas, Ben Burtt, and Roger Barton have begun editing in earnest. Because more than 50 percent of the movie—the digital percent—has yet to be created, Lucas says, "What I'm doing, in essence, is cutting the movie without seeing it. So I guess and I theorize that the editing might be right."

"We're in a weird, scary place right now," McCallum says, "which is normal at this stage. You know, we don't really have a movie yet. We've shot everything that was scheduled, but the digital elements are still to come. What's happening now is that George works with Ben from about 9 A.M. until 1 P.M., primarily on the action sequences. From 1 P.M. until about 2:30, he has lunch upstairs in the animatics department while working on visual effects shots to use as placeholders, so we can actually see the film just before Christmas 'complete.' It'll be very crude, but it will at least give us an indication of where everything is going.

"At about 3 P.M., George works for about three to four hours with Roger, primarily on the dramatic sequences. Together, George, Ben, and Roger are just going straight through the movie, assembling the picture and creating the first rough cut."

Of the three fronts Lucas is attacking, editorial and animatics are two. The third front, of course, is ILM. At this still-early stage, the visual effects juggernaut is continuing, primarily, to transform concepts into digital creatures, sets, and vehicles. ILM's workload will increase dramatically as soon as Lucas begins to turn

over edited sequences—a combination of principal photography, animatics, and concept art. At that point, ILM will start to meld the digital components to the images—characters, digi-matte paintings and so on—eventually showing them to Lucas as "finals": shots deemed complete, which Lucas reviews during "dailies." He may agree that a shot is "final," or send it back for additional work. If it's finalized, the shot is dropped into the cut, where Lucas has to approve it again. Even after this point, shots may change or be omitted as the film evolves.

Each step toward finals is closely monitored by ILM visual effects executive producer Denise Ream and producers Janet Lewin and Jill Brooks. Working hand in hand with visual effects supervisor John Knoll, animation director Rob Coleman, and a growing roster of department heads, they budget and analyze every sequence that ILM receives from editorial and every digital asset they have to create. They then strategize with McCallum and Kathryn Ramos to fine-tune their methodologies.

"Denise's job is to coordinate all the supervisors and make sure ILM has their working spaces, their environments, and everything else that they need to actually start to work," McCallum explains. Lewin deals with the "front end"—modeling, layout, animation, and digital simulation work—while Brooks is producing the technical directors, compositors, and stage work, or the "back end."

"So now I have this brief period up until Christmas, during which my job is to set up ILM," McCallum says. "If you arrive on a set that has a hundred fifty people, and you're not shooting, you still pay those hundred fifty people. In the same way, if you don't make up your mind about a visual effects shot, then you have about three hundred fifty people getting paid to do nothing. A film used to have maybe ten to fifty effects shots; we have at least two thousand. Where you once had a million dollars in effects shots, now you have forty or fifty million dollars' worth. On *Revenge*, the production crew worked for nine months, the shooting crew for three months—but the visual effects crew will work for eighteen months. And even as big as our sets were, we only spent about four and a half million dollars on all of them combined. We'll spend ten million dollars on our digital sets.

"One of the problems with these big visual effects films is that there's always been a distance between the filmmaking community and the effects community. But this has been a happy experience so far because we got ILM involved at the very beginning. They're such an integral part of the crew—the largest part of the crew—and they're doing the most awesome, mind-blowing work. They're all incredibly conscious of what it is that we need, the schedule we're up against, the amount of money we have to spend.

"So it's also a challenge for George," McCallum concludes. "He has to finish the first twenty-five minutes of the film by December 19. Then we have to be ready to move and shake by January 5."

FRIDAY, OCTOBER 31, 2003
ILM: As promised on the set, Lucas has cut together and turned over seven brief Yoda scenes, which amount to ninety-eight shots, for Coleman and his animation team to get started on.

"I'm in a very good place right now," Coleman says. In fact, his department has nearly finished replacing the Episode I Yoda puppet with digital Yoda—an exercise that Lucas and Coleman agreed would serve as a good warm-up—so the animation department is now primed and ready for Yoda's Episode III performance.

Friday, October 31: The following scenes have been turned over to ILM:
Sc. 56: CYQ (Coruscant Yoda's quarters)
Sc. 61, 62, 70: CJC 1 & 2 (Coruscant Jedi Council)
Sc. 171, 172, 173: SAC 2 & 3 (Alderaan space cruiser)
Note: The three-letter acronyms that follow scene numbers are used to designate scene locales; subsequent single digits indicate whether it's the first, second, or third scene to take place in that locale.

TUESDAY, NOVEMBER 4, 2003
ILM: Every day, various departments—layout, digi-matte painting, view paint, CG model making, compositing—meet to discuss works in progress. "We're in ILM mode," Fay David says, explaining that even much of what the Skywalker Ranch art department does is now geared toward helping ILM build assets in the spirit of the original concept art. While still creating conceptual designs when called for by Lucas and the animatics depart-

ment, Tiemens is acting as consultant to ILM's digi-matte painting department, while Church works with ILMers creating CG vehicles. Because the projects are so numerous, ILM also has two of its own art directors: former concept artist Alex Jaeger and Aaron McBride (*Minority Report*, 2002; *Pirates of the Caribbean*, 2003), who both work hand in hand with Church and Tiemens while art directing the CG model shop and CG creatures, respectively.

Today's ILM art department meeting has Church, Tiemens, Jaeger, McBride, and Knoll—who carries a coffee mug saying I KNOW MORE THAN YOU DO—touring the computer graphics department, reviewing digital reconstructions of sets on terminals. The work spaces are informal: One has three aquariums, another has a giant leftover *Star Trek* hull (NCC-1701-A) affixed to the wall; Japanese screens divide some cubicles, while one area has a large sculpture of a soft-drink can hanging over the door.

Talk with the CG modelers reveals that some are wrestling with the ambiguities inherent in the creation of digital versions of real sets. Knoll instructs them to duplicate the inconsistencies of the real-life sets, not to correct them. Throughout the next eighteen months, because he was the only one at ILM to be on set throughout the shoot, Knoll will be a valuable source of reference. "Whenever someone asks me why we didn't do X or Y on the set, which would've made their job easier," Knoll says, "I just say, 'You have no idea what it's like, how intense sets are.'"

McCallum is also quick to note Knoll's importance: "I've been blessed to work with John Knoll over the last ten years."

Although pinned to his office door is a rejection letter from ILM dated January 25, 1985, Knoll's rise here has been rapid. "I always enjoyed movies," he says of his childhood. "And when I'd see things that had to have been manufactured, I thought it was fascinating and I wondered, *How did they do that?* By nine or ten, I was model making. When I was in high school, my dad got an Apple II as part of his university research, and he encouraged my brother and me to use it. I'd get home from school and it was just sitting there. There wasn't

---

Left: McCallum and Wookiee #5 (Axel Dench); #7 (David Stiff); #2 (Steven Foy); #1 (James Rowland); #6 (Julian Khazzouh); #4 (Robert Cope); #3 "Tarfful" (Michael Kingma). Above left: Wookiee catamaran by CG hard-surface modeler Howie Weed, supervised by Pam Choy. Above right: Concept sketches (Jun) and sculpt (Murnane) of a Wookiee ripping apart a droid. Right: Wookiee by CG creature supervisor Aaron Ferguson. "Wookiees are all about hair," viewpaint supervisor Susan Ross says. "Many maps are made to create fur, for color (tip and root), length, density, jitter, and tufting."

any software for it, but there was a built-in basic interpreter, so I learned how to program it [Knoll and his brother Thomas would go on to create Photoshop].

"I had a life-changing experience in May of 1978," Knoll remembers. "My dad had a Society of Nuclear Medicine conference in Anaheim, so he brought my brothers and me out to California. At this point ILM was still down in Van Nuys, and I'd been reading all these magazines about how *Star Wars* was done. On a lark, I picked up the phone book and found a listing for Industrial Light & Magic. I called up and said, 'I'm a model maker and I'm interested in doing this work for a living'; and they said, 'Why don't you come on down.' So my dad dropped me off and I hung out at ILM for a whole day—and boy, that was an awesome experience. I got there in the morning and saw dailies and how the optical department put the elements together; I saw models under construction. It was really cool, and the experience also made it real to me. I thought, *I could be one of these guys!*

"Later, at USC film school, I think I was the only one in the program who hadn't decided they were going to be a writer-director. I was interested in the technical aspects of filmmaking. In the end, I'm a craftsman at heart."

November 5-20, 2003: On the (Virtual) Cutting Room Floor I
While the following scenes have been turned over to ILM...
Sc. 131-132: CJE (Coruscant Jedi entry)
Sc. 138-138A: CTC (Coruscant Jedi Temple control center)
Sc. 167: PMM-1 (Polis Massa Medical Center)

...these scenes have been cut:
Sc. 68-69: CPA-2 (Obi-Wan tells Padmé of his worries about Anakin and that he knows they're in love)
Sc. 71: CPA-3 (Bail Organa and other Senators discourage Padmé from talking to Obi-Wan about their plan to present Palpatine with a petition protesting his handling of the war)
Sc. 73: CCT (Palpatine arrives at the Senate, and Anakin informs him that Obi-Wan "will soon have Grievous's head")
Sc. 74: CSH-2 (Jar Jar greets Anakin inside the Senate, and Palpatine insinuates to Anakin that Obi-Wan's mind has been clouded "by the influence of a certain female Senator")
Sc. 75: CPA-4 (Anakin confronts Padmé, but says he's not the Jedi he once thought he was)
Sc. 76-77: SRC (a Republic cruiser comes out of hyperspace near Utapau)
Sc. 86: KHA (Mace Windu talks with Yoda on Kashyyyk via hologram, telling him of his plans to arrest Palpatine)

During his last semester, Knoll built a motion-control camera for his advanced animation class. As a result, about six months after he graduated, in 1986, one of his professors from USC called and said ILM was looking for a motion-control cameraman. This time, Knoll was hired.

"*Star Wars Special Edition* was the first time I got to work with George," he notes. "I'd put together these animation tests of individual shots and show them to George for his feedback. And George is not a real outgoing, gregarious guy, at least at first. If he hasn't gotten to know you, he doesn't joke around. But as we would continue to work together [on Episodes I

and II], and we got to know each other better, he would be a little more jovial, and humor would start getting injected into the situations."

FRIDAY, NOVEMBER 21, 2003
SKYWALKER RANCH (SR): The animatics department is a long room equipped with a tan couch and comfy white chair, a dozen work spaces with several dozen computers, and black ceiling lamps that extend downward from an arched fifteen-foot-high wood-beamed ceiling. According to

---

Top left: Male lizard modeled by Sunny Wei, technical directed by Kevin Reuter; and painted by viewpaint supervisor Susan Ross (middle right; viewpaint supervisor Elbert Yen is middle left), who explains. "We made separate maps for the front and the back of the feathers. Splines were placed by the modeler and hair was grown along the lines to mimic feathers." Top right: Female lizard by Aaron Ferguson.

pre-visualization supervisor Dan Gregoire, his department is now "under the gun." Lucas's afternoon visits are multiplying and being extended. The intention is to finish sequences and then give them to ILM and say, "Make it real." Using a software program called iViz, the animatics artists are continuing to create low-res digital scenes that ILM will eventually re-create, enhance, and make photo-real. "You load in your models," McCallum explains, "and you have a virtual camera you can actually move around. It helps George plan out a shot in real time."

Above left and right: Two shots from the deleted scene 71, in which Senators discourage Padmé from talking to the Jedi of their petition; (left) Chi Eekway (Katie Lucas), Padmé (Portman), Mon Mothma (Genevieve O'Reilly); (right) C-3PO (Daniels), Giddean Danu (Chris Kirby), Bana Breemu (Bai Ling), Fang Zar (Warren Owens). Top right: The animatics department.

Dan Gregoire was born in Winelander, Wisconsin, and grew up in Minnesota. Throughout his schooling, he benefited from an interest in art that was well served by good art programs and teachers. Like Church, Gregoire was consumed by planes and flying them. The real sea change occurred when his college girlfriend ended their relationship. "If she hadn't broken up with me and left me just completely stranded mentally," Gregoire says, "I'd have never dropped aviation and dedicated the amount of time I did to the computer."

The head of his college's technology education department was William (Bill) H. Brown. Gregoire became close with Brown and, after learning many of the newer software programs of the early 1990s (Illustrator, Photoshop, and others), began instructing Brown's summer classes. "Teaching taught me that I really don't know anything until I try and teach it to somebody else. That made me really learn what I was doing." It also made him the ideal supervisor. Not long afterward, Gregoire worked with David Dozoretz on *Titan A.E.* (2000). Dozoretz had worked on Episode I; when he needed help on Episode II, he called in Gregoire, who had recently finished work on *Moulin Rouge* at Fox Studios, Australia.

In many ways, a visit to the animatics department is like a visit to a virtual set—actually, several virtual sets, as each of the artists is working on a different locale. Although there are specialists within the group, "at this point," Gregoire says, "everybody's expected to do some modeling, texturing, and setup, as well as actually animating and compositing their own shots"—while he keeps busy doing everything from working on a veranda shot and updating the shot-tracking database to "playing IT support for broken or crashing desktops." A quick partial survey reveals who is working on what . . .

Chris Edwards has already completed six thousand frames of animation. "Recently, George's been coming upstairs and for the first time has been hands-on with us," Edwards says. "He sits next to me at my desk so he can stage scenes with Artoo in the Federation cruiser hangar. George has me animate all the characters, placing the cameras as he gets ideas, and then we shoot coverage as you would live action from different angles. He's been experimenting quite a bit. He called up [Francis Ford] Coppola and said, 'I'm shooting my film digitally in the computer—and it goes really fast!' "

Greg Rizzi is working on the opening space battle (or "OSB"). Joshua Wassung is adding Coruscant to the background of one scene, filling in empty spots that are sometimes created in editorial when shots are rotated or minimized. Eric Carney is establishing tracking—essential for the digital cameras—while Nathan Frigard is creating computer models, with complex skeletal rigs designed to work easily with minimal computer memory.

Before getting a job here by responding to a blind listing on the Internet, senior animatics artist Brad Alexander was in the air force for four years loading armaments onto military attack aircraft. When he had the opportunity to show his demo reel to Lucasfilm prior to Episode II, "I ended up staying awake for around five days straight and drank a good ten gallons of coffee, preparing my portfolio and demo reel." In addition to working on the OSB, Alexander is touching up a scene in which Yoda and Obi-Wan watch a hologram, adding animations to computer screens.

Senior animatics artist Euisung Lee (*Titan A.E.; Moulin Rouge*) has also

been concentrating for about six months on the OSB. According to Lee, Lucas has now designated the opening shot as being one minute long, during which he wants Anakin and Obi-Wan to fly in perfect harmony to express their friendship.

To help the department create the OSB's flying sequences, and those throughout the film, Scott Benza has been giving the animatics department flying lessons. ILM's lead animator for *Pearl Harbor* (2001) and responsible for much of that film's aerial action, Benza's presence here is in part the solution to a recent problem.

"There were things George was waiting for that he wasn't getting, and he didn't understand why," Gregoire explains. "I think that perhaps my communication with George wasn't as clear as it could've been in terms of the amount of work he was asking us to do, which meant pulling people off of things to do other things that he wanted immediately. Meanwhile, Rick was going to be paying for a ton of ILM artists who were being specifically hired to do the space battle at the beginning of the year. But if we weren't done with the space battle, George wasn't going to turn it over. We were scheduled to finish it by the end of the year, but it wasn't going to happen.

"So I got on the phone one day with Rick, and he said, 'You've got to get the space battle done by the time we go on vacation or we're in real trouble. George doesn't understand—he's not seeing the shots—what is going on?!' "

"Afterward, I went downstairs to editorial to talk to George and said, 'I just got off the phone with Rick and I need to know what the frustration level is down here. Because he's telling me I have to get the space battle done by the end of the year, which means I can't get to all this other stuff—I just can't do it.' So then we talked about it. George talked. Ben talked. And they said okay; they understood. Shortly after that, things started rolling. He started seeing more stuff. I was going to editorial more often—communication improved. That's also when George started coming up on a daily basis,

---

Top, from left: Senior animatic artist Brad Alexander, and animatic artists Dorian Bustamante, Nick Markel, Hiroshi Mori, Greg Rizzi, Joshua Wassung. Above: Lucas and Knoll, and Dan Gregoire and Lucas.

which helped tremendously. He started heading off problems at the pass, and saw we were working. He said, 'I want to teach you how to fly.' "

THURSDAY, DECEMBER 4, 2003

ILM: Because ILM is still ramping up, dailies take place in a small viewing room within the UJ Building, whose acronym stems from its former existence as a factory where Unknown Jerome's Cookies were made. Following its conversion to an ILM facility, the space became a stage known as Turbo Bay, where parts of *Star Trek II: The Wrath of Khan* (1982), *Congo* (1995), and *Men in Black,* among many other films, were shot.

The assembled—Lucas, McCallum, Knoll, Coleman, Church, Tiemens, David, lead animators, and a few others—are not here to watch footage of what was shot on the set—or what used to be called dailies. Instead, every Tuesday and Thursday morning at eight thirty, they're here to review visual effects work, which could be anything from finals and animation to

digital doubles and cloth sims. On an approximately four-by-six-foot screen, a CG model turnaround of a Jedi starfighter, with burnished-steel parts, is examined. "I like that," Lucas says.

Knoll has a question about digital statues: they could make one and use it twice in different locations. But Lucas would prefer to have them custom-made.

"Nice try," McCallum says.

"Well, I'm trying to save you money," Knoll explains.

"But this is art," Lucas says in mock shock. "Art!"

"The idea for Episode II was to make it for ten percent less than Episode I," McCallum says. "And we did. The next challenge was to shoot Episode III for exactly what we shot Episode I for, and we did—even though, between Episode I and Episode III, there was virtually twenty-four percent inflation. So we're happy with our achievement in Sydney. Everybody worked hard and nobody got greedy. Ultimately, it cost $59

million to shoot, and it will cost $55 to $60 million for the effects, so around $115 million total."

Following Episode III dailies, Lucas, McCallum, and postproduction supervisor Mike Blanchard walk across the parking lot from UJ to C Theatre, where, for the next few months, Lucas's first feature film *THX 1138* (1971) and his *Star Wars Trilogy* will be reviewed pending their release on DVD. Lucas needs to sign off on their restoration processes and enhancements, which he can do only while watching them on C Theatre's large screen.

The lights go down and scenes from the 1977 *Star Wars* are projected. In the detention block shootout aboard the Death Star, a corridor has been elongated and the color corrected. "I've always seen it as this way," Lucas says.

Return of the Jedi's celebration scene on Coruscant has also been extended so that the rebuilt Jedi Temple is now visible in the background. Lucas requests more and brighter lights on the buildings. For the shot in which

Top right: Animatics of the OSB by Alexander. Top left: FGQ.050 (General's quarters, October 13), Alexander combines animatics with plates shot in Sydney. Above: R2-D2 in the Separatist cruiser (visual script); a Jaeger illustration of hangar bay details and refueling crane (middle left, October 23); Eric Carney's animatics for FHR.046 (middle, November 17), ILM's finishing touches (middle right).

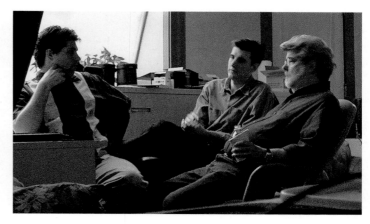

Luke Skywalker sees his father appear as a spirit in the company of Yoda and Obi-Wan, Hayden Christensen has been inserted in place of Sebastian Shaw. Following a brief discussion, Lucas confirms that he does not want to age Christensen, explaining that Anakin has reverted to who he was before he went over to the dark side.

After a pause, Lucas jokes, "What if, behind Yoda, we add . . . Qui-Gon!"

"Oh my God," says Rick.

In order to check color timing, the first two reels of *THX 1138* are then projected. Lucas is happy with the results, and occasionally remarks on his 1971 work: "I loved working with Bobby [Robert Duvall] . . . The cameramen were documentary guys who had never done a feature before . . . Look at these grays!" He mentions how the film was shot almost entirely on location for less than a million dollars with a twenty-five-person crew, and adds, "People have forgotten where I came from."

MONDAY, DECEMBER 8, 2003

SR: Lucas walks upstairs to the animatics department with his usual lunch—a soft drink and a sandwich in a brown to-go box from the kitchen downstairs—which he'll eat while working.

After meeting with Edwards and Wassung, he talks with Gregoire and Alexander about the symmetry involved in the opening space battle. "They're two sets of shots," the director explains, "with the second shot introducing another ship flying in the opposite direction, which the camera follows."

Through a window in the attic, sunlit trees can be seen on a hill, over which turkey vultures circle. Inside, the steady hum of hard drives permeates the long room. Lucas returns to Edwards (*Dinosaur*, 2000; *Treasure Planet*, 2002), whose three-minute film about vegetables battling among themselves for control of a refrigerator first garnered attention from Disney. Like most of the animartists, he has a two-computer setup. Lucas asks him to add a door to the cruiser hangar, so Edwards calls up menus and submenus, rapidly clicking through dozens of virtual windows.

"I have so much respect for Dan and all the animatic crew," McCallum says. "They work under such enormous pressure because they have to make real what George dreams up every day. And often we're talking about forty or fifty shots a day, which means two hundred or two hundred fifty shots a

week, of which only about ten or fifteen will actually be used. But they have to make the shots in order for him to be able to pick them. So they're working ninety- to one-hundred-hour weeks for the whole three years. Often they spend nights. They've brought up their own tents to sleep in. They have alarm clocks so they can be woken up at three o'clock in the morning, after a shot's been rendered by the computer, so they can start rendering another shot. They are true filmmakers, in the virtual sense."

Left: ILM art director Aaron McBride's illustration of the Grievous bodyguards' cloak fastener (November 12). Insets: Hard-surface modeling by Simon Cheung (top), while Moon Kang built their cloaks (middle). Viewpaint by Elbert Yen (bottom). Top left: Gregoire in the animatics department, along with (top right) Carney, Edwards, and Lucas, who would regularly spend two to three hours nearly every afternoon directing the animartists. Right, top: the animatics group, and (below) examples of their animatics. Far right: Wassung and Edwards.

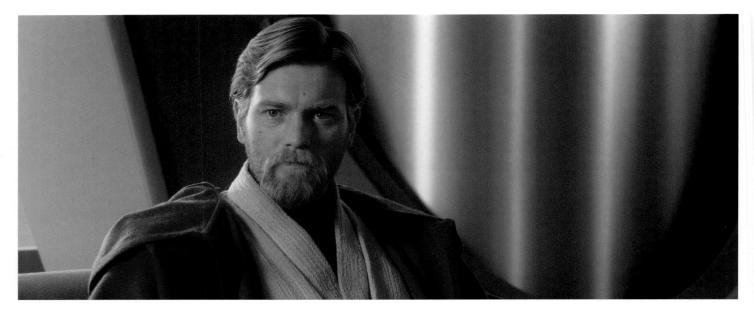

THURSDAY, DECEMBER 11, 2003

ILM: At UJ's dailies, a shot of Obi-Wan sitting, in which the set has been extended over a small bit of bluescreen, is the first visual effects shot final to be finalized by Lucas—and there's small but enthusiastic applause. Only about 1,999 to go.

Lucas and a few of the others are here despite low-grade winter colds. As he occasionally coughs, George makes many adjustments to a shot in which a gunship carries Yoda, Mace, and Obi-Wan through Coruscant airspace. "This lane needs more traffic; the gunship should be coming out of one lane, then merging with another." He pans up, zooms out, and requests other changes. He mentions that he'll soon be ready to hand over more scenes.

"Anything you're ready to turn over, turn over," Coleman says.

On the way to C Theatre for more *Star Wars* and *THX 1138* work, the group passes a flyer announcing a screening of *Howard the Duck* (1986) at ILM, and Lucas comments, "That's how wacky *they* are!"

The Rain People. The two have of course gone on to work together on several projects, including the founding of American Zoetrope, *THX 1138*, *American Graffiti*, *Captain EO* (1986), and *Tucker: The Man and His Dream* (1988).

Today the two sit down with Euisung Lee so the former USC student can show the former UCLA student his virtual directing techniques: "I describe a picture," Lucas starts, "the art department draws it; animatics builds a three-D world . . ."

"So [Lee] translates it," Coppola says, putting his hand on Lucas's shoulder.

"I shoot it like a movie," George says, "then I send it to ILM."

"Do you have to have a hefty computer?"

"Just a desktop PC," Gregoire answers.

"Are you changing the script much, or is it holding up pretty well?" Coppola asks.

"It's holding up."

TUESDAY, DECEMBER 16, 2003

SR: When Lucas arrives in the animatics department, he is accompanied by Francis Ford Coppola. Dressed in a gray suit, Lucas's old friend, former mentor, and fêted director has come over to see how George is directing the film in the computer.

Lucas and Coppola first met at Warner Bros., where Coppola was working on *Finian's Rainbow* (1968). They recognized a kindred spirit in each other, and, shortly afterward, Lucas became Coppola's assistant on

Friday, December 19: The following scenes have been turned over to ILM:
Sc. 1–5: OSB (opening space battle)

Top left: On December 11, Obi-Wan (McGregor) sitting in the Jedi Council chamber is the first Episode III shot finalized. Above left: In ILM's C Theatre, Lucas reviews early animatics of Kashyyyk. After Yoda is attacked (top right) and then tracked by clone troopers (above right), Euisung Lee creates a shot in which a Wookiee emerges from the water à la Martin Sheen in Apocalypse Now *(top middle). Scene 56 from the visual script (right) in which Yoda, Mace, and Obi-Wan discuss Anakin will be cut from the film as of early March 2004.*

Episode III

000065
kvl055 - v01
12-16-03
Artist: Euisung Lee

Episode III

0259
kib030 - v01
Artist: Eric Carney

"I've never been up here before, in this attic," Coppola notes, looking around. "You're doing what you like to do most—having fun."

"I'm making movies," Lucas says. "Some people do storyboards and intellectualize it—I prefer to do it this way." He adds that Robert Rodriguez is doing something similar, and that Spielberg worked in like manner on *A.I.* "You set up your camera, your actors, the action, and then you shoot coverage. Think of it as a disposable camera—you only get one shot. Then I go in with the editor and we cut it together like a regular movie."

When Lucas has to leave the room for a moment, Coppola jokes about kidnapping the entire department so he can use them on his film *Megalopolis*. Lucas returns and, sitting down, says, "I just want to tell a story and make it work."

As they talk, Lucas is also developing a Kashyyyk sequence in which Wookiees ambush clone troopers. "This can be our *Apocalypse Now* shot," he decides suddenly. "Put the camera down on the water."

After a few adjustments, Lee has a Wookiee emerging from the water as Martin Sheen does in Coppola's 1979 film.

"Will you accept this as an homage?" George asks, and Francis seems pleased.

"Are you pretty much on schedule?"

"Well, we're running a little bit behind."

As they go downstairs to view material in editorial, Coppola jokes about the word *pre-visualization*.

"How can it be *pre*?" he asks. "What came before?"

TUESDAY, JANUARY 6, 2004

SR: Tiemens shows Lucas an impressive cyclorama of Padmé's funeral on Naboo. George requests more people, saying it should look like "the Kennedy funeral."

He then goes down the hall to the animatics department, where he sits with Barry Howell, who made his career choice after seeing *Jurassic Park* (1993). "I decided right then and there to focus my attention on CG." He's working on a sequence where Obi-Wan sneaks onto Padmé's ship. The way the shot has been locked down, the engine of the ship is preventing the camera from seeing Obi-Wan. So Lucas asks Howell to move the engine forward and cut off as necessary till the shot works. "When in doubt, cut it out," he says. "You can redesign the ship for the shot—that's the great thing about digital."

Talk turns toward the Mars polar landing, so Lucas and the artists gather round a monitor to look at the first color panoramic photograph of the red planet.

THURSDAY, JANUARY 8, 2004

ILM: Episode III dailies have moved from UJ to C Theatre. While waiting for Lucas's arrival, everyone is quiet, whispering, seated in plush red chairs beneath a scalloped ceiling. The change in venues is due both to the importance of seeing the film as it will eventually appear in movie houses and to the increase in the number of attendees, which from now till the end of production will number in the dozens. Today is also the official turnover of the OSB.

When Lucas arrives, he sits next to Knoll in the second row, with Coleman on his other side. McCallum sits in the first row with Kathryn Ramos and Denise Ream.

Thursday, January 8: The following sequences have been turned over to ILM:
Sc. 59: CCO-1 (Coruscant Chancellor's office)
Sc. 64-65: CJG (Coruscant Jedi gunship)
Sc. 70: CJC2 (Coruscant Jedi Council)

"Our first C Theatre screening," Lucas says.

Editors Burtt (who became a grandfather yesterday) and Barton are also here, exceptionally, as are regular attendees David, Church, Tiemens, and Gregoire. Lucas seems excited: "This is the first thing I've actually seen on the big screen!" he says. "I'm turning over fifty-two scenes to animatics."

"Good. Never let them rest," Knoll says.

"Well, as they go, so go you," Lucas cautions. "We're starting to kick this stuff out."

Above: The "waterfall" animatics of Euisung Lee, as directed by Lucas. Top right: a comic by Episode II concept artist Jay Shuster humorously describes the "history" of animatics. Middle right: Frank Oz first performed the puppetry of Yoda on Monday, August 6, 1979, Shoot Day 108 of The Empire Strikes Back. *A quarter of a century later, he continues to voice the venerable Jedi. Right: "Space battle laser scale and look chart" by Alex Jaeger and OSB painting by Tiemens (inset).*

The lights go down, and, as the familiar music begins with the opening crawl, the energy level in the cinema increases. Images fly by, all CG except for Christensen and McGregor in their cockpits. Many of the shots have new dialogue, with placeholder performances recorded by Burtt. The fourth draft's opening line, "Flying is for droids," has been moved to a minute or more into the action, as much of the script has been reorganized and rewritten. A new theme illustrates how Anakin relies heavily on droids and computers to target the enemy (the opposite of his son, who will use the Force).

After they watch the sequence once, which ends with Obi-Wan crash-landing into the cruiser hangar, the assembled do a second run-through, with explanations, questions, and repeated viewings of particular shots. This routine will become the norm for each turnover from editorial to ILM.

"Our biggest challenge here is readability," Lucas says as they re-view the opening sequence, which feature a potentially confusing array of craft and action. "It may be that some of these shots are a little fast."

In one, he feels a Jedi starfighter is spewing too much blue exhaust, which could prevent people from seeing the other craft. As the starfighters fly between two enormous capital ships, Knoll suggests that it might be nice if they were firing on each other, but Lucas says, "Well, that's okay, except they're on the same side," and laughs. "We just have to make sure the triangles [Republic ships] are attacking the circles [Separatist ships]."

When the missiles carrying the buzz droids arrive on screen, Knoll notes, "We never see where those missiles come from. Is that okay?"

"Yeah, we cut that out. We decided we don't need to know."

When Anakin's starfighter crushes one of the buzz droids against the windscreen of Obi-Wan's cockpit, Lucas says, "The idea is: dead mosquito on window."

"Looking in with a sort of forlorn expression," Knoll adds.

SATURDAY, JANUARY 10–SUNDAY, JANUARY 11, 2004
Although the March pickups have been delayed, animation forges ahead–helped by the fact that Lucas and Frank Oz are able to sync up their schedules so that Lucas is able to tape the latter as Yoda.

"When we got into this little hovel of a recording place," Coleman remembers, "Frank slid right into Yoda, no problem. They would record it ten times with different intonations, and George would say, 'I like that one and I like that one.' Matt [Wood, sound supervisor] would take a minute, and then you could watch the movie with the lines cut right in. So George was able to make sure the reading worked for the length of the shot and for any body or hand actions.

"I was afraid Frank wouldn't be able to sustain his voice hour after hour after hour. He must have drunk two gallons of water, but he kept going for five hours."

MONDAY, JANUARY 12, 2004

SR: Lucas arrives in the animatics department with his lunch, prepared to spend his usual three or more hours. At Wassung's station, he watches an early version of the death of Jedi Aayla Secura. Like fellow animatics artist Nick Markel, Joshua Wassung first met Gregoire at SIGGRAPH, the annual computer graphics industry conference. "Before I left, I was able to give Dan a copy of my work," he recalls, "One week later I got a letter asking me to fly out for an interview. Next thing I knew I was moving cross-country two days after graduating. It was pretty surreal."

After watching Secura in silence, Lucas thinks for a few moments and then decides to reorganize her scene. "We need to start with her and the clones walking through Felucia," he says.

"Staggered column?" asks Gregoire, who's been watching.

"Well, Vietnam," Lucas responds. "She'll send the clones into the bush . . ."

Wassung does so.

"Let them walk for about three seconds, then she stops–"

"And they fan?" he asks.

"All but these three guys," Lucas specifies. "That's when one of the clones gets the call from Sidious." The new footage then merges with the early version: Secura is shot in the back and the camera pulls back as the clones continually fire upon her corpse.

March will be the time when we'll examine what works, what doesn't work, and what we could do better. Of course, we do this soul searching throughout production–right up through 2005–but this is probably the biggest hit we'll take, and it will likely result in our most complicated pickups."

TUESDAY, JANUARY 20, 2004

SR: More visitors have been touring the animatics department. The director of *Akira* (1988), Katsuhiro Otomo, who's finishing up the sound mix of his latest film at Skywalker Sound, came to visit, as did Lucas's old friend and filmmaker Matthew Robbins.

This afternoon, after spending some time with animatics artist Carney, Lucas takes a seat next to Euisung Lee and asks him to slow down Obi-Wan's action as he swings from one pipe to another: "You have to show what's going to happen to him before it happens, otherwise people are confused–and they stop following the action for fifteen seconds–and that can be deadly."

He then reorganizes the layout of the Mustafar landing platform. "The most important thing is to make the landings look good. Then once we get down there, the geography just has to be mostly right," Lucas says, adding, "Continuity is for wimps."

This phrase will be heard often during the next sixteen months, and is born from the fact that *Revenge* will ultimately be able to show only about two dozen landscapes–which need to be as striking as possible.

"You just don't get the camera way back very often," George points out. "Everything else is talking heads against backgrounds. So every wide shot is a signature shot."

TUESDAY, JANUARY 27, 2004

ILM: In C Theatre, as Knoll takes a seat, he receives congratulations for his Oscar nomination (see page 171), as does Jill Brooks, who was the visual effects producer. "It's nice to wake up to that," Knoll says.

The rest of dailies are marked by the delicate balance between the need to get things done quickly and the need to make things work. After Lucas and McCallum take a seat, a CG model of the Imperial shuttle is shown. "Is this a final?" Lucas asks, with some hesitation. "It looks like a final . . ."

THURSDAY, JANUARY 15, 2004

ILM: While Hayden Christensen and Nick Gillard are being motion-captured on ILM's Windward Stage, just across the road in C Theatre, Lucas is saying, "I'm happy to announce that I've cut out one of the completed shots."

This announcement is met by laughter, as nearly everyone here is well acquainted with Lucas's working techniques. They know that, until the film is in theaters, he can and will change it. Nevertheless, the first rough cut is 75 percent complete.

"The end of January is when we'll really start tweaking things and thinking about new scenes to add," McCallum explains. "February and early

January 15: ILM receives 13 nominations from the Visual Effects Society for the 2003 Visual Effects Awards, for its work on: *Pirates of the Caribbean: The Curse of the Black Pearl; The Hulk; Master and Commander: The Far Side of the World; Peter Pan;* and *Terminator 3: Rise of the Machines*. Lucas will receive a Lifetime Achievement Award at the show, which will be held at the Hollywood Palladium on February 18.

January 15-22: The following sequences have been turned over to ILM:
Sc. 6: FCS (FedCruiser Shaak Ti)
Sc. 15: FEH (FedCruiser Elevator Hallway)
Sc. 72: CCL (Coruscant clone landing platform)
Sc. 94: CCS (Coruscant Chancellor's office Sith)
Sc. 121: KVL (Kashyyyk village lake)
Sc. 122: KYE (Kashyyyk Yoda escape pod)

"Move on to the next one," McCallum urges, but too late. A conversation begins about how the shuttle door opens.

In the shot of Anakin waking up after his nightmare, Lucas asks that his mechanical hand catch the sunlight filtering into the room and reflect it. He also decides to change the position of the sun in the background. "Oh no . . . ," McCallum moans.

The producer's reactions come on the heels of a slew of changes made last week, which included new costume designs for Neimoidians; the combining of the planets Cato Neimoidia and Saleucami (bridge world); and the reinstatement of the lemur creatures, who now live on Mygeeto.

Of course, McCallum is well aware of the positive side of Lucas's creativity. "It's the thing about him that has always fascinated me," he explains. "We basically take the same road back and forth to work. I drive home at the end of a hard day, and he drives home. And he comes back to work and I come back—but the stuff that happens to him from the time he leaves and returns is just incredible. In the morning, he'll start off a conversation, 'What if we did this?' Every day, there's a new idea coming in. And it's just a fantastic way to work. It's mind-boggling."

THURSDAY, JANUARY 29, 2004

ILM: Lucas takes a look at CG clone troopers and changes their backpack gear so it's more individualized and jerry-rigged. "The other thing is, the armor on their butts should be scraped," he says.

"If you need any reference, just tell me," McCallum offers.

Following the turnover of the OSB, it's up to the newly formed layout

---

Wednesday, January 28: *The Art of Star Wars*, a new major museum exhibition featuring props, costumes, models, and artwork from Episodes I and II, as well as artifacts from Episodes IV through VI, debuts in Kyoto. The exhibit will travel through Japan until September.

January 30-February 9: The following sequences have been turned over to ILM:
Sc. 7-37: Miscellaneous FedCruiser
Sc. 66: CPV-1 (Coruscant Padmé veranda)
Sc. 67: CGO (Coruscant Galaxies Opera House)

---

department to block out the shots based on the animatics. Headed by Brian Cantwell, this group is the result of a postmortem on Episode II, whose attendees recommended better preparation for the CG work so that questions about choreography and geography could be worked out sooner in the process, saving time and money.

Naturally, the layout department has started with the first shot of the OSB, which features an enormous Republic assault ship. The two Jedi starfighters fly its length and then plunge off its edge, as if it were a waterfall—hence the name of this sequence, "the waterfall shot"—then, as the camera follows them over the edge, the rest of the gigantic battle is revealed far below. After he makes a few adjustments, Lucas approves the layout, and work on the next stages can begin.

Afterward, more of the *Star Wars Trilogy* is examined for the upcoming DVD release. "I can't cope with this," Lucas jokes. "I have too many movies. It's my whole life flashing before me."

THURSDAY, FEBRUARY 5, 2004

ILM: Lucas is about 85 percent done with the rough cut. Outside C Theatre, he remarks to Coleman, "You realize this is an animated movie." Coleman replies that he's already calculated that eighty to eighty-five minutes of *Revenge of the Sith* will be animated, which is the average length of a Disney feature. Inside C Theatre, Lucas finals the first Yoda shot. He then reviews the opera scenes that have just been turned over.

"I think this part of the city should be slightly more Las Vegas–like," he says. For a shot of people walking up the opera house steps, he asks that evening wear be designed. Vehicles will be pulling up, so he requests that space-age limos be created. This expanded scene, he adds, will be part of the pickups.

The interior of the opera, as Lucas describes it, is a big ball of liquid in which there are aliens swimming around with "something" attached to them.

"The Mon Calamari Dancers," McCallum says.

"That's it!" Lucas says, "that's what we'll call them." He also suggests adding "some ETs in the opera seats, throwing popcorn."

January 30-February 9: The following sequences have been turned over to ILM:
Sc. 7-37: Miscellaneous FedCruiser
Sc. 66: CPV-1 (Coruscant Padmé veranda)
Sc. 67: CGO (Coruscant Galaxies Opera House)

Top left: Animatics by Joshua Wassung depict Jedi Master Aayla Secura on Felucia just before she is shot down by her former soldiers. Above left, strip: Lucas directs Euisung Lee's animatics, while Fay David, J.W. Rinzler, and Erik Tiemens look on. Top right: The "inner mechanical layers" of Anakin's arm by Aaron McBride (November 3, 2003). Above: Clone commander variations designed for different theaters of war by Alex Jaeger.

LSJ

Sang Jun Lee
SW3 2. 24. 04
opera female costume #9

TUESDAY, FEBRUARY 10, 2004

ILM: Looking at the animatic of Count Dooku jumping from a balcony to confront the Jedi, Lucas asks for "a more elegant flip. This one's not very Jedi."

The two battle droids accompanying the Count fire, miss and are cut down by Obi-Wan. "You really want these guys?" Coleman asks. "They can't hit the side of a barn!"

"That's what's so funny about them," Lucas says, but then concedes, "We can make them anything you guys like. We'll make them the big droids."

More animatics reveal some changes to the Dooku-Jedi fight: Now the Count levitates Obi-Wan into the air, strangling him with the Force; he then kicks Anakin and flings Obi-Wan across the room. These shots, and some of the old, are marked with an R for "reshoot" (although in most cases it's a "new" shoot or a pickup).

In the last shot, Anakin beheads Dooku, and the latter's head rolls away. "Now, talk to me about this head," McCallum turns to Lucas.

"What kind of rating are we going for?" Coleman asks.

"This is the boys upstairs [in the animatics department] enjoying themselves," Lucas says. "We're somewhere between an extremely hard PG and a PG-13."

"How about a PG-18?" Rick suggests.

"Wait till you get to the end," George counters. "This is nothing."

THURSDAY, FEBRUARY 12, 2004

ILM: As of today, a whiteboard in the UJ building ticks off the numbers:

EPISODE III SHOT STATUS

Total # of shots: 2,000

Finals: 46

Final omits: 1

Shots turned over: 1,031

Shots left to go: 1,954

Finals needed per week: 32

Weeks to go: 59

The "Total #" refers to the number of shots with visual effects in them, which is nearly every shot in the film. "Finals" are those shots deemed complete by Lucas, after reviewing them at dailies. "Final omits" refers to finals that have been dropped because of the film being recut. "Shots turned over" refers to those sent from editorial to ILM.

SKIN DEEP

On January 27, 2004, the Academy of Motion Picture Arts and Sciences will be officially recognizing one of the tools created by ILM: subsurface scattering rendering. On February 14, Christophe Hery will represent ILM in receiving a special certificate of merit from the academy as part of the seventy-sixth annual Academy Awards. "The idea is to simulate the effect of translucency and depict how light penetrates inside the skin and scatters around the different tissues, then comes out at different points," Hery explains. "It opens the door to all different kinds of materials in computer graphics — especially skin. The technique was used on Episode II and will be used more heavily in Episode III.

In addition, several ILM and Skywalker Sound projects have been nominated for Oscars, including *Pirates of the Caribbean: The Curse of the Black Pearl* (John Knoll and Hal Hickel) and *Master and Commander: The Far Side of the World* (Stefen Fangmeier) for Best Visual Effects. *Finding Nemo* (Gary Rydstrom and Michael Silvers) was nominated for Best Sound Editing.

"This is the fun part," Lucas says. "Though I'm struggling to get through the final drama of making the film work, twice a week, I get in ten to twenty shots–which I've been waiting years for. So that's exciting; that's fun. It's like getting stuff in the mail when you were a kid–'Oh, look! I got the Master Spy Ring.' I'm getting these little gifts. Sometimes they're disappointing and you have to send them back to be redone–and sometimes they're fantastic. Then I cut the shots in, so I get two hits: one is when I see it on the big screen, and two is when I actually see it work and see a scene fall together."

TUESDAY, FEBRUARY 17, 2004

SR: Back in the art department, concept artist Sang Jun Lee has returned to work on Episode III, designing costumes for the grandiose opera staircase scene. In his critique of Jun's first sketches, Lucas asks for "an array of things, so they look like they're from different cultures . . . sexier, formal, more glamorous."

During his tour of duty in animatics, he sits with Euisung Lee. It's pouring rain outside. Tiemens sketches while observing. Church and Gregoire keep watch, also sketching, as Lucas directs while eating lunch. All three are here in case Lucas needs them, and to keep track of changes made to the movie. "It's Kamino weather today," Tiemens remarks.

Lucas consecrates about forty-five minutes of his time to a complicated shot. A flying tank must be seen to descend into an Utapau sinkhole and turn toward the camera as it fires two shots, which the camera quickly follows into the hangar, where one gun is destroyed; the camera then drops down to pick up more choreographed combat action.

"Try to make it a nice, consistent, smooth pan," he tells Lee.

On a pop-up screen, Lee complies by plotting the camera's trajectory.

"That'll be cool," Tiemens remarks.

Gregoire mentions that tomorrow Lucas will receive the Lifetime Achievement Award from the Visual Effects Society, which will be handed to him by James Cameron.

000110　　　　　utc730 - v02　　Artist: **Dorian Bustamante**
07-16-04

Tuesday, February 10: Lucasfilm and Twentieth Century Fox announce a September release for the *Star Wars Trilogy* on DVD.

Left: Opera costume illustrations and sketches by concept artist Sang Jun Lee for Lucas's new staircase scene. Above: One of the intricately choreographed animatic frames of UTC.730 (Utapau Tenth-Level control center) by Bustamante.

SBT.790

000107

sbt790 - v02
11-24-03

Artist: Dorian Bustamante

Direction of falling / rolling peices

WEDNESDAY, FEBRUARY 18, 2004

ILM: In C Theatre, Lucas explains that a deceptively simple shot of Padmé sleeping is a combination: blowup, zoom, and rotate. "The art of editing is also how you manipulate images to get the best performances out of the actors," he says. "And what we've done is move that to another level, where we can actually move the characters around within the frame and change what's going on, rather than just cutting from one frame to another."

"George told me that he likes to do what he calls three-dimensional editing," editor Barton explains. "Whereas editors are used to working in a linear mind-set, he'll want to work not only in terms of piecing one shot next to another–but within each frame, he'll be editing it, resizing things, and moving the camera around within the frame. That's something new to me. That's something I'll have to wrap my head around."

Roger Barton grew up in southern California and Oregon. "My dad told me that you have to fight and struggle to get what you want out of life," he notes. After attending Long Beach State, he broke into editing on a documentary called *The Wild West*, which was being cut on a brand-new Avid. The night before his interview, Barton bought a book about nonlinear editing and learned just enough to convince the producer to hire him. "Later, I worked on what was a very difficult film about a sinking ship you may have heard about," Barton jokes.

"We interviewed about sixty-five editors over a period of four months," McCallum says. "Jamie [Forester, postproduction supervisor] and I flew to Los Angeles six times. I made it very clear to every editor. I said, 'Look. You're going to get your own cut while we're shooting the movie. The rest of the time, you're going to be working for George.' "

"I do believe that what comes around goes around," Barton says, "and karma definitely has something to do with why I'm here. Maybe it was also because George felt like he could control me maybe more than a more established, well-known editor. I'd like to think that it was just a natural fit. I consider myself, now that I'm on the movie, to be the luckiest person alive."

TUESDAY, FEBRUARY 24, 2004

ILM: Outside C Theatre is a courtyard where stands "Java the Hutt": a sheet-metal construct where coffee and pastries can be purchased. Before dailies, people congregate outside this venerable institution, milling about or sitting at the one picnic table. Large potted trees dot the asphalt area, most of which are left over from ILM's work on *Jurassic Park III* (2001). An artificial tree, with blue-green leaves and thick fake vines, is from *Planet of the Apes* (2001). Usually McCallum is the first to arrive, followed a few minutes later by Ramos, Brooks, Lewin, Ream, and others.

ILM executive producer Denise Ream began her visual effects career after being hit by a car while jogging. Temporarily unable to do the more physical work of an on-set production supervisor, she eventually found a niche as the optical coordinator at Boss Film Studios, something that made her grandfather–Linwood Dunn, the inventor of the first mass-produced 16mm optical printer (in 1944: the Acme-Dunn Optical Printer for the U.S. Navy's Central Photographic Laboratory)–quite happy. Hired by ILM in 1993, Ream is responsible, among other things, for working with McCallum to build a team that works together well. "I don't think you can underestimate the chemistry involved," she says.

"I wanted working with ILM to be a happy experience," Rick adds. "And I wanted to have somebody I could totally trust, who would be hands-on and really take care of the people who were working for us. The first minute that both Kathryn and I met Denise, we immediately fell in love with her. She was honest; she was straight; she was smart. And she had no problem whatsoever during the next few weeks telling me when I was wrong."

Lucas arrives, gets his coffee, and everyone moves inside, where others are already seated. First up is the layout stage of the Republic embarkation center. Per a Star Destroyer taking off, he says, "I think you can slow it down even more."

"Good. I was hoping you'd say that," Knoll says, pointing out that these ships are more than a mile long and would take a while to go past camera.

February 23-27: The following sequences have been turned over to ILM:
Sc. 70: CJC-2 (Coruscant Jedi Council—this is not the first turnover of CJC-2; some sequences have been reworked and resubmitted)
Sc. 115-116: CPV-2 (Coruscant Padmé's veranda)
Sc. 144: CHO-1 & 2 (Coruscant Chancellor's holding office)

Left: For SBT.790 (space battle tri-droids), Editor McBride shows the damage to the Federation core ship (January 15). Top: Editor Roger Barton and Lucas at work cutting the movie. Middle: Standing in front of Javva the Hutt are: Tiemens, Coleman, David, ILM producer Jill Brooks, ILM president Chrissie England, Kathryn Ramos, (below) Knoll, Lucas, Brooks, Janet Lewin, and ILM VFX executive producer Denise Ream.

Blast Cleaner Piece

Forklift droid turn 180 so back is front and Arms swiveled around facing opposite direction

Eyes Face from Analysis Droid

Tower Omega Pieces

Clone Tank Peice for undercarriage

Tower Omega Pieces

Above: McBride's droid illustrations. Top left: Scene 48 of Mace Windu at the site of the crash-landing (visual script) would be cut and reworked to take place at "Senate office parking entry" as illustrated by Church. Right page: Digi-matte paintings (top) Kashyyyk beachhead by Max Dennison. Middle, from left: Utapau from space by Simon Wicker; rehab center by Jeremy Cook; view from Padmé's apartment by Christian Haley; ILM digital matte supervisor Jonathan Harb. Right: Senate establishing shot by Yusei Uesugi.

SR: George studies Jun's additional opera costumes. He inserts a slit in a skirt, makes a bust metal, changes one dress to black, and adds silver and diamond beads to a skirt—in general, he makes the garbs sexier. "Tell Trisha," he turns to David, "if none of this works, she can do what she wants, but I think we can keep trying. We really need some designs for aliens. We do have a Greedo and a Greedess."

Tiemens suggests a Mon Calamari creature and Lucas agrees. "Yeah, the family of the entertainers."

"We could put Jar Jar in there with a female Jar Jar," Tiemens adds.

"How about if Jar Jar is with a Kaminoan?" Church suggests.

"That could be a good one. I'll think about that," Lucas says and pauses. "Okay. Jar Jar and a Kaminoan. As he's been cut out of the rest of the film"—a comment that leads him to comment on the rough cut in general. He plans on watching it twice: once with the temp music, once without.

"Music is a really powerful source, and, unless it's really right, it can throw everything else off," Lucas notes. "It can get to be confusing as to why something isn't working: Is it the music or is it the way it's cut?"

March 1-11, 2003: On the (Virtual) Cutting Room Floor II
While the following scenes have been turned over to ILM . . .
Sc. 4: CEL (Coruscant emergency landing platform)
Sc. 57-58: CJB (Coruscant Jedi briefing room)
Sc. 42: FRH (FedCruiser ray shield hallway)

. . . these other scenes have been cut:
Sc. 48: CEL (Mace Windu greets Palpatine and the Jedi right after the crash-landing)
Sc. 56: CYQ (Yoda, Obi-Wan, and Mace discuss the dark side in Yoda's quarters)
Sc. 60: CBO (Bail Organa and fellow Senators speak about the Senate)
Sc. 83: UDC (Obi-Wan chooses his lizard-mount, Boga)
Sc. 121: KVL ("crazy" Yoda and Chewbacca ambush an AT-ST)

After the film has been shortened, inevitably, certain information will have been deleted, so he'll then decide how to reinsert key plot points. Though the pickups have been pushed back to August, because the rough cut is taking longer than expected, Lucas is telling the editorial group to "keep up the faith."

TUESDAY, MARCH 2, 2004
ILM: As soon as Lucas takes a seat, the lights goes down, a shot of Anakin with the Jedi Council is projected, and the subject of the sky is discussed.

"We're just going through a whole thing with the backgrounds," he observes.

"I've heard about these machinations," Knoll says.

"Well, this is the same day as the storm," Lucas continues, pointing out that scenes taking place on the same day on the same planet will be related: A storm that occurs in a later scene can be prefigured in an earlier one. (The result is a lengthy time and weather chart that now stretches around two walls of the art department.)

Next up is the partially complete opening waterfall shot. "It'd be nice if, when the starfighters go into the darkness, we could see the interior lights of their cockpits," George says. He also asks that the speed of the ships in relation to the rotation of the planet be worked out, so that it's clear to the audience how fast things are moving.

"It's going to be an amazing shot," Coleman notes.

TUESDAY, MARCH 9, 2004
ILM: A final is projected of Bail Organa in his office. But the first thing Lucas says is: "As of yesterday, this is a DVD shot [that is, it's been cut]. Right now, it's an everything-must-go sale," he adds, explaining that the rough cut—or what is now being referred to as more of a rough "assembly"—is done, and he's now into two to three weeks of reorganizing.

"The first script I wrote had stories for everybody," Lucas notes per the reorg, "and I cut it down and we had a script. But when we cut it together, there were still problems. Finally, I said, 'Okay, let's be even more hard-nosed here and take out every scene that doesn't

have anything to do with Anakin.' But that causes you to juxtapose certain scenes that you were never contemplating juxtaposing before. And these scenes take on different qualities than before, because the scenes were never meant to be next to each other.

"In one case, there was supposed to be a scene with Padmé and Bail Organa between two Anakin scenes, because we were following her story along with his. And when most of those scenes were cut out, suddenly all sorts of weird things started to happen that weren't intended in the script—but in some cases it actually worked much better.

"What happens then is that some of the themes grab hold of each other and really strengthen themselves in ways that are fascinating. You pull things together and suddenly a theme is drawn out because it's in three consecutive scenes instead of just one. Suddenly one theme is infinitely stronger than it was before, so we'll strengthen that theme because it seems poetic."

Above: Anakin (Christensen) in the Jedi Council recorded in Sydney and the reverse-angle final frame (top). The storm clouds behind Anakin are foreshadowed in earlier scenes and evolve in later ones, thanks to the flexibility of digital cinema.

🏵 8 A Diamond in the Rough

FRIDAY, MARCH 12, 2004

ILM: Work here is advancing on multiple fronts. On ILM's Windward Stage, crew are wrapping up the Jedi starfighter (which had been shipped over from Sydney) shoot, providing OSB insert shots. Technical directors, layout artists, CG model makers, and others now have their hands full.

In UJ, Coleman is conducting animation dailies with his lead animators. He tells them that the lemurs are probably out again and that Lucas has said, half seriously, that Jar Jar might be sent to Alderaan (which is blown to bits in *A New Hope*). As the animators file out of the room, John Knoll comes by, excited. "You wanna see an explosion?! Come with me."

Animators and others rush into another viewing station to watch a spectacular fireball created with new technology by R&D technical troubleshooter Willi Geiger, who, according to Knoll, has made a "valve volume fluid sim that they're feeding particles through."

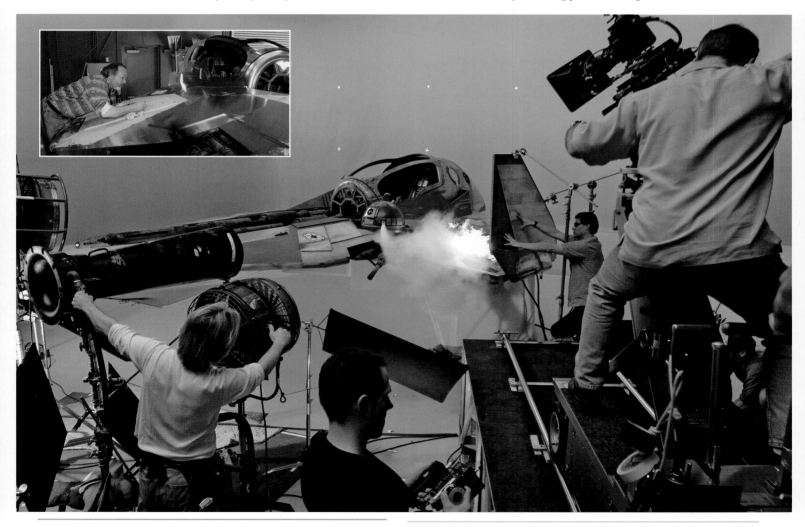

March 29–April 2: The following sequences have been turned over to ILM:
Sc. 94: CCS (Coruscant Chancellor's office Sith–recut with new time of day)
Sc. 78-82: UJA (Utapau Jedi arrival)
Sc. 82A: KJB (Kashyyyk Jedi battle)
Sc. 90A: CJW (Coruscant Jedi war room)
Sc. 153-154: CYE (Coruscant Yoda escape)

Shooting Obi-Wan's starfighter during pickups at ILM are: DP Carl Miller, stage crew Mike Olague and Mark Walas. Knoll supervised these insert shots of boots, cockpit interiors, hands, astromech droids, etc. Inset: To change Obi-Wan's starfighter into Anakin's, model-maker Charlie Bailey helps paint it yellow.

March 15-22, 2004: On the (Virtual) Cutting Room Floor III

While the following scenes have been turned over to ILM . . .

Sc. 49: CSL-1 (Coruscant Senate landing platform)

Sc. 139-140: CLP (Coruscant landing platform Padmé)

Sc. 109: FJB (Felucia Jedi battle)

. . . these scenes are now cut:

Sc. 88-89: CCO-2 (Padmé presents to Palpatine the Senators' petition)

Sc. 6, 7, 8-14, 25, 28, 30, 32, 37-41 (various FedCruiser scenes—Grievous killing

Shaak Ti; Anakin and Obi-Wan using their lightsabers to escape Grievous;

their underwater swim through the generator rooms, with droids in pursuit;

their climb through the vent shaft; many of the R2-D2 hangar gags;

and, following the death of Dooku, many of the Jedi-Palpatine

cliffhangers have been cut)

Left: Burtt's editing work is backed up in a nearby room that is Michael Blanchard's responsibility. "We have four terabytes of storage, because George wants all dailies available from the last two films [principal photography and successive cuts]," Blanchard says. "Avid said it would be impossible to do that, but we did it—and every file is mirrored. George always forces us to come up with a better way of doing things." In addition to his editing duties, Burtt is the sound designer. "I've done something different than ever before," he notes. "I've built a portable sound setup that fits in a suitcase, which enables me to connect to the 5,700 sounds that I've made in the past for Star Wars, which normally reside in the Tech Building library. So far, I've probably made about 150 new sounds, about a tenth of what I'll need, which I test on George. Usually the director of a film doesn't hear these until the last moment, but George hears them as they're created. The final mix will therefore be a performance of sounds that have already been rehearsed."

Above left and right: Sequences cut from the film: FCS.070—The death of Shaak Ti aboard the FedCruiser, as originally scripted and shot in Sydney on August 19, 2003; animatics by Gregory Rizzi, January 15, 2004. FCS.200—Following the murder of Shaak Ti, the Jedi ignite their lightsabers in Sydney; CG droids are added by Nathan Frigard in the animatics department on January 12, 2004. FCS.300—Seeing they're outnumbered, the Jedi use their lightsabers to cut a hole in the floor, and drop to the generator room below; animatics by Euisung Lee, January 9, 2004. FCG.020—The Jedi will extinguish their sabers when they realize they've fallen into a room leaking fuel; animatics by Dorian Bustamante, January 26, 2004. FCG.530—As fuel floods the room, Obi-Wan swims to escape, only to be dragged down by a pursuing super battle droid. McGregor was shot in Sydney on August 14, 2003; animatics by Eric Carney, January 23, 2004.

Right: Responding to Lucas's new scene in the Jedi Temple, Church creates a war room concept on February 9, 2004.

SR: "We cut out another ten minutes of the opening sequence," Lucas says, while visiting the animatics department. "We're trying to get it down to twenty minutes, if we can, from forty minutes."

Other major changes consist of new scenes. After Palpatine reveals to Anakin that he is a Sith, the Jedi now takes this information to Mace Windu. The latter decides to arrest the Chancellor—but leaves Anakin behind. Alone in the Jedi Council chamber, Anakin thinks about Padmé and how the Sith can prevent death. He decides to intervene, hopping in an airspeeder and arriving just as the Windu-Palpatine fight reaches its climax.

"What I like about what George has done is that he's taken this new scene and injected into it more distrust between Mace and Anakin," Barton says. "George will sometimes come up with an idea and quickly write some lines while sitting in the editing room. Then we'll steal frames from

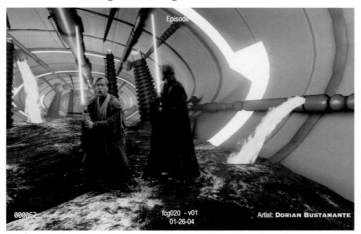

ILM: In C Theatre, Lucas watches reels five and six of *The Empire Strikes Back*, the images flickering across the glasses of the man who made them twenty-four years ago. Though satisfied with the color timing, he mentions that a shot on Bespin will need to be reworked for a future re-release.

SR: In the office next to Barton's, Burtt is editing side by side with Lucas. The setup includes two monitors—one is the Avid, one displays the files—and an HD screen with a 5.1 surround sound system. On the walls are a poster for *El Capitan Blood*, with Errol Flynn and Olivia de Havilland, and Fellini's *La Douceur de Vivre* (*La Dolce Vita*), along with images from reels one through seven. As Ben prepares a sequence for his review, George reads the paper.

"As we've made this trio of films, this process of making things up as we go along has increased," Burtt says. "I think it's satisfying for George to take the characters and the tools, and experiment with them, because he's

different images in the movie and record the dialogue, just so he can get a sense of it.

"I have to admit that sometimes it takes me a couple minutes to understand where George is going with something. He'll have me join pieces of completely different scenes together—but once he's in that zone, I don't want to interrupt. He just wants to put together those images and see if they'll work. Of all the movies I've worked on—and some have been big visual effects movies—they just don't come close to the amount of reinvention that goes on in postproduction here."

developed it all, over many, many years. The way George works—where he shoots and then reshoots—is a real luxury. Historically, only Charlie Chaplin has had this kind of control.

"So I come in every day to help George figure out what he wants. Quite often we're in here for long stretches making things up, quite literally going along until we get stuck—and then saying, 'Now what could happen?' It's like a series of brainstorming sessions. Sometimes it's like having a bored teenager in the back of the car, and we're changing things just because it's stimulating for him. But George certainly doesn't hold on to material because it's sacred. He's very able to look at something and say, 'It's gotta go,' or, 'Let's try something completely different today.'

"His approach is also very close to how someone would do an animated movie. I call it recomposing the movie. You're free to split apart the visual elements within a shot–the people, the objects, the setting–and rearrange them. We put in a shoulder, raise an arm, take out a blink. This is the process we do every day. There isn't a shot or a scene or a moment that isn't deeply affected by this process, and there isn't a day in the editing room where we don't discover something interesting through that process."

FINALS: 91   SHOTS LEFT: 1,914   WEEKS TO GO: 52 (ONE YEAR LEFT!)

THURSDAY, APRIL 1, 2004

ILM: Yoda crawls through a service tube filled with wires, after his defeat at the hands of the Emperor. In his airspeeder, Bail pulls up far below the tube's opening to rescue the Jedi Master, and Knoll asks, "Why does Bail stop two hundred meters under that opening and make Yoda jump?"

Lucas reflects a moment. "Good point," he says, and changes the shot so Yoda has less distance to drop.

SR: Lucas stops by the animatics department to briefly check on things before leaving on a ten-day vacation. He advises Gregoire to have his team work on the establishing shots. He also predicts that they'll have a first rough cut by May. Gregoire wonders if some shots are taking too long to finish.

"Everything is taking too long," Lucas says, only half jokingly. "From this point on, it's a permanent 911."

TUESDAY, APRIL 13, 2004

SR: In the art department, Knoll, Church, Tiemens, Gregoire, and David prepare for a Mustafar meeting. They need to hear from Lucas exactly what he wants and doesn't want logistically, so that work can begin in earnest on assets both in the animatics department and at ILM. Knoll is particularly concerned because *Revenge of the Sith* has many sequences that require lengthy builds for only a few shots.

"It's a house of cards," Tiemens says, "everything is connected."

"Yeah, I know," Gregoire agrees. "I had to redo an entire sequence last night."

Lucas arrives and Knoll says, "Our goal is to get a working map."

"That's why these entry shots are critical," the director responds. "You have to get all the pictures together or you're going to paint yourself into a corner. The theories don't count anymore."

He then points out that there's a problem with the Mustafar environment, because Anakin and Obi-Wan end up on the wrong side of the lava river at the end of the fight. "We have to figure out where in relation to that river they're standing at all times."

"The time to do that is now," Knoll concurs, noting that they have a year to go, which is not a long time.

"I don't think it's a long time," Lucas says. "Not at all."

"You wouldn't consider a 2006 release, would you?" Knoll asks, almost rhetorically. When Lucas replies in the negative, he adds, "Then we'll have to throw a lot of bodies at it."

"The sooner, the better," Lucas says.

Monday, April 5: Lucasfilm announces that Episode III will be released domestically on Thursday, May 19, 2005, with a "near-simultaneous release around the world."

TUESDAY, APRIL 27, 2004

ILM: With forty-eight weeks to go, and 1,973 visual effects shots to finish, people congregate once again in C Theatre. ILM has started what will be months of shooting miniature models (some of which are actually several yards long or tall), including a Kashyyyk tree, Utapau sinkhole, and the Jedi embarkation center. The majority of these miniatures will be scanned using a process called Zenviro, which creates digital environments out of the models, which in turn enables Lucas to place his camera wherever he wants (for locked-down shots, digi-matte paintings will be used).

Later in the day, Lucas, McCallum, Burtt, and Barton watch the second version of Lucas's rough assembly.

April 12-16:
The following sequences have been turned over to ILM:
Sc. 177: SIS (Space Imperial Star Destroyer)
Sc. 178-79: ACB (Alderaan castle balcony)
Sc. 102: CCC (Coruscant Chancellor clones attack)
Note: The present cut is running, without end credits, at 2 hours 11 minutes 23 seconds.

Top: During a miniature shoot of the opera box at ILM are: Jason Snell, DP Carl Miller, model shop supervisor Brian Gernand (behind Miller), Knoll, and match-mover Josh Livingston. Below at work on the Polis Massa crater miniature is veteran model-maker Lorne Peterson. Right: Carl Miller (center), camera assistant Dennis Rodgers (top in white), grip Mike Olague (front at left) and key grip Tom Cloutier (right) on the ILM Utapau miniature sinkhole set.

WEDNESDAY, APRIL 28, 2004

SR: In a follow-up to the April 13 meeting, today's gathering is designed to forever pin down Mustafar geography. Euisung Lee, Tiemens, and digi-matte artist Yanick Dusseault have collaborated for the last two weeks, with the latter two painting on top of animatics derived from concept paintings to create what they hope are the most cohesive and fantastic landscapes possible. If Lucas finds fault with their shot-by-shot breakdown, however, it's back to the drawing board.

After he arrives and examines the angles and backgrounds, it's clear that George likes the presentation.

"Do we have a plan?" Knoll asks.

"We have a plan," Lucas says.

As they walk down the hall to the animatics department, Lucas informs Gregoire that it's Anakin who now kills Shaak Ti in the Jedi Temple while she's meditating.

"I want Anakin walking in there," he says. "Anakin walks around, he kneels down, and then he stabs her."

TOTAL # OF SHOTS: 2,100   FINALS: 135   FINAL OMITS: 35
SHOTS TURNED OVER: 1,255   SHOTS LEFT TO GO: 1,961
FINALS NEEDED PER WEEK: 40   WEEKS TO GO: 48

TUESDAY, MAY 4, 2004

ILM: In the still chilly morning, people clutch hot coffees in front of Javva the Hutt. Fay David arrives and McCallum suddenly motions everyone to be quiet as the public-address system says, "Congratulations to Fay David on her engagement." She receives many smiles and congratulations, and Lucas gives her a hug.

During dailies, Lucas tells Knoll that some birdlike creatures have been cut out of the Felucia sequence. Because that particular creature build is already 60 percent done, John asks if the CG model department can finish it for inclusion in other shots.

"See if you have more time in June next year," McCallum suggests.

"Rick's the boss," Lucas says. "I'm just the poor director."

Clockwise from top left: model-maker Jon Foreman and Rogers work on the ILM Polis Massa observation dome miniature. Wagner works with Jaeger on the Felucia miniature. Model-maker Grant Imahara adjusts the cruiser hangar bay set. Model-maker Carol Bauman works on the Federation battleship gun. Model-makers Fon Davis and Pierre Maurer piece together the hangar bay wall. Above: Evidence of the Mustafar rethink—Tiemens's view of the landing platform and an aerial view—along with a page from the visual script (top right). Right: Wagner and costume archivist Gillian Libbert prepare Amy Allen (Aayla Secura) for her scenes.

THURSDAY, MAY 6, 2004

Crew are preparing for today's pickup shoot featuring the death of Jedi Aayla Secura (Amy Allen). Not surprisingly, the set is nothing but a floor and three walls of green, which will eventually become the exotic landscape of Felucia. There are about a dozen crew, including DP Carl Miller. Concept model maker Danny Wagner, who is also a makeup artist, has just finished transforming Allen into an alien. He says it was a three-hour job; he used Real Creation body inks to turn her skin green.

Lucas arrives with McCallum. While the former studies the camera setup, the latter surveys the general situation while leaning on a ladder. As they prepare a complex shot, Lucas reminisces about making *Raiders of the Lost Ark* (1981), in particular the now famous scene in which Indy dispatches his fancy scimitar-wielding foe. There were "huge crowd control problems," he recalls.

They try the shot, and when Allen fails to show up on camera, Lucas remarks, "We certainly learned something, didn't we?" They simplify and do another take. He asks Allen to change her walk to more of a stalk. Take. Lucas adds a "stop-and-look" to her prowling.

He then explains to Allen her character's death scene (she's shot in the back by clone troopers). Take. She falls. "I like how her feet came back up into camera," Knoll says. Take. Lucas asks her to scream next time. After nine more setups, Lucas concludes, "I know we have great stuff in there somewhere"—and these pickups are a wrap.

PICKUPS: MONDAY, MAY 17–TUESDAY, MAY 18, 2004
FOX STUDIOS, AUSTRALIA
LOCATION: Stage 2
SETS: Bluescreen—Kashyyyk and Cockpit
SCHEDULED SCENES SHOT: Lead Wookiee climbs up on barricade and roars; crane down as Wookiees run away from camera; lead Wookiee rips droid apart; Wookiees run away as tank explodes; front on shot of clone's face through visor—burned makeup
TOTAL SETUPS: 98

McCallum has spent the last week in Australia preparing for this two-day shoot, which Coleman is directing. "The week before the Wookiee shoot," Coleman says, "I met with George and we went over the Wookiee hero shots. In Sydney, I went to Fox Studios on Friday, which was a prep day, and met with Rick in Building 28. It was surreal. Everyone was sitting in the same spot: Virginia [Murray, production coordinator] and Stephen [Jones, production supervisor] were at the same desks, and Rick was in the same office.

"Monday, we shot everyone but Chewbacca and Tarfful. We shot the preparation for the battle and the battle itself, and then I was asked to pick up some clone pilot shots with Temuera Morrison. I was working on adrenaline and nerves."

"George and I gave Rob the shot to direct," McCallum points out. "I know that he wants to direct and I think he would make a great director, because performance is all he's concerned about. But he'd never had the experience of actually dealing with live action; he'd always directed within

Episode III

000064   uww10 - v05
                                05-11-04   Artist: Hiroshi Mori

the computer. But I knew I could trust him, and he did a great job."

Though Coleman had use of only one camera, he was aided by the fact that many of the Australian crew returned for these two days—he had the same focus pullers and crane crew, Simon Harding operated the camera, and Colin Fletcher was back as first assistant director. "He was fantastic," Coleman says. "I couldn't have done it without him."

Animation director Rob Coleman grew up in Toronto, Canada, and has been interested in art since "before I can remember." He loved the Warner Bros. cartoons—particularly the Chuck Jones classics *Duck! Rabbit! Duck!* (1953) and *Duck Amuck* (1953). His parents used to project 16mm films, and Coleman recalls watching *Dumbo* (1941) on a screen in their living room. "You could see these little pictures on the film," he notes, "so it made sense to me that you could create these drawings that would become movies."

After a false start studying journalism, Coleman enrolled in Concordia University, where, because he'd been self-taught up till then, he was inundated by new cinematic experiences. "I remember immersing myself in the Canadian Film Board shorts." He would also spend hours using the school's 16mm analyzing projector to dissect animated films, such as Ryan Larkin's *En Marchant* (*Walking*, 1969) and Zdenko Gasparovic's *Satiemania* (1978).

After graduating, Coleman worked on *Captain Power and the Soldiers of the Future* (1987), which was the first TV show to combine live action with computer animation. One of his mentors, Zlatko Grgic, who was on his deathbed at the time, recommended Rob to Derek Lamb, an Oscar-winning film board director. With Lamb, Coleman worked on *Karate Kids*, a documentary designed to educate street children around the world about

the dangers of AIDS.

Years later, after seeing *Jurassic Park*, whose computer animation changed the lives of so many modern animators, Coleman immediately applied to ILM. At SIGGRAPH, Coleman recalls, "I'll never forget: I checked into the hotel and there was a message from ILM saying they wanted to interview me—I was so happy I went up to my room and jumped on the bed!"

ILM had used six animators for *Jurassic Park*, and though they were looking to expand, Coleman went through a lengthy interview process. When he was finally hired in October 1993, he became ILM's ninth animator. Following his work on *Men in Black*, Coleman was flown out to the set of Episode I, at McCallum's request, to spend some time with Lucas and "see if the chemistry was right."

"I had seen some early work from *Men in Black*," Rick notes, "and I was so bowled over by not only the imagination, but the realization of all the animation. I said, 'We've got to have him. Because this guy is an awesome piece of talent.' Little did I know what an awesome person he is, which means he's also a brilliant manager of his crew."

Friday, May 14: The following scenes have been turned over to ILM:
Sc. 151-152: CSC-3 (Coruscant Senate chamber)
Sc. 168: CRL (Coruscant rehabilitation center landing platform)
The following scenes have been cut:
Sc. 93-93A: UWW 1-2 (Utapau windmill scenes)

Monday, May 17: The Academy of Science Fiction, Fantasy and Horror Films gives its Saturn Award for the Best DVD Collection of the Year to *The Adventures of Indiana Jones DVD Collection*. At this year's ceremony, composer John Williams, who has written and conducted all of the soundtracks for the *Star Wars* and *Indiana Jones* films, receives a Lifetime Achievement Award.

Monday, May 24: Lucasfilm announces that *THX 1138: The George Lucas Director's Cut* will be released on DVD on September 14.

Lucas was looking for an animation director, so, as Rob tells the story, "I spent the next ten days sitting with George trying to be myself." A conversation about the Canadian Film Board indicated a shared love of animation, so, at the end of Coleman's time there, "Rick put his arm around me and said, 'You're the guy.'"

FRIDAY, MAY 28, 2004
ILM: During Friday's animation dailies—which are not part of Lucas's weekly schedule—Coleman announces that the first rough cut was finished as of May 18. And, after watching it, Lucas said that he felt that the character of General Grievous needed further development. If he was a bounty hunter slaughtering Jedi for their lightsabers, Lucas asked, why does he have bodyguards? This week, the director has decided that Grievous should be more cunning than fearsome, a villain who makes others fight for him—unless cornered.

"He's mentioned vampires and spiders," Coleman says. "He's mentioned Nosferatu specifically."

Consequently, as they review some early Grievous animation, Rob asks his animators to make his head more "birdlike," and says that Grievous's fight scenes will skip the animatics department and come straight to the animation department, as time is running out.

THURSDAY, JUNE 3, 2004
ILM, C Theatre: While Knoll and Miller shoot pickups of dignitaries and Senators on the Windward Stage, Lucas reviews a shot of the slaughtered younglings. Coleman, McCallum, and Lucas then discuss Frank Oz's visit tomorrow to record Yoda dialogue for a marketing initiative. Rob and Rick would like to take advantage of his presence to tape the lines for a new

Although they had gone from concept paintings (above left, by Church) and animatics (below left, by Hiroshi Mori), scenes 93 and 93A of the Utapau windmills are cut. Above: Back in Sydney, the Wookiees are caught on tape by Coleman (left). The live-action actors for the two-day shoot are James Rowland, Steven Foy, Robert Cope, Axel Dench, Julian Khazzouh, and David Stiff. Right: Tarfful (Michael Kingma) grabs Dave Elsey on September 16, 2003.

Grievous Cloak Concept #3... EP3 1/12/04 A. Jaeger ILM

Version A.
Less Mucus

Version B.
More Mucus

Grievous Guts Alone
(Outside of Gutsack Membrane)

Yoda-Anakin scene. "I'd have to write the dialogue," Lucas agrees. "I'd have to write it this afternoon, but I can do that . . . I hope."

UJ: During animation dailies, which always follow C Theatre dailies, Lucas has been directing the movie within the movie—aka the animated parts of *Revenge of the Sith*—since late 2003. These meetings are new to the prequel trilogy process, and are specifically designed to give Lucas more one-on-one

Two CG characters are worked out at ILM. Grievous's cloak concepts are by Jaeger (top left), his eye-mucus and guts are by McBride (insets), and his hard-surface modeling is supervised by Pam Choy (above). Yoda's "facial expressions" are crafted by lead animator Jamy Wheless (middle right), while Coleman (top right) and lead animator Tim Harrington (right) create his physical performance—during the Jedi Master's Senate duel with Sidious—by first recording their own motions and then animating them.

time with the lead animators. Thus, in addition to Coleman, McCallum, and the ILM producers, Jamy Wheless, Scott Benza, Glen McIntosh, and Paul Kavanaugh are present. Tim Harrington (*Eraser*, 1996; *Men in Black*), who supervised the Yoda-Dooku duel in *Attack of the Clones*, is here for the first time, as preliminary animation has begun on the Yoda-Palpatine fight.

After going over animation for that confrontation, Lucas reviews a Yoda shot in his new scene with Anakin. "Yoda doesn't look like he's thinking," he notes.

"I haven't found the emotional tone yet—it's not working," Coleman says, so Lucas explains what's going through Yoda's mind: "*My feelings are correct*, Yoda's thinking. *The kid's going to be a problem*. It's not: listen, think, concern—it's immediate concern."

Speaking of Grievous, Lucas says to the group, "We've got a little hissing now . . . We're making him more and more slimy. He's a manipulative coward. He's Dracula Droid." Looking at animation of a Grievous bodyguard on Utapau, he remarks, "This part is all different now; we've changed it around in editorial."

In the back of the room, McCallum leans forward in his seat and takes his head in his hands.

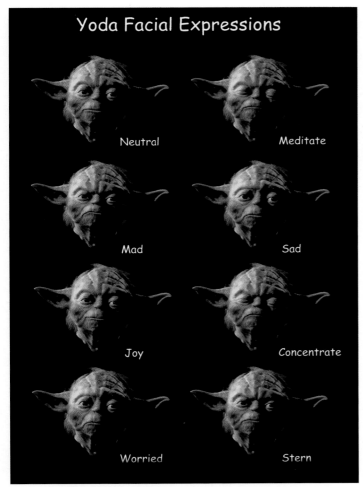

Yoda Facial Expressions

Neutral · Meditate · Mad · Sad · Joy · Concentrate · Worried · Stern

SR: On a wall in the animatics department are the architectural blueprints with the exact Lars homestead set measurements, which were made for Episode II's location shoot in Tunisia. Euisung Lee is using these numbers for animatics of the movie's last shot, which he's preparing as reference for impending pickups. During his short visit, Lucas quickly approves the animatic and leaves.

"So, no new huge changes," Tiemens says, and Lee looks relieved.

TOTAL # OF SHOTS: 2,203   FINALS: 196   FINAL OMITS: 63
SHOTS TURNED OVER: 1,430   SHOTS LEFT TO GO: 2,007   WEEKS TO GO: 44

FRIDAY, JUNE 4, 2004

With Coleman directing, Frank Oz is about to record some lines as Yoda for an international publicity program. In a small, cold room, a microphone is set up for the actor-director. After going over his lines, Oz emphasizes how Yoda has to be himself. "He's not a stand-up comic."

A cell phone rings. It's Lucas, who asks Oz whether he'd mind doing guideline voice-overs for Episode III after he's wrapped the marketing material. Oz says it's "not a problem at all." After audio levels are taken, he puts his head down a moment and comes up speaking as Yoda. Take. "Not good," Oz says, "I'm just getting into it, guys . . ." During the next take, it seems like Yoda has entered the room.

The previous afternoon, Lucas completed writing scene 56:

```
                         YODA
        Premonitions . . . premonitions . . . Hmmmm . . .
                 these visions you have . . .

                        ANAKIN
            They are of pain, suffering, death . . .

                         YODA
        Yourself you speak of, or someone you know?

                        ANAKIN
                     Someone . . .

                         YODA
                 . . . close to you?

                        ANAKIN
                         Yes.

                         YODA
       Careful you must be when sensing the future, Anakin. The
           fear of loss is a path to the dark side.

                        ANAKIN
         I won't let my visions come true, Master Yoda.

                         YODA
       Rejoice for those around you who transform into the Force.
       Mourn them, do not. Miss them, do not. Attachment leads to
              jealousy. The shadow of greed, that is.

                        ANAKIN
                What must I do, Master?

                         YODA
          Train yourself to let go of everything you
                    fear to lose.
```

FGQ290—Tk5—FNEP3-08140 05-20-04

18

FGQ.290

SATURDAY, JUNE 19, 2004

Earlier this week, after showing the first rough cut to a select group from ILM, Lucas decided to show it to Steven Spielberg and Jeff Nathanson, the screenwriter of the former's latest film, *The Terminal* (2004). "Steven saw the rough cut," Lucas says, sitting at home at a table in his kitchen. "I felt I needed to show it to Steven to figure out what the reality was, because we'd earlier had a rough-cut screening for ILM to test the film, and some of the people had strong opinions about things that were contrary to the way I was going. Some people were having a hard time with the reason that Anakin goes bad. Somebody asked whether somebody could kill Anakin's best friend, so that he really gets angry. They wanted a real betrayal, such as, 'You tried to kill me so now I'm going to try and kill you.' They didn't understand the fact that Anakin is simply greedy. There is no revenge. The revenge of the Sith is Palpatine. It doesn't have much to do with Darth Vader; he's a pawn in the whole scheme.

"But then there were larger issues. So I had to ask myself, *What was I trying to say and didn't I say it? Did it just get missed or is it not there?* I had to look at it very hard. I had to ask myself, *Is this how the audience is going to react?* Fortunately, Steven confirmed that most of everything was working. So, I may lose a certain demographic—maybe, maybe not. But I had to make a decision, and I decided that I'm not going to alter the film to make it more commercial or marketable. I have to be true to my vision, which is thirty years old, but I have to be true to it."

THURSDAY, JUNE 24, 2004

ILM, C THEATRE: "Here it is," Knoll says to Lucas—and without any more ado, the hall goes dark and the *final* of the first OSB sequence unrolls.

June 4-18: The following scenes have been turned over to ILM:
Sc. 92-95: UMP (Utapau main city plaza)
Sc. 97-99: CCM (Coruscant Chancellor-Mace fight)
Sc. 124-125: SOS (Space Obi-Wan starfighter)
Sc. 176: DPS (Dagobah pod swamp)
Note: The film at present, without credits,
has a running time of 2 hours, 17 minutes, 59 seconds.

From where the opening crawl will be, the camera pans down, traversing a dense field of stars till a blinding sun is seen rising over Coruscant. Two Jedi starfighters zoom over camera, which then follows them as they accelerate across the beautifully detailed surface of a massively long Republic assault ship, finally plummeting over its side in the waterfall shot. Though sound effects will be added months from now, the sequence continues to dazzle with spectacular imagery and the fantastic maneuvers of the Jedi starfighters as they blast through explosions and debris. It's all over in about forty-five seconds—when there is spontaneous applause.

"I'm dizzy now," Lucas says. "Excellent! I'm sold."

Moments later, as they file out, Denise Ream says to the crew, "Thanks to everyone who worked on that shot."

ILM, UJ: Harrington calls up one shot from a server listing of hundreds. Looking at a moment from the Yoda-Sidious fight, Lucas adds twenty-four frames, or one second, so the audience will understand that Yoda has stopped, in midair, a Senate pod that the Emperor has thrown at him. To accommodate new dialogue, another fourteen frames are "slid" into the sequence where Yoda jumps into Bail's conveniently closer airspeeder.

Reviewing a complex shot that travels from an extreme wide shot into a close-up of the bridge interior of the Federation cruiser as it crash-lands, Lucas says, per composer John Williams, "I know Johnny will make it work."

"Johnny will come up in July and I'll show him the movie," he adds, "And I'll say, *This is what you're up against.* Then he'll come back in September and we'll spot the music. I'll say, *This is what I want here and this is what I want there,* and we'll take notes. Then he'll start composing the music."

TOTAL # OF SHOTS: 2278   FINALS: 293   SHOTS LEFT TO GO: 1985
FINALS NEEDED PER WEEK: 49   WEEKS TO GO: 40

Top left: Animators use a big blue ball to help them animate and simulate Dooku's use of the Force on Obi-Wan. Far left: Animatics by Bustamante of Cato Neimoidia and by Wassung of Jedi Quinlan Vos—the antihero created by Dark Horse comics— on Kashyyyk; early versions of the script had him getting killed in the purge, but the sequence was never filmed. Left, above, and following spread: After years of preparation, the first final frames of the OSB—by Knoll, Coleman, 3-D supervisor David Meny, compositing supervisors Eddie Pasquarello and Pat Tubach, 3-D sequence supervisor Neil Herzinger, lead animators Scott Benza and Glen McIntosh, view-paint supervisors Pam Choy and Elbert Yen, lead 3-D artists David Weitzberg, Willi Geiger, and Jean-Paul Beaulieu, digi-matte painter Joshua Ong, and many others—all led by Lucas.

FRIDAY, JUNE 25, 2004

Additional photography—eleven days of shooting—has now been scheduled from August 23 to September 4 at Shepperton Studios, about an hour's drive from London, England.

"It will be primarily blue- and greenscreen shooting," says McCallum, who will leave soon for six weeks of prep. "There won't be any full sets, but there may be large set pieces. We have four or five hundred shots to

Above and far right: Final frames for FBC.640, with a digi-matte painting by Johan Thorngren and the animatics by Alexander that preceded them (right).

do in two weeks. It's almost like shooting another movie. Pretty much all the principal actors are coming."

"The scheduling of this particular two weeks is very intense," Lucas says. "Trying to get all those people from all over the world back at a particular moment, away from other movies, creates a lot of restrictions on what we shoot. We have three or four dramatic scenes we're going to be adding—that's a lot of shooting—and the rest are pickups."

In order to help ILM finish on time, as of August 3, Roger Guyett (*Saving Private Ryan*, 1998; *Harry Potter and the Prisoner of Azkaban*, 2004) will be joining John Knoll as the second visual effects supervisor (his team will be produced by Janet Lewin, while Jill Brooks will now produce Knoll's team). "In Episodes I and II, we had three supervisors from the very start.

This time we're bringing them in over time, though, right from day one, we had planned on Roger coming on," says McCallum. "Roger will have huge sequences—Kashyyyk and Mustafar—to start with. He's been a godsend."

choices for the opera costumes. Among them are samples for Lucas's costume—he'll be making a cameo on the opera house stairs as Baron Papanoida—as well as those for Amanda Lucas's and her friend Jason Hallikainen's. David explains, diplomatically, that Biggar has pointed out that these fabrics are leftovers from Sydney.

"In other words," Lucas smiles, "approve them—or else!"

TOTAL # OF SHOTS: 2278   FINALS: 466   SHOTS LEFT TO GO: 1812
FINALS NEEDED PER WEEK: 49   WEEKS TO GO: 35

TUESDAY, JULY 13, 2004
ILM, C THEATRE: "How's the cut coming?" Knoll asks.

"We're now adjusting it," Lucas says, of the second rough cut, which he finished on July 9.

"What areas are the most fluid?"

"Reels four and five. They've settled down."

In UJ, the new scene with Yoda and Anakin is reviewed. Frank Oz can already be heard saying, "Fear of loss is a path to the dark side."

"Everything leads to the dark side!" Lucas jokes.

"Even carbohydrates," Knoll agrees.

A shot of Padmé in her coffin reveals that ILM has succeeded in taking away Natalie Portman's pulse, as Lucas predicted they could back on the set.

TUESDAY, JULY 27, 2004
ILM, C THEATRE: "Soon the space battle is going to be over," Knoll says.

"Good," responds Lucas. "Rick is pushing for some reels to be finished by January."

After dailies, Lucas is on the phone to Rick, who's in England paving the way for the pickups. "I'm having Anne type up the script today."

SR: This afternoon in the art department, David shows Lucas fabric

Saturday, July 24: At the San Diego International Comic Convention, the title of Episode III—Revenge of the Sith—is announced to the public and picked up on CNN that night.

WEDNESDAY, JULY 28, 2004
Peter Mayhew is on hand to reprise his role as Chewbacca. Michael Kingma (as the Wookiee general Tarfful) is also here. At 8:30 A.M., a small crew and Lucas are on a greenscreen set. Inside a black tent nearby are three transplants from Australia—Dave and Lou Elsey, and Rebecca Hunt, who have set up a small creatures department.

When called, Mayhew and Kingma walk onto the set—towering over the crew—in their complete Wookiee regalia. "They're incredible," Denise Ream says. "It was an awesome moment," McCallum adds. "Everybody stopped in their tracks. I thought it was beautiful—and Chewbacca gave me a kiss."

Lucas shows Mayhew and Kingma animatics of the scene—a hologram moment on Kashyyyk—the two then return to the tent for final hair adjustments. When they're not before the cameras, tubes running from ice chests into their suits keep the actors cool. While waiting for Miller and his crew to ready the first setup, Lucas talks about multi-element shots in *Return of the Jedi* as compared with today's work.

Top left: Visual effects supervisor Roger Guyett will supervise scenes on Mustafar (digi-matte painting by Brett Northcutt, above) and on Tatooine (visual script painting by Tiemens, top right), among others. Right, middle: The Millennium Falcon *makes a cameo in CSL.005 (Coruscant Senate landing platform), animatics by Bustamante (May 17), courtesy of Lucas. On August 10, Jaeger reverse-engineers the craft, eliminating its rust-colored panels and blast marks (far right)—after all, it's twenty years younger.*

"Dailies used to take a lot longer—and it was almost exclusively discussions about matte lines," he recalls, and then jokes: "I survived the optical compositing era."

"I helped kill it, too," Knoll chimes in, referring to the work he's done to advance computer graphics.

"Wookiees coming out! Everybody in position, please," the 1st assistant director calls out.

The Wookiees climb up on small green boxes, which will eventually be replaced by a lush Kashyyyk environment and a raging Clone War in the background. "You're standing there looking like a bodyguard," Lucas says to Kingma. "There's a lot of commotion, so you can look out at the tanks."

During the take itself, Lucas calls out instructions, "Peter, you can fold your arms . . . tilt your head—great!"

FRIDAY, JULY 29, 2004

"Okay, we're done," Lucas says the next morning after the remaining setups are quickly shot.

"Thank you, Wookiees," the 1st AD says.

The Wookiees bow. Kingma is on his way from Australia to Denmark, where he's trying out for its national basketball team. Mayhew says he feels "fabulous" finally completing his scenes. "It's been a long time. It's great to be doing something I helped start so long ago."

"Uncle Owen will be here in about twelve minutes," Miller announces. And twelve minutes later, Joel Edgerton walks onto the set.

"It's Uncle Owen, looking great," Lucas says. "This is the end of the movie—the very last shot."

After reviewing the animatics with Roxburgh cut in from principal photography, Edgerton walks over to the green ramp that will be the ridge of the crater on Tatooine. "Bring your back foot down a little on the ramp, so it's a little more John Wayne–like," Lucas calls out.

The crew, lights, and cameras are ready, and Lucas directs what will the final shot of the film—the traditional "iris" shot that ends each *Star Wars* episode.

"Okay, we'll try one more," he says, "and . . . Action!"

THURSDAY, AUGUST 5, 2004
ILM: In C Theatre, the first Mustafar final is reviewed—a simple shot of Anakin strangling Obi-Wan—and approved.

In UJ, it's the last meeting before Lucas leaves for England. Animation has begun on Yoda's departure from Kashyyyk and his good-bye to Chewbacca, so Coleman asks what's going through Yoda's head at that point.

"I think he's determined," Lucas says, after a moment's thought. "He suspects that things are bad, but he's thinking about where he's going and what's going to happen."

"By working so closely with Frank Oz and George," McCallum observes, "Rob has totally transformed the performance of Yoda. Everything we ever dreamed Yoda could do, Rob has been able to pull off."

Turning from one CG character to another, Lucas examines a shot that has Jar Jar in the background. "There was a time," he jokes, "when I was going to have Jar Jar walk through every scene, like Hitchcock."

Monday, August 2: The establishment of Lucasfilm Animation Singapore is announced.

An ILM breakdown composited by Mike Conte, of Anakin strangling Obi-Wan in the Mustafar war room: 1. Principal photography; 2. Bluescreen extraction; 3. Digi-matte painting element added; 4. Steam element shot on stage added; 5. Bluescreen over background; 6. Digital rear-wall element added; 7. Window composite and color correction effected; 8. Lightsaber matte added; 9. Final frame.

In the Mustafar control room during Anakin's rampage, Lucas adds a droid getting hit in one shot and falling apart in the next. "It gives the audience a little bit of geography to hang on to," he explains.

SR: Later that afternoon, Lucas is in the animatics department working on the Jedi hangar scene, in which Anakin tells Mace Windu that Palpatine is a Sith Lord. He adds a low sun outside the hangar, so that, in this crucial scene, a sense of light and darkness is evident.

"Anakin should be standing in the light on the edge of the shadow," Lucas says to Alexander. "Anakin is in the sun, but behind him everything is dark."

FRIDAY, AUGUST 6, 2004

SR: Anne Merrifield finishes typing up the "Reshoot Script," which bears today's date. In addition to continuity pickups, Lucas has included miscellaneous dialogue additions—such as this exchange after Anakin kills Dooku:

                    ANAKIN
              It's not the Jedi way.

                   PALPATINE
    It is only natural. He cut off your arm, and you wanted
              revenge. It wasn't the first time.

He adds new scenes like the one in the Jedi hangar as well:

                    ANAKIN
         He won't give up his power. I have learned a
    terrible truth. I think Chancellor Palpatine is a Sith Lord
         [. . .] The one we have been looking for [. . .]
         He knows the ways of the Force. He has been trained
                   to use the Dark Side.

                   MACE WINDU
              Are you sure about this?

                    ANAKIN
         Absolutely [. . .] Master, the Chancellor is very
    powerful. You will need my help if you are going
                   to arrest him.

                   MACE WINDU
    For your own good, you stay out of this conflict. I sense
    much confusion in you, young Skywalker. You carry a great
         deal of fear that clouds your judgment.

                    ANAKIN
               That's not true, Master.

                   MACE WINDU
    We'll see. If what you say about the Chancellor is true,
              you will have earned my trust.

Some of the script has names in place but dialogue listed "to be written," while a key Padmé scene is "to be rewritten."

TOTAL # OF SHOTS: 2,300   FINALS: 540   SHOTS LEFT TO GO: 1,760
FINALS NEEDED PER WEEK: 53   WEEKS TO GO: 33

NOTE: On August 19-20, for the Kashyyyk battle sequences, ILM will shoot the following elements: water planes, tank droid wakes, churning water, and other beach and water assets, some of which will be recorded at the Berkeley Aquatic Park.

Above: Final frames of Count Dooku's death at the hands of Anakin. The Jedi's fall is further illustrated by Lucas's new scene in the Jedi hangar (left, by Tiemens; August 6) in which Skywalker stands on the threshold between sunlight and darkness.

9 Revenge Rashomon-Style

ADDITIONAL PHOTOGRAPHY DAY 1: MONDAY, AUGUST 23, 2004
  LOCATION: Shepperton Studios, England—R Stage
  CREW CALL: 7:30 A.M.
  SET: Chancellor's office/hallway; opera house
  SCHEDULED SCENES SHOT: Palpatine reveals he is a Sith;
  Anakin runs up opera house stairs [NOTE: *Not all scenes shot are listed.*]

Lucas and McCallum sit by side as preparations are made for shooting the enhancements to the scene in which Palpatine seduces Anakin. In addition to the English crew, many of whom have worked on Episodes I or II, some of the Episode III crew are back: supervising art director Peter Russell, "A" camera operator Calum McFarlane, stunt coordinator–sword master Nick Gillard, first assistant director Colin Fletcher, costume designer Trisha Biggar, and others. Though Lucas is using a small on-set crew of forty-four, it's going to be a short, intense two weeks.

Shepperton is a large, sprawling studio where many English TV productions have their home and where many of cinema's legends have worked–Alfred Hitchcock, Stanley Kubrick, Orson Welles, David Lean, and many more–including Lucas, who shot part of *Star Wars* here back in 1976. *Batman Begins* (2005) has just wrapped, and other films are just starting up. Though older, Shepperton is like Fox Studios, Sydney–even more

Top left: Lucas, "A" camera operator Calum McFarlane, and Hayden Christensen; Knoll and McCallum. Above: The giant opera staircase featured the only crowd scene of the pickups and squished the video village into a corner of Stage R. Barry

Howell's animatics of CGO.020 (inset, June 23), using a concept painting by Church, show Lucas in Jun's early costume design concept for his character Baron Papanoida. Next to him is his daughter Katie (Chi Eekway).

so—in its fragile constructions. Its layout seems to obey the laws of urban sprawl, while some structures have the distinct look of abandoned World War II aerodromes. The JAK production office is a tiny room, with cheaply made desks cluttered together and a pervasive smell of tobacco.

The first set is crowded. Actors and crew are wedged into one side of the already smallish R Stage, thanks to the enormous staircase built for the opera scene, which occupies the other half of the stage. Because it's the first day of pickups, the first shot takes some time to prepare. "Close?" McCallum asks Fletcher. "Is Ian here?"

Not long afterward, Hayden Christensen and Ian McDiarmid arrive in their dressing gowns. Lucas shows them on a video monitor the scene as it presently appears—an editorial collage consisting of shots taken from other scenes, dialogue voiced by Burtt, and animatics, which combine into something a little bewildering for the actors.

"You'll keep us right," McDiarmid says to Lucas.

"Yeah, it's difficult, but don't get thrown off by all that," the director reassures. "By the time you guys get dressed, we'll have the set ready."

The video village is the usual setup, but this time Giles Nuttgens is DP, Victoria Pike is script supervisor, and Duncan Blackman is matchmove supervisor. Many of the newer faces actually go way back with either Lucas or McCallum. Nuttgens originally met the latter while focus pulling on *Blackeyes*, and later worked on *Young Indy* as DP.

By 8:30 A.M., Christensen and McDiarmid are in costume and on the set. "Stand by for rehearsal," Fletcher says.

Though a year has passed, everyone, new and old, knows the routine. Lucas explains to the actors that although Anakin is delivering big news—Obi-Wan has found General Grievous—the Chancellor's reaction is personal, not political, and designed to seduce Anakin. "He doesn't talk about whether the war should continue or not—he responds to *you*," George emphasizes to Hayden.

                    PALPATINE
    It is upsetting to me to see that the Council doesn't
       seem to fully appreciate your talents. Don't you
       wonder why they wouldn't make you a Jedi Master?

Wearing her usual long black coat, Biggar arrives and asks Lucas if he had a nice weekend. "I had to write part of the script, *because . . .*," he deadpans, "there were some people who were anxious about what they were going to say."

Unlike the intentionally simple first day of principal photography, today's opera scene involves an ambitious use of costumes and extras, so he indicates the stairs and adds, "This wasn't my idea."

"I was told it was Rick's idea," Biggar says laughing.

As the morning continues, the importance of hairdresser Pip Lund and makeup artist Shane Thomas—both of whom traveled here from Sydney—becomes obvious as questions of continuity arise. "The real question is how much the hair matches—that's always the big issue," Lucas says. Indeed, he and Knoll will consult throughout the next two weeks, verifying that what is about to be shot will match a preexisting plate, or what came before, or what comes after. Continuity problems can be anything from lighting, scale, and angle to choreography, eye lines, makeup, and wardrobe.

Following lunch in the Orangery—a choice of chicken, pasta, or salad—is the afternoon's big opera scene. Creature heads on sticks adorn long tables. Gillard is supervising safety to ensure that no one falls off the roughly ten-yard-high stairs. People who can see in their costumes are placed near the edges. Those who can't see are led to their marks by hand. Opera attendees include everything from enormous "hippo" creatures to scantily clad humanoids. Hidden among them is Anthony Daniels, who, as "Captain" Faytonni, is reprising his brief "human" appearance in *Attack of the Clones*.

"I'm just reminding everyone not to go too close to the edges," Fletcher says. "No closer than you were at rehearsal."

On "Action," they all elegantly ascend the stairs. On Fletcher's cue, Christensen disembarks from a blue placeholder vehicle and races up the steps, maneuvering among the extras. "One more!" Lucas calls out, and a PA immediately yells, "Resetting!"

Though this shot is quickly recorded, its sixty costumes took more than two months to make—requiring the skills of Biggar, her key collaborators, four cutters, and a milliner—while the creatures took two weeks of prep and the services of the Elseys, Rebecca Hunt, prosthetics makeup artist Colin Ware, and their small team.

"George, we're ready for first rehearsal," a PA says, while Lucas and Christensen talk about key scenes to come.

"As for what's written on the page?" Hayden asks.

Above: Day 2 sees Lucas adding to the visual script's illustration of Padmé watching the Jedi Temple burning, intuiting that her husband is somehow responsible. Right: Meanwhile, back at ILM, technicians and crew begin their six-month Mustafar miniature shoot (bottom right, lead model-maker Nick D'Abo).

"I'm open to alternatives," Lucas says. "It's not set in stone." Per the climactic duel, he adds, "I haven't quite figured out how to attack it. I need to come up with something that fits, but the dialogue would have to be short and powerful. You'll have it the day we shoot."

As the last shot is prepped, a PA asks McCallum if it's been a good first day.

"I would've been happier if it we'd finished twenty-five minutes earlier," he replies, "but, considering the extras, it's a good start."

After Fletcher makes it a wrap, a surprise birthday cake is wheeled out for Rick, who lights a cigarette with the candles and then blows them out.

LOCATION WRAP: 19:15   SETUPS: 33

ADDITIONAL PHOTOGRAPHY DAY 2: TUESDAY, AUGUST 24, 2004
LOCATION: B Stage
SET: Padmé's apt; clone & Senate landing platform; Mustafar control center
SCENES SHOT: Obi-Wan tells Anakin that he's a hero; Anakin surveys the slaughter on Mustafar

Having been picked up at 4:15 A.M. and in makeup by 5:15—an hour earlier than anyone else—Natalie Portman is now on the set: a green bench and two arcs, which is all the shot needs of her apartment.

"Okay, here we go—shooting. Bell up!" Fletcher says. "Roll cameras, please."

For this nondialogue scene in which Padmé senses something is wrong, Lucas calls out, "When you decide to get up and go to the window, don't do it as if you heard something. You can actually see the Jedi Temple on fire."

"Okay," Portman says. "Got it."

Looking at the actress on the HD monitor, which appears next to what was shot a year ago on the video monitor, Lucas says, "In the last twelve months, she's really grown up." He walks over to the set and mentions that.

"Thank you," Portman says.

"So I've decided to go back and reshoot the whole movie," Lucas jokes.

Back in the video village, which is, unusually, lodged in a set (the work-in-progress Naboo Skiff), Lucas goes over mentally which Padmé scenes come before and after this one, and talks over the problem with Knoll. He also shows McCallum the difference.

Between setups, Portman sits on a stool reading the latest edition of *The New Yorker* while Lucas sits writing dialogue for the Obi-Wan/Anakin duel, having been inspired during his drive from London this morning.

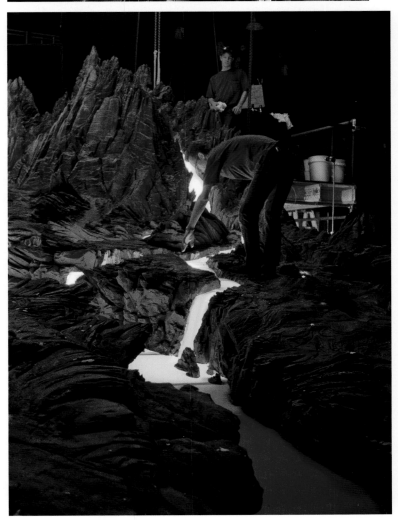

```
                    OBI-WAN
    Much of what I've taught you, you're using against me.

                    ANAKIN
   I should have known the Jedi were plotting to take over.

                    OBI-WAN
      From the Sith!!! Anakin, the Chancellor is evil.

                    ANAKIN
  From the Jedi point of view. From my point of view, the
                   Jedi are evil.
```

"Hot off the presses," Lucas says to Knoll, as he hands the sheets to a PA, who will get them typed up. "Written by hand! None of this digital nonsense for me."

"You! Of all people," Knoll replies.

They finish Portman's scene, and McGregor arrives with Christensen for the next one.

Spotting Ewan, Lucas says, "I couldn't sleep for months!" referring to McGregor's recent around-the-world motorcycle trip.

"I did get bit by a mosquito," McGregor admits, "which the Russian papers picked up."

"How many miles?" McCallum asks.

"Eighteen and a half thousand."

As the actors rehearse the scene, McCallum informs Lucas that he's reserved a week at the end of January 2005 at Shepperton for the next pickups, which will precede the recording sessions with John Williams in early February. "Well, obviously, the more I can do [looping, reshooting, music] at once, the better," Lucas says.

"The better for all of us," McCallum agrees.

A PA hands Lucas the typed-up dialogue on one page of pink paper.

> ANAKIN
> Your combat skills have always been poor, Master. You're called "the negotiator" because you can't fight . . .
>
> OBI-WAN
> It's over Anakin. I have the high ground. Don't try it.
>
> ANAKIN
> You underestimate the power of the dark side.

After lunch, Portman and Christensen stand with miniature motorized fans in hand as makeup prepares them for their close-ups. "In the classic Hollywood tradition," Lucas tells his DP, "light her so she's beautiful."

He then talks with Christensen, noting that he needs a "nice, vicious, crazed close-up" for when Anakin surveys the carnage he's created on Mustafar. He also tells him how, in the editing

room, he changed things around so that "all the subplots now relate to Anakin. It's all knitted much more tightly together."

"Sounds good," Christensen says.

Moments later, after cutting out a few shots he realized weren't necessary, Lucas tells McCallum, "I'm following in the footsteps of John Ford—I'm ripping everything out of the script!" referring to that director's legendary method of dealing with producers who felt he was going too slowly.

Anthony Daniels arrives, ready to resume his role under armor as C-3PO, who is resplendent—so much so that Knoll is afraid that the camera will catch reflections of cameras and equipment in his metal.

"I remember having a fit about this in Sydney," he says. "There's too many people on the set. I can see every one of them reflected in his head."

"Well, go have a fit," Lucas says.

Knoll leaves the video village to find a remedy, and Lucas and McCallum both call out, "Giles!"

When the DP comes over, Lucas says to him, "John wants to have a fit."

The upshot is, they tone down the golden droid's reflection factor.

CAMERA WRAP: 18:44   SETUPS: 31

ADDITIONAL PHOTOGAPHY DAY 3: WEDNESDAY, AUGUST 25, 2004
LOCATION: B Stage
SET: Mustafar landing platform, locker room, secret landing platform
SCENES SHOT: Anakin chokes Padmé; Obi-Wan dispatches Grievous

For the moment just before Anakin assassinates the Separatist leaders, Christensen is having trouble putting on his hood.

"It's the hood's fault," Lucas calls out from the village.

Though a seemingly minor gesture, the donning of the cowl must look seamless and menacing. After another flubbed take, Lucas walks over to help layer the pleats correctly. The next shot, in which Vader espies

Top right: Church's concept art of July 19, 2004, depicts the Naboo skiff's "medbed." Peter Russell's art department built the set based on the drawings, and the new scene was filmed on August 25, 2004, with McGregor, Daniels, and Portman—who wears a costume designed by McCaig in December 2002. Above right: Obi-Wan (McGregor) slips into the locker/closet aboard the Naboo skiff in another new scene. Right: Fletcher, DP Giles Nutggens, Lucas, Daniels, and McCallum.

Padmé's ship, has Anakin taking *off* his hood, which goes without a hitch.

The following setups are for one of the new scenes, and take place in an actual set of the Naboo skiff interior. Although relatively small, the skiff set has one thing that almost none of the sets had in Sydney: a ceiling.

In the first shot, Obi-Wan must hide in a utility closet—and jokes abound.

"R2-D2 walks by and hears someone banging on the door who can't get out," Lucas says, "but moves on."

"Or," McGregor offers, "I disappear into this small cupboard where they keep the mops. Light-years later, I emerge as Alec Guinness!"

As the jokes continue, they inadvertently reveal that the closet is mysteriously and unrealistically empty of objects, so Lucas, Peter Russell, and art director David Lee quickly come up with something to make it more lived-in. A few minutes later, the closet contains some air-conditioner hose and a few plastic containers.

"I'd like to try that little Jedi thing with my hand when I'm inside," McGregor says, "to close the door." Lucas agrees, and the shots are quickly recorded.

Wearing the costume that concept artist Iain McCaig drew up nearly two years ago, Portman lies on the skiff's bunk for a scene in which Obi-Wan checks on her condition after Anakin has attacked her. While they set up, unit photographer Keith Hamshere snaps some stills. In 1975, when Lucas was still in search of a location for his desert planet, Hamshere showed him and *Star Wars* production designer John Barry photographs of a recce he'd done in Algeria for Stanley Donen's *The Little Prince* (1974). Hamshere's first Lucasfilm job was on *Indiana Jones and the Temple of Doom* (1984). He went on to do *Young Indy*, *Willow* (1988), *Radioland Murders*, and the first two prequels.

"He's the best in the business," Knoll says.

At 2:50 P.M., McGregor, Christensen, and Portman watch edited footage of the Mustafar landing platform scene. With Lucas and company, they'll soon be recording bits of missing continuity, created by changes made during editing: an over-the-shoulder shot here, a bit of dialogue there.

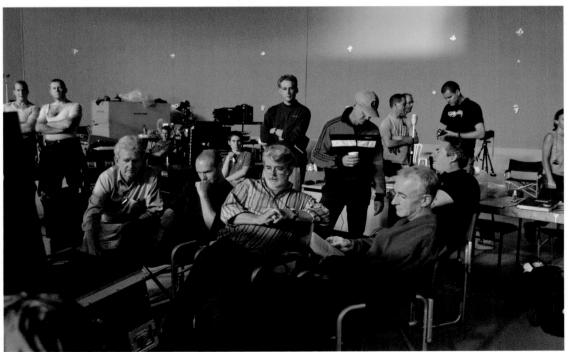

"You need my shoulder?" Christensen asks, incredulously.

"Well, we're going to turn around and do the emotional part, too," Lucas says. "And we need your lips to make a *w*."

"Fantastic," the actor says.

As the afternoon ticks by, Knoll remarks to Lucas that doing partial scenes isn't as exciting as shooting complete scenes.

"But when we get back to editorial," Lucas points out, "there is nothing better than patching this material into the film."

CAMERA WRAP: 19:27
SETUPS: 42

ADDITIONAL PHOTOGRAPHY DAY 4: THURSDAY, AUGUST 26, 2004
LOCATION: B Stage
SET: Mustafar volcano edge
SCENES SHOT: Anakin and Obi-Wan talk while dueling; Obi-Wan looks
on in horror as Anakin becomes toast

As crew prepare to shoot the new dialogue Lucas has written for the duel on Mustafar, the director explains to Hayden, "Basically you're arrogant—at one point I had you say to Obi-Wan, 'I could've beat you when I was ten years old.' "

Second AD Deborah Antoniou, who also made the flight from Australia, walks up to Lucas and whispers, "Just a gentle reminder about your costume fitting tonight, is that still okay?"

"No, but I'll do it anyway," he says, referring to preparations for his cameo.

"You're a gentleman," she smiles and departs.

For the dialogue sequence, McGregor and Christensen are standing on four-foot-wide blue disks, which can be rotated by stagehands. At first, however, they have a hard time judging at what speed to turn them—so when Christensen says, "You can't fight!" he also happens to be jettisoned from his disk.

"Well, you can't fly!" McGregor jokes.

In the village, someone inquires how the disks are able to float on lava.

"Does it make sense?" McCallum responds. "No. Will it work in the movie? Maybe."

Production moves on to Obi-Wan's new line just before he slices off Anakin's limbs. To prep him, Lucas shows McGregor the edited sequence on one of the monitors. "I cut out Anakin's line, 'Help me, Master,' " he explains. "I didn't want him to be redeemed."

"But the end stays like that?" he asks, referring to the sequence as a whole.

"Yeah."

"Good," says Ewan, who seems to have been impressed with the scene's quality even in its rough form.

"When you get the sound and the music in there," Lucas says, "it'll be really powerful."

CAMERA Wrap: 19:10   Setups: 52

ADDITIONAL PHOTOGRAPHY DAY 5: FRIDAY, AUGUST 27, 2004
LOCATION: B Stage
SET: Senate landing platform, Chancellor's office
SCENES SHOT: Fight up to where Palpatine changes to Sidious

"Good morning. It's good to be here," Samuel L. Jackson says to Lucas. Today's key scene, which will take a couple of days to shoot, is the end of the Mace-Palpatine fight. The Jedi Master is winning when Anakin arrives, but Palpatine, as the scene has been rethought, now seizes the occasion to exaggerate his weakness in order to force Anakin's hand—after which Palpatine kills Mace.

Although the emotional context of the scene is complex, the set is simple: just a section of the window in Palpatine's office—the niche in which Mace corners the Chancellor. McCallum is here early making sure everything is on track, while Lucas sits alone in the video village studying the already cut material.

PALPATINE
You are not one of them, Anakin. You must choose. Don't let
him kill me [. . .] I am your pathway to power to save the
one you love.

MACE WINDU
Don't listen to him, Anakin [. . .] I am going to end this
right now [. . .] He is too dangerous to be kept alive [. . .]

ANAKIN
He must live . . . I need him . . .

A combination of elements show Windu's death: (above) he and other Jedi arrive in a final frame; (top right) in one of the pickup shots, fencing double Michael Byrne (Palpatine) cuts down Kit Fisto; Carney's May 7 animatic of CCM.340 (top, far right) shows the window shattering . . .

Thursday, August 26: ILM completes the first "hero" Mustafar motion control shot—an "incredibly complicated and messy process," according to Janet Lewin, "because we have to get the lava flow to look just right, especially in the wide establishing shots." Jedi Temple miniature elements are also being shot, and prep continues on the Utapau hero wall, as well as the Kashyyyk beach, hologram room, and tree.

because we're dealing with things that aren't so obvious. The audience knows Anakin is going to turn to the dark side, but the things that he's struggling with are so subtle that it may be hard for people to understand why his obsession to hold on to Padmé is so strong."

Jackson and McDiarmid join Lucas in front of the monitor to review the scene.

"It's coming together," he says. "But the only scene I hadn't thought through enough is the scene we're reshooting today."

"The fight itself was fine," Lucas says. "The problem was that the final confrontation between Mace and Palpatine wasn't specific enough in terms of Anakin, so we're working to make his story, his conflict sharper—I have what I call two sharp 'right turns' in the movie," he adds, "and they are very hard to deal with. For the audience, it's a real jerk, because you're going along and then somebody yanks you in a different direction. Anakin turning to the dark side and killing Mace is a very hard right,

. . . while a final frame of Palpatine (McDiarmid) and Windu (Jackson) has Yanick Dusseault's digi-matte painting of Coruscant in the background (middle). Thinking he has won, Windu winds up his death blow in a pickup shot (above).

"It makes it easier for Anakin to come in later in the fight," McDiarmid notes.

The actors rehearse in their dressing gowns and then adjourn for final costume adjustments, while Lucas and Knoll continue to examine the footage. When Palpatine easily strikes down Mace's three associate Jedi at the outset of the scene, Knoll says, "Look at this—Mace brought the B-team!"

"You have to be either Mace or Yoda to compete with the Emperor," Lucas says. "If Anakin hadn't got all beat-up, he could've beat the Emperor."

"But Mace was going to arrest Palpatine," Knoll says, "and a few moments later he says Palpatine's too dangerous to live. What happened?"

"Mace was going to do the right thing by arresting him, but after Palpatine does the lightning, he changes his mind."

Jackson and McDiarmid return, final checks are completed, and cameras roll.

"You're under arrest, my lord!" Jackson threatens. Towering over Palpatine, he booms, "You old fool!!"

For the moment when Anakin arrives, Lucas explains the situation to Christensen: "You almost come a second too late. You're rushing over to make sure that nothing happens—but your anticipation is that they're going to hurt each other. When the lightning starts, things are getting worse from your point of view. And when Mace is going to kill him, you have to act."

Fletcher calls action and the large fans ruffle the Jedi cloaks.

"You have lost!" Jackson intones above the machines.

After a couple of takes, Lucas asks Jackson to add a hand gesture that warns Anakin to back off as he prepares to execute the Sith.

For the end of the conflict, Jackson screams over and over as he's fried by Sith lightning.

"He's pretty good at that electrocution business," Knoll remarks.

"Yeah, but I want him to do a little bit more before turning away from the camera," Lucas says.

After Jackson adjusts his performance, completing another convincing death scene, the crew applauds.

CAMERA WRAP: 18:24   SETUPS: 40

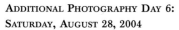

ADDITIONAL PHOTOGRAPHY DAY 6:
SATURDAY, AUGUST 28, 2004
LOCATION: B Stage
SET: Naboo main square, Chancellor's office, Jedi Council
SCENES SHOT: Sio Bibble walks in Queen's funeral procession; Sidious laughs while attacking Mace; Anakin sits alone in the Council chamber

Ian McDiarmid is in his Darth Sidious makeup as crew prepare for different angles and sections of the Mace-Palpatine-Anakin showdown. Christensen does his usual push-ups to warm up. He is staying with Nick Gillard in Brighton, so Gillard jokes about writing a book titled, *Darth Vader Is Living in My Basement.*

During McDiarmid's close-ups as Sidious, as he unleashes his pent-up fury on the doomed Jedi, the power of the actor's performance is impressive. There is applause and hoots of joy after he screams out, "Power! *Unlimited power!*" twisting his face with unmitigated delight at his sadistic victory.

"Ian should have added, *Sucker!*" Gillard says.

Lucas asks for more wind to match earlier shots, and McDiarmid performs his victory a few more times, each time eliciting positive reactions from the cast and crew.

"I tell you," Lucas says to those in the video village, "this is as good a villain as we've ever had. Darth Sidious emerges in this one."

He walks to the set after shooting is done, and says, "Brilliant!"

"Well, it's the moment for that," McDiarmid observes.

"I can't wait to see it on the big screen."

After lunch, with the clock ticking, McCallum asks a PA, "Where's Hayden?"

"He's dressing."

"Tell him we're desperate."

Christensen arrives a few minutes later, ready for the moment in which Anakin submits to Palpatine's temptation:

> ANAKIN
> I will do whatever you ask. Just help me save Padmé's life. I can't live without her. I won't let her die.

"It's basically *Faust* in the end," Lucas explains. "This is the one where you make a pact with the devil. And that usually leads to the same end: You cannot change the inevitable. If you try, you're basically going against the cosmos or however you want to define that."

After the first take, Lucas says to Christensen, "When you get to 'I won't let her die,' I need you to say it with real determination."

After the next take, Hayden asks, "It's more in that direction, right?"

As Lucas climbs up the stairs to the set, he responds, "Yeah. Also the words should be hard to get out."

Take. "Don't turn up the volume; just grit your teeth," George says.

After the next take, Lucas asks, "You want to go straight into one more?" and Christensen does another.

"Great. Really good—one more like that," the director says. "Those were at exactly the right levels"—but Christensen has to wait while they alter the lighting, so he says to Fletcher, "As soon as possible," in order not to lose the moment.

"One more right away," the actor asks after the previous one.

Take. "That was fantastic, Hayden. Fantastic," Lucas says. They do another one. "That was fantastic, too. You want to go right into one more?"

"Yes, please," Christensen says.

After the final take, McDiarmid walks over to Christensen and pats him on the shoulder.

Next on the Call Sheet is Anakin in the Jedi Council chamber, brooding on his and Padmé's destiny. While Nuttgens gets the lighting in place, Lucas and Knoll talk at length about how they're going to make Christensen fit into the already shot plate of the Jedi Council. McCallum listens for a few minutes and then says, "John, I have a great idea. Let's just shoot it and work it out later."

He continues watching and waiting, becoming slightly concerned about how long the setup is taking. "Can we do it?" he asks Fletcher.

"Yes, let's do it," Fletcher says. Twenty minutes later, however, other problems have developed.

Meanwhile, director and visual effects supervisor continue their debate,

with the latter pressing his point. Lucas finally asks, "What are you going to do if, after you put him in the plate, Anakin walks into the middle of a [digital] chair?"

Knoll thinks for a moment and says, "Beg for mercy."

As Christensen takes his place in the minimal set, Lucas counsels him: "Try and increase how uncomfortable you feel as the shot goes on. Try to think back on the Darth Plagueis story—run that through your head."

As they move into close-ups, Lucas says, "Take it one step further: You realize that by telling the Jedi about Palpatine being a Sith that Padmé is going to die. Basically, you just killed her."

They do several takes of Christensen effectively exteriorizing Anakin's internal pain, which will shortly push him over to the dark side.

"Showing how much Anakin and Padmé care for each other is one of my weak points," Lucas admits. "Expressing that is hard to do. It's really hard in the end to express the idea, *I'm so in love with you that I would do anything to save you; I'd give up everything—friends, my whole life—for you*, and make that real—make that stick—and say it in *two* minutes, which is all the time this film has for it. If I had a whole movie, I could probably manage it. But I can't go deep into the psyche of these people beyond a certain stylistic reality I've created for myself. It wouldn't work.

"It's also a very difficult structural issue," he adds. "And when I created it, I knew I wanted two hard right turns—it's designed to be that way—and I knew I was taking a real chance that it wasn't going to work. But you have to see if you can make it work. If it doesn't, well, then I'm going to get skewered for it. But if I can make it work, it'll be neat; it'll be good."

CAMERA WRAP: 17:45   SETUPS: 32

ADDITIONAL PHOTOGRAPHY DAY 7: MONDAY, AUGUST 30, 2004
LOCATION: R Stage
SET: Jedi Council, Kashyyyk hologram, Jedi gunship, Jedi war room, Mygeeto
SCENES SHOT: Anakin tells Mace about Palpatine; Jedi cut down by Palpatine

Because of budget constraints, the Jedi Council chamber is being shot in sections. The first group of five chairs is placed on their marks and Yoda is unwrapped—to reveal a truly deranged version of himself—which will be used only for camera reference and eye lines.

"Have you seen Yoda's expression?" Knoll asks Lucas. "It's priceless."

"Somebody has to get a photo of that," Lucas agrees, and Knoll adds, "Something's definitely wrong with the universe."

ANAKIN (cont'd)
My loyalty belongs to both sides.
~~I don't wish to join either.~~ I
can't tell you any more.

            PADMÉ
I understand.
He takes her in his arms
            ANAKIN
~~And~~ *mostly* I'm afraid of losing you.... ~~I'm afraid of my visions~~
            PADMÉ
That won't happen...

She looks him in the eye.

            PADMÉ
~~That won't happen~~ *I believe you can protect me against anything.*

Top left: McDiarmid (Sidious) is reshot as he fries Windu with Force lightning, and Jackson (Windu) is reshot as he falls onto a blue mattress supervised by Gillard. Top right: A final frame of the hologram in which Anakin kneels to Sidious. Above right: Jackson casts a quizzical eye on a disturbed Yoda puppet. Above left: Lucas's efforts to write how much Anakin and Padmé feel for each other is evident in his script revisions.

After a week of shooting, Lucas says he feels "good." But today turns out to be trying.

While Phillip Wade (Plo Koon) and Tay Bayliss (Stass Allie) are being touched up by creatures department technicians, Silas Carson (Ki-Adi-Mundi) and Jackson arrive. "You're a hologram from Mygeeto listening to Yoda on Kashyyyk," Lucas says to Carson, who seems perplexed by the director's relatively esoteric vocabulary.

"I had no clue what George was talking about," Carson would later confess.

"Okay, the next shot is of Agen Kolar and Anakin," Fletcher says, and the chairs are reoriented. While waiting, there's a fair amount of joking that Mace Windu isn't really dead, and that, during the credits, he could perhaps crawl back through the window, with his clothes just a bit singed.

"Yeah," Jackson says, "Mel Gibson could do it: *The Resurrection.*"

During rehearsals, he asks what "Utapau" is. "It's a planet," Lucas replies.

"Oh, next to Badda-Bing?" Jackson says.

Between shots, Jackson explains that he travels with "a stack of comic books and a stack of Hong Kong movies." He also talks with Lucas about additional photography.

"There are some directors who think it's an affront to reshoot and that it makes them look stupid," Lucas says. "But it's a natural part of the process."

"Even as an actor, you know sometimes that what you're saying isn't connected to anything," Jackson agrees.

"Well, sometimes you take a risk and then you come back and fix it."

"*You* have that luxury."

"This is more like the theater, where you're constantly improving the material."

"There is only one director I know who claims to know exactly what he's doing all the time," Jackson says.

"I'd rather think of myself as not knowing what I'm doing."

It is gradually becoming very hot on stage. About 250 kilowatts are raining down on the crew, and the air conditioner has developed a problem, but Knoll says, "No matter how hot we're shooting, I always think this is nothing like Tunisia."

Another problem develops when the head of the camera crane malfunctions. Lucas instructs the crew to put the camera on "sticks," a tripod, to avoid waiting for repairs. As they set up the Jedi war room, crew measure the length of the room's table.

"Sixteen feet?" Lucas asks, incredulous.

"Yeah, that's the diameter according to ILM," Peter Russell says.

"I think that six is a zero," Lucas points out, and the table is adjusted accordingly.

Middle: Crew prepare to shoot a Jedi Council scene. Above and bottom: The doomed pair share a few tender moments in final frames of Padmé's veranda (digi-matte painting by Christian Haley) . . .

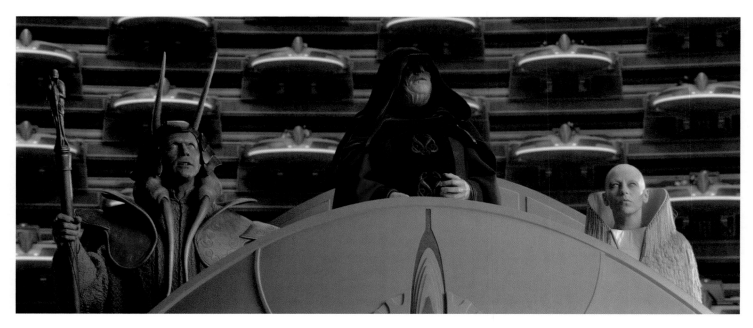

Hours later, Fletcher informs the crew that work will continue till eight. In an open electric car outside, Hayden, Jackson, and others are sprawled about, waiting.

CAMERA WRAP: 20:13   SETUPS: 46

ADDITIONAL PHOTOGRAPHY DAY 8:
TUESDAY, AUGUST 31, 2004
  LOCATION: F & B Stages
  SET: Alderaan space cruiser, Obi-Wan starfighter, Mustafar control room, Senate
  SCENES SHOT: Mas Amedda on cruiser monitor; Sidious approaches Yoda on the floor

*S*tar Wars fans know that beneath the armor of bounty hunter Boba Fett was actor Jeremy Bulloch. Today Bulloch is on the side of the heroes, playing a pilot in Bail Organa's space cruiser—the cockpit of which is the one other complete set of this eleven-day shoot. Lucas decided to put Bulloch in the film "some time ago. We were just looking for a place to put him and this seemed like the best choice," he explains. "Now he's more than just a mysterious conundrum."

Jimmy Smits has also arrived for his one day of pickups, and he walks onto the set with McGregor, joining Lucas for a look at the animatics of the scene.

"Ben's doing his best work," McGregor remarks, referring to Burtt's valiant placeholder voice-overs.

They run through a rehearsal, but when it's time for Yoda to speak, nothing happens.

"Did Yoda die?" Lucas inquires.

It turns out that nobody had written down Yoda's dialogue for someone to read off-camera, so Lucas does so. During the first take, however, 3rd AD Eddie Thorn's reading is so . . . English, that everyone breaks up laughing.

The next bit of laughter occurs when Anthony Daniels, in the rehearsal for C-3PO's last scene, appears towing a red vacuum cleaner on wheels behind him, which is ostensibly for R2-D2 reference. After a take and a missed cue, Daniels, encased in his armor, walks up to the camera and says, "I can't hear a word anyone is saying."

The scene completed, Lucas gives the thumbs-up to Daniels.

"It's only been twenty-five years," George says.

"And we're still not getting it right," Anthony jokes.

"Thank you—thank you for everything," Lucas says and they shake hands.

CAMERA WRAP: 19:22   SETUPS: 52

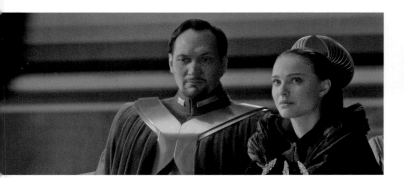

. . . but the tide soon turns as (above and bottom) Palpatine ushers in the Empire, to Padmé's horror. Middle: Jeremy Bulloch as the pilot of the Alderaan starcruiser.

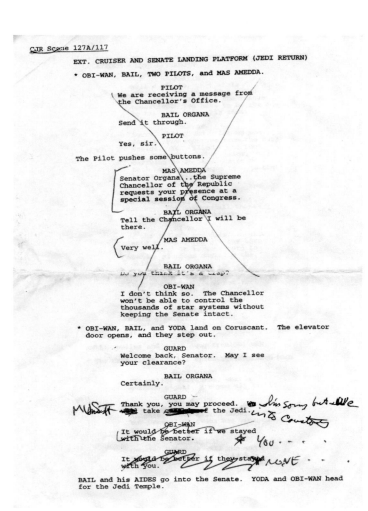

```
CJR Scene 127A/117
       EXT. CRUISER AND SENATE LANDING PLATFORM (JEDI RETURN)
   * OBI-WAN, BAIL, TWO PILOTS, and MAS AMEDDA.
                          PILOT
              We are receiving a message from
              the Chancellor's Office.

                       BAIL ORGANA
              Send it through.
                          PILOT
              Yes, sir.
              The Pilot pushes some buttons.
                       MAS AMEDDA
              Senator Organa...the Supreme
              Chancellor of the Republic
              requests your presence at a
              special session of Congress.
                       BAIL ORGANA
              Tell the Chancellor I will be
              there.
                       MAS AMEDDA
              Very well.
                       BAIL ORGANA
              Do you think it's a trap?
                          OBI-WAN
              I don't think so.  The Chancellor
              won't be able to control the
              thousands of star systems without
              keeping the Senate intact.

   * OBI-WAN, BAIL, and YODA land on Coruscant.  The elevator
     door opens, and they step out.
                          GUARD
              Welcome back, Senator.  May I see
              your clearance?
                       BAIL ORGANA
              Certainly.
                          GUARD
              Thank you, you may proceed.
              We'll take _____ of the Jedi.
                          OBI-WAN
              It would be better if we stayed
              with the Senator.
                          GUARD
              It would be better if they stayed
              with you.

     BAIL and his AIDES go into the Senate.  YODA and OBI-WAN head
     for the Jedi Temple.
```

(handwritten annotations on script:) MACE; I'm sorry but we'll into Country; * YOU . . .; NONE

(handwritten note at bottom:)
IF A SPECIAL SESSION OF
CONGRESS THERE IS EASY FOR
US TO ENTER THE Jedi TEMPLE
IT WILL BE

ADDITIONAL PHOTOGRAPHY DAY 9: WEDNESDAY, SEPTEMBER 1, 2004
LOCATION: B Stage
SET: Trade Federation cruiser, Chancellor's office, Jedi return, Senate chamber
SCENES SHOT: Jedi running down corridor; Dooku uses the Force to hurl Obi-Wan

---

Above left: 3rd AD Eddie Thorne's "sides" contain the lines for Yoda that Lucas hastily scribbles. Above right: Lucas and Daniels once again for the last time. Right: In a new scene Organa (Smits) and Obi-Wan (McGregor) are stopped by blue guards, but Obi-Wan does the ol' mind trick. Lee (Dooku) in final frames (top right) and in a pickup shot using the Force (below). Far right: A final frame of a new scene shot at Shepperton of Anakin leading clone troopers to the Jedi Temple (digi-matte painting by Vanessa Cheung).

Every morning, many of the crew—Lucas and McCallum among them—gather at the Orangery between 7 and 7:30 A.M. to eat a typical English breakfast of eggs, sausages, bacon, and baked beans. Today, waving away their electric car and driver, Rick says, "Let's walk to the stage."

"Yes. It's the first day of the rest of your life," Lucas says. "Put out that cigarette and let's walk."

Once on the set, Lucas says to Gillard per a shot in the elevator shaft, "This is your shot—but I need to get it in fifteen minutes."

"You'll get it in ten," Gillard replies.

McGregor joins Lucas in watching the dailies sent over from ILM.

"I find the filming of it gets in the way of the watching of it," remarks Ewan, enjoying the brief show. After he departs, Lucas expresses concern to Knoll and McCallum that he's not receiving enough final shots.

"We'll stay on schedule," Knoll says, "but we don't want to get into numerology."

"It's about trying to get a sense of the movie," Lucas counters.

"We need a reel by December 1," McCallum says.

"It's going to have to be the first reel," Lucas says, and Knoll promises that ILM will hit the thousand-shot deadline of October 31.

After lunch, 2nd AD Deb holds the blue curtain open so that Christopher Lee can enter. Dressed as Count Dooku, he hugs Lucas. They then watch animatics of Dooku's fight with the Jedi. "It's really that one shot," Lucas says, referring to the moment when Dooku uses the Force to bring a balcony down on Obi-Wan's leg.

They do a take. Lucas walks to the set. "That wasn't quite right, was it, George?"

"Come out a little more decisive," Lucas suggests. "It's almost in one motion: You turn and bring your hand up—and then you can push it down with energy."

Take. "Try one with a little more malice and evil," Lucas calls out from the video village. Take. After Lucas gives him the okay, Fletcher

announces, "Well, that's it."

"Thanks for everything; you've been terrific," Lucas says to Lee.

" 'Farewell. God knows when we'll meet again,' " Lee replies, quoting Shakespeare.

CAMERA WRAP: 18:45   SETUPS: 52

ADDITIONAL PHOTOGRAPHY DAY 10: THURSDAY, SEPTEMBER 2, 2004
LOCATION: R Stage
SET: Utapau caves and sinkhole, Senate chamber, Mygeeto
SCENES SHOT: Anakin and clones; Sidious and Anakin after Mace is killed; Sidious robe is now on

As Christensen marches forward, simulating Anakin's walk to the Jedi Temple to massacre the Jedi, a corner of the blue carpet is blown up by the fans. Christensen stops midstride and fixes it. "He might be evil," McFarlane says, "but he's still neat."

Later, it's another key hood-donning moment, this time as Palpatine changes into the Emperor/Darth Sidious. After a failed attempt, Lucas calls out, "Don't worry—Ewan and Hayden had their hood moments, too." After a few takes, Lucas walks over to Ian and says, "For the end of this dialogue, you can become contemplative—and then stronger with, 'Do what must be done, Lord Vader.' "

"When he changes into Sidious," McDiarmid would note, "it's his Mr. Hyde moment."

CAMERA WRAP: 19:18   SETUPS: 45

ADDITIONAL PHOTOGRAPHY DAY 11: FRIDAY, SEPTEMBER 3, 2004
LOCATION: R Stage
SET: Utapau, Yoda's quarters, Mustafar landing platform
SCENES SHOT: Utapaun sidekicks; Anakin talks with Yoda; Anakin frowns at younglings; death of Shaak Ti

Lucas is wearing a colorful, festive shirt today. "I thought I'd celebrate," he says. "My last day of shooting after thirty-five years."

After a couple of short pickups, production readies for the new Yoda-Anakin scene. The set consists of one cushion and a blue wall with slats in it to create the necessary lighting.

"No human can let go," Lucas would say of this scene. "It's very hard. Ultimately, we do let go because it's inevitable; you do die and you do lose your loved ones. But while you're alive, you can't be obsessed with holding on. As Yoda says in this one, 'You must learn to let go of everything you're afraid to let go of.' Because holding on is in the same category and the precursor to greed. And that's what a Sith is. A Sith is somebody that is absolutely obsessed with gaining more and more power—but for what?

September 13: *Star Wars: Clone Wars* receives an Emmy Award for Outstanding Animated Program (for Programming One Hour or More) at the fifty-sixth annual Creative Arts Emmy Awards.

Left: In the last shot of the pickups, Obi-Wan (McGregor) clings to a rock face. Above left: Anakin seeks the help of Yoda, but winds up killing Shaak Ti (Oli Shosan). Above right: Fletcher coaches the Jedi younglings; McGregor, Christensen, and Lucas share a light moment, as do Ian and Hayden; Lucas and McCallum depart—the last Call Sheet reads, "To everyone on the Cast and Crew: Thank you so much for your hard work; we've had a fantastic time—it's been great working with you!—Rick, George, Brian [Donovan], Colin and Deb. P.S. Thanks for working on the Bank Holiday—sorry we couldn't pay you for it! (only joking!)"

Nothing, except that it becomes an obsession to get more.

"The *Jedi* are *trained* to let go. They're trained from birth," he continues. "They're not supposed to form attachments. They can love people—in fact, they should love everybody. They should love their enemies; they should love the Sith. But they can't form attachments. So what all these movies are about is: greed. Greed is a source of pain and suffering for everybody. And the ultimate state of greed is the desire to cheat death."

As Christensen prepares himself, 3rd AD Thorn confides, "I'll be reading Yoda, but I'm not doing the voice."

"Why not?" Hayden asks.

"Because the crew's been laughing at me the whole week," Thorn says. "Is that okay?"

"Okay," Christensen replies.

"Let's shoot it!" McCallum calls out—but crew have to work on the positioning of the chairs and getting better striped lighting on Anakin.

"Hayden," Fletcher says, "sorry. Ten minutes." And Christensen leaves the set to talk to some friends who are visiting.

About a quarter of an hour later, the first take is completed. "Can you feel the light on you?" Lucas calls to Christensen. "Try and keep that light in your eye." Take. "Bring your head down just a bit more so it's in that little shaft of light." Take—and for this last take, Thorn does the Yoda voice.

"Beautiful!" Lucas says, and there is applause for Christensen—and for Thorn.

While discussing the upcoming Jedi youngling scene with Lucas, Fletcher says, "I think with the kids, the best thing to do is to set up and shoot the rehearsal."

Lucas agrees, also deciding to shoot the scene in the Jedi Council chamber. Knoll thinks that might be too many scenes there, and suggests the Jedi Temple archives.

"I'm going to put it in the Council Chamber," Lucas says. "It has the right symbolism—and it's night," he adds, as Nutggens arrives. "So whatever light coming in is from the outside. And as the kids move, they go in and out of the light."

Much later, the kids are ushered in, each outfitted in a tiny Jedi costume. Fletcher explains to them that Anakin will come into the room. "And then we'll run away?" one boy asks, while, on the other side of the set, Lucas says to Christensen, "You come in and you just smile."

The last shot of additional photography is of McGregor on a cave wall as he emerges from a watery sinkhole. McCallum smokes a cigarette while the camera crew tilts the camera to make the wall look steeper than it is—until Knoll and others say it's too much. "All right," Lucas says. "Straighten it up a little bit—the peanut gallery is refusing to accept that."

"More water on the wall, please," Rick says, and they do a take.

"Should I try one more?" Lucas asks.

"Yeah, get Obi-Wan's hair and beard wetter," Knoll suggests.

"Okay."

Take.

"Cut. Print. Wrap!" Lucas says.

"That's a wrap," Fletcher says to applause. As everyone celebrates, he adds, "Folks, it's been a great two weeks. It's been a pleasure working with you," and hugs Lucas. "Thank you, George. It was good fun."

CAMERA WRAP: 19:29   SETUPS: 44   TOTAL SETUPS: 469
NOTES: Additional UK shooting completed today.

ILM begins churning out finals, of Boga the Utapaun lizard (top left), Wookiees in battle (above left), Obi-Wan in the Jedi Temple circuit room (top right) and in the Temple control room with Yoda (above right). It's here that the two will decide on one last battle with the Sith.

TUESDAY, SEPTEMBER 14, 2004

ILM: Lucas is back in UJ after taking a week off to attend a premiere of *THX 1138* in Deauville, and things proceed as they did before. With his sense of invention unabated, he reviews Grievous once again. "We might hear little clicks as he unlocks his arms," George says, discussing how the droid general's two arms become four.

"What I kind of like is you don't know what he's doing," Knoll agrees.

"It's like he's spinning the sabers," Lucas continues, discussing how the general might use his two upper arms. "He pulls the lower two back, and pushes the other two lightsabers forward, spinning them. We haven't cut it yet, so let's see if we can expand the fight and make it more than it was."

SR: Yesterday was Lucas's last visit to the animatics department. "It felt

weird, melancholy," Fay David says. By October's end, there will be only three left there. Dan Gregoire has already moved on to Steven Spielberg's *War of the Worlds*.

Though still editing with Lucas mornings, Ben Burtt is now spending afternoons at Skywalker Sound. Sitting in a fairly large office, which he shares with Matt Wood, Burtt is encircled by equipment. Every day, he consecrates at least an hour to research and development, so he's already devised 590 new sounds, including "buzz droids talking and Grievous's chariot." On Monday, when the first reel will officially be turned over to Burtt from editorial, sound editor Tom Meyers will start cutting in sounds both new and old. Lucas will begin coming over for reviews in November.

"We're doing some Artoo stuff at the moment," Burtt says. In fact, for the first time since 1981, he is making new sounds for R2-D2. "I was a little afraid to go back. It was a moment in time," he adds. "Fortunately, I had my notes and I had my 1971 synthesizer, which I'd stored in the crawl space under my house. And through the miracle of Howie Hammerman [a Lucasfilm veteran], it now works again. My intention is to give Artoo a fresh voice."

TOTAL # OF SHOTS: 2,300   FINALS: 700
FINALS NEEDED PER WEEK: 57   WEEKS TO GO: 28
NOTE: The third rough cut is running, without end credits, at 2 hours 29 minutes 51 seconds.

FRIDAY, OCTOBER 8, 2004

SR: In his large, somewhat circular office, McCallum is having a brief consultation with Mike Blanchard. On one table, amid myriad books on cinema, is an Episode I ILM crew shot. In boxes are tapes of all formats and correspondence from around the globe. On the mantelpiece are *Star Wars* collectibles and a RICK MCCALLUM PRODUCER toy, which was given to him as a joke.

Across the corridor from his office sits Ardees Rabang, who has been McCallum's assistant for nearly ten years; she handles everything from production crises to organizing the actors' menus to scheduling

McCallum's travel. "He calls me his 'little mom,' " Rabang says. "Rick used to be notorious. His assistants used to hide, because you could hear him yelling and screaming. But he's a lot more relaxed now."

"Our present cut is running at about two hours, twenty-five minutes," McCallum says of third rough cut, finished October 1, "and we want to try and get it down to two hours fifteen without losing any scenes, just by trimming. Francis has seen it, and George has talked with him. And what happens next is that on Wednesday, John Williams and Steven Spielberg are coming up to watch the film. Then Spielberg will leave, after talking with George, and the rest of that day and the next, George and John will spot the film. They'll work with music editor Kenny Wannberg, who's done all six. He's actually retired, but he's coming back to do this; he's been a good-luck charm and is a lovely guy.

"The rest of the month will be spent on really focusing on the digital stunt work, and ILM will just continue finishing shots. By November 7, George will have the picture pretty much locked down, at which point we can decide if we're going to do any more pickups. The looping will take

Yoda's duel with the Emperor in a final frame (top left), in early ILM cloth sims (right-hand strip, by Todd Widup, Scott Jones, and Greg Killmaster), and in early animatics directed by Steven Spielberg featuring giant HoloNet screens transmitting their duel across the galaxy. "Anytime a creature changes major poses," notes cloth sim supervisor Juan-Luis Sanchez, "like from lying down to standing, it is difficult." Far left: George Lucas (Baron Papanoida) and his daughter Katie Lucas (Chi Eekway) are prepared by Gillian Libbert for their cameo in the Galaxies opera staircase scene, filmed in November 2004, months after the crowd scene was shot at Shepperton. An early version of the Baron's costume is by concept artist Sang Jun Lee (left).

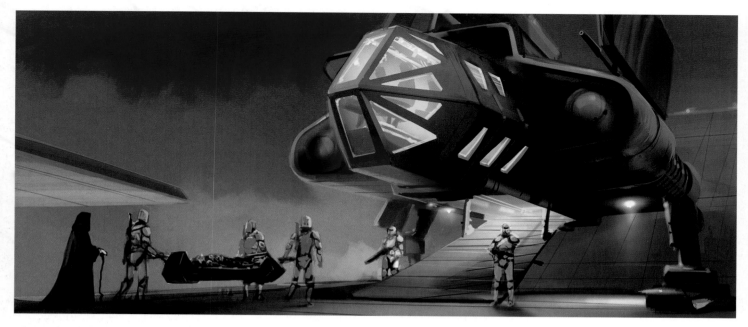

place in London, in mid-December, and on February 2, we start to score for approximately three weeks—and then we have the horror of doing all the foreign versions, trying to make the day-and-date release.

"Usually when you finish a movie, you get sick," he adds. "You've been running on adrenaline for so long. After we do all the press events, I'm going to say, 'I'm shattered.' And then it'll be a very strange feeling. The people you've worked with, and grown up with—everyone will move on. I've always been connected to John and Rob—and Ben, of course, I've been with for fifteen years. That's the sad part. It's emotionally wrenching.

"But the most important thing for me, personally, when the film is released, is that it's a breakthrough in terms of being visually breathtaking and emotionally powerful, so that the people involved in this—Gavin, and David Tattersall, Trisha, and ILM, and Ben, and everyone else—who have done extraordinary work and who have never been acknowledged—what I'm hoping is that their work is recognized."

TUESDAY, OCTOBER 12, 2004

ILM: In UJ, Lucas is reviewing an animation of Yoda as he surveys Dagobah from his vessel at the end of *Revenge of the Sith*. Rob asks George if he's looking too sad.

"Yeah," Lucas responds. "Yoda should bring his head up faster. He should look around because this is his new world. I think the word here is *wise*. Yoda has to have a *we will have our day* look on his face. He is going to persevere."

EPILOGUE: The Compassion of the Jedi

George W. Lucas was born on May 14, 1944, in Modesto, California. After graduating from the University of Southern California, he directed *THX 1138*, *American Graffiti*, and four *Star Wars* films. He has executive produced Francis Ford Coppola's *Tucker: The Man and His Dream*, Jim Henson's *Labyrinth* (1986), Ron Howard's *Willow* (1988), Lawrence

Episode III

000121   crc010 - v04
05-06-04   Artist: Nick Markel

Episode III

0001   crc150 - v01
04/09/04   Artist: Eric Carney

Episode III

0132   crc190 - v02
04/09/04   Artist: Eric Carney

Episode III

0147   crc210 - v01
04/08/04   Artist: Eric Carney

The transformation of flesh-and-blood Vader into mostly mechanical Vader, as seen in the visual script (being taken from Mustafar to the rehabilitation center, top left) and in a final frame, as droids operate on him (left).

Top: The operation continues in Markel's animatics for CRC.010 (May 6, 2004), and Vader's new life-sustaining suit is revealed in Carney's animatics for CRC.150 (April 8, 2004). The two Sith converse in a final frame (middle), and then Vader breaks free in Carney's animatics for CRC.190 and CRC.210 (above).

Kasdan's *Body Heat* (1981), Akira Kurosawa's *Kagemusha* (1980), Walter Murch's *Return to Oz*, Paul Schrader's *Mishima* (1985), Steven Spielberg's *Indiana Jones* trilogy, and of course the other two *Star Wars* films. He has helped pioneer several visual effects breakthroughs, began what became Pixar Animation, and spearheaded digital filmmaking.

With seven months of work left on *Revenge of the Sith*, though it's impossible to speak of it as complete, certain observations can be made. For three years, a nonstop barrage of art and ideas, created by an incredibly talented group of core collaborators, has gone through the filter of Lucas's mind, inspiring certain conceits and mixing with his own. The ultimate design of the movie's scripts, sets, vehicles, characters, and shots is the expression of a writer-director whose vision is at once popular and

abstract—the detached eye of the documentarian and the intensely, almost idiosyncratically emotional lens of the man.

The two *Star Wars* trilogies share many characters but have different structures. Instead of telling another heroic coming-of-age story, Lucas has crafted in the prequels a historical drama, at whose center is Anakin Skywalker. His story is tragic; that of the Republic-turned-Empire, uncom-

Top left: In this shot, Padmé's body will be delivered to Naboo, which exists here as a digi-matte painting by Yanick Dusseault, who explains, "a grayscale shading of the 3-D geometry was constructed as a base for the painting process" (inset). The following dawn a funeral is held for the former Queen (final frame, above, with digi-matte painting by Paul Huston). However, there is a new hope in her and Anakin's son, Luke, who will be cared for on Tatooine (final frame, right)—all envisioned by Lucas (above right), who began this last shot back on September 7, 2000.

fortably familiar. Anakin begins as a nine-year-old boy who is physically enslaved. He ends the prequel saga a spiritual and mental slave to the Emperor, who is his metaphorical if not biological father. First seen in Episode I as beset by a crippling bureaucracy, the Republic Senate is, by the end of Episode III, a rubber stamp for the Empire. As the locale for the duel between the Emperor and Yoda, the Senate finally becomes what it has always been: the physical manifestation of the eternal conflict between totalitarianism and democracy.

But the end of *Revenge of the Sith* is not the end of Anakin, whose story really closes when it merges with those of his children, Luke and Leia, in *Return of the Jedi.*

"It really has to do with learning," Lucas says. "Children teach you compassion. They teach you to love unconditionally. Anakin can't be redeemed for all the pain and suffering he's caused. He doesn't right the wrongs, but he stops the horror. The end of the saga is simply Anakin saying, *I care about this person, regardless of what it means to me. I will throw away everything that I have, everything that I've grown to love—primarily the Emperor—and throw away my life, to save this person. And I'm doing it because he has faith in me; he loves me despite all the horrible things I've done. I broke his mother's heart, but he still cares about me, and I can't let that die.* Anakin is very different in the end. The thing of it is: The prophecy was right. Anakin was the chosen one, and he does bring balance to the Force. He takes the ounce of good still left in him and destroys the Emperor out of compassion for his son."

Anakin Skywalker's final confrontation with the Emperor occurs during Luke's first confrontation with the Emperor, which complements his father's dealings with the same man many years earlier. Indeed, the life of the father and the life of the son are commentaries on each other. One of

Lucas's tendencies, evident throughout his films, is to tell simultaneous stories, many of which are interconnected.

"I come out of editing, and that's probably part of it," Lucas says. "I think I have a short attention span and that's probably part of it, too. [laughs] It's just my nature.

"The *Star Wars* saga is like a symphony, which has recurring themes," he adds. "You have one theme orchestrated in a particular way and place, which then comes back orchestrated as a minor theme somewhere else. There are these little threads running through things that are constantly turning events on their head. You see two people confronting the same things, with different ends. It's a rhythm. I like the idea of seeing something from different perspectives. An advantage I have in this particular situation is that I have literally twelve hours to tell a story. It has the epic quality of following one person from the time he's nine years old to the time he dies. It's Anakin's story, but obviously there are many other characters in that story—his children, his best friend—and their stories carry through. So this isn't just a tune—it's a symphony. When you do it as a symphony, I think, it actually becomes beautiful."

Don't miss the exciting online FINAL CHAPTER to THE MAKING OF STAR WARS: REVENGE OF THE SITH, detailing the work that continued even after the book was done. This exclusive material is available at www.readstarwars.com.

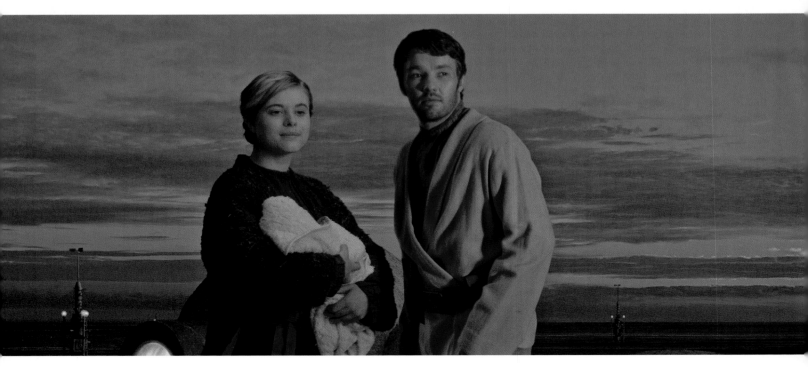

Creating the Visual Script

At Skywalker Ranch, on Monday, June 23, 2003, art department supervisor Fay David calls an emergency meeting. While finishing his fourth draft of the script, Lucas has decided that the corresponding visual script needs a lot more detail. The purpose of this latter reference document is to give actors, on-set technicians, and the Sydney art department a better idea of what the finished sets—post visual effects—will look like. Lucas has therefore asked for the visual script to cover every scene, and in alarming detail—given that the artists must finish paintings for the first thirty days of principal photography by Wednesday evening, with the balance due not long afterward.

To create most of these paintings—and create them quickly—the artists form an assembly line: (1) they read the scene, carefully noting all of its visual elements;

(2) Derek Thompson then composes shots in storyboard-like sketches, with black-and-white values, and places the file on a server; (3) either Michael Murnane, Robert Barnes, Feng Zhu, or Sang Jun Lee takes the file and does a character pass—i.e., putting in character details; (4) either Zhu or T.J. Frame do an ID (industrial design) pass to make the environment detailed and three-dimensional; (5) Tiemens or Church then do a composition and lighting pass, adding washes of color and checking it against the time of day specified in the script. Examples of finished visual script pages are found throughout the book.

Acknowledgments

Very special thanks to George Lucas, for his input and generosity over the past three years; and to Trisha Biggar and Gavin Bocquet, for tours and insights into their respective departments; Ben Burtt, for his refined thoughts about editing and sound; Tippy Bushkin, for her great documentary footage; Ryan Church, for many concept-art sneak previews; Rob Coleman, for a memorable Indian dinner; David Craig, for his learned help; Anthony Daniels, for a conversation about the ends and beginnings of *Star Wars;* Fay David, whose help was simply invaluable; Nick Gillard, for a talk about the character of dueling; Dan Gregoire, for letting me stand around; Pablo Hidalgo, for the mind-boggling continuity conversations in Foodles; John Knoll, for his great panoramic photos; Christopher Lee, for recalling his adventures during the making of *The Three Musketeers;* Iain McCaig, for unforgettable car-pool conversations; Tina Mills, for taking care of the thousands of images; Kathryn Ramos, for her notes on the manuscript; Erik Tiemens, for—among many, many others—the painting of Skywalker Ranch; and to everyone else who gave a helpful word or hint. At Del Rey, to Keith Clayton, Mark Maguire, Sylvain Michaelis, and Steve Saffel; and at Lucasfilm, to Amy Gary, Howard Roffman, and Sue Rostoni—for making the book readable and beautiful—and in particular to Iain Morris, who oversaw the design process with his usual skill and panache and eleventh-hour heroics! And much thanks to Hayden Christensen, for the many lucid conversations. *And very special thanks to Rick McCallum—none of this would've been possible without his unstinting support from day one.*

Top left and right: Anakin vanquishes Count Dooku, and Palpatine vs. Yoda, from the visual script. Above: Parts of the symphony: in Episode VI, Darth Vader, Emperor Palpatine, and Luke Skywalker; in Episode III, Chancellor Palpatine, Anakin Skywalker, and Obi-Wan Kenobi. Opposite page: Death droid by Tiemens. Following page: (left) Tenggren's continuity script shows the changes made on the set during the final Anakin–Obi-Wan scene in Sydney, Monday, September 1, 2003. (right) Props dresser Jeremy Fuller takes a sledgehammer to the Trade Federation cruiser hallway—the fate of nearly all the sets.

Index

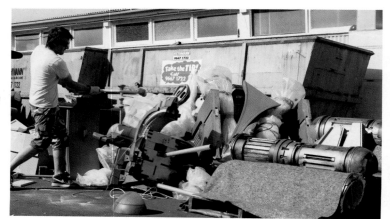